THE SAME GOD WHO WORKS ALL THINGS

The SAME GOD
Who WORKS ALL THINGS

Inseparable Operations in
Trinitarian Theology

ADONIS VIDU

WILLIAM B. EERDMANS PUBLISHING COMPANY
GRAND RAPIDS, MICHIGAN

Wm. B. Eerdmans Publishing Co.
4035 Park East Court SE, Grand Rapids, Michigan 49546
www.eerdmans.com

Published 2021
Printed in the United States of America

27 26 25 24 23 22 21   2 3 4 5 6 7

ISBN 978-0-8028-7443-6

Library of Congress Cataloging-in-Publication Data

Names: Vidu, Adonis, author.
Title: The same God who works all things : inseparable operations in Trinitarian
   theology / Adonis Vidu.
Description: Grand Rapids, Michigan : William. B. Eerdmans Publishing
   Company, 2021. | Includes bibliographical references and index. | Summary:
   "An exposition and defense of the dogmatic rule of the inseparable opera-
   tions of the Trinity"—Provided by publisher.
Identifiers: LCCN 2020033819 | ISBN 9780802874436
Subjects: LCSH: Trinity.
Classification: LCC BT111.3 .V535 2021 | DDC 231/.044—dc23
LC record available at https://lccn.loc.gov/2020033819

For Hannah

Contents

Acknowledgments

The seeds of this book were first planted during my work on an earlier project on the theology of the atonement (*Atonement, Law, and Justice: The Cross in Historical and Cultural Settings*, Baker Academic, 2014). At that time it became clear to me that the interpretation of any act of God, such as the atonement, must first recognize the uniqueness of divine agency. Two concepts bring out this uniqueness more than any others: divine simplicity and inseparable operations. My 2014 book addresses, very modestly, the first one. To my surprise I discovered that no book-length treatment existed of the doctrine of inseparable operations. While important article- and chapter-length contributions already existed, a full-scale articulation and defense of the doctrine did not exist. Where the present attempt is at all successful, it builds on previous work in the area of patristic and medieval theology (Lewis Ayres, Michel Barnes, Gilles Emery, Khaled Anatolios, and others).

The burden of making a contribution to such an important area of Trinitarian theology would have been unbearable were it not for the unfailing support of a number of fellow wayfarers. I was fortunate enough to be writing this book at a time of great enthusiasm for the doctrine of the Trinity within the Evangelical academy. I benefited from the keen critical minds of a circle of friends who love to talk about the Trinity: Josh Farris, Mark Hamilton, James Arcadi, Carl Moser, Derek Rishmawy, Fred Sanders, Oliver Crisp, J. T. Turner, Luke Stamps, Matthew Emerson, Gregg Allison, Eduardo Echeverria, Charles Twombly, Josh Malone, Tom McCall, Kyle Claunch, Tyler Wittman, Keith E. Johnson, Scott Harrower, Austin Freeman, Rafael Bello, Chris Woznicki, Adam Johnson, Josh McNall, Lucy Peppiatt, Joanna Leidenhag. A number of colleagues at Gordon-Conwell have patiently read through sections of the manuscript, in particular Sean McDonough, Jack Davis, Rick Lints, Gordy Isaac, Kirsten Sanders, and Patrick Smith. A number of wise and seasoned Trinitarian theologians have kindly provided invaluable feedback at various points along the way, of whom I should mention Bruce D. Marshall, Paul Molnar, Neil Ormerod, Matthew Levering, Kevin Vanhoozer, William J. Abraham, and Najib Awad. Several research assistants provided incredible support along the way, including Mark Hertenstein, Ross Alan MacDonald, Cameron Brock, Greg Parker, and Andrew Johnson. Heartfelt gratitude goes out to Michael Thompson, who supported this project from its proposal stage and who has been a constant encourager along the way. Thanks to James Ernest and Laurel Draper at Eerdmans for the excellence and fine tuning so much needed by this manuscript.

I owe a double debt of gratitude to the Trustees and Administration of Gordon-Conwell, as well as to my faculty colleagues who filled in for me during two semester-long sabbaticals. Without Gordon-Conwell's generous sabbatical program, books such as this one would be impossible to conceive.

I have left the deepest debt for the end. As all writers know, a tremendous emotional investment enters into any writing project, especially the longer ones, such that almost everything is affected and shaped by it, including the most important thing, family. My wife, Adriana, and my daughter, Hannah, have accepted to share me with this long-standing project. Our conversations were often finding their way back to the topic of inseparable operations. This book has shaped and molded me for the past six years or so, hopefully mostly for the better, although evidently not on every occasion. This project would not have been the labor of love it is were it not for their steadfast support, encouragement, and thoughtful contribution. During these six years, my daughter Hannah has grown to be the beautiful and smart young lady that she is. This book has often carried me away from her mentally. By dedicating it to her, I want to close the circle, returning to what matters most.

Introduction

Classical Trinitarianism confesses that *opera trinitatis ad extra sunt indivisa*. This principle functions as a dogmatic rule in descriptions of divine action in the world. With some notable exceptions, most theologians today would affirm this principle. However, in actual use a number of obviously conflicting interpretations may be observed. Some understand the principle minimalistically, to imply that there is no conflict between the economic works of the triune persons. Others understand *indivisa* to imply that the three work "in concert," that they stand behind each other's actions, that they act collectively, or otherwise that they cooperate. Still others insist that the indivisibility of divine triune action means that the persons do not undertake separate actions—not simply that they do not act without each other's support (this much is trivial), but that one cannot even individuate distinct actions of the persons.

It goes without saying that achieving some clarity with regards to this principle is a vital theological task. Still, beyond a small number of articles and individual book chapters, no large-scale exposition and discussion of this rule has so far been attempted. The task is not of marginal significance for the rest of Christian doctrine since the proper elucidation of divine action is fundamental to understanding the claims of the faith. For that same reason, it is an undertaking that must be assumed with fear and trembling. At stake are doctrines at the heart of our faith. A wrong move at this most foundational level will corrode large swaths of Christian teaching.

That God acts in the world is universally affirmed in Christian theology. Beyond this point there is much disagreement: Does God act merely providentially, or are there special divine actions in the world? Much energy is currently expended on the question of special divine action—that is, on whether God intervenes in the space-time continuum and, if so, what form this "intervention" takes. We will not wade into this important discussion although we are not entirely indifferent to it; however, the paucity of consideration for the Trinitarian dimension of divine action needs immediate correction. This study can be a first step in this direction in that it clarifies the theological question of what it means for the Trinitarian God to act. It must not be supposed that we are already familiar with the notion of divine action, much less Trinitarian action. God is not an item in the world, and therefore we must tread carefully here. Beyond the epistemic difficulties that God's transcendence poses regarding his action, God's Trinitarian nature also qualifies divine action.

We are calling the doctrine of inseparable operations a *dogmatic rule*. Nodding toward Wittgenstein's conception of "theology as grammar," we admit that we are not aiming at comprehension of triune agency. Just as language fails at describing God perfectly, so it cannot hope to capture the essence of divine action. Nevertheless, since we are called to witness to the reality of God's dealings with us, we must take on the hard task of speaking about the unspeakable and describing the indescribable. When we refer to the doctrine of inseparable operations as a grammatical rule, we mean that its function is primarily that of normalizing and qualifying other more basic descriptions. The primary meanings of these descriptions are retained but qualified. Taken in this form the doctrine of inseparable operations functions in a way similar to analogy. Whereas analogy qualifies univocal meaning, the inseparability principle qualifies actions, descriptions, and ascriptions. For example, when the action of salvation is ascribed to the Son (on a first order level of predication), under the rule of inseparability it is also ascribed to the Father and the Spirit.

However, this continual chastening of language is not made with the hindsight of perfect vision. The fact remains that we do not have an insight into the essence of divine action. But then why has classical Trinitarianism insisted on the strict application of this rule? The primary reason has been fidelity to scriptural revelation! Contrary to what some might expect, the inseparability rule in its classical interpretation—or what we call here its "hard version"—is grounded in Scripture, not in speculative deduction from the unity of divine essence. The conviction of the earliest exponents of the rule has been that Scripture ascribes the selfsame actions to the Son as much as to the Father and the Holy Spirit. In fact, it was precisely under the influence of this observation that the doctrine of the Trinity developed, including the notion of the irreducible distinctions between the persons. It is Scripture that calls for a kind of reading that does not divide the actions of the triune persons.

Such an indivisibility, however, is without equal in the finite world. For this reason, we cannot probe its depths, we cannot explain it; we lack the capacity for understanding it; we can only attest to it in faith. It cannot be stressed enough that the current volume must be understood as a modest exercise in theological grammar rather than an impetuous explanation and representation. We do not claim to be able to "explain" triune inseparable action, to show how it functions, to lay bare its logic, or to discover its essence. As a grammatical exercise, the most we can aim at is at adjusting the uses of our language. The conviction behind this is that there is a point to grammar because it aims to regulate language use, yet without the presumption of an exact mapping of language unto the divine reality.

Laws, and in particular laws of grammar, go out of use not because they are falsified by new discoveries, since laws do not so much make assertions as they make assertions possible. They go when they are no longer considered useful, when better ways of organizing and framing the material are invented. Many contemporary Trinitarian theologians are of the opinion that the inseparability rule, in its hard version, is passé. The conditions of the language of theology have changed to such an extent that it is no longer necessary to enforce it, they say. There are, it is being suggested, much better ways of making sense of the data of Scripture and of Christian practice. The enduring value of this rule, in their opinion, is the general idea of noncompetitiveness and cooperation between the triune persons. Apart from this *soft* reading of inseparability, the rule is not only past its usefulness, but it positively stifles progress in God-talk. A critical mass of such objections has been reached, such that it is wise for the defender of the rule to accept the burden of proof. We intend to do precisely that. Distinguishing between *hard* and *soft* inseparability—the former meaning that every *act token* of any Trinitarian person is also an act token of the other persons, the latter meaning only that the divine persons participate in shared and collective actions together—we will argue for the former against the latter.

We start our volume with a biblical theology of inseparable operations. Were it not for the fact that Scripture itself ascribes specifically divine actions to Christ and the Spirit, they would not have been identified as divine. But is "God" a singular being, a kind, or a trope? The question of the character of Jewish monotheism becomes in this context very pressing. If to Jesus is ascribed only a *type* of actions that other divine figures also undertake, hard inseparability fails to follow. There are two fundamental ways in which Jesus can be identified with "divinity": either by ascribing to him covenantal actions, or covenant-related activities, or by ascribing to him the very act of creation. Both of these kinds of ascriptions are made in Scripture, but with varying implications for our thesis.

Scripture not only ascribes the self-same actions to the Father and the Son, it also irreducibly distinguishes the persons. A theology of inseparable operations must take the unity and distinction between the persons as equally basic. We discuss this with special reference to the Gospel of John. We then conclude the first chapter with exegetical observations about the unity between the risen Christ and the Pentecostal Spirit.

Chapter 2 surveys the development and abrogation of the inseparability rule. We discover the fact that in the development toward Trinitarian monotheism the biblical evidence for inseparable operations was the factor that convinced strict monotheists to allow for real distinctions between the persons within the unity of God. Far from being a mere deduction from a metaphysical concept of unity, the doctrine of inseparable operations was in fact the pillar on which the very distinction between the persons was established. Not only was this doctrine regarded as a biblical necessity, but in the Christological controversies up to the seventh century it became an issue of vital religious importance. The reason why the doctrine of inseparable operations has become so counterintuitive today has not a little to do with its reception in modern theology, and in particular in much of the modern Trinitarian resurgence. During the past century the rule has gone from being part of the very foundation of Trinitarian dogma to being dodged as one of its greatest vulnerabilities. Knowing the story of this recent disenchantment with the rule helps us identify the signal grievances and difficulties, thus setting the agenda for the rest of the book.

Before addressing the various objections to the doctrine, we pause in chapter 3 to explain the metaphysical logic of the doctrine, primarily along two vectors. Ontologically, we explain what triune causality means and why the Trinity only operates inseparably in the economy. We then assess the implications of this triune causality for our knowledge of the divine persons. The doctrine of *appropriation*, the great corollary to the rule of inseparability is discussed here. Finally, since we have suggested that the classical construal (in East and West) of the relationship between persons and nature is interwoven with the doctrine of inseparable operations, an alternative social-Trinitarian model must now be assessed. Taking Richard Swinburne as one possible social Trinitarian construal of operative unity we appraise the success of his proposal.

From the fourth chapter onward, we begin to test hard inseparability against various doctrines and the specific objections they generate. The common theme throughout these next chapters is whether hard inseparability possesses explanatory power in relation to the Christian confession, or is it falsified by it? To put it differently: Does this grammatical rule still apply to the first order Christian statements? Is it still able to organize and regulate them? These various discussions will also indicate the fecundity of the rule for a fresh look at the individual doctrines. Far from seeking to be innovative, however, our aim is to retrieve a classical Trinitarian lexicon for these dogmatic *loci*.

The first such discussion, quite naturally, is the doctrine of creation. Perhaps the most pivotal doctrine in the development of Trinitarian theology, creation also sets up a challenge for hard inseparability: can it account for its biblical inflection according to which the Father creates through the Son and the Spirit? Is the logic of inseparability able to accommodate the *"through* Christ," the *"by* the Spirit," and the *"from* the Father"? Or will it inevitably see in these distinctions separations and therefore swipe them to the side? Much modern theology attacks the inseparability rule for forcing an approach to the doctrine of creation through the Son that effectively depersonalizes the mediation of creation. Much is at stake in this discussion of a first theological *locus*. The doctrine of creation establishes the unsurpassable ontological difference between God and everything else. The signal fear of the inseparability tradition begins to emerge here—namely, that it is the very transcendence of God that is neglected by the ascription of divisible operations to the persons of the Trinity.

The second test for the rule is whether it is able to respect the doctrine of the incarnation of the Son alone (chapter 5). This is perhaps the most fundamental objection to the rule. If every act token of the Son is also the act token of the Father and the Spirit, shouldn't it follow that the Father and the Spirit were also incarnate? This objection forces us to reckon with the metaphysics of acts and states. It will emerge that this test demonstrates not the weakness, but the inestimable religious significance of the inseparability rule. Another related objection will be discussed at this point: Given the particular understanding of divine action (as the production of created effects), doesn't this render the human nature of Christ extrinsic to the Son, with the consequence that it doesn't truly reveal the Son in his personal distinction?

Chapter 6 continues the theme of Christology, this time attending to the works of the incarnate Son. Whereas the previous chapter discussed the hypostatic union, here we turn to the operations that follow from the union. Are the operations of Christ merely appropriated to the Son, or do they properly belong to him? It is not difficult to understand why some would be concerned by the thought of a "mere appropriation," since it is precisely in the operations that the person is thought to be most manifest. Thus, if the operations of Christ do not belong exclusively to the Son, how can they reveal the Son in particular? Indeed, how can the Son be himself without proper operations? We are clearly dealing with the same family of objections: no exclusive personal operation, therefore no revelation of the person itself. In addressing these concerns, we shall have to evaluate how actions pertain to persons and to natures, but also the particular arrangement of the divine and human natures in the incarnation, all within strict Chalcedonian limits. Again, we hope, it will emerge that the rule of hard inseparability does not inhibit true scriptural confession, but instead it is able to mine its most profound depths.

The religious significance of this rule comes out perhaps most clearly in our discussion of the atonement (chapter 7). The approach is somewhat different here. Rather than taking a particular confessional statement and using it to test the sustainability of the rule, this time we are assuming the rule is healthy and are using it to test a particular doctrine. The aim of this chapter is fundamentally critical, with only a hint of a positive construal. Building on the foregoing work, we are asking how the operations of the Father and those of the Son need to be related in the act of atonement. Can the Son, as man, do something (e.g., die) which enables the Father to do something else (e.g., forgive)? This yields a Trinitarian correction of a particular account of penal substitution, a doctrine that otherwise we consider to be indispensable. An inseparable-Trinitarian account of atonement must be very alert about the way in which the actions of the persons are coordinated, or rather about how the persons are related in the unity of their operation. More specifically, it must resist either separating the action tokens of the triune persons, or making the actions of one person depend upon the actions of another, or making the actions of the divine nature depend on the actions of the human nature. The rule of inseparability together with traditional theistic and Trinitarian concerns have, we shall see, quite clear implications for these relations.

The atonement, we shall see, cannot simply be about the actions of the Father and the Son. Rather, if atonement is about the at-one-ment of God and humanity, the work of Christ must be *intrinsically* coupled to the pouring out of the indwelling Spirit. The Spirit cannot be left out of the at-one-ment; doing so would make the latter a farce. But the Spirit is often seen as merely an extrinsic reward for Christ's obedience, received upon his ascension. So one must try to account for the presence and operation of all Trinitarian persons in the atonement. One must also account for another fact: the conditioning of the arrival of the Spirit upon the departure of Christ (chapter 8), which raises another objection: If the persons act inseparably, why must one person leave before another can descend? Engaging with this complicated question takes us again into the territory of the logic of the divine missions, particularly to the manner in which the human nature of Christ is instrumentalized and transfigured by its being caught up in the life of the Trinity. A constructive conclusion follows from this discussion, which observes the inseparability rule and also identifies the proper place of the humanity of Christ in the sending of the Spirit.

This brings us to our final test case for the inseparability rule: how it accounts for the personal indwelling of the Spirit (chapter 9). The problem is posed in the following manner: How can the Spirit be said to indwell the believer in his *proprium*? Is there a similarity between the "incarnation of the Son alone" and the "indwelling of the Spirit alone"? Is the indwelled believer in possession of the divine person as himself, or only in possession of gifts *appropriated* to this divine person?

The cumulative effect of these various dogmatic engagements will hopefully be to exhibit the continued vitality of the rule of inseparable operations and to persuade the reader that the rule is properly biblical, that it can handle objections coherently and clearly, and finally that it is fecund in terms of its resources for additional constructive work in dogmatics.

CHAPTER 1

A Biblical Theology of Inseparable Operations

The fundamental questions of a biblical theology of inseparable operations concern, first, the manner of the participation of Jesus Christ and the Holy Spirit in the agency of the one God, and second, the relation between the agency of the incarnate Son and the Holy Spirit. This first chapter treats each of these questions. As articulated by tradition, the doctrine of inseparable operations holds that Father, Son, and Holy Spirit share the divine agency of the one God. But what kind of singularity characterizes this one God? Before attempting to analyze conceptually the coherence of the doctrine, its origins in biblical monotheism have to be elucidated. The kind of unity that Trinitarian agency possesses must ultimately derive from the kind of unity characteristic of the biblical God.

THE NATURE OF JEWISH MONOTHEISM

A generation ago the nature of Jewish monotheism was not a burning research question. Scholars investigating the origins of Trinitarian theology were primarily asking whether it could be shown that Jesus and the Holy Spirit were originally described with language appropriate only to the God of the Old Testament. The question remained whether Jesus and the Spirit were somehow included in the identity of this one God of Israel. It was assumed at the outset that Jewish monotheism was of a strict kind. This assumption is no longer universally shared today. This makes a significant difference to our investigation. The kind of divine unity into which Jesus and the Spirit are included by New Testament writers determines the nature of their agency.

Two claims recently made about the nature of Jewish monotheism bear directly on our topic. First, attention has been properly called to the practical nature of Jewish monotheism. In contrast to an Enlightenment preoccupa-

tion with divinity in the abstract,[1] Jewish monotheism is concerned fundamentally with God as he relates to Israel. N. T. Wright helpfully distinguishes
between an inward-looking monotheism, focused on an analysis of the one
God, and an outward-looking monotheism, stressing the relation between
the one God and the world.[2] He goes on to summarize the nature of Second
Temple monotheism thus:

> Monotheism of the second-Temple Jewish kind, as we saw, was the belief
> not so much that there was one supernatural being rather than many, or
> that this God was a single and indivisible entity, but that the one true God
> was the creator of the world, supreme over all other orders of being, that
> he would be judge of all, and that in between creation and final putting-
> to-rights he had a single purpose which arched its way over the multiple
> smaller stories of creation and, not least, of Israel.[3]

It is important, however, not to make too much of this distinction and
suppose that Second Temple Jewish monotheism makes *no* theoretical claims
about the unity of God. A number of writers have been suggesting that monotheism is fundamentally a matter of *whom to worship*, and less a matter of
how many possible objects of worship there are. Thomas McCall, for instance,
writes that "monotheism is not primarily concerned with integers, or with
questions of how many tropes of divinity there are; it *is* centered on exclusive allegiance to the only Creator and Ruler."[4] Reframing the question along
praxiological, as opposed to propositional lines, McCall's monotheism is more
permissive: "While there is no precedent in Second Temple monotheism for
the inclusion of more than one 'personal' agent in the worship that rightly
belongs to YHWH, *neither is there anything that prohibits it*."[5]

This leads us to the second recent claim about the nature of Jewish monotheism. A number of writers have been steadily dismantling the received narrative of a unique God, articulating a porous notion of divinity. The view is
not entirely new, having been first articulated by Wilhelm Bousset in his 1903
Die Religion des Judentums im neutestamentlichen Zeitalter. Bousset had held

---

1. See Nathan MacDonald, *Deuteronomy and the Meaning of "Monotheism"* (Tübingen:
Mohr Siebeck, 2012).
2. N. T. Wright, *Paul and the Faithfulness of God* (London: SPCK, 2013), 627.
3. Wright, *Paul and the Faithfulness of God*, 638.
4. Thomas McCall, *Which Trinity? Whose Monotheism? Philosophical and Systematic
Theologians on the Metaphysics of Trinitarian Theology* (Grand Rapids: Eerdmans, 2010), 60.
5. McCall, *Which Trinity*, 61, emphasis mine.

that in the postexilic period Jews became interested in all kinds of intermediary beings on account of a growing sense of divine transcendence. In his wake we now recognize a certain Jewish comfort with all kinds of celestial beings of quasi-divine status. This is indeed a helpful development, clarifying that monotheism does not entail an unpopulated heaven occupied by a single supernatural being.

Many of these beings serve in all kinds of mediating roles. Larry Hurtado, for instance, distinguishes between different kinds of mediators: personified divine attributes such as Word and Wisdom; exalted patriarchs such as Enoch and Moses; supreme angels such as Michael.[6] P. G. Davis, in turn, classifies these beings along different "patterns of mediation": past mediators, such as Abraham and David, forming what he calls a "legacy pattern"; present mediators such as Gabriel, forming an "intervention pattern"; and future mediators, such as Elijah or the Son of Man, forming a so-called "consummation pattern."[7]

The existence as such of these mediators is certainly not problematic for the standard picture of strict Jewish monotheism—though it poses questions about the unique mediating role of Jesus Christ. However, a number of authors have suggested that their roles seriously challenge the standard picture. According to Aubrey Johnson, God must not be conceived as an Enlightenment isolated individual but "as possessing an indefinable extension of the Personality which enables Him to exercise a mysterious influence upon mankind."[8] He identifies various "extensions" of the divine personality: the Word (Isa 55:10–11); the Name of God (Num 6:22–27; Pss 20; 54); the Ark of the Covenant (Num 10:35–36; 1 Sam 4:5–8; 6:20). Each of these "mediators" seem to be identified with YHWH himself. Moreover, Johnson argues that there is an "oscillation" between the One and the Many in the manner in which the Scriptures refer to God.[9] He finds further evidence for this in the mysterious figure of the Angel of YHWH, who is "frequently indistinguishable from Yahweh Himself" (cf. Gen 12:4; 16; Judg 6:11–24), but also the three angels who appear to Abraham by the terebinths of Mamre (Gen 18). This "is but another aspect

---

6. Larry Hurtado, *One God, One Lord: Early Christian Devotion and Ancient Jewish Monotheism* (London: SCM, 1988), 17–18.

7. P. G. Davis, "Divine Agents, Mediators, and New Testament Christology," *Journal of Theological Studies* 45, no. 2 (Oct. 1994): 479–503.

8. Aubrey Johnson, *The One and the Many in the Israelite Conception of God* (Cardiff: University of Wales Press, 1942), 20.

9. Johnson (*The One and the Many*, 23–24) points to an ambiguity of translation of the end of Ps 58, for example, as well as to 1 Sam 4:5–8, although in this case the oscillation between singular and plural is placed in the mouth of the Philistines.

of that oscillation as between the individual and the corporate unit within the conception of God."[10]

In his *The Open Heaven: A Study of the Apocalyptic in Judaism and Early Christianity*, Christopher Rowland, an important scholar of the origins of Christianity, asserts the possibility of a distinction within the very identity of God within Jewish theology, between what we may call the primordial or transcendent God and an appearance of God in human form. In Genesis 18 and 32 we find "an angelic being who in some sense was regarded as communicating the appearance of God himself and who sometimes appeared in the form of a man."[11] Rowland sees a connection between this anthropomorphic deity and Ezekiel 1:26 and 8:2, but also Daniel 7:13. With H. L. Balz, he identifies "two divine figures" in Daniel 7, but he thinks that such a separation already takes place between Ezekiel 1:26 and 8:2. "What has happened [in Ezekiel] is not so much the splitting up of divine functions among various angelic figures but the separation of the form of God from the divine throne-chariot to act as a quasi-angelic mediator."[12] He continues, "The similarity which exists between Ezekiel 8:2 and Daniel 7:13 lies in the fact that both verses refer to heavenly figures and speak of them in quasi-divine terms."[13] By the time we get to Daniel 10:5, something significant has already happened: "What we have here is the beginning of a hypostatic development similar to that connected with divine attributes like God's word and wisdom."[14]

Both Johnson and Rowland suspect that such distinctions, oscillations, and ambiguities in the reference to God and his agency indicate that Jewish monotheism is a lot more nuanced than traditionally it was supposed. Already there are developments that ascribe quasi-divine functions to angels (Rowland) or imagine the divine personality as extensible to various angels, humans, objects, or groups. Not only is God understood to employ various intermediaries, but these also appear to bear the divine name, to be addressed as God, to be at least revered, if not outright worshipped. Are these nuances sufficient to suggest that Jewish monotheism is indeed much less strict than commonly assumed?

Crispin Fletcher-Louis's *Jesus Monotheism* makes precisely such a case. He continues to build the case against a strict Jewish monotheism of the

---

10. Johnson, *The One and the Many*, 33.

11. Rowland, *The Open Heaven: A Study of the Apocalyptic in Judaism and Early Christianity* (London: SPCK, 1982), 95.

12. Rowland, *The Open Heaven*, 97.

13. Rowland, *The Open Heaven*, 97.

14. Rowland, *The Open Heaven*, 100.

Second Temple period, adding at least one other intermediary being who seems to straddle the border between divine and nondivine. In the *Similitudes of Enoch*, "Adam carries or expresses the divine identity in a way that warrants the angelic worship of him. But in all the diverse witnesses to the story there is no suggestion that Adam should be included in the creative work of God."[15] This means, for Fletcher-Louis, that the distinction between divine and nondivine is not exactly coterminous with the distinction between Creator and creature. Adam can be divine without also being Creator. That is possible because, according to this author, God "shared his identity or nature with others."[16]

Fletcher-Louis builds his case on much the same range of intermediary beings who seem to be in some way treated as quasi-divine. Instead of a clear Creator-creature distinction, he finds God extending his identity to all other kinds of beings. But on what basis can Fletcher make such a significant metaphysical claim? It appears that the key concept for him is presence. He points to God's presence on earth, in a temple, in the ark, and elsewhere as a demonstration of this extensive identity. We need to reject, he insists, a "decidedly modern notion of identity,"[17] such as the one Richard Bauckham works with, as we shall see momentarily, that "God is a discrete, impermeable, Cartesian self."[18] The primary sources, in his opinion, point to another model: "that God is willing and able to share himself and (something of) his identity with a few specifically chosen entities."[19]

In other words, it is fundamentally mistaken to define God's identity over and against creation and creatures in an oppositional way. According to this definition, God is defined as whatever caused the entirety of contingent reality. Such a way of individuating God, Fletcher-Louis claims, omits the very presence of God within creation. Such a presence is not oppositional and it "miss[es] the shape of the Bible's own way of thinking. To simplify matters grossly: The Temple consists of *concentric zones* of holiness and there

---

15. Crispin Fletcher-Louis, *Jesus Monotheism*, vol. 1, *Christological Origins: The Emerging Consensus and Beyond* (Eugene, OR: Cascade, 2015), 144.

16. Fletcher-Louis, *Jesus Monotheism*, 297. He identifies four classes of texts which indicate various figures with whom God shares his identity and divinity: (1) divine creatures as creative agents, e.g., Wisdom and the Logos as created entities yet belonging to the divine identity; (2) divine angels; (3) divine and deified human beings; (4) worshipped divine agents.

17. Fletcher-Louis, *Jesus Monotheism*, 305.

18. Fletcher-Louis, *Jesus Monotheism*, 305.

19. Fletcher-Louis, *Jesus Monotheism*, 306.

is no one 'line' dividing God, who resides in the holy of holies, from the world outside."[20]

Only such a view of identity ensures divine freedom, it is further claimed: "It is precisely because he is absolutely distinguished from, different in kind to, the rest of reality, and free from all external constraint, that God is able to enter into and take on the nature and identity of that reality, even on occasion, taking that reality up into his very own self. . . . This is the 'fluidity' of divine being that makes the gods what they are."[21] Now, "any sharing or delegation of divine being and nature comes at the gracious initiative of this one God; it is not forced upon him by the already-determined rules of the divine hierarchy."[22]

James McGrath agrees that the evidence suggests "'bluriness' . . . as to whether a figure was intrinsic to the divine identity or separate and subordinate hereto."[23] His conclusion:

> It is thus possible that Jews, like others in this period, believed that the highest God created all things and was the source of a hierarchy of being which has its origins in him and which proceeds from him through the Logos, angels, humans and various other forms of life and existence.[24]

This has clear implications for the agency of these beings. "The result is that the agent can not only carry out divine functions but also be depicted in divine language, sit on God's throne or alongside God, and even bear the divine name."[25] This implies a very fluid border between the Creator and creature.[26]

The implications of the conclusions of Fletcher-Louis, McGrath, and Rowland for the topic of Trinitarian agency are considerable. If the indigenous Jewish monotheism can accommodate, as these authors argue, multiple beings who bear the divine name, carry out divine functions and roles, and even receive various sorts of devotion, then the claim that Jesus (and the Spirit) receives the divine name, is worshipped, and carries out divine actions need

20. Fletcher-Louis, *Jesus Monotheism*, 309.
21. Fletcher-Louis, *Jesus Monotheism*, 310.
22. Fletcher-Louis, *Jesus Monotheism*, 313.
23. James McGrath, *The Only True God: Early Christian Monotheism in Its Jewish Context* (Urbana: University of Illinois Press, 2012), 13.
24. McGrath, *The Only True God*, 13.
25. McGrath, *The Only True God*, 14.
26. According to McGrath, such a border only firms up after the emergence of the Christian doctrine of *creatio ex nihilo* during the third century (*The Only True God*, 92).

not entail that he shares the single agency of YHWH. Jesus could then be easily slotted into the manifold intermediary positions without requiring any modification of Jewish monotheism itself.[27]

But are these conclusions warranted by the evidence? We believe there are formidable arguments against such a softening of Jewish monotheism. Bauckham makes a coherent case against this "fluid" monotheism. The proponents of the latter position have failed to sufficiently focus on the uniqueness of God and have played fast and loose with their designations of "divinity." As we have seen, Fletcher-Louis tends to draw a direct line from observations of divine presence to conclusions about an extended identity of God. Bauckham argues that, on the contrary, Second Temple Jews were strict monotheists and in general had quite "clearly articulated criteria" by which to identify God.[28] The "practical monotheism" of these Jews considered God to be "significantly identifiable."[29] They knew who their God was: He had a name, a character; he acted, spoke, and related to others. He was a character in a story. The criteria for singling out the unique identity of God are two: First, he is identified in relation to Israel; secondly, he is identified in relation to the whole of reality, as its single Creator.

For our purposes, the criteria that individuate God in relation to the rest of reality are the most significant. In this respect "God had no helper, assistant or servant to assist or to implement his work of creation. God alone created, and no one else had any part in this activity."[30] Applying this criterion to other intermediary beings yields categorical and uncontested conclusions: "There is no suggestion, anywhere in the literature, that principal angels or exalted patriarchs participate in the work of creation. They are clearly created beings."[31]

Bauckham makes an important yet common-sense distinction. It is one thing to say that God makes himself present through a variety of entities, personal and impersonal; it is quite another to relativize his very identity to these individuals. It needs to be said unequivocally that such a confusion between presence and extended identity is simply logically fallacious. While an agent may *make himself present* in different ways in different relational contexts, he

27. It is significant that most of these authors, but McGrath in particular, attempt to minimize the Jewish opposition to the earliest Christian claims about Jesus's identity with God (McGrath, *The Only True God*, 69, discussing John 10:33).

28. Richard Bauckham, *Jesus and the God of Israel: God Crucified and Other Studies on the New Testament's Christology of Divine Identity* (Grand Rapids: Eerdmans, 2009), 3.

29. Bauckham, *Jesus and the God of Israel*, 6.

30. Bauckham, *Jesus and the God of Israel*, 10.

31. Bauckham, *Jesus and the God of Israel*, 14.

remains altogether *individuated* by other criteria. Quite simply, there needs to be an individually existing substance in order for this substance to engage in relationships and to extend its presence. While one's presence is certainly extensible, it seems unclear in what sense one might conceive of one's identity being extended in a literal sense.

While both God's identity and his presence are *known* relationally (rather than in the abstract), it does not follow that they are both also *constituted* relationally. In fact, to claim that in his identity God is self-sufficient and dependent on himself alone is precisely the reason why God alone is to be worshipped. Hurtado has consistently driven this point in his own defense of the strictness of Jewish monotheism. God is to be worshipped alone because he alone deserves to be worshipped. Thus, "even though the writings of this period describe this or that chief agent in quite exalted language, it is not at all clear that the persons who produced these writings believed that Jewish piety demanded the recognition and veneration of a particular figure as God's chief agent."[32]

It would be quite beyond the purview of this chapter and book to make a substantive contribution to the debate over the strictness of Jewish monotheism. The data we have presented show that there is in fact a debate over the question of Jewish precedents to either binitarianism or polytheism. Such evidence is particularly interesting for the light it sheds on the Jewish conceptions of divine agency, even if it hasn't reached the critical mass to revolutionize the traditional picture of Jewish monotheism.

First of all, researchers remain unpersuaded that the language of Word and Wisdom entails anything more than personifications of the divine attributes. The one reference to Wisdom's role in creation (Prov 8:22–31) is scant testimony for such a significant metaphysical claim as the existence of a separate created being next to God. Researchers are quite right to claim that this kind of expression neatly fits with Jewish poetic expressions.

On the issue of the Angel of the Lord, while it seems quite clear that there is a strong identification between him and God himself (Gen 16:13; Judg 6:14; 13:21–22), this need not entail more than the angel's status as the chief of God's intermediaries, mediating the divine intimacy, power, and authority to the persons that he is sent to. The distinction between the Angel of the Lord and the Lord himself is clearly established (Exod 23:23; 32:34; 2 Sam 24:16; 1 Chr 21:27; Zech 1:12). Equally clear remains the subordination of the angel to the

---

32. Bauckham, *Jesus and the God of Israel*, 19.

Lord himself. While the angel is *perceived to be the very presence of YHWH himself,* he is subordinate to YHWH.[33]

Finally, there is the linguistic oscillation between singular and plural in references to God (El, Elohim, etc.). While to speak of a "divine council" is not in itself problematic for monotheism, as long as the subordinate status of the other "gods" is maintained, some authors have argued that YHWH himself is but a member of the divine council, one of the sons of El Elyon.[34] These authors point to a tradition of the "sons of God," which indicates a possible polytheistic origin of Jewish devotion (Gen 6:2, 4; Deut 32:8; Job 1:6; 38:7; Ps 29:1; 58; 82; 89; Dan 3:25). A key text here is Deuteronomy 32:8, where the Masoretic Hebrew reads "When the Most High (עֶלְיוֹן) apportioned the nations, when he divided humankind, he fixed the boundaries of the people according to the number of the sons of Israel (בְּנֵי יִשְׂרָאֵל)." The Qumran text, however, has "sons of God" instead of "sons of Israel," while the Septuagint has "angels of God." On the Qumran reading of this text, favored by Barker, among others, "Elyon the High God had allocated the nations to the various sons of God; one of these sons was Yahweh to whom Israel had been allocated."[35] Such a reading is extremely counterintuitive and impossible to reconcile with the whole tenor of Deuteronomy, especially 32:39 ("See now that I, even I, am he, and there is no god beside me; I kill and I make alive; I wound and I heal; and there is none that can deliver out of my hand"), as Bauckham points out.[36] Instead, the reading corroborated by overwhelming evidence in early Judaism is that "the Most High and YHWH are the same. In his exercise of universal sovereignty over the nations (as the Most High), he allocates them to the heavenly beings of his entourage ('the sons of God' in 4QDeut), but reserves Israel for his own direct rule (as YHWH the covenant God of Israel)."[37]

The work of Alan Segal further bears out the claim that Jewish theology was quite unambiguous in its affirmation of a single divine being. His influential book *Two Powers in Heaven* charts various rabbinic responses to the

33. For additional work on this, see J. E. Fossum, *The Name of God and the Angel of the Lord: Samaritan and Jewish Conceptions of Intermediation and the Origin of Gnosticism* (Waco, TX: Baylor University Press, 2017); A. S. Malone, "Distinguishing the Angel of the Lord," *Bulletin for Biblical Research* 21, no. 3 (2011): 297–314.

34. E.g., Margaret Barker, *The Great Angel: A Study of Israel's Second God* (Louisville, KY: WJKP, 1992), 4.

35. Barker, *The Great Angel*, 6.

36. Bauckham, *Jesus and the God of Israel*, 112.

37. Bauckham, *Jesus and the God of Israel*, 112. Cf. 113 for the evidence for this in early Judaism.

so-called "Two Powers" heresy. Segal shows a determined rabbinic reaction against not only dualistic heresies, but also against cosmologies with partnering deities. Crucially, such a reaction dates to the second century AD; it not only addressed Gnostic sects but seems to have been aimed at Christians too. "The earliest isolatable rabbinic opposition to 'two powers,' then, is not against ethical dualism, but against a principal angel or mediator. While it seems possible that the angelic or anthropomorphic creature has some relation to the problem of theodicy, the helping angel is in no way evil."[38] Segal notes that "The rabbinic response to the heresy is clear: The rabbis appeal to Scripture to show that God is unitary. Deuteronomy 6, Isaiah 44–47, and Exodus 20 are used by the rabbis to show that God is unique."[39]

Segal's conclusions seem to imply several things. First, second-century Jews appear to be quite protective of their strictly monotheistic stance, not accepting interpretations of certain problematic scriptures that have been twisted to support "two powers." Secondly, there was, after all, significant Jewish—and in particular rabbinic—opposition to Christian claims prior to the debate over Gnosticism in the third century. Early Christianity, then, was quite clearly (and correctly) perceived as introducing a significant modification to Jewish monotheism. Finally, Segal confirms that rabbis apparently not preoccupied with a theoretical monotheism were perfectly able to understand and refute the problematic propositional implications of alternative construals.

We may now return to the two considerations this section took up. First, on the question of the practical nature of Jewish monotheism, the bifurcation between a praxiological, doxological monotheism and a propositional, metaphysical one is a red herring.[40] While Scripture does not enter sophisticated metaphysical debates about the nature of ultimate reality, its doxological single-mindedness is predicated upon certain beliefs it held about the singularity, uniqueness, and absolute sovereignty of the one God of Israel. Astute Jewish monotheists, without being primarily speculative metaphysicians, understood clearly the theoretical underpinnings of their praxis. In relation to the second consideration, postexilic monotheists had a clear and distinct manner of referring to God, of picking him out of a range of possible referents. They understood that the sovereignty of God and his sole divinity was perfectly compatible with the existence of other celestial beings, being their Creator and

38. Alan Segal, *Two Powers in Heaven: Early Rabbinic Reports About Christianity and Gnosticism* (Leiden: Brill, 1977), 149.

39. Segal, *Two Powers in Heaven*, 79.

40. Cf. also Wright, *Paul and the Faithfulness of God*, 632.

Lord. But it is quite misleading to claim that they lacked prohibitions against worshipping additional personal entities together with YHWH.

Although we favor the judgment that Second Temple Judaism was strictly monotheistic, it must be admitted that its understanding of divine agency is considerably sophisticated. While God creates without availing himself of any supporting intermediary, he relates to creation sometimes directly and sometimes through intermediaries, either angels or personified attributes. It is within this nuanced framework that we must ask how Christ's agency is related to the agency of the one God.

The remainder of the chapter uses Bauckham's twofold criteria of individuation for God: first, in relation to Israel; secondly, in relation to the whole of reality. We will show that the New Testament clearly portrays Christ as assuming in a comprehensive way the totality of God's agency toward his people Israel, to the point that Christ represents the expected YHWH, returned to his people. Secondly, and partly as a result of this, to Christ is ascribed the divine activity of creation, precisely the one act where YHWH works directly and without intermediaries. As a result of this double-pronged individuation, it follows that Christ is identified specifically with the one agent who is the object of Israel's monotheistic devotion. To Christ are ascribed precisely the selfsame actions that are operated by YHWH himself. However, to say that Christ assumes the operations of YHWH is only one side of the coin. Christ receives these works from the Father; the Spirit does as well, from the Father and the Son. Within the very unity of operation, a distinction is established between the Father, from whom the works originate, the Son, by whom the works are done, and the Spirit, in whom they are finalized. John articulates this theology most clearly. The final section in this chapter, therefore, will explore the Johannine theology of inseparable operations where this unity in distinction and distinction in unity is most clearly, though not uniquely, articulated.

Jesus and the Spirit Identified with the God of Israel

Fundamentally, the issue of the inseparable operations hinges biblically on the correlation of the respective actions of the Father, the incarnate Son, and the Holy Spirit. The difficulty, however, is that unlike the Incarnate Son, the Father and the Spirit are not embodied persons and consequently not empirically accessible. Since God is transcendent Being one cannot ostensibly refer to a phenomenally present agent. One only has empirical access, so to speak, to the effects of the actions themselves. From the experience of these effects one infers a divine agency as their uncreated cause. While God has indeed appeared in various theophanic events, it is generally assumed that such visible appearances, although mediating the divine presence in a special way, are not to be identified with God without remainder. The various appearances (Abraham's three visitors, the angel that wrestled with Jacob, the burning bush, etc.), in virtue of their mediating function, receive the worship and reverence that is due to God, yet no illusion persists that they might in some way be numerically identical with the divine being.

This being granted, the question before us is the relation between the actions of the only embodied divine agent, Jesus Christ, and two other sets of actions without embodied agents. Given such a disembodied agency, it is not hard to see why the identification of the divine agent is not an entirely straightforward matter. If I may be permitted an inapposite analogy, the situation parallels crime cases in which there is empirical access to the effects of the criminal agency (say, a dead body) but not to the criminal himself. Solving a crime is a matter of discovering the agent behind the action, of attributing an action to a particular agent. Of course, one generally assumes that a crime has been committed by an embodied agent, who can (in principle) be apprehended. Not so in the case of divine actions (as our study will indeed reveal later on): The agent remains empirically inaccessible and only identifiable through his effects.

Except in the case of Jesus Christ. The logic and in fact the rationale of earliest Trinitarian theology is very much the logic of pairing the actions of an embodied agent (Christ) with the actions of a disembodied agent (YHWH) in a way that is facilitated by the actions of another disembodied agent (Holy Spirit). Trinitarian theology arose because the three sets of activities—namely the activities attributed by consensus to YHWH alone, the activities ascribed to Jesus Christ, and the activities experienced as those of the Spirit—were thought to originate from a single, though differentiated, agency.

The difficulty in the case of a transcendent, disembodied agent is that one cannot identify this agent by ostensive reference, such as by pointing. It is only possible to single out the agent of those actions identified (for various reasons) as divine by a sort of a causal approach. Certain actions are regarded as being uniquely able to single out this divine agent; they serve as sufficiently discriminating criteria of reference. Bauckham, we saw, identifies two such criteria for singling out the divine agent: actions by which God creates, sustains, redeems, and ultimately judges his covenant people; and secondly, the primordial act of creation. These sets of actions are ascribable to God alone and thus can serve as *discriminating descriptions* of the agent. When precisely the same sets of actions are ascribed to Jesus Christ, the implications are straightforward:

Jesus is identified with YHWH, since YHWH is the only possible agent of those actions.

The present section charts the New Testament ascription to Jesus of precisely those divinity-discriminating actions familiar to Jewish believers. The question will then be raised as to what the data can be taken to demonstrate or imply. We will argue that, taken by itself, this first criterion is not a sufficient basis for the doctrine of inseparable operations and needs to be supplemented by Bauckham's second criterion.

Before moving on to the data, a cautionary note is required. The literature on biblical Christology and Pneumatology and on the biblical foundations for the doctrine of the Trinity is vast. There are various approaches present in the field, from title Christology, to Trinitarian formulae, to analysis of patterns of worship, and so on. It must be understood that the burden of this chapter is *not* to show the biblical coherence of the doctrine of the Trinity. Ours is a much more modest aim: to scope the literature for approaches with direct implications for Trinitarian agency. Even with such a narrow objective, there is much material that will be neglected. Nor will we be able to enter very deeply into the scholarly discussion pertaining to every bit of data. Our aim is to paint with a relatively broad brush, demonstrating the clear ascription to Jesus of singularly divine actions.

We may start with Paul. There is a growing consensus that Paul is advocating a high Christology, assuming the divinity of Christ. The fact that he remains a committed monotheist while asserting the divinity of Christ is also increasingly acknowledged (cf. Rom 1:19–20; 9:6; 11:33–36; 1 Cor 15:23–28). In one of the landmark texts, Paul is understood to be intentionally adapting the *Shema* of Deuteronomy 6:4 to include Jesus in its confession of the oneness of God. He writes, "yet for us there is one God, the Father, from whom are all things and for whom we exist, and one Lord, Jesus Christ, through whom are all things and through whom we exist" (1 Cor 8:6). Paul's point in context seems to be granting the Corinthians' intellectual knowledge—that "there is no such thing as an idol in the world, and that there is no God but one" (1 Cor 8:4)—but resisting monotheism as mere head knowledge. One's confession of the oneness of God should be followed in practice by adherence to the way of the Lord Jesus Christ. Thus, as Chris Tilling notes, Paul appears to be glossing "God" with "Father" and "Lord" with "Jesus Christ."[41] Tilling sees the Corinthian believers as intellectual, or even metaphysical, as opposed to properly

41. Tilling, *Paul's Divine Christology* (Grand Rapids: Eerdmans, 2012), 83.

relational monotheists. Paul's adapting of the *Shema* makes it impossible to be a monotheist without following the way of Jesus Christ:

> Precisely in a context that contrasts the monotheistic "knowledge" of the Corinthians with the relational "necessary" monotheistic knowing of love for God, Paul includes Christ directly in this relational dynamic, and does so by employing a text in Deuteronomy that was central to the daily prayer life of Jews and to the relationship between YHWH and Israel.[42]

Anthony Thiselton concurs with this analysis:

> A static metaphysical monotheism disengaged from discipleship is not enough. . . . For all things, including Christian existence, take their origin from God as a gift, and since the one God is the goal of our existence, the means by which this comes about is that it is one Lord Jesus Christ through whom all things come, and he is the means of our existence.[43]

Monotheism gets redefined around Christ. That means that the Old Testament deeds normally ascribed to God get to be attributed to Christ as well. Later on, in chapter 10, which should be seen as forming a unity stretching back to chapter 8, Paul makes some startling statements about the pre-existent Christ. Urging the Corinthians to avoid Israel's mistakes, he claims that Israel "ate the same spiritual food, and all drank the same spiritual drink. For they drank from the spiritual Rock that followed them, and that Rock was Christ" (1 Cor 10:3-4). In the same vein, Paul writes (1 Cor 10:9), "We must not put Christ to the test, as some of them did and were destroyed by serpents."

However we interpret this overlaying of Christ upon the agency of YHWH in relation to these wilderness events,[44] Paul could not have been unaware of the resonances of this *agency toggling*. This is further amplified by applying Old Testament language of jealousy to Jesus (1 Cor 10:22).

Referring to 1 Cor 8-10, N. T. Wright quips,

> A small step for the language; a giant leap for theology. Jesus is not a "second God": that would abrogate monotheism entirely. He is not a semi-divine

42. Tilling, *Paul's Divine Christology*, 91.

43. Anthony Thiselton, *The First Epistle to the Corinthians* (Grand Rapids: Eerdmans, 2000), 638.

44. For an excellent discussion of this see Anthony T. Hanson's *Christ in the Old Testament* (London: SPCK, 1965; repr., Eugene, OR: Wipf and Stock, 2011). He discusses the additional texts of 2 Cor 3:7-18 and Rom 10 (25-47).

intermediate figure. He is the one in whom the identity of Israel's God is revealed, so that one cannot now speak of this God without thinking of Jesus, or of Jesus without thinking of the one God, the creator, Israel's God.[45]

Wright concludes that "Paul has redrawn this monotheism quite dramatically around Jesus himself"[46] such that one is now "compelled to use Jesus-language for the one God."[47]

Wright's claim is compatible with Bauckham's Christology of divine identity, but, as the former sees it, it develops and strengthens the eschatological dimension of monotheism:

Central to second-Temple monotheism was the belief . . . that Israel's God, having abandoned Jerusalem and the temple at the time of the Babylonian exile, would one day return. . . . This act, still in the future from the perspective of the pre-Christian Jews, was a vital part of what they believed about "divine identity."[48]

And thus it is this "long-awaited return of YHWH to Zion" that is "the hidden clue to the origin of Christology.[49] Wright finds this identification of Jesus with the returned YHWH to be operative in several texts, briefly summarized here. He relies much on Second Temple conceptions of Wisdom as the mode in which YHWH will return to Israel (cf. Sir 24). In Galatians 4:1–11, which is, according to Wright, a "compact exodus story,"[50] the sending of the Son and the spirit of the Son echoes the sending of "wisdom to dwell in the midst of Israel, as the mode by which, in Ben-Sirach, Israel's God was to come back and dwell in the Temple at last."[51] The same motif of wisdom, as present for example in the Wisdom of Solomon 9, is alluded to in the sending "of the one who is God's own second self."[52]

Colossians 1 and parts of 2 identify Christ with the fullness of God (Col 1:19; 2:9). God, dwelling in Christ, "reconcile[d] to himself all things, whether on earth or in heaven, making peace by the blood of the Christ" (Col 1:19–20). Much the same thought is conveyed by 2 Corinthians 5:18–19a: "All this is from

45. Wright, *Paul and the Faithfulness of God*, 666.
46. Wright, *Paul and the Faithfulness of God*, 644.
47. Wright, *Paul and the Faithfulness of God*, 655.
48. Wright, *Paul and the Faithfulness of God*, 653.
49. Wright, *Paul and the Faithfulness of God*, 653.
50. Wright, *Paul and the Faithfulness of God*, 656.
51. Wright, *Paul and the Faithfulness of God*, 656.
52. Wright, *Paul and the Faithfulness of God*, 660.

God, who through Christ reconciled us to himself and gave us the ministry of reconciliation; that is, in Christ God was reconciling the world to himself." The agency clearly belongs to God here, yet not in a way that makes Christ a mere instrument.

Wright finds further traces of the theme of the returned YHWH in 2 Corinthians 3–4: "To speak of seeing 'the glory of God in the face of Jesus the Messiah,' in the context of a long discussion of Exodus 33–34, can only mean one thing. *The God who abandoned Israel at the exile, because of idolatry and sin, but who promised to return one day, as he had done in Exodus after the threat of withdrawing his 'presence,' had returned at last in and as Jesus the Messiah.*"[53] The echoes of the Spirit writing the law on the hearts is strong in 2 Corinthians 3:3: "You are a letter from Christ delivered by us, written not with ink but with the Spirit of the living God, not on tablets of stone but on tablets of human hearts." Here too, the conflation of the divine agency with Christ's agency is hard to miss.

Finally, Philippians 2:6–11 further strengthens Wright's case. He finds in verse 11 ("so that at the name of Jesus every knee should bow, in heaven and on earth and under the earth") an allusion to Isaiah 45, which is part of the segment of chapters 40–55 which is "perhaps the central statement of the return of YHWH to Zion."[54] The most important thing, however, is that

> Jesus is not a new God added to a pantheon. He is the human being in whom YHWH, Israel's one and only God, has acted within cosmic history, human history and Israel's history to do for Israel, humanity and the world what they could not do for themselves. Jesus is to be seen as part of the identity of Israel's God and vice versa.[55]

The Spirit can be included into this expanded divine identity of the returned YHWH. Paul's temple imagery is especially apt to accommodate his understanding of the Spirit as the divine Shekinah, returned to dwell among the people (1 Cor 3:16; 6:18–20; 2 Cor 6:16; Eph 2:19–22; Rom 8:9–11). The inclusion of the Spirit himself in the divine agency and identity is seen in 1 Corinthians 12, where the divine agency is glossed as that of the "Spirit" (verse 4), of the "Lord" (verse 5), and of "God" (verse 6). A tritheistic interpretation of this

---

53. Wright, *Paul and the Faithfulness of God*, 679 (original emphasis).

54. Wright, *Paul and the Faithfulness of God*, 683. See, for example, Isa 40:9, 10, 12–26; 43:2; 45:23; 46:13; 51:5.

55. Wright, *Paul and the Faithfulness of God*, 683–84.

verse, Wright comments, "would have made entirely the wrong point within the present argument for unity."[56]

Gordon Fee concurs with this interpretation of the Spirit as "the eschatological renewal of God's presence with his people,"[57] finding similar echoes of Exodus and the construction of the tabernacle, filled with the glory of God (Exod 40:35). In later Jewish literature, Fee notes, the motif of the divine presence "was specifically equated with 'the Holy Spirit of the Lord' (Isa 63:9–14; cf. Ps. 106:33), a language and theme Paul himself deliberately echoes in Ephesians 4:30."[58]

Working with much the same data, Tilling argues that the logic of Pauline Christology is not so much the inclusion of Christ in the identity of YHWH (per Bauckham), as much as it is what we would call a *relational or functional equivalence*. The relationships that obtain between Christ and the church or the Christian are described with the same language used to describe the relationships between YHWH and Israel:

> This pattern of Christ-relation language in Paul is only that in which a Jew used to express the relation between Israel / the individual Jew and YHWH. No other figure of any kind, apart from YHWH, was related to in the same way, with the same pattern of language, not even the various exalted human and angelic intermediary figures in the literature of Second Temple Judaism that occasionally receive worship and are described in very exalted terms.[59]

For Tilling the net result is that Paul affirms a high Christology based on Jesus's assuming in relation to the church the functions that YHWH has in relation to the people of Israel.

The synoptics display a similar confidence about the divine identity of Jesus Christ. In keeping with our focus on material relevant to the doctrine of inseparable operations, the following data appear to be relevant. Matthew understands the work of John the Baptist as a fulfillment of Isaiah's expectation of the return of YHWH (Matt 3:3; Isa 40:3). The divine authority of Jesus is evident in his nature, miracles, and exorcisms (briefly discussed below), but

---

56. Wright, *Paul and the Faithfulness of God*, 723.

57. Gordon Fee, "Paul and the Trinity: The Experience of Christ and the Spirit for Paul's Understanding of God," in *The Trinity: An Interdisciplinary Symposium on the Trinity*, ed. Stephen T. Davis, Daniel Kendall, SJ, Gerald O'Collins (Oxford: Oxford University Press, 2003), 67.

58. Fee, "Paul and the Trinity," 67.

59. Tilling, *Paul's Divine Christology*, 73

especially in the extraordinary claim to forgive sins (Matt 9:5–6)[60] and in his lordship over the Sabbath (Matt 12). Jesus appears to be included in the divine identity by taking over divine prerogatives, such as giving rest (Matt 11:28), an apparent allusion to Exod 33:14. The participation of Jesus in the divine identity is modulated through the language of sonship (Son of Man, Son of God: Matt 17:1–11; Son of David: Matt 22:41–45). While Jesus often refers to the "Son of Man" in the third person, causing scholarly speculation that Jesus was himself expecting another eschatological figure, there is growing consensus in the scholarship that Jesus understood the title to apply to himself (Matt 26:2, 45). The language of the Son of Man refers, of course, to the vision in Daniel 7 about a human figure on the divine throne, which Matthew picks up in 25:31–32, where the Son of Man performs the eschatological judgment. Now eschatological judgment properly belongs to God alone, which Matthew seems to be aware of, given his clear allusion to Ezekiel 34.

To conclude this concise excursus on Matthew, Jesus is seen as fundamentally the eschatological Son of Man in whom the kingdom of God is inaugurated. He mediates the divine presence by performing actions that come under the prerogative of YHWH alone.

Mark continues the same theme of the identity between Jesus and YHWH, in particular by his deployment of the language of *kyrios*.[61] Daniel Johansson argues that there is a deliberate ambiguity in the reference of *kyrios*, either to Jesus or to God throughout Mark. He argues that "the ambiguous use of *kyrios* is intentional and serves the purpose of linking Jesus to the God of Israel *so that they both share the identity as* kyrios."[62] There is a "complex view of *kyrios* found throughout Mark," Johansson argues, "there is one *kyrios*, and yet two figures, God and Jesus, share the same name and title."[63]

Additionally, Bauckham points out that the "parallelism of 'your [i.e. Jesus's] way' and 'the way of the Lord' (where 'Lord' represents the divine name YHWH in the text of Isa 40:3) is an instance of the common early Christian practice of applying to Jesus Old Testament texts that use the divine name. God's name refers, not to divine functions, but to the unique divine identity."[64]

Michael Bird also finds the *kyrios* language significant and concludes that

60. Additional references for Christ's action of forgiving sins: Mark 2:10; Acts 5:31; Col 3:13. See in conjunction with Jonah 2:9.

61. E.g., Mark 1:2–3.

62. Daniel Johansson, "Kyrios in the Gospel of Mark," *Journal for the Study of the New Testament* 33, no. 1 (2010): 102.

63. Johansson, "Kyrios," 119.

64. Bauckham, *Jesus and the God of Israel*, 265.

"it would be incorrect to infer that Mark conflates Jesus and God; even so, it is reasonable to surmise that Jesus and God modulate together under the designation *kyrios*."[65]

Mark also ascribes exclusively divine actions to Jesus. He forgives sins (Mark 2:1–12); he commands nature (Mark 4:41; 6:50–51); he exorcises demons (Mark 5).

The practice of applying to Jesus the divine name is also observed in Luke. Kavin Rowe argues that it is theologically significant, in light of "the monotheistic exclusivity of the divine name."[66] There are two significant names or titles used in Luke: *kyrios* and *sōtēr*.[67] The latter title is used in the Septuagint almost exclusively for the God of Israel, becoming a fundamental component of his identity. *Kyrios* also clearly refers to YHWH. In Luke 1:5–38 *kyrios* clearly designates YHWH; then, in 1:43 Mary is addressed as "mother of my Lord." Rowe comments, "This is the first time Jesus himself appears in the narrative, and it is at this point that Jesus takes on the title/name *kyrios*."[68] Such an "overlapping resonance of *kyrios*"[69] is indeed similar to what is going on in the synoptics generally.

There are additional data directly bearing on the doctrine of inseparable operations in John, to which we will pay due attention below. It is a matter of some debate how the early church came to affirm the divinity of Christ (and the Spirit)—and ultimately to affirm the doctrine of the Trinity—given the assumed monotheism of the religious cradle in which the church emerged. As we have shown, speculation about the identity of God (ontology) is derivative of the knowledge of God's activities (economy). The analysis of divine actions, and in particular the actions of the Father, the Son, and the Holy Spirit, constitutes the premises of the eventual ontological conclusions.

Douglas Campbell helpfully distinguishes three types of arguments for Christology, respectively deployed by Bauckham, Hurtado, and Tilling. Bauckham's is an argument from *predication:*

65. Michael F. Bird, *Jesus the Eternal Son: Answering Adoptionist Christology* (Grand Rapids: Eerdmans, 2017), 88.

66. Kavin Rowe, "Luke and the Trinity: An Essay in Ecclesial Biblical Theology," *Scottish Journal of Theology* 56, no. 1 (2003): 9. For more on this from Rowe, cf. his "Biblical Pressure and Trinitarian Hermeneutics," *Pro Ecclesia* 11, no. 3 (2002): 295–312, passim. See also Brevard Childs, *Biblical Theology of the Old and New Testaments: Theological Reflection on the Christian Bible* (Minneapolis: Fortress, 2011), 363–64.

67. Christ is also called "our God and Savior" in Titus 2:13 and 2 Peter 1:1.

68. Rowe, "Luke and the Trinity," 14.

69. Rowe, "Luke and the Trinity," 14.

Certain predications were strictly reserved by Jews for their single, transcendent deity, for example, his name, along with fundamental creative, redemptive, and eschatological judging activities. He then argues that some of these predications were attributed to Jesus by Paul, from which it follows that Jesus is included by Paul within the divine identity.[70]

Campbell suggests the following syllogistic structure for the argument:

1. For all Jews, activities A, B, and C, are only predicated of God.
2. The early Christians, who were Jews, predicated activities A, B, and C of Jesus.
3. Therefore (other things being equal), the early Jewish Christians held Jesus to be God.[71]

Hurtado's argument, on the other hand, is an argument from *devotional practice*, with the following logical structure:

1. All Jews believed only God was to be worshipped.
2. The early Christians, who were Jews, worshipped Jesus.
3. Therefore (all things being equal), the early Jewish Christians believed Jesus was God.

Tilling, thirdly, formulates an argument from *relational patterns*. His approach canvasses the whole pattern of "Jesus-relations"—that is the language that Paul deploys to speak about the relationship of Jesus to Christians, or the church—and finds it to be equivalent to the language used to describe the relations between God and Israel. Campbell suggests the following logical structure:

1. God ← practices of his people in this relationship
2. Christ ← practices of the Corinthians and Paul in this relationship
3. Therefore, Christ is functioning as God did (and does).[72]

We might add to this Wright's own argument, which is also a form of argument from *predication*:

---

70. J. Douglas Campbell, foreword to Tilling, *Paul's Divine Christology*, xiii.
71. Campbell, in Tilling, *Paul's Divine Christology*, xiii.
72. Campbell, in Tilling, *Paul's Divine Christology*, xvii.

1. YHWH had promised that he will return to his abandoned people and perform activities A, B, and C.
2. Jesus performs activities A, B, and C.
3. Therefore (all things being equal), Jesus is YHWH returned to his people.

A number of observations need to be made about these arguments. Hurtado's approach seems the least germane to our discussion since it appears to be focusing not on divine activities as much as it does on devotional practices. It is a more phenomenological approach, designed to yield conclusions about the experience and perceptions of the Christians.

Bauckham's argument is perceived by some scholars to run into difficulties associated with his concept of divine "identity." Campbell, for instance, believes that it suffers on the front end given his more rigid approach to Jewish monotheism. Arguments such as those of McGrath, Fletcher-Louis and others seem to allow for the predication of A, B, C to other entities besides YHWH. It has become more difficult, some argue, to sustain his first premise. To put it in terms of our discussion, some find it hard to accept the premise that there is only one (disembodied) agent to whom certain activities must be exclusively ascribed. Bauckham's approach, however, if successful can best differentiate between the one transcendent God and every other supernatural entity that might claim the praises of men. His critics think it difficult to make such discrimination based on the observation of various activities.

Given this difficulty, scholars like Tilling prefer to focus not on the presumed dividing line between God and the rest of reality, and those activities reserved for the Creator, but on the covenantal activities whereby God is identified in terms of his relationship with Israel. Tilling offers one such approach. He is convinced that exegesis yields the conclusion that Paul related to Jesus (and understood the church to relate to Jesus) in precisely the same way that Israel relates to God. The focus here is not strictly speaking on divine activities, neither is it just on the devotional experience and practice of the church, but on "relation."

While there is much that is extremely helpful and illuminating about Tilling's approach, it is insufficient to establish the divinity of Jesus Christ, much less an incipient Trinitarianism. Tilling at most is able to point to what we have called a relational or functional equivalence. In a relational equivalence, the *type* of relations that obtain between X and Y is the same as the relations that obtain between Z and Q. To use a mathematical example: 2 is to 4 what 16 is to 32. There is no implication here at all that X must be Z. Now it would be a different matter, though still not sufficient, if Tilling's Q would be Israel, not the church or Christians in general. In that scenario he would be arguing that the relation between God and Israel is equivalent to the relation between Christ and Israel. But Tilling is not saying that. As a result, his argument can only show that there is some functional equivalence between Jesus and God. Still, Jesus and God may be completely different agents and divine entities.

Wright's argument, on the other hand, while still focused on identifying God in relation to Israel (as opposed to the whole of reality) seems to yield the most helpful results. Jesus is quite clearly identified with the singular God of Israel, who has returned as he has promised, revealing himself in the process as the one God, which is Father, Son, and Holy Spirit. His argument is tighter than Tilling's since he is suggesting not only that Jesus shares the same *type* of relations to the church that God has, but that he shares precisely the same *token* relation that exists between YHWH and Israel. In other words, Jesus precisely is the one YHWH to whom Israel had been related and whom they were hoping to see return. If Wright's analysis is correct, a certain model of inseparability will obtain for Trinitarian operations, much tighter and affirming a single agent. On the other hand, Tilling's approach only seems to require a looser account of inseparability.

Before moving on to the next set of criteria that identify God, what may we conclude from the scriptural observation that certain activities that belong exclusively to YHWH are operated by Jesus?

First, the question about the nature of monotheism remains clearly in the background. If there are multiple possible agents of those types of actions, then predicating this or that action of Jesus does not seem to firm up his divine identity, unless by that we mean that he might belong to a pantheon of divinities.

Second, certain questions remain about the validity of the inference from (a) Only God does A, B, C to (b) Whoever also does A, B, C must be God. The difficulty is generated by a rich pattern of mediators and intermediaries, from angels to patriarchs and others. For example, Daniel Kirk suggests that by casting Jesus in the role and in the activities normally ascribed to God, it does not follow that he is the same as God, identified with him. It need only mean that Christ is an "idealized human being" operating under the power of the Holy Spirit.[73] In other words, a form of adoptionistic Christology is fully consistent, so the argument goes, with the ascription to Jesus of divine activities (of forgiveness of sin, miracles, final judgment, etc.). We shall revisit

---

73. J. R. Daniel Kirk, *A Man Attested by God: The Human Jesus of the Synoptic Gospels* (Grand Rapids: Eerdmans, 2016), 325–80, esp. 371–80.

in due course the question of the relationship between the operation of Jesus and that of the Holy Spirit. For now, however, this point suggests the necessity of applying the second set of criteria specified (and preferred) by Hurtado. To rehearse: If Christ's ontological relationship with YHWH is only ascertained from an analysis of the covenant-sustaining activities of Israel's God, it still remains possible that Christ is the highest form of intermediary, the most exalted mediator, replicating the divine functions to perfection through the power of the Holy Spirit. But Christ would still only be an agent of God, but not *the* divine agent. There is, however, an additional set of data that identifies Jesus's relation to YHWH from the perspective of his sharing in the absolutely singular divine action of creation. To this we must now turn.

Jesus Identified with the Creator

Not only are God's covenant-related actions ascribed to Jesus Christ, but so is YHWH's creative activity itself. This is a step of momentous significance and the strongest possible biblical support for the doctrine of inseparable operations. By ascribing to Jesus the singular act of creation, he is understood as operating not simply the same action *types* as YHWH, but the quintessentially divine action *token*, namely God's act of creation itself. It does not follow from this alone that every other action *ad extra* is inseparably common to all the triune persons, but this is a key step toward the ontological identification of Jesus with YHWH.

The Old Testament and Second Temple Jewish literature consistently describe God as being the sole creator. In the statement of eschatological monotheism that starts in Isaiah 40 there is a clear link between the ultimate victory of God and his creational sovereignty:

> Who has measured the waters in the hollow of His hand, and marked off the heavens by the span, and calculated the dust of the earth by the measure, and weighed the mountains in a balance and the hills in a pair of scales? Who has directed the Spirit of the LORD, or as His counselor has informed Him? (Isa 40:12–13)

Bauckham comments:

> Isaiah 40:13 is most immediately a statement of creational monotheism, declaring YHWH to be unique in that he created the world without any collaborators or assistants. This incomparability as the sole Creator of all things

is closely related, in the rest of Isaiah 40–55, to the eschatological monotheism that expects him to make his unique deity known to all the nations.[74]

He is categorical that "in the uniquely divine role of creating all things, it was for Jewish monotheism unthinkable that any being other than God could even assist God (Isa 44:24; Sir. 42.21; 4 Ezra 3:4; 6:6; Josephus, C. Ap. 2.192; Philo, Opif. 23)."[75]

Outside the canon, one encounters little possible dissent to this view, that God created without any assistants or intermediaries. Christopher Rowland calls attention to 4 Ezra 6, where "there appears to be evidence that God shares his act of creation with another being, for the division between the waters is said to take place as a result of the delegated act of the spirit of the firmament."[76] However, besides the extracanonical nature of this source, the division of the waters could possibly be included as a component of *creatio secunda* and not of the primal act of calling things into being out of nothing.

It could be argued that the distinction between the creation of primal matter and *creatio secunda* cannot be projected backward into a literature that had not yet formulated the doctrine of *creatio ex nihilo*. James McGrath in particular has called into question the standard conception of creational monotheism. He argues, as we have already noted, for a more fluid border between God and creation. Prior to the formulation of the doctrine of creation out of nothing, God was generally understood to create out of pre-existing matter, by reining in chaos, as it were. The idea that God brings order to the primordial chaos through intermediaries is not ill fitting in Second Temple Judaism: "In the available Jewish texts that date from the first century of the Christian era, there is no evidence that belief in a supreme mediator or agent of God was controversial within Judaism."[77] McGrath admits that "these entities, further down the hierarchy of being, were created by and dependent on the Creator."[78] However, he concludes that, while God may be understood as ontologically prior, this does not translate into an ontological uniqueness: "What should be clear is that creational monotheism attributes an ontological priority to the Creator God, but not necessarily an absolute ontological 'uniqueness,' at least in the sense that later theology would come to define it."[79]

---

74. Bauckham, *Jesus and the God of Israel*, 194. Cf. also Isa 45:18–25.
75. Bauckham, *Jesus and the God of Israel*, 102.
76. Rowland, *The Open Heaven*, 148.
77. McGrath, *The One True God*, 48.
78. McGrath, *The One True God*, 18.
79. McGrath, *The One True God*, 18.

McGrath thus suggests that ancient Jewish cosmology was quite comfortable with a variety of intermediary beings, all ultimately dependent upon God, and some of them would have served as mediators of creation itself, understood as the controlling of chaos. There is thus no clear dividing line between a single being who is responsible for the single act of creation, and more of a continuum in which creation is a *type* of activity shared by a plurality of beings.

It is curious that the only evidence that McGrath supplies is the conception of Word or Wisdom of God. Going against an almost universal consensus in the scholarly literature, McGrath entertains the thought of Wisdom as "a literal, preexistent divine person or *hypostasis.*"[80] It is doubtful, however, that there is any evidence behind this interpretation. The ideas of Wisdom and Word are quite clearly personifications of divine attributes and are not to be confused with other celestial hypostatic entities, such as angels and powers, which are quite clearly distinct from God and placed outside of the divine identity.

Additionally, we find it difficult to understand how God's ontological uniqueness does not follow upon his ontological priority, except in the case of a form of Neoplatonic type of monism, or a form of process theology. While the doctrine of creation out of nothing may not have been explicitly formulated until the third century in Christian circles, and not until the Middle Ages in Judaism, it does not mean that it had not been already implicit in the theology of the divine uniqueness and sovereignty over creation. Thoughtful Jews would have found it very easy to understand the principled difference between God and everything else.

A similar attempt to weaken the consensus about creational monotheism is found in the work of Fletcher-Louis. He argues against Bauckham's claim that there was no room in Judaism for sharing in the divine act of creation:

> Already in Gen 1, God delegates to parts of creation a creative role in the making of the cosmos. God commands the earth and the waters to create and they do so, on three occasions (vv. 11, 20, 24). This and other features of OT creation traditions lead a growing number to speak now of a creaturely co-creativity in biblical theology.[81]

This is true but trivial. As we have pointed out, it goes without saying that God may have used instrumental causes in his work of arranging the features of the cosmos. It is undeniable that there is a strand in the biblical witness that

---

80. McGrath, *The One True God*, 48.
81. Fletcher-Louis, *Jesus Monotheism*, 145.

describes creation in the language of the organization of chaos.[82] A cocreative
activity of man must also be acknowledged, either in terms of procreation, the
naming of the animals, or cultural creation. None of this contradicts the essential claim, presupposed clearly and sometimes clearly stated (as in Isa 40), that
the primal act of creation belongs exclusively to God since there was no one
else he could have shared it with. Even the supernatural personal entities, to
return briefly to McGrath, which God might have used in his act of structuring
the cosmos must have themselves been brought into being at some point.

Fletcher-Louis further argues against Bauckham's strict dividing line between Creator and creation. However, it is truly striking how little evidence he
is able to provide. Indeed, the only serious argument he can provide is from
Sirach 24, where Wisdom both plays the role of creator as well as speaks of
God as "my creator" (Sir 24:8–9).[83] Again, this may be readily dismissed as
personified-attribute language (cf. also Prov 8:22).

Additional evidence that Judaism clearly understood the singularity of the
creator God is provided by Alan Segal's study of "two powers" heresies. He
points out that "two powers" (or "many powers") heretics might have appealed
to texts such as Genesis 1:26–27; 11:7; Deuteronomy 4:7; 2 Samuel 7:23[84]—which
use the grammatical plural in their descriptions of certain divine creative activities—to speculate about the existence of other deities through whom God
might have worked. The rabbinic reaction to these texts, however, is categorically in defense of creational monotheism, often appealing to the immediate
vicinity of the problem texts (such as an appeal to Deuteronomy 4:34 to refute
heretical interpretations of 4:7), or to the grammatical singular as a corrective
and control for the plural.[85]

We may conclude from this that the case against creational monotheism is
very weak. It remains the case that Jews of the Second Temple period and into
the first century of the Christian era remained convinced that God was the
only creator, even though he may have worked through created intermediaries.
In light of this, the ascription to Jesus of the unique act of creation can only
have one possible implication: that Jesus is so thoroughly and completely identified with YHWH that God's actions are Jesus's and Jesus's actions are God's.

---

82. This is particularly the case in prophetic literature, e.g., Isa 29:16; 45:7, in wisdom
literature, e.g., Job 3:8; 7:12; 9:13; 26; 40:15–24; Ps 74:13–15; Ps 139:7–12; Ps 89:1–14.

83. Fletcher-Louis, *Jesus Monotheism*, 297.

84. To this might be added Amos 4:13, where some suspected a distinction between the
"one who forms the mountains" and the one who "creates the wind."

85. See Segal, *Two Powers*, 116–22.

We must now review the New Testament teaching on Christ's participation in the act of creation.

A good place to start is with the Gospels as a record of Jesus's works. There is no explicit statement of Christ's *Schöpfungsmittlerschaft* (mediatorship in creation) in the synoptics themselves. However, scholars have seen implications of Christ's creatorship in various kinds of miracles, in particular the nature miracles, healings, and exorcisms. For our purpose it will suffice to focus on the nature miracles. Among these the lordship of Christ over the waters of the sea is particularly suggestive of his possible role in creation itself.

Jesus's calming of the storm is recorded by all synoptics (Mark 4:35–41; Matt 8:23–27; Luke 8:22–25). In each of these testimonies, Jesus's power to still the sea provokes fear and raises the question of his identity: "Who then is this, that even the wind and the sea obey him?" (Mark 4:41). Sean McDonough maintains that "the suppressed answer, as has often been noted, lies in a cluster of Old Testament verses: God is the one who stills the sea, whether at the exodus (Ps 105:9 LXX), or in his ongoing maintenance of the created order (Pss. 65:8; 107:25–32)."[86] He also finds echoes of a similar question in Ps 89:8–9. Additionally, he surmises that "echoes of the creation of the world might have been heard by some, since the controlling of the chaos waters was an integral part of the initial ordering of the cosmos. But the synoptic authors do not make the equation explicit."[87]

A second episode involving waters is found in two of the synoptics (Mark 6:45–52 and Matt 14:22–33). Both Mark and Matthew record the episode of Jesus's walking on the water immediately after the feeding of the five thousand. The disciples apparently failed to draw the appropriate conclusions from the feeding, as Mark records: "They were utterly astounded, for they did not understand about the loaves, but their hearts were hardened" (Mark 6:51–52). Matthew records the additional detail of Peter's attempt to sea-walk, which he works into a point about faith: "O you of little faith, why do you doubt?" (Matt 14:31). Matthew's event finalizes with the boaters worshipping Christ, saying, "Truly you are the Son of God" (Matt 14:33).

Davies and Allison find very significant Christological implications in this pericope.

---

86. Sean McDonough, *Christ as Creator: Origins of a New Testament Doctrine* (Oxford: Oxford University Press, 2011), 25.

87. McDonough, *Christ as Creator*, 25.

Jesus both walks on the sea and subdues its rage, and these are acts that the OT assigns to Yahweh himself. In other words, Jesus here exhibits an authority which the Jewish Scriptures associate exclusively with the deity. The fact speaks volumes. In addition, Jesus is bold enough to refer to himself with the loaded and numinous "I am." In view of all this, it does not quite suffice to say that, for our author, God has acted through Jesus the Messiah. It seems more accurate to assert that, in Matthew's gospel, God actively shares attributes characteristic of himself with another, his Son. The step towards the later ecumenical creeds, which affirm Christ's deity, appears undeniable.[88]

McDonough contends that

here the clearest parallel is the Septuagint Job 9:8: "the one who stretches out the heavens alone, and walks on the sea as if it were dry land." . . . That this precise verse from Job may be in view is supported by the further allusion to Job 9: 11: "If he were to go beyond me, I would not see, and if he passed me . . . by I would not know." This helps explain the curious note in Mark 6:48, "and he meant to pass them by". . . . With these allusions in play, the identification of Jesus with YHWH becomes evident. This is a theophany every bit as much as the storm-stilling.[89]

That a high Christology is implied by these episodes is challenged by J. R. Daniel Kirk: "Both the idea of power over the waters and the hopes for abundant provision of food are aspects of the Jewish cultural canon that are taken up in the descriptions of idealized figures such as coming Messiahs or Davidic kings."[90] It is not unusual, Kirk argues, for an ideal human person, as representative of God on earth, to share in various divine powers and functions. What Jesus does, in other words, is simply "playing the role of Israel's God [which] is precisely what idealized human figures do."[91] We should therefore not conclude anything more from these events than is necessary. He cautions that these miracles are not reserved for Jesus alone, but he invites other human beings to share in them, referring to the participation of the disciples in the feeding,[92] to which we might

88. W. D. Davies and Dale C. Allison Jr., *The Gospel According to Saint Matthew* (Edinburgh: T&T Clark, 1991), 2:512.
89. McDonough, *Christ as Creator*, 26.
90. Kirk, *A Man Attested by God*, 433.
91. Kirk, *A Man Attested by God*, 442.
92. Kirk, *A Man Attested by God*, 454.

add Peter's partly successful water-walk, as well as the promise made by Jesus that "whoever believes in me will also do the works that I do; and greater works than these will he do, because I am going to the Father." (John 14:12)

Kirk self-consciously employs a particular type of argumentation: "I have regularly had recourse to one particular line of argument: if a human being does the things that Jesus does, then Jesus' performance of such actions is no indication of ontological distinction."[93] His ontological deflationism is, in our view, a good caution. We must be careful not to base a divine Christology *solely* on such ascriptions of divine functions to Jesus. Certain divine action types are participable by humans. The question is whether there are action types or tokens that are unparticipable, not just by humans, but by any other beings except God himself.

It is not, however, a controversial statement that the testimony of the gospelers is informed by their understanding of the finalized Christ event. Events such as the stilling of the sea and Jesus's walking on water appear in hindsight, after the penny has dropped, so to speak, as bearers of the full range of Christological implications, which were not in full view at the time of these events.

With Paul (and, of course, John) the ascription of primal creation to Jesus Christ is explicit. We may pause to consider two passages that are by now familiar. We have already noted Paul's inclusion of Christ in the *Shema*, in 1 Corinthians 8. This identification of Jesus with YHWH implies that Christ participates in the uniquely divine act of creation: "Yet for us there is one God, the Father, from whom are all things and for whom we exist, and one Lord, Jesus Christ, through whom are all things and through whom we exist" (8:6).

It is tempting to see in the "through whom" (*di' hou*) a mere instrumental causality. Christ would then appear as God's chief agent, short of being included in the very identity of God himself. However, Bauckham helpfully points out that Paul is taking over a common "Jewish description precisely of God's unique relationship to all other reality," which also appears in Romans 11:36: "From him and through him and to him are all things" (*hoti ex autou kai di' autou kai eis auton ta panta*).[94] "That God is the instrumental cause (*dia*) as well as the agent or efficient cause (*ek*) of all things well expresses the Jewish monotheistic insistence that God used no one else to carry out his creative work, but accomplished it solely by means of his Word and/or Wisdom."[95]

---

93. Kirk, *A Man Attested by God*, 453.

94. Cf. Heb 2:10.

95. Bauckham, *Jesus and the God of Israel*, 215. The forms *di'* and *ex* are variants of *dia* and *ek*, respectively, with no change in meaning.

In Colossians 1:16 Paul repeats the theme of Christ's mediatorship of creation: "For by him all things were created, in heaven and on earth, visible and invisible, whether thrones or dominions or rulers or authorities—all things were created through him and for him." This clearly indicates primal creation, since the *ta panta* announces exhaustiveness.[96]

That Christ is named the "firstborn over all creation" (*prōtotokos pasēs ktiseōs*) need not denote any subordinationist positioning of Christ as the first of God's creatures, since Paul goes on to stress that all things have been created through him. What we find here is the theme of the unity between the Creator, Providential Lord and the Redeemer (cf. 2 Cor 4:6). The same Christ through whom the world was created is the one in whom "all things hold together" (Col 1:17), and through whom all things are reconciled to himself (1:20).

Other New Testament material could be adduced in support of the conclusion that Christ participates in the uniquely divine and singular act of primal creation.[97] We may conclude this brief discussion of Christ's participation in creation with the following conclusions. First, it is beyond reasonable doubt that Old Testament religion had by the time of the New Testament either consolidated or was in the process of consolidating a creational monotheism, which held that reality as a whole was created by a single being, and this was the God of Israel. There is no *class* of "divine" beings or even a hierarchy of divine beings. We found that Bauckham's line between divine and nondivine is the same as the line between Creator and creation. God is a unique being, upon whom all other beings, without exception, are ontologically dependent. While the idea that all other beings came into existence from nothing should not be projected back into the Old Testament, its germinal seed is necessarily and sufficiently determined by other explicit Old Testament beliefs such as the ones just outlined.

Thus, when the act of creation is ascribed to Christ he is identified with the only possible referent of this description, YHWH himself. There just aren't any other possible beings X that might satisfy the description "X created the world." While space must be left for other beings, angelic or otherwise, to participate in *creatio secunda*, Christ is held by Paul and others to have been responsible for primal creation itself.

The prepositional language (*ex, en, dia, eis*) is not neatly distributed between God the Father and the Lord Jesus Christ. Paul is quite able to ascribe *through him* to the Father (Rom 11:36), as well as to Christ (1 Cor 8:6; Col 1:16).

96. This holds even if McDonough is right that the *archē* in Col 1:18 "almost certainly refers to Christ's role in the new creation, rather than in primal creation" (McDonough, *Christ as Creator*, 85).

97. In particular Heb 2:10.

This undercuts, as we shall see in later chapters, attempts to view Christ simply as a secondary, instrumental cause of salvation, while the Father is the efficient cause. At the same time, the language of *from whom, by whom, through whom, for whom*, and so forth does reveal something about the operational relations between Father, Son, and Holy Spirit. To that aspect of the biblical teaching about inseparable operations we will turn momentarily. Up to this point we have sought to establish the fact that Jesus's actions identify him with YHWH, the God of Israel. Such a worldview-shaping identification is precipitated precisely by the ascription to Jesus of actions exclusively attributed to God. However, this might leave the impression that there remain no distinctions between YHWH and the Lord Jesus Christ. To rectify this treacherous appearance we must eventually turn to the manner in which Scripture renders the distinctions between Father, Son, and Spirit in the context of describing their inseparable actions. However, before moving in that direction, it must be noted that the New Testament affirms not only the inseparability of Christ and the Spirit respectively with the Father, but the inseparability of Christ and the Spirit.

INSEPARABILITY OF CHRIST AND SPIRIT

Trinitarian inseparability does not only extend to the relations between the Father and the Son on the one hand, and the Spirit and the Father on the other. Equally inseparable are the operations and persons of the Son and the Spirit. It is only possible to point out a few of the most important narrative indications of this inseparability in the life of Jesus, followed by the inseparable presence of the risen Christ and the Spirit in the experience of the earliest communities.

The Spirit is present in the life of Christ from his very conception (Matt 1:18; Luke 1:35). The framework for this constitutive association between the incarnate Son and the Spirit is given by the eschatological expectation of God's anointed (Isa 11, 42, 61). While the connection between sonship and the anointing with the Spirit will become commonplace in the epistles, the Gospels associate this in particular with the baptism of Jesus (cf. Mark 1:9–11). John had already stoked the expectation that one will come whose baptism will be far superior to his, a baptism with Holy Spirit and fire (Mark 1:8; Matt 3:11; Luke 3:16), also hearkening back to the Isaiah and Joel prophecies. Interestingly, in light of our conclusions to the previous section, Myk Habets finds a "most obvious reference . . . to the activity of God's Spirit in creation, just as Gen. 1:2 spoke of him 'brooding' over the waters."[98] As we have seen, to speak about

---

98. Myk Habets, *The Anointed Son: A Trinitarian Spirit Christology* (Eugene, OR: Pickwick, 2010), 135.

the Spirit in this sense is to refer to nothing else but YHWH in his relations to creation, or his people.

The presence of the Spirit upon Christ is without measure (John 3:34); it is a permanent presence and endowment. Jesus's ministry commences with his proclamation of the Spirit's anointing (cf. Isa 61:1). Whether this recognition of the Spirit's empowerment follows upon his recognition of his divine sonship or the other way around need not detain us at this point. It is sufficient to recognize that Christ's entire ministry is governed by the Spirit, whom Jesus himself recognizes as being at work in it. The link between Jesus's sonship and his empowerment by the Spirit is nevertheless fundamental. James D. G. Dunn's caution is admirable here: "We would do better to treat consciousness of sonship and consciousness of Spirit as two sides of the one coin. We cannot say that one gave birth to the other, and to build dogmatic conclusions on the priority of one or other is to build on sand, without foundation."[99]

The whole range of Christ's experience and vocation is stamped with the presence of the Spirit. He obediently resists temptation through the Spirit (Mark 1:12-13; Matt 4:1-11; Luke 4:1-13). Christ's great works are executed in the power of the Spirit, which is supposed to demonstrate to John the Baptist that he is indeed the one whom he expected as the Spirit-anointed figure of Isa 61:1. The exorcisms performed by Christ too are in the authority of the Holy Spirit (Mark 3:22-30; Matt 12:24-32; Luke 11:15-23), with Jesus implying that blasphemy against him and his power is a direct blasphemy against the Holy Spirit (Mark 3:29). The same could be said about Christ's passion (Matt 27:50; Luke 23:46; John 19:30; Heb 9:14), and his resurrection (Rom 8:11; 1 Pet 3:18).[100]

It is a fair conclusion to say that prior to his resurrection and ascension, Christ is, as Dunn puts it, "a man determined by the Spirit."[101] Christ's earthly sonship appears to be constituted throughout by the Spirit, such that there is no aspect of Christ's life, ministry, and passion that is not under the direct auspices of the Spirit. The polarity is reversed, however, as a result of the resurrection, specifically in the experience of the Pauline Christians, such that, again echoing Dunn, "his relationship was reversed and Jesus became the determiner of the Spirit."[102] What has happened?

The seeds of this *Christological determination of the Spirit* reside in the sayings

99. J. D. G. Dunn, *Jesus and the Spirit: A Study of the Religious and Charismatic Experience of Jesus and the First Christians as Reflected in the New Testament* (Grand Rapids: Eerdmans, 1997), 66.

100. For more detail on these various events, see Habets, *The Anointed Son*, 118-87.

101. Dunn, *Jesus and the Spirit*, 325.

102. Dunn, *Jesus and the Spirit*, 325.

of Jesus about the conditioning of the sending of the Spirit on his own ascension. This connection is made primarily by John (7:39; 16:7). The writer comments that the Spirit "was not yet" (*oupō gar ēn Pneuma*), which can be translated "was not yet given," or simply "was not yet" because Jesus had not been glorified. In one of his farewell speeches, Jesus comforts his disciples to the effect that it is for their benefit that he goes away, for unless he goes away the Advocate won't come.

Thus, the coming of the eschatological Spirit (not the Spirit breathed on the disciples by the preascension Jesus in John 20:22) seems to be conditional in some way upon Jesus, whether his person or his work. Peter explains this in his Pentecost sermon thus: "Being therefore exalted at the right hand of God, and having received from the Father the promise of the Holy Spirit, he has poured out this that you yourselves are seeing and hearing" (Acts 2:33). The Pentecostal Spirit, then, first inhabits and empowers Christ, then is again received as a fulfilled promise from the Father, and then is poured out by Christ.

This is in keeping with the Old Testament expectation, reinforced by John the Baptist's proclamation of one who will baptize with Spirit. What is truly intriguing, however, is that Christ doesn't seem to simply pass on the Spirit, passively as it were. Rather, he himself becomes *in some sense* constitutive of the Spirit. He does not merely *reflect* but positively *inflects* the Spirit.

The biblical *locus classicus* for this idea is the Pauline concept of "Spirit of Christ," or "Spirit of his Son" (Rom 8:9; Gal 4:6; Phil 1:19). According to Mehrdad Fatehi, it is possible to distinguish broadly between several schools of interpretation here. The majority of scholars see in this concept some reference to the presence and activity of the risen Christ in believers, usually on the analogy of the Spirit of YHWH in the Old Testament. Just as the Spirit mediates the presence of YHWH, so the Spirit mediates the presence and activity of Christ.[103] A second school interprets the "Spirit of Christ" as the Spirit that was at work in Christ, "which was somehow impressed and defined by Christ's character, and which now produces the same character (specifically, eschatological sonship)."[104] This second interpretation, favored by Dunn and Geoffrey Lampe, does not suppose that the risen Christ is in any way present with the Spirit in believers.

In Romans 8:9-10 Paul writes, "You, however, are controlled not by the sinful nature, but by the Spirit, if the Spirit of God lives in you. And if anyone

---

103. Mehrdad Fatehi lists Gunkel, Deissmann, Hamilton, Hermann in *The Spirit's Relation to the Risen Lord in Paul: An Examination of Its Christological Implications* (Tübingen: Mohr Siebeck, 2000), 204.

104. Fatehi, *Risen Lord*, 204.

does not have the Spirit of Christ, he does not belong to Christ. But if Christ is in you, your body is dead because of sin, yet your spirit is alive because of righteousness." The context is that of an argument about life as sons of God, which he equates with life in the Spirit. Understanding the Spirit in what Fatehi argues is a close analogy with the Spirit of YHWH, Paul connects our sonship with Christ's sonship.

In Galatians 4:6, we encounter the same theme of sharing in Christ's intimate relation with the Father through the Spirit: "Because you are sons, God sent the Spirit of His Son into our hearts, the Spirit who calls out, Abba, Father." The Spirit does not merely mediate Christ, who is otherwise at some distance. Rather, the argument works, in both Romans and Galatians, because it includes the idea of incorporation into Christ. Thus, it is Christ who lives in me (Gal 2:20), we have been baptized into Christ, clothed ourselves with Christ (Gal 3:27), as a result of which we are all one, Jews and Gentiles, in Christ Jesus (3:28).[105]

In addition to this designation, peculiar to Paul, two other references seem relevant in this context. In an argument about the possibility of resurrection, Paul says, "So it is written: 'The first Adam became a living being'; the last Adam, a life-giving spirit" (1 Cor 15:45). He directs an argument against a heretical approach to the eschatological resurrection, according to which it had already happened, yet not in a bodily sense. In response, Paul appeals to the fact of Christ's resurrection but also to the experience of the risen Christ by the Corinthians. Paul contrasts the first Adam, who was a living being, with the second Adam, who became a life-giving Spirit (*Egeneto . . . eis pneuma zōopoioun*) through the resurrection. Fatehi concludes that "by calling the risen Jesus 'a life-giving πνεῦμα' he re-defines the Corinthians' experience of πνεῦμα in terms of Christ. That is, he elucidates that their pneumatic experiences were experiences of the risen Christ. . . . Thus Christ is the *source* as well as the pattern of the Corinthians' pneumatic experience."[106] Because the risen Christ is the form of their charismatic experience, their warped conceptions of a disembodied spirituality are to be abandoned.

A final textual instance, surrounded by much interpretive disagreement, is 2 Corinthians 3:17: "Now the Lord is the Spirit (*ho de Kyrios to Pneuma estin*),

---

105. In Philippians 1:19, the other remaining instance, the concept of "Spirit of Jesus Christ" is less explicitly developed and we hesitate to draw what can only be tenuous conclusions. Fatehi and others have pointed out some intertextuality with Ps. 35, but the designation does not seem to play an explicit logical role in the passage, unlike Galatians 4:6 and Romans 8:9–10.

106. Fatehi, *Risen Lord*, 283.

and where the Spirit of the Lord is, there is freedom." A legitimate question rises as to whether *Kyrios* refers to the risen Christ, or to God (as in 2 Cor 3:16). Fatehi defends the former, more traditional interpretation and concludes that Paul is operating a "dynamic identification"[107] between the two. "This would mean that the Spirit, when viewed in its capacity as the Spirit of Christ, does not refer to the risen Lord as he is in himself, but as he communicates his power, his life, his will, his very presence, to his people."[108] This would fall along the same lines as the role of the Spirit in relation to YHWH in the Old Testament, yet including an ontological aspect, which goes beyond a mere functional identification.

> In other words, one should not speak merely of the Spirit playing the role of Christ, or of the Spirit only representing Christ. Rather, there is a sense in which the risen Lord himself is actually present and active through the Spirit which is hardly imaginable without there being some ontic or onto-logical connection between the two.[109]

Thus, while there are ontological implications of this identification, it is not a modalistic or unitarian identity without remainder. Although it may be prudent not to make too much dogmatic use of 2 Corinthians 3:17, a sufficient scholarly consensus can be discerned around the following observations on this issue.

First, it is undeniable that Christ operates through the Spirit. This does not mean that he occupies a merely passive role in relation to the work of the Spirit during his life. He gathers the plenitude of the Spirit, possessing him without measure. In his postresurrection, postascension work, Christ and the Spirit become inseparable. Christ is experienced through the Spirit, but at the same time charismatic experience is Christologically formed.

Secondly, there is a reversal of the polarity between Christ and the Spirit. Whereas the preresurrection Christ is empowered by the Spirit, the post-ascension Christ becomes a sender of the Spirit, yet in such a way that his own reality and presence are also communicated.[110] Dunn has called Christ

---

107. Fatehi, *Risen Lord*, 305.
108. Fatehi, *Risen Lord*, 304.
109. Fatehi, *Risen Lord*, 305.
110. Karl Barth, *Church Dogmatics*, vol. 4, bk. 3, trans. G. W. Bromiley (Edinburgh: T&T Clark, 1961), 291–96. On this score, Barth's observation that Christ's own prophecies about his return, which he seems to think will happen during the lifetime of his contemporaries, can only be taken seriously if we do not exclude a "return" of Christ together with the Spirit.

a "determiner of the Spirit." His rendering of the place of Christ in relation to the Spirit is particularly suggestive:

> The character of Jesus became as it were the archetype which the eschatological Spirit filled, the "shape" which the Spirit took on as mould, the shape which the Spirit in turn stamps upon believers. To change the metaphor slightly, in Paul's view the man Jesus became a sort of funnel or nozzle through which the whole course of salvation history flowed—whatever passed through that nozzle came out at the other end in the shape of Jesus, transformed into his image.[111]

The Works of the Trinity in the Gospel of John

The Gospel of John contains a unique presentation of the unity of action between the Father and the Son as the main argument for the unity of Jesus with the Father. Remarks about the unity of operation between the Father and the Son (and the Holy Spirit) are scattered throughout the book; here we will be focusing on the three discourses about works, in chapters 5, 10, and 14. Naturally, we will ask what are the ontological implications of the language about the unity of action in these discourses. A minimalist position, represented by McGrath, suggests that Jesus emerges as the fundamental agent of God and that claims about unity with the Father, and claims about the Father being at work in Jesus, make perfect sense in a framework of *agency*,[112] with no need for a further ontological identification of Jesus with YHWH. On this view, the unity of action is by way of representation, delegation, or simply agency. It will be shown that this minimalist position cannot account for the language of mutual indwelling—"the Father is in me," "I am in the Father." If it is accepted that the works discourses imply a strong unity between Jesus, as the Son of God, and the Father, the question is what is the nature of this strong unity. Since, as it will be shown, the works discourses imply both an operative unity between the Father and the Son as well as a real distinction between them, one way to resolve this tension is to think of the Son as a *second being* alongside of the Father, yet

---

Thus, Christ's resurrection, Pentecost, and the final return are three modes of the return of Jesus Christ. It is not accidental that one of the primary reasons for Barth's position is his affirmation of the inseparability rule.

111. Dunn, *Jesus and the Spirit*, 325.

112. Note that the term is here used in a different sense than our previous usage. McGrath uses "agent" in the sense of one acting *on behalf of* another, as a representative or intermediary. We have used "agent" in the sense of one's being responsible for a particular effect.

in absolute perichoresis with him. The argument is made that there are good grounds in John for this position. The end of this section, then, will assess this position, which sometimes can go by the name of social Trinitarianism, and suggest that it encounters fatal obstacles, both dogmatic and exegetical.

John 5

The occasion for the discourse on works in John 5 is the healing at Bethesda on the Sabbath day. This provokes "the Jews" to seek him out and accuse him of breaking the Sabbath (5:16). Jesus's initial response to their attack was to invoke the fact that God himself is working on the Sabbath, an allusion to the well accepted claim that God continues to sustain the world into being, even on the Sabbath, to give life, and to maintain the moral government of the universe. But Jesus has the audacity to include himself in these divine activities: "My Father is working until now, and I am working" (5:17). The claim does not stand by itself, but it follows a work in which Jesus restores the fullness of life and health to an invalid. This work, however, is not deemed a satisfactory proof by the Jews, who go on to add another charge to the initial one: "He was even calling God his own Father, making himself equal with God" (5:18).

The second count of the accusation leads to Jesus's speech, prefaced with "Amen, amen": "The Son can do nothing of his own accord, but only what he sees the Father doing. For whatever the Father does, that the Son does likewise" (5:19). This verse is perhaps the most invoked textual ground for the doctrine of inseparable operations, being routinely deployed in patristic Trinitarian apologetics. It therefore deserves special attention here as well. Jesus goes on to say that the reason why this is true is because of the Father's love for the Son and his showing him all that he is doing. Among the kinds of things that the Father is showing the Son are raising the dead (5:21, 25) and judgment (5:22, 27). These are exclusively divine prerogatives (as we have also noted previously). So, if the Jews are seeking salvation, they can find it only through the Son, to whom the Father has entrusted these prerogatives.

How are we to interpret this? What does it mean that the Son can do *nothing* on his own, but *only what he sees the Father doing*? This is clearly not a statement about *some* works of the Son, but an absolute statement of *total* dependency of the Son on the Father. Rudolf Bultmann notes that the negative part of the statement "attempts to guard against the mistaken view that the Revealer can be understood as a human person apart from his divine commission."[113]

---

113. Rudolf Bultmann, *The Gospel of John: A Commentary* (Philadelphia, PA: Westminster Press, 1971), 248.

Neither is it possible to interpret this in terms of a *second divine being* alongside God. There are possible Jewish precedents for this sort of "imitation." C. H. Dodd mentions the Philonic doctrine of two fundamental powers or attributes of God, creative goodness and kingly authority, both activities being mentioned in this text, specifically the power to give life and the prerogative of judgment.[114] However, more interesting is Charles Barrett's suggestion of an echo of Metatron, the exalted angel of 3 Enoch,[115] who seems to also carry out what he hears: "Whatever word and whatever utterance goes forth from before the Holy One, blessed be He, Metatron stands and carries it out. And he establishes the decrees of the Holy One, blessed be He" (3 Enoch 48C:10). But the dissimilarities must also be pointed out: He is also instructed by other heavenly princes (3 Enoch 10:5); moreover, Metatron himself, upon (unintentionally) causing Acher to worship him, is given "sixty strokes with lashes of fire."[116]

Bultmann surmises that the framework in which John communicates the thought is certainly that of a Gnostic myth, of a human being ascending to be shown heavenly realities and then returning to instruct people and carry out a divine commission. However, the content of what John communicates utterly dismantles the mythological framework.

> All these expressions [that he does the will of the Father, etc.] assert what at the very beginning was asserted by καὶ θεὸς ἦν ὁ λόγος: the Father and the Son may not be considered as two separate persons, whose work is complementary to each other, while the Father—as in the myth—remains in the twilight of that which lies beyond history; nor as two separate persons united in their purpose; rather all these expressions assert that the activity of the Father and the Son is identical.[117]

While Bultmann does not do enough justice to the distinction between the persons, he is right that the distinction cannot be grounded in activities that are exclusively proper to them since everything the Son does he does in utter dependence upon the Father, who in fact is "doing these works" (John 14:10). Also, while we may not wish to describe the language of "seeing" as "mytho-

---

114. Charles H. Dodd, *The Interpretation of the Fourth Gospel* (Cambridge: Cambridge University Press, 1968), 323.

115. Cf. Charles Barrett, *The Gospel According to St. John*, 2nd ed. (Philadelphia: Westminster, 1978), 259.

116. H. Odeberg, *3 Enoch or the Hebrew Book of Enoch* (Cambridge: Cambridge University Press, 1928), 45.

117. Bultmann, *The Gospel of John*, 251.

logical," it can be argued that it is not a literal language, for some very good reasons. First, as applied to God, who is not a material being, seeing can only be figurative. Secondly, it would imply an absurd duplication of everything the Father does: two creations, identical human beings, and so on.[118]

Herman Ridderbos also helpfully points out that "seeing" and "hearing" alternate in the Gospel between present and the future: "From this alternation it is clear that in 'seeing' and 'hearing' we are dealing with neither just a 'program' that the Father has given the Son once for all to carry out nor with incidental ad hoc instructions, but with the continuing agreement of the Son's speech and action with the Father."[119]

Clearly every action of Jesus is an action that originates with the Father in some sense. Jesus carries out no actions that are not also actions of the Father. This would not have been construed by the Jews as a statement of modesty, but quite the contrary as a lofty claim of equality with the Father. At the same time, however, it has the effect of undercutting the accusation that "he is making himself equal with God" (John 5:18). Central to Jesus's defense strategy is to invoke the indivisibility of his and the Father's works: Everything he does he only does because he has received it from the Father. But what does this apology refute about the accusation? Is Jesus refuting the accusation that he *is* equal with God? Or is he only refuting the accusation that he is *making himself* equal to God?

McGrath argues that Jesus's discourse on his sharing the actions of the Father is only intended to refute that he is usurping the role of God, yet without any hard ontological implications of identity between him and the Father. He argues that the Jews have fundamentally misunderstood Jesus to be saying, "I am YHWH." They would not have had any problem with the claim that a human being can exercise eschatological judgment.[120] It is not having these prerogatives as such but usurping them that would have been the problem for the Jews: "The

118. Some scholars (e.g., Dodd) have suspected an allusion to a parable of an apprentice and his teacher, echoing Jesus's youthful carpentry days. We are persuaded, however, by George Beasley-Murray who points out that "there are too many statements in the Gospel in the same vein to make it probable." *John* (Nashville: Thomas Nelson, 1999), 75.

119. Herman Ridderbos, *The Gospel of John: A Theological Commentary* (Grand Rapids: Eerdmans, 1997), 192. Cf. also J. Ramsey Michaels, *The Gospel of John* (Grand Rapids: Eerdmans, 2010), who is equally skeptical of the presence of a parable here, and instead thinks the emphasis lies on the idea of "imitation." For the reasons mentioned above, the concept of "imitation" is equally problematic.

120. James F. McGrath, *John's Apologetic Christology: Legitimation and Development in Johannine Christology* (Cambridge: Cambridge University Press, 2001), 98–99.

issue . . . is whether Jesus is God's appointed agent who bears God's name and authority, or an upstart who claims divinity for himself (or has it claimed for him by his followers), and who is misusing God's name and insulting God."[121]

Consequently, Jesus's apology seeks to demonstrate his "commissioning as God's agent" by highlighting his obedience to the Father. McGrath thus argues that Jesus behaves from the very beginning as one that bears the divine name. The divine name is not received upon the successful completion of his mission (as in Phil 2:6–11, for instance), but it is something the possession of which is not in tension with obedience. This makes perfect sense, McGrath argues, if we think of Jesus as God's appointed agent, carrier of the divine name. But to bear the divine name is not, for McGrath, to be YHWH himself, as we have seen in previous sections.

> The Fourth Evangelist works within the context of the dynamic monotheism of first-century Judaism and makes use of many areas of flexibility within that monotheism to present Jesus as God's legitimate agent, the one whom he sent, who carries out his will and bears his name, and who is thus worthy to be respected and obeyed even as one would respect and obey God himself.[122]

So what is at stake here—in McGrath's view—is not monotheism, which is not threatened by a human being having divine prerogatives or even bearing the divine name. Rather, the question is whether Jesus really is God's appointed agent or a usurper. Thus, for McGrath, the logical role played by the inseparable action texts is to demonstrate an obedience that is proper to God's appointed agent. To say, as we will see in John 14:10, that it is the Father who is doing these works only implies that Jesus is faithfully carrying out the commission he has received.

The text, however, seems to be claiming much more than McGrath's agential unity. There is a breaking up in the agency motif, without parallel in the literature. Continuing the theme of life-giving power, Jesus claims that "as the Father has life in himself, so he has granted the Son also to have life in himself" (5:26). The agency motif is clearly surpassed here since an agent only carries out a command and is utterly passive and receptive. Now life and authority (5:27) are not simply carried by Jesus, but *inhere* in him. Christ is not a mere representative, an agent of God, but the one in whom the power and authority of God reside.

---

121. McGrath, *John's Apologetic Christology*, 107.
122. McGrath, *John's Apologetic Christology*, 114.

This is as clear a claim of equality with God as could be conceived; it cannot be made from within the agency framework suggested by McGrath, in which divine prerogatives are merely delegated and not inherently possessed. Of note here is Paul Rainbow's very intriguing comment: "This is why the Son has life not 'through' the Father as the efficient cause of his existence, in the way the world does . . . but rather 'because of' the Father, as his exemplary cause."[123] Presumably, for Rainbow, *through* would mean a cause that is independent of that which is caused. We will return to the distinction between efficient and exemplary causes in later chapters. The point Rainbow wishes to make is that there is a distinction between the dependency of the world on the Father/God, and Christ's dependency on the Father. He continues:

> To be θεός, to have life in oneself, belongs to God alone. It belongs to both Father and the Son, but it belongs to the Father intrinsically and to the Son by gift. Aseity is of the Father, and he communicates it to the Son. . . . Were the having of life in oneself the original, independent property of both, there would be not only two eternals, but also two principles, fathers, powers in heaven—two gods.[124]

The Father and the Son both have life in themselves, which means, to return to Bauckham's formula, they both belong to the identity of the one God. Yet now we learn that within this single identity there is giving and there is receiving.

Thus, there is no tension between Jesus's equality with God and his dependency on the Father. It will be argued at a later point that such a tension would obtain were Jesus and God two distinct beings in their own right. However, within the unity of the one God of Israel, assumed throughout in John, a confession of unity with the Father ("I and the Father are one") can follow in the same context after "the Father is greater than I" (John 14:28).[125]

By way of a brief conclusion to our discussion regarding John 5, it must be said that Jesus's claim of an inseparable operation with the Father is not aimed at clearing up the Jews' misunderstanding. He really is claiming equality with God![126] But the kind of equality he is claiming does not imply independence

123. Paul Rainbow, *Johannine Theology: The Gospel, the Epistles, and the Apocalypse* (Downers Grove, IL: IVP, 2014), 101–2.

124. Rainbow, *Johannine Theology*, 102.

125. Cf. also John 10:29–30.

126. Additional corroboration that Jesus claimed divine prerogatives and was consequently regarded as having blasphemed may be found in Darrell Bock, *Blasphemy and*

from the Father! There is another way of imagining equality with the Father, which as Bultmann has so rightly sensed the Jews weren't aware of: "They can only conceive equality with God as independence from God, whereas for Jesus it means the very opposite."[127]

John 10

The first speech of John 10 presents Jesus as the sheep's gate. Here Jesus continues a theme he has started in chapter 5, and which is in fact replete throughout the Gospel, of the familiarity that those who belong to him have with his voice. Those who do not belong to him (an allusion to the "Jews" who oppose the Johannine community of the implied author) do not believe his words but rather seek their own praise. On the other hand, the sheep that belong to Christ have been given to him by the Father. There is a mutual knowledge of each other—Christ of the sheep and the sheep of Christ—which is parallel to the mutual knowledge that exists between the Father and Jesus (10:15). Jesus again mentions the "charge" (10:18) that he has received from the Father. But again this charge is in perfect equilibrium with Jesus's inherent authority: "I lay down my life that I may take it up again. No one takes it from me, but I lay it down of my own accord. I have authority to lay it down and I have authority to take it up again. This charge I have received from my Father" (10:17–18). Predictably enough, these words rile the Jews once again, although this time the accusation is not as clear as in chapter 5 (10:20–21).

The second speech of the tenth chapter of John is apparently connected to the first one but takes place during winter, at the Feast of the Dedication. The Jews apparently have had enough of the suspense and press Jesus to come clean on his messianic status. Jesus's response appeals to the works again: "The works that I do in my Father's name bear witness about me, but you do not believe them because you are not among my sheep" (10:25–26). Jesus again alludes to his prerogative to grant eternal life (also hinted at in his assumed authority to lay down his life and take it up again) to his sheep.

In verses 29 to 30 he justifies his status in relation to his sheep by an appeal to the Father: "My Father, who has given them to me, is greater than all, and no one is able to snatch them out of the Father's hand. I and the Father are

---

Exaltation in Judaism: The Charge Against Jesus in Mark 14:53–56 (Grand Rapids: Baker, 1998), 68; Morna D. Hooker, *Son of Man in Mark: A Study of the Background of the Term "Son of Man" and Its Use in Mark's Gospel* (London: SPCK, 1967), 173.

127. Bultmann, *John*, 245.

one." There is some debate here as to whether "one" should be taken to imply an ontological unity or just a functional unity: Jesus and the Father are one "hand," under whose protection the sheep are safe.[128] The functional unity makes it easier to accommodate the Father's being "greater than all." On the other hand, 10:16 clearly indicates that the flock has one shepherd: "So there will be one flock; one shepherd."

The Jews do not seem to have read the claim functionally; they react quickly and attempt to stone Jesus (10:31). The situation is defused by Jesus confounding them by an appeal to Psalm 82:6, where Scripture apparently refers to a created being, whether human or heavenly, by the designation "god." All the more so, Jesus argues, should the "one whom the Father consecrated and sent into the world" (John 10:36) be called the Son of God. This is followed by another appeal to the works of Jesus that are the works of the Father. Finally, Jesus repeats his call for them to believe in his works (10:38). The implication of this belief in the works of Jesus is a knowledge and understanding that "the Father is in me and I am in the Father." (10:38)

To draw some brief conclusions from this sequence of speeches, we may assert that Jesus includes himself in the identity of God as a shepherd. He receives his sheep from the Father, and he and the Father act together and inseparably as one protecting hand, from which no one may snatch their sheep. The mutual indwelling of Jesus and the Father is strongly suggested, Jesus himself argues, by the testimony of the works themselves. This provides additional corroboration against McGrath's thesis that the unity of works need not imply more than authorized agency. Bauckham rightly comments on 10:30 that

> the "in-one-another" language refers to the uniquely intimate communion that unites the Father and the Son. This strongly supports the view that the unity between the Father and the Son is not just their unity of will in Jesus' mission from the Father, the unity of words and works by which Jesus conveys what he has heard from the Father and does the works of the Father.[129]

Rather, this language "points to a relational intimacy of Jesus and the Father within the identity of the one God."[130]

128. Andrew Lincoln, *The Gospel According to St. John* (Grand Rapids: Baker Academic, 2013), 306.

129. Richard Bauckham, *Gospel of Glory: Major Themes in Johannine Theology* (Grand Rapids: Baker Academic, 2015), 33–34.

130. Bauckham, *Gospel of Glory*, 33–34.

John 14

The fourteenth chapter of John's gospel presents one of Jesus's farewell speeches, addressed to his disciples alone, which begins with Jesus telling them that he is going to prepare a place for them. He tells them that they know the way to where he is going (14:4), which puzzles Thomas. This provides the occasion for another one of Jesus's "I am" statements in verse 6: "I am the way, the truth, and the life. No one comes to the Father except through me." The implication is that he is going to the Father and the disciples are also going to the Father, but the way to the Father is only through the Son. He then reasserts the principle he had enunciated earlier, that knowledge of him entails knowledge of the Father (14:7). Having known Christ, the disciples can be said to have known the Father.

That in seeing Jesus one actually sees the Father is the religious truth that Philip isn't prepared for, leading him to ask his "uncomprehending"[131] and "dull-witted"[132] question: "Lord, show us the Father and it will be enough for us" (14:8). Yet another opportunity for Jesus to rehearse his inseparable operations theology! The question does not make sense. It is even perplexing: How can you even ask about this, Philip? It ought to have been obvious on the basis of the works that I have done: "The words that I say to you I do not speak on my own authority, but the Father who dwells in me does his works" (14:10).

Again the thought of mutual indwelling is closely connected to the concept of inseparable operations, as has been the custom throughout John. Barrett, Andrew Lincoln, and McGrath all fail to draw the necessary ontological implications of this combination (mutual indwelling plus inseparable operations). Barrett argues that Philip fails to understand the revelational unity between Jesus and God (a thought he shares in fact with Bultmann). While he grants that the "Father is in him and is in fact the agent of his works," he does not appear to draw the full ontological consequences of this.[133] Lincoln, similarly, only sees a "Jewish notion of authorized agency, whereby the one who is sent represents completely the one who sends. Since Jesus is the one whom the Father has sent, in seeing him one sees the Father."[134]

However, the additional thought of mutual indwelling radically stretches the agency framework. We therefore side with Andreas Köstenberger and Scott

131. Barrett, *John*, 459
132. Lincoln, *John*, 391.
133. Barrett, *John*, 459.
134. Lincoln, *John*, 391.

Swain's assessment that the *shaliah* figure—that of an authorized agent who bears the honor of the sender—in rabbinic Judaism is insufficient to account for the kind of union between Father and Son displayed in John. Moreover, they significantly point out that the *sui generis* nature of the Son's agency is presented in the prologue, in contrast with the agency of John the Baptist. They conclude that "the two agents belong to qualitatively different classes."[135] John is one who bears witness about the light but who was not the light himself. It may be reasonably surmised from this that while the concept of agency does play a part, its explanatory value is limited. Köstenberger and Swain go on to suggest that the category of Father-Son is much more appropriate and in fact very much at home here in John:

> What John makes explicit everywhere is that the kind of ordered, obedient agency that presupposes an equal status between sender and sent one is the kind that obtains pre-eminently between a father and a son, between the Father and the Son. The kind of agency exhibited by Jesus in John's Gospel is a distinctly divine-filial agency.[136]

Shaliah agency is perfectly able to account for subordination and obedience but utterly incapable of dealing with Jesus's answer to Philip. If *shaliah* determined the framework, Philip's question would have been perfectly appropriate and in fact timely. On the other hand, the Father-Son relationship is able to account both for obedience, as it is appropriate for a Son, as well as for unity and equality.

The dynamic of the relationships between Father, Son, and Holy Spirit is astoundingly glimpsed in the following few verses. It is impossible to do complete justice to their complexity at this stage, but they will be revisited later. The mutual indwelling between Father, Son, and Holy Spirit is particularly obvious here. Moreover, the inseparability of their operations provides the glue that prevents the tension between equality and subordination to degenerate into sheer contradiction. Jesus announces a sequence of events that includes his disappearance and then his return, but only in a way that is visible to his disciples. "In that day you will know that I am in my Father, and you in me, and I in you" (John 14:20). The debates about which precise eschatological picture is being drawn here are as yet unresolved, but it appears that at the

---

135. Andreas Köstenberger and Scott Swain, *Father, Son, and Spirit: The Trinity and John's Gospel* (Downers Grove, IL: IVP, 2008), 120.

136. Köstenberger and Swain, *Father, Son, and Spirit*, 121.

very least Jesus is announcing an invisible return somehow connected to the coming Spirit. The manifestation of Jesus is conditioned by the disciples' love. This is strangely parallel to the Father's showing Jesus his works on the basis of Jesus's love for the Father. Similarly, those who love God will obey his commandments (14:15). Consequently, Jesus will manifest himself to them (14:21), but also the Father, together with Jesus, will be manifested (14:23). That this manifestation is not merely an extrinsic one is suggested by the language of dwelling: "We will come to him and make our home with him" (14:23). The parallelism between verses 15 and 23 is hard to miss, indicating that there will be an ongoing indwelling of the three, Father, Son, and Holy Spirit. Each of their presences entails the presence of the other two. Knowledge of each one entails knowledge of the others. As Dodd put it, "Knowledge and vision of the Father, of the Son, and of the Paraclete are equipollent."[137]

It is precisely this mutual indwelling, this inseparability, which must be kept in view as the background to 14:28: "If you loved me, you would have rejoiced, because I am going to the Father, for the Father is greater than I." Stripped of this background of mutual indwelling and inseparable operations, texts such as 14:28 have a decidedly subordinationist bent, as indeed they were read by Arians and others in the first few centuries. However, given this mutual indwelling, which is such a trademark of Jesus's discourses in John, it is impossible to read these "greater than I" texts in a subordinationist manner since, quite simply, the Father has no properties or actions that are not already shared with the Son (except the property of being a Father to the Son). Rainbow is again very astute:

> The Father has granted to the Son to be all that he is and to do all that he does. Therefore it is not in respect of any particular divine attribute, nor of the complete round of them, that the Son acknowledges him superior, but only in having received from him the grant and commission that follows from it. In that respect, the Father comes first, always has, and always will.[138]

It thus appears here that the notion of the inseparable being and operations of the Father and the Son undercuts readings of this text that imply any ontological subordination. Moreover, the same notion, in which the Son has life in himself from the Father and receives his operation from the Father, underscores the irreducible *taxis* that obtains within the one being of God between the Father, the Son, and the Holy Spirit.

137. Dodd, *Fourth Gospel*, 165.
138. Rainbow, *Johannine Theology*, 113.

Distinctions among Persons in John

It may seem as if the above undermines the real distinctions between the divine persons, by refusing to recognize their proper operations. The argument implies that there is a single personal agent (comprised of Father, Son, and Holy Spirit), who acts inseparably, rather than three distinct agents. At this stage in our inquiry we will assess the evidence available in John's gospel for multiple personal agents. The data present a real challenge to our thesis, yet they cannot be addressed at this time beyond raising some issues.

McCall formulates the challenge in his *Which Trinity? Whose Monotheism?* He argues that Second Temple monotheism does not prohibit the "inclusion of more than one 'personal' agent in the worship that rightly belongs only to YHWH."[139] To speak of Jesus as being included in the identity of the one God need not mean that Jesus retains no personal agency of his own. Indeed, what we see in the Gospels is precisely the opposite. "The actions of the (incarnate) Son are distinct from those of the Father."[140] Additionally, they use first and second person indexicals in their reference to each other. In John 17 they are most clearly portrayed as distinct agents, who interact with one another and demonstrate mutual love for each other. Also, "Jesus shows awareness of sharing in the glory of the Father in a pre-incarnate state."[141] In this same pre-incarnate state, the Son makes a decision to become incarnate. Hence, "it will not do, then, simply to attribute the distinctness of the Son's will and consciousness to his *humanity*. It is the pre-incarnate Son who willingly humbles himself and empties himself. It is not the case that the Son is distinct with respect to consciousness and will because he is incarnate; rather, he is incarnate because he is a distinct person prior to the incarnation."[142]

All of this is apparently brought out by John 17. Jesus is aware of the "glory he had with [the Father] before the world existed" (17:5). Jesus recognizes that he has received a commission from the Father (17:8, 12), that he was sent by the Father (17:3, 8, 18, 23). He understands that his time has come to return to the Father (17:11). Jesus declares his love for the Father and is aware of the Father's love for him (17:26), even from before the foundation of the world (17:24).

Even more interestingly, the love and the unity between the Father and the Son are to be reflected in the love and the unity between the apostles. He

---

139. McCall, *Which Trinity?*, 61.
140. McCall, *Which Trinity?*, 64.
141. McCall, *Which Trinity?*, 70.
142. McCall, *Which Trinity?*, 71.

prays "that they may be one, even as we are one" (17:11). He then repeats this thought, praying for the unity of new converts, this time with more nuance: "that they may all be one, just as you, Father, are in me, and I in you, that they also may be in us" (17:21). Again he repeats and expands on this idea in John 17:22–23, this time explaining the unity: "I in them and you in me, that they may become perfectly one, so that the world may know that you sent me and loved them even as you loved me" (17:23). Finally, Jesus prays for the transfer of the Father's love for his own Son to his followers: "that the love with which you have loved me may be in them, and I in them" (17:26).

Social Trinitarians argue that the unity that exists between believers can be understood as analogical to the unity that exists between the Father and the Son, with John 17 serving as the most important biblical evidence. However, it bears pointing out that Jesus's expansion of his initial analogy in John 17:11 is always relative to the indwelling of the Father and Son in the believers themselves. The basis for their unity, in other words, is precisely the fact that believers are "in us" (17:21) and also that Christ is in them and the Father is in Christ (17:23). The thought of a simple parallel between the social unity of the believers and the social unity of Father and Son is really not there. Rather, the transition from the unity of Father and Son is made to the unity of the church only on the basis of the presence of Christ in the church. The significance of all this is that the unity between Christians is only a cipher for the unity between the triune persons if we exercise a great deal of caution. Bauckham seems to exercise precisely this caution here: "We do not have to conclude that the unity of the Father and the Son is no more than the kind of unity that can exist between human persons, but only that there is a resemblance."[143]

What may be surmised from the above? We will return to the discussion of social Trinitarianism in some of the material below. We will restrict our comments to one issue upon which this interpretation ultimately stumbles. The greatest difficulty with assigning proper actions to the persons of the Trinity is that, given the ascription of acts of obedience to the Son, and authority and greatness to the Father, it is hard to avoid the implication of an ontological, or at least functional, subordination of the Son to the Father. It will be very hard

---

143. Bauckham, *Gospel of Glory*, 35. Interestingly, Bauckham declares himself sympathetic to social Trinitarianism, despite his emphasis on monotheism and the Christology of divine identity. He defends it from the charge of tritheism: "This is not tritheism, nor is it a purely 'moral' union of will, because the three Persons do not exist prior to their relationships but are constituted as persons in those relationships" (38). It is difficult to understand, however, how a divine person can both have an independent personal agency and be constituted at the same time as a personal agent in those relationships.

not to take the references to the Father being greater than the Son to entail, for distinct beings, or distinct personal agents, such a hierarchy.

Now, one may of course argue that such obedience is perfectly voluntary. Royce Gruenler, in his commentary on John, *The Trinity in the Gospel of John: A Thematic Commentary on the Fourth Gospel,* reads the subordination language "as a genre of language by which Jesus dramatically and ironically describes his voluntary servanthood on behalf of the divine Family in the redemptive program."[144] The difficulty with this reading is that it makes the obedience language ontologically vacuous in the sense that it doesn't reveal anything about the eternal Son. If the decision about who dictates and who obeys is a purely voluntary decision, not grounded in the eternal life of the Trinity, then the incarnate Son's obedience has no revelatory status. Moreover, it may have been the case that any other member of the Trinity might have become incarnate without alteration to the pattern of relationships observed in Scripture. On the other hand, it is much too risky for a social Trinitarian to admit that the Son's mission is grounded in an immanent Trinitarian pattern of some kind, since any such pattern obtains between distinct agents and therefore risks ranking them.

To summarize, if we insist, with McCall and others, on ascribing proper actions to the Son, then we will also have to ascribe to him a preincarnate obedience to the Father. This obedience is either purely voluntary, and therefore not revelatory, or it is grounded in some eternal state of affairs, in which case it comes dangerously close to subordinationism. The advantage of the principle of inseparable operations is that it prevents the ascription to any divine person of actions and properties by which they may be differentiated from one another as distinct agents or beings. As will be shown, the doctrine of inseparable operations suggests that the obedience ascribed by Scripture to the Son is predicated in relation to his having a human nature, but it is a predication that captures something of the eternal relationship between Father and Son that takes place in the unity of their eternal being. It remains to be seen whether the theology of inseparable operations is not itself fatally flawed by appearing to confuse the persons.

CONCLUSION

It was not our intention to provide a comprehensive analysis of the biblical doctrine of the Trinity. Instead we directed our attention to the biblical inclu-

---

144. Royce Gruenler, *The Trinity in the Gospel of John: A Thematic Commentary on the Fourth Gospel* (Grand Rapids: Baker Book House, 1986), xv.

sion of Christ and the Spirit in the identity of YHWH, premised upon their sharing in the divine agency. We discovered that one of the primary ways in which Scripture speaks of the divinity of Christ and the Holy Spirit is through the practice of ascribing uniquely divine actions to them. Recent scholarship, however, questions the very category of "uniquely divine actions" by problematizing the precise nature of Jewish monotheism. If there is a whole class of divine figures who operate divine *action types*, then ascribing to Christ these divine operations can neither bear the load of a high Christology, nor underwrite a hard version of the doctrine of inseparability. In this scenario, Christ at most shares a type of divine actions with other divine personal agents.

Upon closer inspection, we have found that the softened monotheism of some modern scholars does not match either the biblical or the historical data. While a certain delegation to lesser celestial beings is possible, enabling these to mediate divine presence and even to command worship, there is a particular divine action that is by definition utterly unique and impossible to delegate: the act of primal creation itself. We have found that while certain covenantal activities permit a certain mediation by other figures—whether they be personified attributes, angels, or even created realities (the burning bush)—the act of creation is not delegable in this way. For this reason, the action of creation firmly establishes the ontological distinction between God and everything else: Only God creates, without any help, even if other beings may be called to share in some manner in what in time came to be called *creatio secunda*.

When to Christ are ascribed not only divine covenant-related activities, but the very activity of creation, the implications are unavoidable. In this case, Christ doesn't simply act out a set of divine action types, which at least in theory might be delegated to or shared with other beings; but to Christ is ascribed the primeval act of creation itself, the very establishment of a reality outside of Godself. Christ's lordship over nature triggered in the minds of the apostles echoes of Genesis. For the church fathers a few decades later, this was to be a central argument for the recognition not only of his divinity but also of his inseparability from the Father.

To say that Christ creates is the same as saying that God creates. The act of creation establishes the absolute boundary between *ad intra* and *ad extra*, between God and everything that also exists alongside God. Looking "up," beyond this absolute boundary there is only a single being, only one God, one Lord. Israel, and the whole world, must hear that "the Lord our God, the Lord is one!" (Deut 6:4). No amount of celestial figures can attenuate the ontological gap between God and the world. Scripture tolerates no competitors to God on either side of this border. Nor does it tolerate the blurring of the border into either a monism or a Neoplatonism. Creation is not a gradual falling away from God but the punctual act whereby a reality external to God is freely posited.

God does enlist and commission other agents to execute his will. But it is a theological blunder of the highest caliber to explain the agency of Christ in this framework. While these agents can be legitimately seen as conveying God's presence, the manner in which Christ conveys the divine presence is qualitatively different. Where these act as mere instruments of God, Christ is not a mere instrument. In the act of primal creation there are no available instruments to use: God creates through Godself. Additionally, even though Christ acts from the Father in his discharge of covenantal duties, he does it with an authority that resides in himself and is not merely delegated: He came to give life, as one who has life in himself! This tension between receiving his actions from the Father and inherently owning them is exactly the dynamic of inseparable operations! The framework of commissioned agency affirms the former but neglects the latter. On the other hand, modalism omits the former and affirms the latter. In Christ, all the fullness of the deity resides intrinsically yet, as we shall argue, does so in a particular personal mode, a mode of receptivity, as having come from the Father.

Christian theology could not tolerate the suggestion that Christ belongs to a class of divine agents, even if quantitatively superior to them. Rather it was compelled to affirm that whoever has seen Christ has seen the Father. He is not simply one agent or being with whom God chose to share his identity. He is the selfsame creator God, prior to all distinction between creator and creation. His identification with the Father is an essential rather than an accidental reality. They are the same Lord, God, and creator. Thus, the history of God's self-presenting through a series of delegated agents culminates not with an even more superior agent, but with God's Son, with the ultimate and supreme gateway to the Father, who shares in everything with the Father. In Christ YHWH had finally returned.

CHAPTER 2

The Rise and Decline of Inseparable Operations

The doctrine of inseparable operations emerged in the forge of the doctrine of the Trinity itself; it did not debut as a deductive consequence from the unity of the divine substance, but it was the very crutch of the doctrine of triunity itself. In much twentieth-century and contemporary theology, Trinitarian inseparability is analyzed more along the lines of cooperative or collective action, which may be called *soft inseparability*, rather than the *hard inseparability* evident in patristic and medieval theologies of one will, one power, one energy. The story of the emergence and decline of hard inseparability will be told in this chapter. The doctrine of inseparable operations quickly becomes the faith of the church during the first four centuries, being cast in the fire of Christological and Trinitarian controversies. It is consolidated through Augustine's and Aquinas's work on appropriation and the divine missions. It proves of decisive value in the monothelite controversies of the seventh century. However, hard inseparability is disowned precisely by the so-called Trinitarian resurgence of the twentieth century. Theologians of the Trinitarian resurgence do not merely neglect it; they explicitly dismantle it. Thus, from being an ingredient in a robust patristic doctrine of the Trinity, the doctrine of inseparable operations came to be regarded as a handicap that needed to be overcome.

Naturally, some modern critics of this doctrine will argue that they are rejecting only a sub-Trinitarian understanding of inseparability and that the witness of the tradition points to a soft, as opposed to a hard, inseparability. So, our present task is not simply to show the universal acceptance of the doctrine. Rather, it must be shown that our hard version of the doctrine faithfully approximates its original function and meaning. To that end, this chapter spotlights four separate scenes: first, it will be argued that the earliest understanding of inseparability, developed by Athanasius, Didymus, and the Cappadocians was of the hard variety. Second, we will take note of Augustine's and Aquinas's formulations of the doctrines of appropriation and the divine missions in connection to their debugging of the received doctrine of (hard) inseparability. Third, we will pause for a moment to observe the received doctrine at work in the monothelite controversies of the seventh century. Finally, we shall take stock of the modern objections to the doctrine of inseparability in the work of several contemporary and modern theologians.

The Patristic Emergence of the Doctrine

Teaching on the doctrine of inseparable operations certainly did not emerge with Athanasius (AD 296–373). Already around the year 260, Pope St. Dionysius (259–68) in his doctrinal letter to Bishop Dionysius of Alexandria condemns the errors of both Sabellians and Marcionites, the latter of whom "divid[e] and partition the one God into three separate powers and divinities." Pope Dionysius insists that

> These men somehow preach three gods since they divide the sacred unity into three different hypostases completely separate from each other. It is necessary that the divine Word be one with the God of all and that the Holy Spirit remain in God and dwell in him. There is every reason, then, that the divine Trinity be brought together and united in unity, as in one supreme point, that is, the almighty God of all things.[1]

Pope Dionysius's condemnation of "three separate powers" is representative of the theological consensus of the first centuries, and of what will become pro-Nicene theology. There is no question that the doctrine of inseparable operations has a good patristic pedigree. The real issue is which version of inseparability the church fathers had in mind. In what follows, then, it will be argued that Athanasius, Didymus, the two Gregories and Basil all affirm versions of hard inseparability.

Athanasius often deploys a form of argumentation, later to be perfected by the Cappadocians, that moves from a common operation to a common and indivisible nature. In his letters to Serapion, he is concerned to show the divinity of the Spirit by an appeal to his sharing in the same grace of the Father and the Son: "For there is one grace from the Father which is perfected through the

---

1. Heinrich Denzinger, *The Church Teaches: Documents of the Church in English Translation*, ed. and trans. John F. Clarkson (Rockford, IL: Tan Books and Publishers, 1973), 282 (Denzinger, 48).

Son in the Holy Spirit."² There is an inseparability of the Son and the Spirit in the communication of this grace, which forces us to affirm both the divinity of the Son and that of the Spirit. It is thus inconsistent to affirm only the divinity of the Son but not that of the Spirit, as the Tropici did. Employing a popular imagery for the Trinity, he argues that the Son and the Spirit accomplish the same illumination of the believer:

> Thus the Father is Light and his Radiance is the Son . . . and so we are also permitted to see in the Son the Spirit in whom we are enlightened. . . . But when we are enlightened in the Spirit, it is Christ who enlightens us in him. . . . And again, the Father is the Fountain and the Son is called the River, and so we are said to drink of the Spirit. . . . But when we drink of the Spirit, we drink of Christ.³

Summarizing this form of argumentation, Athanasius points out that the Trinity is "indivisible in nature, and it has one activity."⁴

The kind of unity and inseparability, moreover, seems to be of the "hard" variety. Referring to 2 Corinthians 13:14, where Paul enumerates the grace of Christ, the love of God and the fellowship of the Spirit, Athanasius writes, "This consideration also shows that the activity of the Triad is one. The Apostle does not mean that the things which are given are given differently and separately by each Person, but that what is given is given in the Triad, and that all are from the one God."⁵

The appeal to the sameness of operations is made by Didymus as well in his treatise *On The Holy Spirit*.⁶ Speaking about the common grace of the Trinity, he uses the term "a single reception of the Trinity" on the basis of the same 2 Corinthians text, "since whoever receives the grace of Christ has it as much by the Father's administering as by the Holy Spirit's bestowing" (75). He concludes, "Therefore, the fact that there is a single grace of the Father and the Son perfected by the activity of the Holy Spirit demonstrates that the Trinity is of one substance" (76). He then points out that the love of the Son is not

---

2. Athanasius, *Ad Serapion*, in *Works on the Spirit: Athanasius's* Letters to Serapion on the Holy Spirit, *and, Didymus's* On the Holy Spirit, trans. Mark DelCogliano, Andrew Radde-Gallwitz, and Lewis Ayres (Yonkers, NY: St. Vladimir's Seminary Press, 2011), 1.14.

3. Athanasius, *Ad Serapion* 1.19.

4. Athanasius, *Ad Serapion* 1.28.

5. Athanasius, *Ad Serapion* 1.31.

6. Didymus, in *Works on the Spirit*, trans. DelCogliano, Radde-Gallwitz, and Ayres. Hereafter numbers indicate section numbers.

different from the love of the Father (77) and that therefore "the activity of the Father and the Son and the Holy Spirit is the same. But those who have a single activity also have a single substance" (81).

The argumentation is very clear: Things that have the same activity have the same substance; things that have different activities have different substances. If the Father, the Son, and the Holy Spirit all bestow grace, assuming that the action of "bestowing grace" can only be accomplished by the divine substance, they must all share the same divine substance.

Now it is still possible, at least in principle, that the divine persons share not in the *action token* of bestowing grace but rather in the *action type* of bestowing grace. In other words, this is not so much a singular action but a type of actions, much like "walking," or "speaking." Human beings all share in these action types, but from this it does not follow that they share the same indivisible substance. Accordingly, it might mean that the Father bestows his particular grace, and then the Son and the Spirit bestow their own particular graces. Such an interpretation, however, is very much contrary to the tenor of what Didymus is doing in this treatise, not to mention the absurdity of such a view. It would be tantamount to saying that the Father saves some, and the Son and the Spirit others.

If it is difficult to speak about action types in the case of the salvific types of actions in which the members of the Trinity share, it is absolutely impossible to do so in the case of the paradigmatically unique act of creation. Reflecting on the conception of Christ by the Holy Spirit, Didymus does not find it "particularly astonishing that the Holy Spirit is the maker of the Lord's body, since along with the Father and the Son he creates all things which the Father and the Son create: *Send forth your Spirit, and they are created* [Ps. 104.30]" (145). Here it is being explicitly stated that the Father, Son, and Spirit share the same action tokens; they together create the same things.

Now it remains possible that the same action token might be composed of a number of sub-action tokens, much like the action token of "building the temple" is composed of many action tokens, such as "digging the foundation" or "laying the bricks." In that case the possibility would remain that the divine persons share the unity of a collective action. But such an approach is foreclosed in the case of the action of "creating." Given the fact that creation is *ex nihilo*, there are no preparatory acts of creation. Creation, one might say, is a basic divine act that is not further divisible into other subcomponent actions. Thus, to say that the Father, Son, and Spirit create the same things is to ascribe a unity to their operation that is neither of the collective kind, nor of the type kind. That is, there is no division of labor in the act of creation.

It is thus not accidental that the involvement of the Son and the Spirit in the act of creation was so significant in the debates with the Arians and the Tropici. Athanasius in particular leverages the biblical doctrine that God creates through his Word to argue for the divinity of the Son.

In his *Orations against the Arians*, Athanasius challenges the view that the Son was a creature yet above other creatures.[7] In the process he assumes a strict distinction between created and uncreated beings. Appealing to John 5:17 ("The Father works and I also work"), he writes that "it is proper to the Word to work the Father's works and not to be external to Him" (II.20). "But if what the Father worketh, that the Son worketh also, and what the Son createth, that is the creation of the Father, and yet the Son be the Father's work or creature, then either He [the Son] will work His own self, and will be His own creator (since what the Father worketh is the Son's work also), which is absurd and impossible; or, in that He createth and worketh the things of the Father, He Himself is not a work or creature" (II.21). Athanasius clearly shows here why it is contradictory to hold both that everything the Father does he does through his Word; and that the Word is a creature of the Father.

Moreover, if the Word is a creature, then the Word itself must have been created by some Word. But that means that there is another Word in God, different from the Son. This can only mean that the Word must be internal to God, "the proper offspring of His essence" (II.22).

This line of argumentation is significant. For if God creates by the Word, then it cannot be that the triune persons have their own and proper action tokens of creation, for in that case there would have to be three Words in God. There must be, therefore, a fruitfulness of the divine essence itself. The Word cannot be something external to God, for in that case God himself would not be creator:

> But if there not be a Son, how then say you that God is a Creator? Since all things that come to be are through Word and in Wisdom, and without This nothing can be, whereas you say that He has not That in and through which He makes all things. For if the Divine Essence be not fruitful itself, but barren, as they hold, as a light that lightens not, and a dry fountain, are they not ashamed to speak of His possessing framing energy? And whereas they deny what is by nature, do they not blush to place before it what is by

---

7. Athanasius, in *Nicene and Post-Nicene Fathers*, series 2, vol. 4, ed. Philip Schaff and Henry Wace (Peabody, MA: Hendrickson, 1999). Hereafter the discourse and paragraph are indicated.

will? But if He frames things that are external to Him and before were not, by willing them to be, and becomes their Maker, much more will He first be Father of an Offspring from His proper Essence. (II.26.2)

Khaled Anatolios summarizes this point well: "Athanasius advances with syllogistic force to his conclusion: if the Word is creator and the Word is extrinsic to the divine essence, then the creative energy of God is extrinsic to the divine essence and God cannot claim the title 'Creator' as properly his own."[8]

The establishment by Athanasius of the divinity of the Son proceeds by an argument that the Son must be internal to the divine essence and not a creature and thus external to it. It is significant that in the course of this argument, a certain logical connection has been established between the internal fruitfulness of the divine essence (the procession of the Son) and its external fruitfulness (creation). The linchpin is the biblical notion that God creates through his Word and that whatever the Son does the Father does also, and vice versa.

The relationship between these two "productivities" is an interesting question. Creation is spoken into being; the Word too is spoken, or breathed out. Athanasius, fending off Arians, is concerned to establish the noncreaturely status of the Son. He will thus insist that the Father does not beget him by will. If the Son is begotten by will, then one would have "to seek another Word, through whom He too has come to be, and was begotten together with all things, which were according to God's pleasure" (*Against Arians*, III.61). Of note here is, again, the logic of the processions and its implications for the essential attributes. The procession of the Son has to be by nature, not by will (III.65). However, if it is a production by nature, according to which power of nature? Isn't will a power of the divine nature itself? Whatever is produced by the divine essence, it is produced through the Word, that is, through the Word that is intrinsic to this divine essence. Yet the Word itself is not a creature of the Father, being begotten not by will.

It is perhaps unreasonable to expect Athanasius to have a fully worked out understanding of the dynamic between essential and notional properties. The distinction between understanding and will was rather incipient in his own work and would only achieve maturity a few centuries later. The notion of a procession by way of an essential operation would only later develop. However, Athanasius appears to be grasping at precisely these distinctions by anchoring the external productivity of God in his internal productivity. The Cappado-

---

8. Khaled Anatolios, *Retrieving Nicaea: The Development and Meaning of Trinitarian Doctrine* (Grand Rapids: Baker, 2011), 116.

cians, Gregory Nyssen in particular, will be shown to further strengthen the continuity between the two productivities.

As opposed to Arius, Eunomius accepted the divinity of the Son but held that he was of an inferior degree of divinity compared to the Father. The response required by this position was clearly different than the anti-Arian reaction. Whereas Arians would argue that the Son was a different and inferior being to the Father, Anomoean theology held that the Son had an inferior degree of divinity to the Father. Starting from the observation that the Son is a work of the Father and creation is a work of the Son, they concluded that where there are two different works, there must be two different energies (activities). Because the work of the Son (creation) is inferior to the work of the Father (the begotten Son), there must exist a variation in their energy. However, they would not conclude from this a variation in the being of God.

Against this notion, the Cappadocians appealed to the unity of the divine willing as part of a broader appeal to the doctrine of divine simplicity. In the process, the doctrine that there is a single will in God is decisively consolidated in pro-Nicene theology. Gregory Nazianzen affirms this unity of the divine being in a powerful summary of his Trinitarian doctrine:

> We have one God because there is a single Godhead. Though there are three objects of belief, they derive from the single whole and have reference to it. . . . They are not sundered in will or divided in power. You cannot find there any properties inherent in things visible. To express it succinctly, the Godhead exists undivided in beings divided. It is as if there was a single intermingling of light, which existed in three mutually connected suns.[9]

If this sounds social Trinitarian, a theme to which we will return, Gregory distinguishes the unity of the Godhead from the unity of universal human nature, where "the universal is only a unity for speculative thought. These individuals are widely separated from one another by time, temperament, and capacity."[10] Moreover, "each of the Trinity is in entire unity as much with himself as with the partnership, by identity of being and power."[11] If there is a possibility of something resembling social Trinitarianism here, it must include the unity of the essential properties of willing and power.

9. Gregory Nazianzen, *Oration* 31.14, in *On God and Christ: The Five Theological Orations and Two Letters to Cledonius* (Crestwood, NY: St. Vladimir's Seminary Press, 2002).
10. Nazianzen, *Oration* 31.15.
11. Nazianzen, *Oration* 31.16.

Responding to the Anomoean exegesis of Jesus's words, "let this cup pass from me, yet not my will, but yours be done," Nazianzen insists that they do not indicate the presence of a separate will in the Son (interestingly, he does not appeal to the distinction between the human and the divine wills of Christ), but precisely the opposite: "This would give the sense 'Not to do my own will,' for what is mine is not distinct from what is yours but belongs to both you and me, who have one will as we have one Godhead."[12]

Basil affirms that the will of the Son is not separated from the will of the Father: "His power is perfect in all that he has accomplished, and we will in no way separate it from the will of the Father."[13] Yet in this movement of the one Trinitarian will, from the Father to the Son, there is no interruption or interval: "In this way goods come to us from God through the Son who works these goods for each one more swiftly than reason can grasp. Neither lightning nor light in the air has so swift a motion. Nor do the sharp movements of the eyes or that of thought itself. Rather, each of these completely falls short of the divine energy when it comes to swiftness."[14]

While there is an order in the circulation of the same divine will from the Father to the Son, "his own will is received in unity and without interruption from the Father" and hence "we should think of a sharing of will that reaches timelessly from the Father to the Son in a way suitable for God, as, for instance, some figure appears in a mirror."[15] This does not indicate a different will, for it is the same will that is received from the Father, and it remains the will of the Father.

The same goes for power and for energy: "For if he is without difference in substance, he will also be without difference in power, and for those whose power is identical, the energy is also identical."[16] It appears from this that Basil treats the power that is shared between them as an essential property. Gregory Nyssen affirms in his *Against Eunomius* that power resides in the nature and that the nature is constituted by the three persons.[17]

The will-power-energy triad is evidently at work in the Cappadocian response to Eunomius. Against his concept of degreed divinity, Nyssen remarks

12. Nazianzen, *Oration* 30.12.

13. Basil, *On the Holy Spirit*, ed. S. M. Hildebrand (Crestwood: St. Vladimir's Seminary Press, 2011), 8.18.

14. Basil, *On the Holy Spirit* 8.19.

15. Basil, *On the Holy Spirit* 8.20.

16. Basil, *On the Holy Spirit* 8.19.

17. Gregory Nyssen, *Against Eunomius*, in *Nicene and Post-Nicene Fathers*, series 2, vol. 5, ed. Philip Schaff and Henry Wace (Peabody, MA: Hendrickson, 1999), 2.6.

that "simplicity in the case of the Holy Trinity admits of no degrees. In this case there is a mixture or conflux of qualities to think of; we comprehend a potency without parts of composition."[18]

It is the same energy and the same power and the same will that can produce different works. Nyssen easily counters the Anomoean logic of "different works therefore different energies" by showing that the same energy can in fact produce works of different values. But, as is the case, there are no different energies in the Trinity,

> for if there existed any variation in the energies, so that the Son worked His will in a different manner to the Father, then (on the above supposition) it would be fair to conjecture from this variation, a variation also in the beings which were the result of these varying energies. But if it is true that the manner of the Father's working is likewise the manner always of the Son's, both from our Lord's own words and from what we should have expected a priori . . . if, I say, it is true that in all respects the Father from Whom are all things and the Son by Whom are all things in the actual form of their operation work alike, then how can this man hope to prove the essential difference and separation between the working of the Son and the Father?[19]

Nyssen is advancing an argument that concludes, from the unity of energy or the unity of works, sameness of power. As Barnes shows, the logic holds only if by power we mean the sort of power that resides in an existent, and not a power that can be delegated, or passed on to others. Powers such as seeing reside in an existent, in this case the eye. Thus, as Barnes explains, "if the power to create is in fact a power, then it is connatural to God, and, as part of His nature, creating can no more be delegated than an eye can delegate seeing, or fire delegate burning. Wherever one finds the power of producing, one must also find God, just as wherever one finds seeing or burning, one must also find an eye or fire."[20]

Barnes has put his finger on something critical in Nyssen: the continuity between the internal divine productivity and the external, creative productivity. The two activities are grounded in the same power. Thus, Nyssen aims to refute the Anomoeans by showing that the obvious difference in degree between the

---

18. Nyssen, *Against Eunomius* 1.19.

19. Nyssen, *Against Eunomius* 1.27.

20. Michel René Barnes, *The Power of God: δύναμις in Gregory of Nyssa's Trinitarian Theology* (Washington, DC: Catholic University of America Press, 2001), 234.

begetting of the Son and the creation of the world need not separate the powers. For it is the same productive power that generates the two activities.

Barnes explains that creation and generation "are both activities of the divine power and nature, but each activity is the specific property of a particular person of the Trinity: the Father generates the Son, and the Son creates the cosmos."[21] To say that they are activities of the same power, however, need not imply qualitative equivalence. The Son is uncreated yet begotten, while the world is created.

This continuity of productive power is significant because it denies the possibility that the Trinitarian persons each have their own powers. If the very generation of the Son takes place by a power that belongs to the divine nature and not exclusively to the Father, there can be no other power that any divine person may possess exclusively. Thus, inquiries about the "social" character of the Cappadocian doctrine of the Trinity must respect the exacting grammar of their doctrine of divine power.

It is in this light that we have to interpret Nyssen's position regarding the begetting of the Son by the will of the Father, a position shunned by Athanasius. Whereas for Athanasius to hold that the Father generates the Son by will appears Arian, since it would seem to imply another Word prior to the Word, by which the willing takes place, Nyssen is not as concerned about the risks involved. Two reasons may be suspected to have mitigated this risk. First, the strong emphasis on the presence of a single will in the Trinity means that the Father's willing is not different in its being from the Son's willing except in the manner of its "circulation" from the Father to the Son and the Spirit. Secondly, partly as a consequence of their engagement with Eunomius, the Cappadocians are careful not to reify the will as something standing over against the divine persons.[22] To say that the Son is begotten by will is not to insert a third between the Father and the Son, but simply to specify the manner in which the Son proceeds from the Father. Of further note is the manner in which this exercise of the will is strongly connected to the operation of the divine nature itself. Nyssen argues that there is a concurrence between the natural operation and the "choice" of the Father. He adduces the example of a fire and its radiance:[23] It is as if, by pure speculation, the fire could will its

21. Barnes, *Power*, 247. He quotes from *Against Eunomius* 4.4: "If they agree that one activity [of creation] is exercised by the Divine power without passion, let them quarrel about the other: for if He creates without labor or matter, He surely also begets without labor or flux."

22. See Nazianzen, *Oration* 29.6.

23. Nyssen, *Against Eunomius* 8.2.

own radiance. This doesn't make the radiance contingent, Nyssen holds. Even more interesting is Nyssen's appeal to the notion of God's essential goodness: "The Divine Nature, then, is never void of good; but the Son is the fullness of all good and accordingly He is at all times contemplated in the Father, Whose Nature is perfection in all good."[24]

The thought that the Father wills the begetting of the Son is then counterbalanced by the thought that the will is common to the divine persons, that what is willed is connected to the essential divine goodness. The regulating factor throughout much of Nyssen's response is an appeal to the doctrine of divine simplicity. As Anatolios has shown,[25] just this kind of appeal makes it difficult to assent too simplistically to social-Trinitarian readings that naively hold that the Cappadocians "start" with the persons in their doctrine of the Trinity. As we have seen, the persons themselves do not subsist apart from the essential properties, power and will, which are shared. This is not to say that the persons are mere products of the Divine nature either.

Indeed, representing the precise relations between the persons and the divine essence is as difficult as comprehending the processions themselves. The Cappadocians do not imagine that "the uniquely indissoluble nature could be expressed by evanescent speech"![26] Rather, they hold, "we use facts connected with him to outline qualities that correspond with him, collecting a faint and feeble mental image from various quarters. Our noblest theologian is not one who has discovered the whole—our earthly shackles do not permit us the whole—but one who has gathered in his mind a richer picture, outline, or whatever we call it, of the truth."[27] Trinitarian theology is best understood as mining the semantic depth of the Scriptures. It does not purport to comprehend the divine being, its processions, and its immanent relations. Rather, on the basis of Scripture it defines and delineates a number of dogmatic rules for its proper reading.

One such dogmatic rule is the doctrine of inseparable operations. The writers we have canvassed all affirm the unity of the divine will, divine energy, and divine power. It is also evident that they are rejecting accounts of this unity in terms of cooperation, since there are no hypostatic wills or hypostatic powers on the basis of which such partnership might take place. At the same time, there are important distinctions between the *modalities* in which the essential

---

24. Nyssen, *Against Eunomius* 9.2.
25. Anatolios, *Retrieving Nicaea*, 218–20.
26. Nazianzen, *Oration* 30.17.
27. Nazianzen, *Oration* 30.17.

properties of will and power exist in the persons. There is an *order* in the reception of will and power, and in fact all essential properties, from the Father to the Son and the Spirit. However, simplicity prevents the partitioning of this power or the division of the one divine will. Thus, it is by the same power that the Son and Spirit come forth from the unbegotten and that the Trinity creates. The presence of the same power, however, does not preclude the distinction between the manners of subsistence of this power in the persons. The Trinity is simple but differentiated. In the same way, the divine activity *ad extra* is one, yet not without personal distinctions.

In the work of Augustine and Aquinas the inseparability rule is successfully tested against biblical and dogmatic scenarios. In the process, it establishes certain dogmatic precedents in the form of corollaries, such as the doctrine of appropriations. Until the Trinitarian resurgence of the twentieth century the rule and its corollary were considered to be adequate to the manifold witness of Scripture and Christian experience.

AUGUSTINE AND AQUINAS ON MISSIONS AND APPROPRIATION

It is a fact acknowledged by the critics of the inseparability tradition that Augustine favors a hard account of inseparable operations. We need not be detained with further documenting this. He treats the doctrine as an aspect of the "catholic faith"[28] into which he was catechized. Yet he finds himself having to answer a number of objections to the doctrine. For this reason, and because of the explicit attention he gives to the elaboration of the doctrine, it may be said that with Augustine we are in the debugging phase of the development of the doctrine of inseparable operations. The doctrine has been received; now certain problems and what he calls "puzzles"[29] need to be solved. In the process of debugging the doctrine, two clear principles will crystalize: the doctrines of appropriation and of the missions of the Son and Spirit. In the wake of Augustine, these doctrines will be developed in the Western tradition.

Augustine's *Letter XI* to Nebridius represents one of the earlier stages of his work on the Trinity.[30] Already at this time he has to respond to an important

---

28. Augustine, *Tractate*, in *Nicene and Post-Nicene Fathers*, series 1, vol. 7, *St. Augustine: Gospel of John, First Epistle of John, and Soliloquies*, trans. John Gibb and James Innes (New York: Cosimo, 2007), 20.3; cf. also 18.6.

29. Augustine, *The Trinity*, 2nd ed., trans. Edmund Hill, OP (Hyde Park: New City Press, 1991), 1.8.

30. Augustine, *Letters 1–99*, trans. Roland Teske, SJ, ed. John E. Rotelle, OSA (Hyde Park: New City Press, 2001).

objection to the doctrine of inseparable operations, from which it seems to follow "as a consequence that the whole Trinity assumed human nature; for if the Son did so, but the Father and the Spirit did not, there is something in which they act separably."[31] This is perhaps the most fundamental hurdle for a hard conception of triune inseparability and it will be discussed more fully in chapter 5 below. Augustine's treatment of the objection is at this stage still incipient, but it indicates the broad contours of his later doctrine of appropriations.

He starts by distinguishing in each substance between "these three things: first, that it is; next that it is this or that; and third, that as far as possible it remains as it is."[32] The second of these represents form, or mode of existence. He then explains that the Son's mode of existence has to do with training, and with the intellect, being the eternal Logos. However, in the incarnation we have "the effective presentation to us of a certain training in the right way of living." Hence, "it is not without reason that all this is ascribed to the Son."[33]

This appeals to a logic of fittingness, although admittedly Augustine is neither precise nor elaborate at this stage. That is, the incarnation appropriately is said to belong to the Son since the form, or the mode of existence, of the human nature is such that it provides a certain model of spiritual life. Yet the incarnation is not exclusively the Son's under all descriptions of the object. Its being "ascribed" to the Son does not indicate a strict logical elucidation, but rather a range of appropriateness within what may be truthfully said about a phenomenon. Augustine explains that "although the constituent elements may be many, some one nevertheless stands out above the rest, and therefore not unreasonably claims a right of possession, as it were, of the whole for itself."[34]

This hesitation to strictly ascribe the incarnation to the Son is motivated by a certain caution with regard to the relationship between theology and economy. Augustine understands the self-communication of God to consist in a certain adaptation to our needs and limitations. Accordingly, strict equivalences between manifesting effects and transcendent cause will not be found. Language will therefore find it impossible to strictly represent the realities it intends. So Augustine writes that

> wherefore, although in all things the Divine Persons act perfectly in common, and without possibility of separation, nevertheless their operations

31. Augustine, *Letter* 11.2.
32. Augustine, *Letter* 11.3.
33. Augustine, *Letter* 11.4.
34. Augustine, *Letter* 11.4.

behooved to be exhibited in such a way as to be distinguished from each other, on account of the weakness which is in us, who have fallen from unity into variety. For no one ever succeeds in raising another to the height on which he himself stands, unless he stoop somewhat towards the level which that other occupies."[35]

The incarnation only appears to present to us *just* one of the divine persons, the eternal Word. Such an appearance is fitting, for the end of the incarnation pertains to the illumination of humanity, leading to the restoration of the divine image in man. And yet this ascription should not be understood in a strict sense, to the exclusion of the presence of the Father and the Spirit in the incarnation. Since the triune persons are inseparable from each other in substance, the sending forth of the Son cannot entail his becoming untethered from the Father.

Sermon 52 reveals a maturing conception of inseparable operations,[36] as Lewis Ayres notes.[37] The objection to which he responds is identical: given that "the Son, not the Father, suffered; the Son rose again, not the Father. So either admit that the Son does something without the Father, or else admit that the Father too was born, suffered, died, rose again."[38]

Augustine is much more convincing and precise in his response. He admits that "the Son indeed, and not the Father, was born of the Virgin Mary," but he introduces a distinction that is going to prove decisive downstream, between created effects, which are to be commonly ascribed to the Trinity, and a certain possession of these effects by one of the persons alone. He continues: "But the birth of the Son, not the Father, from the Virgin Mary was the work of both Father and Son. It was not indeed the Father, but the Son who suffered; yet the suffering of the Son was the work of both Father and Son. It wasn't the Father who rose again, but the Son; yet the resurrection of the Son was the work of both Father and Son."[39]

Augustine cannot find an analogy for the idea of three things that are "indicated separately, operating inseparably" except in the human psyche and its faculties of memory, understanding and will. This famous analogy is not

35. Augustine, *Letter* 11.4.

36. Augustine, *Sermons: III (51–94) on the New Testament*, trans. Edmund Hill, OP, ed. John E. Rotelle, OSA (Hyde Park: New City Press, 1992).

37. Lewis Ayres, "'Remember That You Are Catholic' (serm. 52.2): Augustine on the Unity of the Triune God," *Journal of Early Christian Studies* 8, no. 1 (2000): 39–82.

38. Augustine, *Sermon* 52.7.

39. Augustine, *Sermon* 52.8.

intended to facilitate an understanding of the Trinity itself—that is, to balance diversity and unity as other such analogies are wont to do. Rather, it's strictly intended as an illustration of the possibility that the three persons may be indicated or manifested separably even while they operate inseparably.

These faculties are each designated separately by the words "memory," "understanding," and "will." But it is impossible to utter these words without drawing together on all of these faculties. "So too, the Trinity produced the flesh of Christ, but the only one of them it belongs to is Christ. The Trinity produced the dove from the sky, but the only one of them it belongs to is the Holy Spirit. The Trinity produced the voice from heaven, but the only one it belongs to is the Father."[40]

The notion of "belonging" to just one person, as in the flesh of Christ belonging to Christ alone, is an improvement over his earlier rather timid ascription of the incarnation to the Son in terms of fittingness. The human nature belongs to the Son in the sense that it indicates the Son. It manifests the Son. Yet here again it must be remembered that even though the Son is manifested separably, the other two persons inseparably act.

By the time Augustine writes *De trinitate* he has a fully worked out account of the divine missions. He explains that there is a twofold sense of the mission of the Son: "the Son of God is not said to be sent in the very fact that he is born of the Father, but either in the fact that the Word made flesh showed himself to this world. . . . Or else he is sent in the fact that he is perceived in time by someone's mind."[41]

There is a certain epistemological intention behind the missions of the Son and the Spirit. The missions are ordered to the knowledge, or to the manifestation, of the divine persons. But the persons must be manifested separably on account of our weakness: "It is to make us aware of the trinity that some things are even said about the persons singly by name; however, they must not be understood in the sense of excluding the other persons, because this same three is also one, and there is one substance and godhead of Father and Son and Holy Spirit."[42] We know that there are three irreducible "persons" in the Trinity because of their separate manifestation. However, this separate manifestation must not obscure their inseparable working, and thus their sameness of substance.

The dynamic of unity and diversity within the Trinity results in particular constraints upon language. Augustine, together with the tradition, dis-

40. Augustine, *Sermon* 52.22.
41. Augustine, *The Trinity* 4.28.
42. Augustine, *The Trinity* 1.19.

tinguishes between substance terms (or names) and relational names. The former indicate the whole being of God, with its substantial properties. The second refer to the properties of the persons themselves. The distinction became essential in the refutation of Arianism, which took "being begotten" as a substantial term, implying both the inferiority and the separateness of the Son. An exacting grammar of predication emerges, according to which strictly speaking only relational names can be applied exclusively to the persons. Only the Son is begotten; only the Son is Word; only the Spirit is proceeding, or spirating. This seems to result in an austerity of descriptions with regard to the triune persons, an austerity that doesn't seem to characterize scriptural descriptions, which do characterize the persons with names such as Creator, Lord, power and wisdom.

This problem is tackled in books 5–7 of *De trinitate*. Augustine selects as his primary test case Paul's description of Christ as "the power of God and the wisdom of God." (1 Cor 1:24). He asks in what way can Christ be called the power of God. Noting that power and wisdom are properties of the divine nature, he rejects an interpretation according to which the Father is wise with the wisdom that is specifically the Son's,[43] or powerful with a power that is the Son's property. As Edmund Hill explains,

> The text Christ the power of God and the wisdom of God faces us with the possibility that perhaps all substantive predications, like goodness, greatness, and eternity, which do not seem to differ in quality from power or wisdom, should be treated really as quasi-relative predications, in such a manner that the Son is to be considered as the power, wisdom, goodness, greatness, and eternity by which the Father is powerful, wise, good, great, and eternal.[44]

This discussion concerns us because it is asking about the grammar of predicating properties to the triune persons. A chief concern underlying this discussion in *De trinitate* is the preservation of the simplicity and unity of God. Augustine is asking whether "the Father is not powerful or wise taken singly, but only taken together with that power and wisdom which he has begotten."[45]

---

43. Augustine notes that some orthodox theologians have suggested this view, in their refutation of Arians (*The Trinity*, 6.1). On some interpretations, this is an account that is similar to Athanasius's; cf. Leithart, *Athanasius*, Foundations of Theological Exegesis and Christian Spirituality 1 (Grand Rapids: Baker Academic, 2011), 86–87.

44. Hill, in Augustine, *The Trinity*, chapter description, 205.

45. Augustine, *The Trinity*, 218.

Per simplicity, however, this would be absurd: "But if the Father too who begot wisdom becomes wise with it, and if for him to be is not the same as to be wise, then the Son will be a quality of his, not his offspring, and there will no longer be absolute simplicity in God."[46]

What is Augustine doing here, beyond "tying himself inextricably in knots for the pure pleasure of then extricating himself from the tangle"?[47] He is trying to figure out the logic of predicating attributes to a triune yet simple God. If the Son is the Father's own wisdom, then the Father taken by himself is not wise, except through the begetting of the Son. But then the Son appears to be a quality of the Father, which the Father begets. The unity and simplicity of the divine nature appears to be threatened by the predication of a substantial property to just one of the persons of the Trinity, in this case the Son. Matthew Levering explains Augustine's argument: "If the Son is the Father's power and wisdom, how can the Father and the Son be said to have one and the same substance? If only the Son were powerful and wise, then only the Son would be God. The Father would participate in the Son's power and wisdom, rather than being powerful and wise."[48] For this reason it cannot be said that any triune person has any substantial attribute that the other persons do not have. According to Augustine's and Athanasius's logic, this would partition the divine essence and surrender divine unity. More importantly, however, it would falsify the scriptural predications of substantial attributes to all Trinitarian persons.

The only attributes that are properly to be attributed to the persons are relational attributes, such as being unbegotten, begotten, and spirated. This rule must be strictly observed if one wishes to retain the unity of the divine substance. As Hill explains: "If God is powerful by the power of Christ, i.e. if power is a 'relationship name,' why not other attributes?"[49] It is important to understand that any substantial attributes can be in principle appropriated to any of the divine persons.[50]

The doctrine of appropriations does not supply a set of criteria for further distinguishing the persons from each other. Instead, it stipulates a number of grammatical and semantic rules that pertain to proper predication of substantial attributes to the persons. Augustine understands that the persons are given

46. Augustine, *The Trinity*, 7.2.

47. Edmund Hill, *The Mystery of the Trinity* (London: G. Chapman, 1985), 104.

48. Matthew Levering, *The Theology of Augustine: An Introductory Guide to His Most Important Works* (Grand Rapids: Baker, 2013), 164.

49. Hill, *Mystery*, 104.

50. See Hill, *Mystery*, 105. We discuss the nature of appropriation in the next chapter.

to us distinctly, that is, they are manifested for our knowledge distinctly, yet without operating separately. Such a separate operation would entail distinct natures. Augustine understands Trinitarian reflection as a form of semantic ascent, where the self-manifestation of God in Christ is understood under the discipline of Scripture. That the Father, Son, and Spirit always operate together we learn from Scripture, by faith. Such an indivisible operation is not manifested as such for our senses. Faith receives this truth and thus leads our mind from the sense impressions of the distinct manifestations to the understanding of the underlying unity. There is no implication here that unity is superior to distinction in the Trinity. The ascent does not imply leaving behind the diversity of the relations and processions. On the contrary, insisting on the unity leads to a truer understanding of the persons themselves, since their deepest identity lies not in autonomy but in unity.

Next we turn to Thomas Aquinas's contribution to the doctrine of inseparable operations, the most distinctive aspect of which is his clarification of the corollary of appropriation. He explores the concept of appropriation in his commentary on Lombard's *Sentences* and in *Summa Theologiae* 1 question 39, articles 7 and 8. The two presentations will be briefly introduced here.

In the commentary on the *Sentences* he insists that the procedure of appropriation is not without a basis and therefore does not lack appropriate controls. There must be a kinship between the appropriated attribute and the person. So, wisdom is appropriated to the Son because it has a kinship with his character as the Word. Similarly, goodness has a kinship with the Spirit's personal character as love. This means that the procedure is not entirely subjective. Its basis, as Gilles Emery observes, lies in what Thomas calls "congruence,"[51] which is something that would obtain even in the absence of the human knower. In appropriation, then, a real objective feature of reality is identified.

Thomas also insists in the same context on the utility of appropriation from the standpoint of the human knower. Appropriation has the function of a disclosure of the faith. As Emery explains, "Once the properties of the persons have been laid down, appropriation enables us to supplement our presentation by way of their essential attributes."[52] However, it must be made clear that "The [appropriated] essential attributes do not open the way to a sufficient knowledge of the persons. Nonetheless, we observe in the appropriated [attributes]

51. Gilles Emery, *The Trinitarian Theology of Thomas Aquinas*, trans. Francesca Aran Murphy (Oxford: Oxford University Press, 2007), 318.

52. Emery, *Trinitarian Theology of Thomas Aquinas*, 322.

some kind of likeness to the persons, and this is how an appropriation has the quality of a disclosure of the faith, however, imperfect."[53]

It is this second, disclosive dimension of appropriation that Thomas elaborates in the *Summa Theologiae*. Referencing 1 Corinthians 1:24 he writes:

> For the manifestation of our faith it is fitting that the essential attributes should be appropriated to the persons. For although the trinity of persons cannot be proved by demonstration . . . nevertheless it is fitting that it be declared by things which are more known to us. Now the essential attributes of God are more clear to us from the standpoint of reason than the personal properties; because we can derive certain knowledge of the essential attributes from creatures which are sources of knowledge to us, such as we cannot obtain regarding the personal properties. . . . As, therefore, we make use of the likeness of the trace or image found in creatures for the manifestation of the divine persons, so also in the same manner do we make use of the essential attributes. And such a manifestation of the divine persons by the use of the essential attributes is called appropriation.[54]

Thomas rehearses here the restrictions on our knowledge of the divine persons through creation. The persons cannot be known from their work in creation since that work is according to their common power as an essential attribute.[55] But the process whereby we come to know the persons presupposes the knowledge of the essential attributes we derive from the creatures.

It is not easy to follow the analogy he makes at the end of the paragraph just quoted. There is first a natural knowledge of God's essential properties as cause, derived from our knowledge of his creatures. In intellectual creatures the resemblance between cause and effect takes the form of an image. Following Augustine, Thomas's tradition has identified this image with the notion of intellect, or reason. So the human intellect is a trace of the divine intellect. We surmise that God is an intellectual being by analogy with his creatures. But the knowledge chain does not stop here. For it is possible to identify relational distinctions within the human intellect, between the word and its principle, which in turn "gives us an analogy of faith through which to grasp the eternal procession of the divine Word, as other from the Father."[56]

---

53. Aquinas, I *Sent.* d. 31, q. 1, a. 2, quoted in Emery, *Trinitarian Theology of Thomas Aquinas*, 323.

54. Aquinas, *Summa Theologica*, trans. the Fathers of the English Dominican Province (Westminster, MD: Christian Classics, 1981) 1, q. 39, a. 7.

55. Aquinas, *ST* 1, q. 32, a. 1.

56. Emery, *Trinitarian Theology of Thomas Aquinas*, 330.

Aquinas then seems to be arguing that just as we can use the trace of God in the human psyche to illuminate the distinctions between the persons, so we can use other essential terms—such as power, wisdom, goodness—to illuminate the personal character of the hypostases. It must be made clear, though, that the personal distinctions, just as in the case of the psychological analogy, must already be known—from revelation and by faith. Knowledge that there are three in God may not be derived from a natural unpacking of the dynamics of the human psyche. On the other hand, once the theologian has worked through the personal distinctions, he can now turn to these essential attributes to further shed light on the persons' character.

In *De Veritate*, Aquinas defines appropriation as "nothing other than to draw what is shared towards what is proper."[57] This is a particularly apt description of what is going on in appropriation, which we may understand as a stretching of the language beyond the immediate application of a term such that a new vision, a new insight, may be gained. The semantic ascent to the knowledge of the persons must start with a knowledge of the divine substance, since the notion of the person necessarily includes that of the divine substance, the person being a *subsistent relation* within it. The procedure of appropriation leads to a change in the cognitive content of the essential attribute, from its being considered in the abstract, as applied to the substance, to its being appropriated, in which case it includes the person's character. At no stage, however, does the knower drop sight of the unity of the divine substance. It is for this reason that we must be speaking of a semantic ascent within the unity of a single concept referring to a single reality, such as "wisdom" referring to the singular divine *wisdom*.

Appropriation, for Thomas, does not identify a distinct referent for an appropriated attribute. The reference remains the same: the singular divine perfection. Nor does it introduce a new concept of equivocal meaning. Rather, it is the same concept, applying the same reality, creating a deeper understanding or insight in the knower. Aquinas's Trinitarianism is not austere in regard to the descriptions of the persons. While it is true that the only properties exclusive to the persons are those indicating origin, what is to be known and believed about the persons, what can and must be contemplated about them, is in fact endless. For the Son is not simply "begottenness" but "begotten wisdom," "begotten power," and so on. The Spirit, in turn, is not simply "spiration," but "spirating wisdom," and "spirating power." It is only the grammar that is austere, while the actual use of language in contemplation is ever new and of no end.

---

57. Thomas Aquinas, *Quaestiones Disputatae de Veritate*, trans. Robert Mulligan, SJ (Chicago: Henry Regnery Company, 1952), q. 7, a. 3.

Aquinas's perspective on the knowledge of the divine persons dovetails with his account of the divine missions. The doctrine of inseparable operations heavily informs that of the divine missions. At this stage only a preliminary presentation will be given to demonstrate the doctrine's consolidation.

The treatment of the divine missions in the *Summa Theologiae* is the theme of Question 43 of the *prima pars*. The first article explains that "the notion of mission includes two things: the habitude of the one sent to the sender; and that of the one sent to the end whereto he is sent."[58] A mission entails a hypostatic procession, to which a created effect is added. On the one hand, the person sent does not stop proceeding from the sender. The one sent never leaves, so to speak. On the other, the one sent does not arrive at a place from which he was previously absent (a. 1, ad. 2). A mission involves "a new way of existing in another" (a. 1, *responsio*).

By these distinctions, Thomas intimates that the mission represents, in a way, an extension of a procession, which is to say a new way of existing of a divine person in another created reality. This new relation must observe important metaphysical and Trinitarian rules. Responding to the charge that a mission involves the Trinitarian person in change, Aquinas explains that the change is in the creature, not in the divine person.[59] To speak about a new relation is to say that the relation is real in the creature, and only conceptual in God. This is to say that the relation becomes constitutive for the created effect only.

We may represent this relationship on the analogy of a needle that is attracted and attached to a magnet. The needle becomes magnetized in the process, all the while the magnet remaining itself. Certain created realities are "drawn" to participate in the processions, in the sense that they mediate the processions and manifest them.

Since the missions extend the processions, it can be said that they are in a certain sense *proper* to the sent persons. But this needs to be carefully explained. Since a mission has two dimensions: the procession and the created term, there is a sense in which the missions are proper to the persons, since the processions are separable: the Son is born only of the Father; the Spirit proceeds from the Father and the Son; the Father is unbegotten. Thus, in respect of the procession that it extends, a mission is always proper to the person sent. But if a mission is regarded in terms of the created effect, which is drawn

58. Aquinas, *ST* 1, q. 43, a. 1.
59. Aquinas, *ST* 1, q. 43, a. 2, ad. 2.

to extend the procession, and insofar as this term is the effect of the common divine causality, all Trinitarian persons participate in the mission.

This is, in fact, Augustine's explanation of the baptism of Jesus in terms of the whole Trinity producing the flesh, the voice, and the dove, but these belonging separately to only one of them. Aquinas thus expands Augustine's notion of "belonging" to signify the fact that a created term extends the procession of the person to which it belongs. This captures the sense that the mission is not a mere manifestation—theophanies are manifestations—but a relationship of union, an actual drawing into the divine life of created realities.

The notion of appropriation, then, does not always apply to the reality of the missions. To understand that, one has to understand the various dimensions of causality that Aquinas employs, a topic that will be covered in chapter 4, on the doctrine of creation. At this stage it should only be noted that a mission is not, strictly speaking, an operation. A mission is the extension of the mode of existence of a divine person to incorporate a created reality. The Son comes to exist in the human nature of Jesus Christ. The Spirit comes to exist in the soul of the faithful. The whole Trinity will come to indwell those who love and obey God (John 14:23). As internal operations, the processions *sunt divisa*, are divisible.

Now a mission may result in operations, that is, in effects of efficient causality. Insofar as certain effects flow from a mission, appropriation has its jurisdiction. Additionally, insofar as the term of the mission is created, it is the operation of the whole Trinity. This raises a fundamental question: while the formation of the human nature of Jesus Christ may be relatively easily understood as the work of the whole Trinity, should Christ's operations also be understood as only appropriated to the Son? On the other hand, if it were admitted that Christ's human actions properly belong to the Son alone, and aren't merely appropriated to him, does the inseparability rule still stand? Our theological journey will have to pause for those discussions in due course.

The reality of the divine missions focuses the critical question in regards to the inseparability doctrine. On the one hand, the missions are said to extend the processions and to make the persons known. On the other hand, the missions imply the existence of a created reality,[60] which is understood to be the effect of the inseparable divine causality. This may feel like what is given with

60. In Eastern Orthodox doctrine divine action is not conceptualized in terms of created effects exclusively, but rather in terms of the uncreated divine energies. For an excellent account of this difference, see David Bradshaw, *Aristotle East and West: Metaphysics and the Division of Christendom* (Cambridge: Cambridge University Press, 2004). For the relevance of this distinction to the doctrine of inseparable operations, see Adonis Vidu,

one hand—the manifestation of Trinitarian diversity—is taken with the other since all created effects are properly the work of the whole Trinity. Modern theology will find this situation intolerable, squarely laying the blame at the feet of hard inseparability. Those arguments and objections will be schematized in the final section of this chapter. Not, however, before we canvass another scene in which the doctrine of inseparable operations plays a fundamental role, this time in the eastern corners of Christendom, during the seventh century.

Christ's Two Wills and Two Operations

The development of Trinitarian theology secured the doctrine that the Trinity has a single operation *ad extra*. It also fortified a particular association between nature, operation, and will. These did not belong to the hypostasis, but to the divine nature. In Christology, this was to play a fundamental role, resulting in the clarification of the relationship between the activity of God *ad extra* and the activity of Christ.

The post-Chalcedonian Christological landscape was largely divided between two camps. On the one hand were the Nestorians, who had been defeated at Ephesus and Chalcedon. However, a growing party among the victors were the Monophysites represented by Severus. These argued for a single operation of Christ. The primary impetus for this was coming from Cyrillian Christology, which proclaimed the single subject of the two natures. As such, to this one subject, the hypostasis of the Word, were to be attributed both the sufferings and the miracles. Interestingly, Nestorians had also initially affirmed a single operation in Christ—as their way of salvaging the unity of his person. But there was a gradual shift, as Jaroslav Pelikan notes,[61] among the Nestorians away from the single operation and toward dual operations. By the seventh century a discussion ensued about whether there were two operations in Christ. This proved extremely divisive, at a time when the empire could afford no more tension, in light of the growing external threats to Christianity. The *Ecthesis*, which proclaimed a single will in Christ, was supposed to pacify the situation, allowing both kinds of language, or rather preventing talk of operations altogether. There was one subject in Christ—and this should suffice.

"Triune Agency, East and West: Uncreated Energies or Created Effects," in *Perichoresis* 18, no. 1 (2020): 61–79.

61. Jaroslav Pelikan, *The Christian Tradition: A History of the Development of Doctrine*, vol. 2, *The Spirit of Eastern Christendom (600–1700)* (Chicago: University of Chicago Press, 1974), 69.

Despite the judgment of some historians of dogma, such as Adolf von Harnack, these struggles were not unnecessary quibbles over unessential matters. Neither did it appear so to the church at the time. The fundamental reason had to do with the relationship between certain operations of Jesus—such as his praying, his obedience, his angst in the face of the cross—and the divine affirmations—such as his continued and unbreakable unity with the Father, his divine power, his omniscience. How is it possible that the same subject can both be in unbreakable unity with the Father and experience forsakenness? In other words, it was difficult to duck one's head in the sand and stop talking about these, as the *Ecthesis* required, precisely in light of the many questions that were being raised. The fault line was precisely that between theology and economy. This relationship was too important to be left unresolved. The problem was that it could not be settled by an appeal to Scripture or with an appeal to the dogma of the fathers. However, it could be decided by an appeal to the framework erected during the Trinitarian controversies, which associated will and operation with nature.

The champion of the dyothelite and dyoenergetic doctrine was Maximus the Confessor. Although it is brimming throughout his oeuvre, Maximus most clearly deploys his Trinitarian logic of the two wills and two energies of Christ in his *Disputation with Pyrrhus*. His opponent, Pyrrhus, is convinced that Chalcedonian orthodoxy, which affirms the unity of the person of Christ, must entail the singularity of Christ's will and operation. Because Christ is a single person, that of the eternal Word, so he must have a single will and operation. Against this apparently commonsense position, Maximus invokes a battery of arguments, both biblical and theologico-philosophical.

Maximus's first move is to attack what is (for us today) the intuitive position that will belongs to person. Distinguishing between willing and the mode of willing, he argues that the former, like seeing, is proper to a nature. He would call this "simple willing," or "natural will."[62] It is precisely the doctrine of the Trinity that compels him to locate will in the nature:

> For if one suggests that a "willer" [person] is implied in the notion of the will, then by the exact inversion of this principle of reasoning, a will is implied in the notion of a "willer." Thus, wilt thou not say that because of the one will of the superessential Godhead there is only one hypostasis, as

---

62. Maximus the Confessor, *The Disputation with Pyrrhus of Our Father Among the Saints, Maximus the Confessor*, trans. Joseph P. Farrell (South Canaan, PA: St. Tikhon's Seminary Press, 1990), §§17, 19.

did Sabellius, or that because there are three hypostases there are also three wills, and because of this, three natures as well, since the canons and definitions of the Fathers say that the distinction of will implieth a distinction of natures? So said Arius![63]

Here we find Maximus not defending but assuming the claim that a distinction of wills in the Trinity implies a distinction of natures. Pyrrhus then argues that the wills should be understood as composed, meaning that the human and the divine will compose a higher, theandric will. Maximus responds that a composition of the wills would lead to an ultimate composition of the natures, which would yield the thought that Christ has a (composite) nature he does not share with the Father: "Thou dividest Him from the Father by means of this composite will, for a composite will characterizes only a composite nature."[64]

Pyrrhus reluctantly concedes the point that Christ's wills are natural and seeks no further proof of this. However, he continues to wrestle with the relation between the two wills in Christ. He appears persuaded by the monothelite claim that Christ only had a human will "by appropriation."[65] Thus, Christ is not said to possess a human will but to assume the will of others as a form of sympathy, by relation only and not as a property. What Pyrrhus fears is the opposition between the two wills, divine and human. The appeal of the monothelite position is that "Christ formed our will in Himself,"[66] which Pyrrhus cannot square with Christ's having a natural human will. If a will is natural, how can it be formed?

Maximus understands very well that at stake here is the "whole mystery of the Economy,"[67] which will be shown to be a mere illusion if the Son did not take unto himself our nature complete with all its faculties. Our salvation rests on just this complete union:

Because the same Person was wholly God with the humanity, and wholly man with the Godhead. The same Person, as man, subjected human nature in Himself, and through Himself, to God the Father, showing Himself as the flawless image and pattern for us to imitate in order that we may voluntarily draw nigh unto God, the Author and finisher of our salvation, no longer willing anything apart from that which He willeth.[68]

63. Maximus, *Pyrrhus*, §15.
64. Maximus, *Pyrrhus*, §27.
65. Maximus, *Pyrrhus*, §56.
66. Maximus, *Pyrrhus*, §66.
67. Maximus, *Pyrrhus*, §65.
68. Maximus, *Pyrrhus*, §73.

There is no contradiction between the two wills, Maximus continues, because Christ's human will is natural rather than gnomic. The natural human will of Christ is entirely moved by his divine will. In his human will Christ does not deliberate about the good. As Dumitru Stăniloae explains, his natural human will desires the good in general, as is the case for all human beings. The concrete good was known by the hypostasis, which was divine, and yet he acted by taking into account the will for the good that is proper to his human nature.[69] Maximus supports an instrumentalization of the human nature of Christ, whereby the eternal Word brings about divine things through the instrument of his human nature, and human things through his divinity. Crucial here is the fact that Christ advances and perfects his humanity not through a deliberative will, which implies that he "advanced through ignorance before learning whatever He learnt,"[70] something that is Nestorian for Maximus. Rather, Christ's growth and the gradual deification of his humanity took place as a consequence of the hypostatic union. In appealing to the hypostatic union, Maximus is making yet another overture into the doctrine of inseparable operations. We shall indulge this ample quotation here:

> Furthermore, those who have rejected the proposition that the will is natural must say either that it is hypostatic or contrary to nature. But if they say it is hypostatic, then the Son shall have a different will than the Father, for a characteristic of any given hypostasis characterizes only that [particular] hypostasis. But if they [say the will is] contrary to nature, then they make Him destroy His own essence, since things contrary to nature destroy what is natural.
>
> But I will gladly question them on this as well: doth the God and Father of all will as Father, or as God? But if He willeth as Father then His will is different from the will of the Son, for the Father is not the Son. But if He willeth as God, and the Son, and the Holy Ghost, are God as well, then they must affirm that the will is [a property] of nature, in other words natural.
>
> Further, if the will be one, then, according to the teachings of the Fathers, the essence is one. So, if there be one will of the Godhead and humanity of Christ, then they are compelled to say that there is one and the same essence. How then, being so impious, can they follow the Fathers?
>
> And again, if wherever there be one will there be no evident distinction of natures, then those who say that there is one will perforce do not make

---

69. Dumitru Stăniloae, in *Părinți și Scriitori Bisericești* 81 (Bucharest: Editura Institutului Biblic si de Misiune al Bisericii Ortodoxe Romane, 1990), 308n152.

70. Maximus, *Pyrrhus*, §105.

a distinction of natures in Christ. Conversely, they that affirm a distinction of natures do not affirm one will, provided that they observe the norms of the Fathers.[71]

Maximus concludes that monothelitism invites a confusion between humanity and divinity. Yet it is only by keeping to this distinction that one can make sense of the economy. He shows that texts such as Hebrews 10:7-9 (referencing Ps 40) make sense only by keeping in mind the distinction of wills: "He thus delights to do the will of the Father, not according to His deity, but according to His humanity, for the Father's will is also His will, since He is also God by essence."[72] Similarly, referring to John 5:21, "For as the Father raises the dead and gives them life, so also the Son gives life to whom he will," Maximus opines that "it is not possible to say that this referreth to the human nature of Christ. Thus, the Saviour taught us that just as the Father, being God, giveth life to the dead by His will, so also the Son, being of identical essence and will with the Father, giveth life to whom he will."[73]

Having convinced Pyrrhus that there are two wills in Christ, Maximus switches in the second half of the disputation to an argument about the two energies in Christ. Here again the rationale is fundamentally inspired by the doctrine of inseparable operations. The first argument largely parallels the argument about the wills. If there is one work in Christ, and this work is hypostatic, it would follow that Christ has a different work than both the Father as well as the Virgin Mother.[74] But that would break both his unity with the Father and his communion with humanity, since different works indicate different essences. Moreover, if persons and energies mutually entail each other, consistency would demand "either to say that because of the one operation of the Holy Godhead there is one Person as well, or because of its Three Hypostases that there are three operations."[75]

Such was the strength of the consensus on the doctrine of inseparable operations that in a situation as labyrinthine as this, it showed the way. Everyone, including the Nestorians and the Monophysites, accepted the assumption that

71. Maximus, *Pyrrhus*, §§106-9.

72. Maximus, *Pyrrhus*, §137. Interestingly, the very same texts are interpreted by, e.g., McCall as referring to the pre-existent Christ.

73. Maximus, *Pyrrhus*, §142.

74. Maximus, *Pyrrhus*, §162. Granted, Maximus's logic is deficient and circular on this point, since he must already assume that works belong to nature in order to infer a break with the Virgin's humanity.

75. Maximus, *Pyrrhus*, §166.

the works of the Trinity *ad extra* are indivisible.[76] That meant that operation and will belonged to nature. In turn, that signaled that Christ has two natural wills and operations.

The designation "natural" is important here, since it allows for the possibility of a single "personal" operation and a single "personal" willing. That personal mode of operation is not the ontological substrate of the operation, which belongs to nature, but the mode of operation, and the mode of will (or the willing itself), in this case, the object of will.

Stăniloae clarifies this distinction between the will and the willer. The will belongs to nature; the willer is the person.

> The willer is the person or the hypostasis. The will belongs to nature. Nature demands its fulfilment, but the person fulfills it. The person concretely accomplishes the demand of nature, as the hypostasis is the realized or concrete form of the nature. In Christ, the human nature is not realized in a separate hypostasis, but in the hypostasis of the Word, or it receives concrete, hypostatic realization together with the Word. His hypostasis, therefore, in addition to the properties of the divine nature, receives those of the human nature. From this point of view, it is composed, but it is at the same time one.[77]

The notion of a compound operation and of a compound will was also rejected by John Damascene, despite the apparent support it received from Pseudo-Dionysius. Again, the backbone of the argumentation came from the doctrine of inseparable operations, as Damascene illustrates: "Should we speak of one compound will in Christ, then we are making Him distinct from the Father in will, because the will of the Father is not compound. Accordingly, it remains for us to say that only the Person of Christ is compound, in so far as it is composed of His natures and His natural properties as well."[78]

There can be no confusion between the two operations. Damascene formulates another argument from the nature of action as the perfection of a potentiality, via Nyssen,

---

76. See Maximus, *Chapters on Knowledge*, 2.1; John Damascene, *The Orthodox Faith*, in *Writings: The Fount of Knowledge, The Philosophical Chapters, On Heresies & On the Orthodox Faith*, ed. F. H. Chase (Ex Fontibus, 2015), 1:8, 183, 186–87.

77. Stăniloae, in *Părinţi şi Scriitori Bisericeşti*, 81n133.

78. Damascene, *On the Orthodox Faith*, 3:14, 302; cf. 307–8.

who says: "Things having one operation vey definitely have the same potentiality, also." For every operation is the perfection of a potentiality. Moreover, it is impossible for there to be one nature, potentiality, or operation
belonging both to an uncreated nature and to a created one. And, were we
to say that Christ has one nature, we should be attributing the passions of
the intellectual soul to the divinity of the Word—fear, I mean, and grief,
and anguish.[79]

Thus, Christ did the divine things humanly and the human things divinely.
Although there are two natural operations, these "mutually indwelling operations"[80] always commune with each other toward a single goal. Naturally,
this requires a fairly sophisticated distinction between operator, operation,
and what is being operated. Damascene provides that in *On the Orthodox
Faith* 3:15. Pope Leo had earlier distinguished somewhat rigidly between Christ
acting as God and his acting as man. This did not highlight so much the functional unity between the operations and wills, their coalescing together.

Again, this accounted not only for the distinction between the operations
and the wills, but also for the unity between them in practice. How does this
work in practice? Here we have an insight into the most profound mystery
of all. This is the very descent of God into the world. It is not a mere case of a
causative divine agency, moving things around in the world of time and space;
it is the very divine being united hypostatically with humanity, acting as God
through humanity and deifying the very operation of the human nature. This
is precisely the reason why God became man, so that man might become God.
Deification shows itself to be the heart of the mystery of salvation, enacted in
the incarnation and passion of our Lord.

In this union, the motion of the creature does not spring from the creature
itself, since the creature does not exist prior to its assumption by the Word. Yet
the creature is assumed as a whole, not in part, possessing the fullness of its
properties and operations. The creature is not blotted out or muted in the act
of assumption or in the union itself (in two natures, not from two natures).
It retains its integrity as a human creature. Yet now everything it does and it
experiences, it experiences as God. Conversely, everything God does—the
healing and salutary energies that he bestows upon this creature and the rest
of creation—flows through this creature's human operations, human will, hu-

---

79. Damascene, *On the Orthodox Faith*, 3:14, 306–7.
80. Charles C. Twombly, *Perichoresis and Personhood: God, Christ, and Salvation in John
of Damascus* (Eugene, OR: Pickwick, 2015), 76–87.

man body, and human reason. There is nothing pertaining to these assumed properties, however, that is sinful. Fallen they may be, disrupted by disease and death, but not alienated because not sinful. The mystery and power of the union lies precisely in this, as it was recognized by both parties, in fact: that the Word did not stop being the Word and Lord of Heaven; that he bent the heaven to come down; that his union with the Father and the Spirit was unbroken.

This controversy and its outcome show that, in fact, the doctrine of inseparable operations played a fundamental part in preserving and unpacking the significance of the heart of our faith. The Son has a single operation with the Father and the Spirit *economically*. Operation belongs to nature, not to the hypostasis primarily. If it belonged to the hypostasis, we would have an operation of Christ that would be fundamentally different from the operation of the Father and the Spirit, since it would involve his submission to the Father, his prayer, his fear in the face of death, and so on. This, indeed, does not seem to be the saving and powerful action of God, but rather of a demigod, an Arian figure.

No one in this controversy entertained the possibility that somehow the doctrine of inseparable operations would be faulty. Rather, it was by showing that certain positions entailed the rejection of this assumption, that these were shown to be unacceptable. In the process, however, the deep significance of the doctrine was being showcased. The Trinity acts as a differentiated unity within the economy such that there aren't different operators, or at least not operators that act independently of one another. There are neither different operations nor different things being operated by different operators. In acting as man, the Son does not stop operating as one of the Trinity, that is, indivisibly with the Father and Spirit. Damascene in particular stresses that "even after the Incarnation He has the same operation as the Father."[81] His divine activity instrumentalizes his human activity (the priority of the divine nature). It is precisely this unbreakable and indivisible unity with the divine operation that ensures the very deification of the human operation and human nature of Christ. Were the Son's divine operation notionally distinct from the operations of Father and Spirit, it would mean that he is no longer in continuity with them; it would lead to a mythological account of the incarnation (basically the Arian position).

The doctrine of inseparable operations had thus demonstrated its Christological and soteriological fecundity. Maximus and Damascene had rightly intuited that apart from this inseparable unity with the Father (and the Spirit),

---

81. Damascene, *On the Orthodox Faith*, 3:14, 307.

Jesus would be reduced to a mythological hero. Were Jesus to act as a Nestorian *homo assumptus*, his unity with the Father would be lost, he would be a mere human being graced by the Father, like the saints and the angels. Were he to have a single operation, this too would sever him from the Father, who had not become incarnate and thus would have a distinct operation.

It is essential to observe here how the fact that the Father and the Spirit did not become incarnate does not prevent them from continuing to share economic operations with the Son! John Damascene in particular makes this explicit, stressing the ongoing inseparability of the Son with the Father even after the incarnation. That is because the Son retains his divine operation, inseparable from the Trinitarian operation. But he adds on a human operation that remains essentially his, while being energized from the divine side. Thus, what remains peculiar to the Son in his incarnate activity is precisely the personal mode of action, precisely as Son. But this, it is important to note, does not constitute a distinct operation, only a distinct mode of the same operation (coming from the divine nature, which instrumentalizes the human).

It is hard to miss the significance of this coordination between dyothelite and dyoenergetic Christology and the doctrine of inseparable operations: The natural human operation of Christ is actualized in the mode of sonship—which consists in an unbreakable unity with the Father. The alienated human operation is deified and shares in the unbreakable divine unity. This human operation cannot stop receiving from the Father its impulse, which it accepts in obedience. It no longer resists its natural desire for God, but now it favors the development of its inherent virtue; it no longer tries to escape the gravitational pull of the Trinitarian communion. It only exists in the mode of sonship, which is to say, in the mode of receptivity to the Father.

The Abrogation and Amendment of the Inseparability Rule in Contemporary Theology

The resurgence of Trinitarian theology during the twentieth century included, for some, a questioning of the doctrine of inseparable operations, despite its impressive conciliar credentials.[82] Karl Barth repositions the doctrine of the

---

82. The doctrine of inseparable operations is affirmed at the Council of Constantinople (681) as well as at Toledo (638, 675, 693). For the council documents, see Josef Neuner and Jacques Dupuis, eds., *The Christian Faith in the Doctrinal Documents of the Catholic Church* (London: Collins, 1983), paragraphs 635–36 (for Constantinople), and paragraphs 315, 630, 633 (for Toledo).

Trinity at the beginning of his *Church Dogmatics*, including a subscription to the inseparability rule together with the attendant corollary of appropriation. Others, like Wolfhart Pannenberg and Jürgen Moltmann, give reformulations of the doctrine. On the Catholic side, Karl Rahner introduces certain amendments to it. Throughout contemporary Trinitarian conversations, however, the universal applicability of the rule is being challenged. At this stage it is helpful to understand what the objections are. Many of the particular revisionary proposals will be dealt with in some detail below.

Beyond doubt, the principal kind of objection to the rule is epistemological: It blocks knowledge of the divine persons. If every work *ad extra* is common to the divine persons, it is both impossible to distinguish between the persons— let us call this the *individuation problem*—or to know them in their personal character—the *personal description problem*. In this case, both the distinction as well as the personal characteristics are matters of speculation, almost entirely disengaged from the Trinitarian work of creation and reconciliation. Hence, the rule, far from leading to the doctrine of the Trinity of persons, in fact leads us away from it, quarantining it to metaphysical speculation. It is no surprise that, once the Trinity is disengaged from our experience of reconciliation, the doctrine becomes a point of dead orthodoxy, with little import for Christian experience.

The very demise of the doctrine of the Trinity, its languishing as an appendix in Friedrich Schleiermacher's *Glaubenslehre*, may have been facilitated by a rigid application of this rule, coupled with a principled priority given to *Deo uno* as opposed to *Deo trino*. Of note is the invocation of the rule by Maurice Wiles to conclude that "our Trinity of revelation is an arbitrary analysis of the activity of God, which though of value in Christian thought and devotion is not of essential significance."[83] Noting that neither the Scriptures nor the fathers distinguish between separate activities of the triune persons, the distinctions between them can only be a matter of propositional revelation. Once such a notion of revelation has been discredited, however, there remains no compelling reason to insist exclusively on the threeness of God. "If there is no distinction whatever in the activity of the Trinity towards us, how can we have any knowledge of the distinctions at all?"[84] According to Wiles, Scripture does not individuate the persons precisely because it ascribes to them the same activities. The only way to individuate them, however, is on the basis of what the

---

83. Maurice Wiles, "Some Reflections on the Origins of the Doctrine of the Trinity," *Journal of Theological Studies* 8, no. 1 (April 1957): 104.

84. Wiles, "Origins," 103.

persons are recorded to have said, as well as on the basis of the propositional teaching of the Gospels and the epistles.[85]

From the opposite side, Christoph Schwöbel concurs with the conclusion: If the rule stands, "precisely what is excluded in this way, however, constitutes the necessary conditions for individuating actions and for identifying agents."[86] Our very ability to tell the Father, Son, and Spirit apart from each other and thus to affirm their irreducibility seems to be jeopardized on this account (*the individuation problem*).

Schwöbel's assumption is that "persons" can only be individuated on the basis of distinct actions. The problem of individuating divine persons is clearly of a different kind than the problem of individuating human agents. By definition divine persons are transcendent and thus, not being objects in the world, our access to them is to a certain extent inferential or indirect. We infer them from their effects or manifestation in the world. However, if always every effect is ascribed to the same unique agent—God, or the Trinity as a whole, or the divine essence—we have no other basis for individuation. Interestingly, this also seems to leave out the verbal and propositional dimension of this manifestation.

Colin Gunton echoes these sentiments:

> The particular persons, Father, Son and Spirit, must each have their own attributes, their own distinctive characteristics, or they would be indistinguishable from one another, and so theologically perform no function. If the persons are functionally indistinguishable—that is, indistinguishable in their modes of action—there seems little point to the doctrine of the Trinity.[87]

Gunton agrees that we can only know agents from their actions, which therefore would reveal what is proper to the persons: "Persons are those particular beings—hypostases—whose attributes are manifested in particular kinds of action, such as love, relationality, freedom, creativity."[88] He admits that this is a univocal account of "person": "What it is to be a human person is in this

85. For an extensive and perceptive discussion of the necessity of propositional revelation for the knowledge of the Trinity, see Fred Sanders, *The Triune God* (Grand Rapids: Zondervan, 2016), 46–68. He argues for an inner unity between act and word in revelation.

86. Christoph Schwöbel, *God: Action and Revelation* (Kampen: Kok, 1992), 52.

87. Colin Gunton, *Act and Being: Towards a Theology of the Divine Attributes* (Grand Rapids: Eerdmans, 2003), 27.

88. Gunton, *Act and Being*, 146–47.

case identical with what it is to be a divine person, and therefore the word means the same at the levels of creator and creation."[89]

Gunton insists that one must reckon with the distinctive *forms of action* or *kinds of action* of the persons. It is not entirely clear what Gunton recommends, but he is aiming his objections both at the classical rule as well as at Reformed dogmaticians who have applied it to ascribe creation to the Father, redemption to the Son, and sanctification to the Holy Spirit. These theologians were guilty of "the chief pitfall" of the doctrine of inseparable operations, "which effectively prevents them from distinguishing the forms of action of the distinct albeit inseparable persons."[90]

Against what Gunton appears to regard as an appropriation approach in Reformed dogmatics, he suggests we should think of the different kinds or forms of action that the persons have. Creation, reconciliation, and sanctification are not to be appropriated to the Father, Son, and Spirit respectively. Rather, these actions are fundamentally the work of the Father, who operates through his hands, the Son and the Spirit. A clear distinction between their different *forms of action* yields appropriate personal descriptions:

> We need an account of the kind of person the Father is in creating, redeeming and sanctifying—and anything else essential to an account of the economy of the divine action—and the kind of persons that the Son and the Spirit are in mediating that action as the Father's "two hands" and therefore as the Father himself in action through their particular action. We need, that is to say, a distinction in terms of initiation and mediation rather than of actions in the economy, which are indeed the work of the whole Trinity, undivided, certainly, but not homogenous or monotonous.[91]

It is not entirely clear precisely what Gunton regards as proper to each person. He admits that they do not have distinct *actions*. The notion of a *kind of action* or a *form of action* is left without a clear explanation. Gunton agrees that "we must avoid talk of *individual*—non-perichoretic—agency,"[92] but then he asserts that the Son and the Spirit are "particular agents."[93] This is not the time to critically engage with Gunton's positive proposal, which clings to some notion of inseparable operation, differently construed to be sure. At this juncture,

89. Gunton, *Act and Being*, 147.
90. Gunton, *Act and Being*, 139.
91. Gunton, *Act and Being*, 139–40.
92. Gunton, *Act and Being*, 144.
93. Gunton, *Act and Being*, 145.

Gunton's objection to the traditional understanding of inseparability must be acknowledged. It derives from the claim that the rule makes it impossible to distinguish—or individuate—the persons (i.e., the *individuation problem*), and also from the claim that it would result in impossibly austere descriptions of the persons (i.e., the *personal description problem*).

Catherine Mowry LaCugna, a Roman Catholic theologian who has done much for the recovery of interest in Trinitarian theology, has also taken aim at the rule:

> Augustine's principle, which follows logically from the starting point in the divine unity instead of the economy of salvation, tends to blur any real distinctions among the divine persons and thereby formalizes in Latin theology the break between oikonomia and theologia.[94]

LaCugna agrees that under this rule the persons cannot be "single[d] out . . . in relation to a particular activity"—*the individuation problem.*[95]

It is fundamentally the balance and order, in theological knowledge, between the immanent and the economic Trinity that needs to be addressed. Theology has been crippled by an account that starts with the divine unity instead of starting with the diversity of persons as manifested in the economy. LaCugna treats the rule as a logical inference from divine unity, rather than a datum of revelation itself. On the other hand, "it is clear that if a theology were to begin from and center itself on the economy . . . it would have no need for a doctrine of appropriations."[96] As she reads the tradition, the doctrine of appropriations is needed in order to maintain the divine unity. She writes,

> The Bible attests to the uniqueness of the missions of Son and Spirit in the economy of salvation, and Scripture remains the firm foundation for all statements about the unique identity of the persons in the economy of salvation. . . . The mission of the Son to become incarnate belongs properly to the Son as Son. The Spirit is the one sent to make the creature holy. Each of these is a proprium, an identifying characteristic of a unique person, and as such cannot be appropriated.[97]

---

94. Catherine Mowry LaCugna, *God for Us: The Trinity and Christian Life* (New York: Harper, 1993), 99.

95. LaCugna, *God for Us*, 99.

96. LaCugna, *God for Us*, 100.

97. LaCugna, *God for Us*, 100.

It must be underscored at once that, although there may be some ambiguity in the tradition over this, Aquinas had also insisted on the nonappropriated character of the missions. When considered in terms of the procession, a mission is not appropriated, but unique to the person sent. That is why the Father has no mission, because he does not proceed. LaCugna ignores the important distinction between *mission* and *operation* at this particular point. However, every mission entails an operation, since every mission includes a created effect, which—as created—is produced by the common Trinitarian efficiency.

This brings us to another set of objections, of the epistemological kind. The Western tradition tends to speak about divine operation in terms of the *production of an effect*. The missions imply such an operation, insofar as they extend a procession to include a created effect. To a modern sensibility this sounds suspiciously depersonalizing. To speak about divine action merely as the production of "created effects" seems to evacuate personal agency from the action. While the divine transcendence is certainly observed, it makes it difficult to understand how we are related to distinct persons, if the missions entail only created effects that are arbitrarily connected to this or that person.

James P. Mackey condenses this critique:

> Once again a flat and undifferentiated formula, if rigidly applied in accordance with its own logic, will yield only the sense that the one God "creates" voices, clouds, fire, or human flesh, to make visible one of the "persons" and to reveal them thus in their relationships to one another, but no visible means of manifestation has, or could have, any intrinsic relationship to a particular person.[98]

Karl Rahner feels that the problem is compounded by Aquinas's insistence that any of the divine persons might have become incarnate. This seems to entail that there is no *intrinsic connection* between the created effect, the human nature of Christ, and the eternal Son. If the relationship between the eternal Son and the created effect is merely extrinsic, how may the person truly be known in its own *proprium*? Rahner thus presses the point that the self-communication of God must entail more than simply created effects. "The one God communicates himself in absolute self-utterance and as absolute donation of love. . . . He does not merely indirectly give his creature some share

---

98. James Mackey, *The Christian Experience of God as Trinity* (London: SCM, 1983), 157–58.

of himself *by* creating and giving us created and finite realities through his omnipotent *efficient* causality."[99]

Rahner, unlike LaCugna, does not wish to overturn the inseparability rule. But he insists that "the axiom is absolutely valid only where the 'supreme efficient cause' is concerned. . . . Not-appropriated relations of a single person are possible when we have to do, not with an efficient causality, but with a quasi-formal self-communication of God, which implies that each divine person possesses its own proper relation to some created reality."[100] These statements will be unpacked to some extent below. To be noted here is Rahner's careful distinction. If we are to think of operations in terms of the divine efficient causality, then these operations are indeed indivisible. However, this is not the only kind of relation that may obtain between divine persons and the world. In fact, the incarnation provides us with "a dogmatically certain 'instance' for a (theoretically at least not impossible) economic relation, proper to each person, of the divine persons to the world. Such a relation entails the possibility of a real communication, in salvation history, of the whole Trinity as such to the world, therefore of the identity of the economic and immanent Trinity."[101]

God not only operates as one, but, Rahner argues, the divine persons donate themselves as such in certain relations to creation. This form of causality is labelled *quasi-formal* by Rahner. We find such a self-communication paradigmatically in the person of Jesus Christ, where the Son gives himself and becomes the form of the human nature of Jesus Christ. Such a relationship of self-donation is not sufficiently captured by any account of efficient causality, and thus simply by the notion of created effects. It remains true, for Rahner, that the human nature of Christ was created by that divine efficiency, yet at the same time it receives its *form* as the incarnate Lord from this relationship that it has exclusively with the person of the Son.

Rahner, then, does not abrogate the rule, but limits its application, by introducing an exception to it. The question, of course, is whether his explanation of this self-donation of the Son in terms of quasi-formality is an adequate one. But, certainly, Rahner too adds his voice to the growing discontent about the rule. The fundamental objections have thus been formulated: The inseparability rule (1) makes it impossible to individuate the persons; (2) condemns theology to austere descriptions of the persons simply in terms of their relations of origin; and (3) depersonalizes divine action and fails to account for

99. Karl Rahner, *The Trinity*, trans. Joseph Donceel (London: Burns and Oates, 1970), 36.
100. Rahner, *The Trinity*, 77.
101. Rahner, *The Trinity*, 27.

the self-donation of the distinct persons to created natures, as in the case of the incarnation of the Son and the indwelling of the Holy Spirit. Each of these objections are tackled from a variety of angles below, as they relate to specific doctrinal loci: creation; incarnation; Christ's action, passion, and ascension; the coming and indwelling of the Spirit.

CONCLUSION

The history of the inseparability rule is intertwined with the history of Trinitarian theology. During the earlier development of the latter, the former was a foundation stone of the Trinitarian edifice. Beings that have the same power and the same operation must have the same substance. Scripture ascribes common operations to the Son and the Spirit, whether it is the same grace or the same salvation, but most fundamentally the same token act of creation. In the second and third person was experienced nothing less than the very activity of God, yet unlike any other delegated activity. Christ and the Spirit must be part of the very identity of God, internal to his substance, lest one fall either into Arianism or Anomoeanism.

Throughout, the transcendence of God played a constitutive role. The fact that one of the Trinity has become incarnate did not stifle this affirmation of divine transcendence. The incarnate Son remains the transcendent Son. Mythological interpretations of the incarnation are prevented by attending to the grammar of the divine missions: The person who is sent never leaves; and he never arrives where he wasn't already. The development of the doctrine of the divine missions by Augustine and Aquinas enabled them to solve certain objections to the inseparability rule: How do we make sense of the incarnation of the Son alone? Don't we observe the divine persons acting separably at Jesus's baptism?

The consolidated Trinitarian orthodoxy held an important implication for later Christological and anthropological conversations—it paired will with nature! In the dynamism of person and nature, will carries over into person from nature. There is thus a single natural will and a single natural operation in God. The persons share the same operation and the same will, although these subsist in the persons according to the manner in which they possess the divine substance. How foreign this naturalization of will must be to the modern mindset! Modern anthropology locates will in personal existence, hoping to preserve the freedom and the self-expression of the person. The result is the evanescent existence and superficial identity of the modern self, utterly unmoored from its ontological substrate. If, however, personal identity is secured not by one's nature but by one's personal choices, suspended above nature and not originating from it, the will itself having become divorced from nature, then the personhood and personal identity of Father, Son, and Spirit can only be revealed and established by their unique personal activities.

Modern theology, then, regards the old inseparability rule as a vestige of a backward culture, where an unemancipated will belonged to nature by definition. This no longer accords with our current intuitions about personhood and freedom. An operation that is entirely natural and a will that is also entirely natural cannot permit the development of personal uniqueness. And so it is with the doctrine of the Trinity as well: A budding personalism begins to undermine the traditional arrangement, ultimately leading to the divorce of will from nature. With will now a personal property, there must be three wills and three operations in the Godhead. The primary interest of modern Trinitarianism is to recover the personal distinctiveness of the triune hypostases, correcting the perceived one-sidedness of the traditional emphasis on unity. Personal identity must lie in personal action. The question, though, is whether in doing so it has not sawed off one of the Scriptural branches on which the Trinitarian edifice rested. The patristic and medieval consensus, on the other hand, roots the person and thus personal action deeply in the nature. Thus, personal distinctiveness cannot be established by abstracting from the nature and its essential operations. Divine persons in particular are to be only conceptually distinguished from the divine substance. The persons and the substance are "equiprimordial." The next chapter aims to make explicit the metaphysics and theo-logic of inseparable operations.

CHAPTER 3

Unity and Distinction in Divine Action

The primary reason for the confession of the doctrine of inseparable operations is that it is a datum of revelation. To Christ and the Spirit are ascribed uniquely divine actions. Such an ascription cannot be accommodated within the framework of intermediaries, whether these are other gods, or subdivine beings, for the reasons we have been unpacking, chief among which is the implication of Christ in the unique act of creation. Attempts to ascribe creation to an intermediary being inevitably imply that the Father is not Creator. The development of Trinitarian theology in the first few centuries held tight to the conceptual rule of inseparable operations and applied it consistently and across the board.

The fact that the rule is primarily a revelational datum does not prevent the exploration of its conceptual coherence. The present chapter picks up that task, with the aim of showing the consistency of the rule with Trinitarian doctrine more broadly construed. Trinitarian monotheism and the doctrine of inseparable operations mutually entail each other. That is, one can argue from the exegetical datum of inseparable operations to the doctrine of the Trinity. This is the trajectory initiated in Scripture and continued in pro-Nicene theology. But, as an inductive approach, this cannot lead to a universal rule. From the fact that to Christ and the Spirit are ascribed some of the operations of the Father, even if we include here the quintessentially divine operation of creation, it does not immediately follow that all operations must be shared.

Modern suspicions about inseparability focus on this point precisely, as we have seen: if there aren't distinct operations in addition to common ones, we would lack a basis for discerning the personal identity of Father, Son, and Spirit. It is therefore incumbent upon us to explore this relation of mutual implication in the opposite direction. Now we must ask: does Trinitarian monotheism require that all economic operations of God be inseparable? Can the scriptural observations be generalized into a rule?

Triune Causality

"A thing acts in so far as it is in act," Aquinas wrote.[1] By no means an esoteric principle of the Common Doctor, this axiom merely expresses the simple idea that the activity of a particular thing is determined in its nature by the kind of thing that it is. A rock can't speak, but it can break; water can flow, but it can't break; and so on. The kinds of actions, or action *types* that an agent may do, are directly related to the range of possibilities inscribed in its nature. We have observed early Trinitarian principles deploying this principle to argue from a certain kind of activity to a certain kind of power to a certain kind of nature.

In examining the activity of the triune God in the economy, the same principle must be observed. Since actions are grounded in natures, the nature of the action is determined by the nature of the agent. There is something of an epistemic circularity here, which we have in fact encountered throughout our journey. The knowledge of the nature of God, of the fact that he is one substance in three persons, is derived precisely from divine revelation, and thus from a divine action. At the same time, we have just suggested that a divine action may only be understood by starting from the divine nature. The threat of a vicious circularity is making some theologians anxious enough to force a resolution. Thus, some insist that the divine nature is simply known from its actions. But this supposes that the nature of the divine actions is accessible and plain for all to see. Equally pernicious is the opposite attempt: to find almost a divine necessity flowing from nature to activity.

The second part of this chapter picks up the problem of the knowledge of divine actions. We will only tackle this issue, however, after dealing with the ontology of the divine actions, in keeping with the above principle. The reason for this is not merely that epistemology should follow ontology. There are material concerns about any attempt that proceeds to speak about the nature of God in terms that involve the economy and thus created realities.

While it is natural that one starts with the divine economy and proceeds to an understanding of the immanent Trinity, the knowledge of the divine economy should be regarded as provisional, as a sort of first naïveté. Having "known"

---

1. Aquinas, *Summa Theologiae*, trans. the Fathers of the English Dominican Province (Westminster, MD: Christian Classics, 1981), 1/2 q. 18, a. 1, ad. 2.

the immanent Trinity by way of the economic operations, one must return, in a second naïveté, to the economic works. Thus, our principle does not yield a simplistic and unidirectional application but rather a creative tension, whereby the immanent pole is ascribed a principled priority, with full awareness that the two poles cannot be divorced and are unavailable apart from one another.

The reason why it must be insisted that the external operations of God must ultimately be understood only on the basis of the immanent relations, or of the processions, has to do with the difference between Creator and creation. John Webster concurs that the contemplation of God's *ad extra* activity must begin with a contemplation of *ad intra* activity in order to preserve the creature-Creator distinction. God enjoys a plenitude of life *in se*, having no need of creation. There is an absolute ontological difference between God and creation, which qualifies any understanding of God's economic acts. The danger in allowing the economy to absolutely dictate our understanding of divine action, to take the economic *acta* as some sorts of givens that can be grasped in themselves with ease, risks thinking of the identity of God as in some sense dependent upon the world. Webster concludes that "the creator can be conceived neither by thinking of him as in some fashion continuous with the world, nor by conceiving of a purely dialectical relation between uncreated and created being; both continuity and discontinuity turn the divine difference from creation into a relative or comparative property and so make creation intrinsic to God's fullness."[2]

The reason why *ad extra* data must not be taken as a "given" is that it necessarily entails God in "real relations" with creation. By "real relations" we understand relations that are constitutive in some sense of the being of God, becoming properties of the divine being itself. God's speaking to Moses, for instance, seems to suggest that God has become an object of Moses's hearing and knowledge. Being mindful of the divine transcendence, it must be remembered that, although such activities manifest the being of God, God is not collapsed into finite being.

Theologians of the Western tradition have often found it useful to speak about divine action in terms of created effects precisely as a cautionary measure. To say that God acts in the finite world is simply to say that certain "created effects" are caused by the transcendent God. And so it must be remembered that in producing finite effects, God does not himself become a finite cause.

2. John Webster, "Trinity and Creation," in *God and the Works of God*, vol. 1 of *God Without Measure* (Edinburgh: T&T Clark, 2018), 91.

The danger in regarding the economy as a given lies precisely in supposing that one can transition with ease from the effects to the cause of these actions. Yet the ontological gap intervenes between the divine causality and the created effects as well. This is not to say that there is no resemblance between the divine cause and the created effects, only that this is a matter for analogical and not univocal thinking.

Bruce Marshall puts it quite bluntly: "Our understanding of how the three persons are one God must not be infiltrated or 'contaminated,' as it were, by terms and concepts that refer only to the economy. The economy of salvation as such contributes nothing to understanding either the distinction or the unity of the divine persons."[3] What Marshall means is that there is a certain dynamic of unity and distinction between the divine persons in economic action. If we take the economy as normative for our full understanding of the divine action, we risk making elements that are finite to be determinative for divine action and identity. It must immediately be kept in mind that the particular relations (unitive or distinctive) between the divine persons in the economy are always and inevitably couched in finite and created terms. The Father saying, for example, "This is my Son whom I love; with Him I am well pleased" (Matt 3:17) necessarily involves audible effects, movements of the air and sound waves. Similarly, Christ's obedience and submission to the Father's will also involves created conditions, particularly an assumed human nature.

Here is the difficulty: If the persons are defined by the relations they have with each other, it may appear as if the very identity of the triune persons is not only manifested, but is positively shaped by their economic interactions. But this cannot be the case. God's identity cannot be thought to depend in some way on what happens in the economy, even on what he himself achieves in the economy. Marshall is quite right to write that "whatever distinctions the persons of the Trinity exhibit among themselves in the actual economy would obtain in just the same way were there no economy at all, and no decision to have one."[4] What Marshall in fact claims is that the particular manner in which unity and distinction, and thus essence and supposits, obtain and are maintained in God cannot be in any way seen to depend on anything outside of God. This does not mean that the economy provides no clues for the immanent Trinity—we will address this in the second half of this chapter.

There are immediate implications for our inquiry. Our experience of "divine

3. Bruce D. Marshall, "The Unity of the Triune God: Reviving an Ancient Question," *Thomist* 74, no. 1 (2010): 17.
4. Marshall, "The Unity of the Triune God," 15.

acts" cannot be taken to be epistemically basic or absolute in any way. Since God does not become a finite cause, since he has not exhausted himself in finite reality, but remains transcendent, the nature and reality of the divine acts in history is not fully expressed by what may be experienced. There is a depth to this divine activity that may only be contemplated from above, so to speak, or from the direction of the immanent Trinity, or the processions, as we shall see.

The Thomistic tradition has expressed this insight through the dictum that the divine operations *ad extra* follow from, and are grounded in, the immanent processions. The argument in progress is that by starting from the processions we may find a truer description of the relationship between unity and diversity in divine action. One would mistake the shadow for the thing if one were to take the diversity visible in the economy at its face value and then proceed to establish the divine unity. Some may think this is a respectable historic tradition of moving from the three to the one. As we will show, while there may indeed be such a tradition, it is not the one often supposed to be.

Divine action *ad extra* does not wear its meaning on its sleeve. Its true nature is only accessible from the direction of the self-sufficient and yet abundantly overflowing divine life. Only by making our beginning with the processions will we properly be able to bear witness to the divine economy. We are not claiming that the processions can be comprehended. Such is a promise that will be made good in the beatific vision alone. Rather, we are expressing a principled directionality in our knowledge of divine operations. Failure to regard actions from the perspective of the processions invites mythologizing the agents, regarding them as objects in the world.

A detailed analysis of the Trinitarian processions would be beyond the scope of our text. We will restrict ourselves to making some observations based on the dogmatic consensus achieved in the formulation of Trinitarian doctrine. The outcome of the church's struggle for the doctrine of the Trinity has been the twofold affirmation: numerical unity of the divine substance; real distinction of the three persons. It must not be assumed, however, that the church succeeded in *comprehending* the relationship that exists between the persons and the substance. Theological insight into this sacred reality proceeds sometimes by affirmations but mostly by negations. The apophatic character of Trinitarian doctrine is quite appropriate, given the reality it fearfully contemplates. Basic Trinitarian concepts cannot be directly explained and fully defined. The darkness of ignorance necessarily envelops them. In this case theological progress takes the form of a gradual purification of our speech about God, by stipulating grammatical rules rather than shining the light of comprehension on transcendent realities.

Fundamental Trinitarian concepts such as that of "person" remain analogical when applied to God. The same may be said about the divine substance. The notion of person is particularly important for our study since it is the persons who are the subjects of acting. It is supposits who act, not natures. The persons are the agents of the divine operations *ad extra*. But the question remains: what is the nature of the action that they undertake together? In particular, what is the dynamics of unity and distinction that pertains to such an action? Should one conceive it after the model of a cooperative or collective action, where individual persons have their own individual acts as part of a broader collective unity? Or should one speak rather of a single agency, with no individual operations undertaken by any of the persons?

The argument we have been making, by no means original, is that the answer to this question is to be sought not from an investigation of the external actions themselves, but rather by starting with what the church has confessed about the dynamics of immanent Trinitarian unity and distinction and only thereafter moving to the external activity. From a human angle, from below, it is true that what we appear to encounter are three sets of personal operations: those of the Father, of the Son, and of the Holy Spirit. It is also often supposed that it is precisely the distinction between these operations that establishes, for our knowledge, the distinction of the persons. It is a mistake to rush to such a conclusion, as was shown. It is at least in principle possible that the filter of finite reality brings the diversity of persons in disproportionate focus, elongating their shadows, so to speak, to the detriment of their unity. If our axiom is correct, a proper description of the nature of external action must await the clarification (as far as is possible) of the immanent nature of God.

We must therefore exercise proper caution before validating a univocal concept of "person," and personal action which seems to be suggested by the *apparent* distinctions between the operations of Father, Son, and Holy Spirit. This is precisely what we have seen happening in the modern unravelling of the doctrine of inseparable operations. The concept of person, and its implied concept of agency (and causality) must obey the grammatical rules of Trinitarian doctrine.

In the wake of the conflict with Arianism, it was established that the Son and the Holy Spirit proceed from the person of the Father, but within the unity of the divine substance. Athanasius had successfully demonstrated that unless these processions are internal, the Father cannot claim properties such as those of "Creator," given that the work of creation is ascribed by Scripture to the Son. Since the work of creation is "carried out" by the Son, the Father can only be also Creator if the Son is immanent to the Father and not a separate substance from him.

The West has been particularly taken with the psychological analogy developed by Augustine, though even here it must be recognized that it is not the only way the West elaborates on the procession of the Son and Spirit. The usefulness of the psychological analogy pertains to the fact that in intellectual substances there is an internal procession of the Word as a result, or rather as the form of the intellectual activity of that substance. While the East does not privilege the psychological analogy to the same extent, it is by no means ignorant of it. However, it is often counterbalanced with other images and metaphors, usually that of the sun and its rays of light, or even biological generation, as we have seen in Nyssen, for example. It remains the case quite clearly, however, that it is the universal conclusion of creedal Trinitarianism that the processions of the persons are immanent, or that they remain internal to the substance, neither separating the substance nor multiplying it. The impression that the East emphasizes the persons while the West stresses the essence is caricatural, as Orthodox theologian Lucian Turcescu states: "In contrast to a widespread, misinformed opinion of the twentieth century, the Cappadocians did not state a priority of persons over the substance, but kept the two together in worshipping God as Father, Son, and Holy Spirit."[5]

Not only are the processions internal to the substance, but by no means can one subordinate the persons to the substance, or the substance to the persons. Instead, an *equiprimordiality* must be affirmed of substance and persons. The persons are not the product of the substance, which would entail a fourth reality above the persons. Neither is the substance the product of the persons, which would entail the absurd conclusion that the Father produces his own substance in begetting the Son, a conclusion that John Zizioulas realizes he must make, though he refuses to see the absurdity.[6]

Failure to observe what may be called the rule of equiprimordiality can easily lead to a personalism that severs the ties of person with nature and can hardly retain the substantial unity of God except in voluntaristic terms. On the flip side, undue emphasis and privileging of nature or substance can result in depersonalizing the Trinity, such that all its activity, being natural, is necessitated. The activity of the persons would be in that case entirely imposed

---

5. Lucian Turcescu, *Gregory of Nyssa and the Concept of Divine Persons* (Oxford: Oxford University Press, 2005), 60.

6. John Zizioulas, *Being as Communion* (Crestwood, NY: St. Vladimir's Seminary Press, 1985), 43.

upon them by this "fourth reality," the divine substance. The equiprimordiality of substance and persons upholds both the full divinity of the persons and the oneness of God.

The triune persons are not a different reality from the divine essence. Thus, in addition to equiprimordiality, one must speak of numerical identity between person and essence. As John Owen has put it, "a divine person is nothing but the divine essence, upon the account of an especial property, subsisting in an especial manner."[7] The distinction between the persons and the essence is not real but only conceptual. On the other hand, the distinction between the persons themselves is, against Sabellianism, a real distinction. In fact, the rule of equiprimordiality of essence and persons is a corollary of the rule of the identity of persons and essence. Each triune person is fully and wholly God. The diversity of the persons does not partition the simple divine substance, each person fully sharing in the same substance.

It is particularly instructive that even for the Cappadocians the procession of the Son and the Spirit takes place by way of what we may call essential activities. Arguing against the personalistic trend epitomized by Zizioulas, Chrysostom Koutloumousianos demonstrates that neither the Cappadocians, nor John Damascene, Maximus the Confessor, nor any other Eastern Father, sets the person of the Father himself as primordial in relation to the divine essence. There is no monarchy of the Father, but rather a monarchy that is shared by all the persons in virtue of their sharing the one divine essence.[8] The impression of a monarchy of the Father can be explained when one takes into account what Gregory Nazianzen, for example, responds to, namely to refute the heretical reification of will.[9] The stress on the priority of the Father is in the context of an arguing that the will of the Father is not a separate reality from the Father. The intention was never to say that the Father alone is the source of the divine essence.

Koutloumousianos argues that the distinction between the persons is something secured precisely within the divine substance, not by the person of the Father alone. It is not simply the person of the Father, who freely wills to have a Son and thus freely generates the triune substance, as Zizioulas has it. Rather, the distinction between the persons is established precisely by the "essential divine causality," which "furnishes the distinction between the hy-

---

7. John Owen, *Communion with God* (Edinburgh: Banner of Truth, 1965), 407.

8. See for example Gregory Nyssen, *Against Eunomius* 8.2.

9. Chrysostom Koutloumousianos, *The One and the Three: Nature, Person and Triadic Monarchy in the Greek and Irish Patristic Tradition* (Cambridge: James Clarke, 2015), 17–18. See Gregory Nazianzen, *Oration* 29.6–7.

postatic properties, only to ensure that no kind of priority is acceptable within the deity."[10]

It is not the personal will of the Father that lies at the foundation of the Son's procession. Indeed, Koutloumousianos argues, there is no personal will (gnomic will) in the Trinity, but only essential will. The will of the Father to send the Son and the will of the Son to be sent are numerically the same will. The same goes for the love of the Father for the Son—it is the same as the Son's love for the Father. The communion that exists between the persons is not predicated on the more basic personal attributes of will and love, but rather it is a "natural perichoresis" which is the "natural outcome of co-essentiality."[11]

It follows that not only in the Western tradition is the procession of the persons a "function" of essential divine causality, but in the East as well.[12] To reiterate, this does not mean that the essence begets the persons. Aquinas is quite clear on this point. There is no impersonal activity of the essence. But the persons act within the unity of the divine essence, and on the basis of their shared nature, with its shared natural properties: will and intellect.

We must then be clear about the meaning of the dictum, *opera trinitatis ad intra sunt divisa*. It does not indicate that within the immanent life of the Trinity there are three separate agents who each have a separate will, a separate knowledge, and a separate love for the others. Rather, it indicates that *within the essential divine causality* there obtain real and irreducible distinctions, that there are subsistent relations that distinguish and define the persons over against each other yet never against the substance.

Whatever differences still remain between the Eastern and Western accounts of the processions, and between various subtraditions within these broader approaches, it is an undisputed fact, as we have seen in chapter 2, that both regard the external operations of the Trinity as being indivisible. The logic of this goes all the way to the very constitution of the triune persons themselves. The processions themselves, although personal (from person to person), are not independent of, but presuppose the medium of the essential divine causality.

Given that there is one divine essence and that the persons share the essential properties, whenever the persons act, they act on the basis of their shared nature and through those shared essential powers. Immanently, the

---

10. Koutloumousianos, *The One and the Three*, 28.

11. Koutloumousianos, *The One and the Three*, 45.

12. See, for example, Turcescu's comments on the correlativity of the processions and essential divine goodness (*Gregory of Nyssa and the Concept of Divine Persons*, 90).

relations (paternity, filiation, spiration—active and passive) constitute the persons as such. It is for this reason that the operations *ad intra* are said to be divisible, namely that the relations establish the processions. The identity and personhood of each person are constituted by the relations each has with the other persons. In fact, these are nothing but those subsistent relations, since everything else is shared.

But the persons must be constituted in their plenary perfection apart from any involvement in creation. They must each have their fullness in their relations with one another. The Son has his perfection as he proceeds from the Father, by way of intellect, as Word and image. The Spirit has his own perfection as he proceeds from the Father and the Son, by way of will, as love and gift. Now, and this is the pivotal move in this argument, if the persons are identified with the relations, if these are relations that subsist in the unity of an intellectual substance, and if other relations, contingent and economic, were to obtain between the persons—where there would be a to and fro, a giving and a taking—then the very identity of the persons would also depend in some way upon these contingent and finite realities. Divine immutability, perfection, and aseity would be jeopardized by the extension of the personal identity to include such relations in terms of the created order.

This is one reason why it cannot be supposed that there are divisible operations between the persons at the level of the economy. Divisible operations are only possible for divine persons in terms that are constitutive of their very identities. The reason for this has already been established: The persons are nothing but the subsistent relations. For such divisible operations cannot be operations in terms of different essences or substances. The persons do not have these different substances. The only difference between their actions, then, would be in terms of relations within the unity of the divine substance. But such relations cannot be accidental in a simple God; they must subsist substantially, and therefore they would be definitive of the very identity of the persons—not just a narrative identity, so to speak, but ontological identity. In fact, given the fact that God is pure act, it is impossible to distinguish between a narrative identity and an ontological identity. God is what God does.[13]

The above argument can also be stated in terms of two problematic options. Separate economic activities can be of either of two sorts. Either these are activities predicated in terms of different substances or they are activities and causalities within the same substance. The first option is problematic since it entails an abandonment of classical monotheism. The second is also prob-

---

13. For this reason Thomas insists that relations with creation are not real.

lematic since it brings created factors into the very constitution of the divine persons and substance.

If the persons proceed immanently within the divine nature by way of the essential divine causality, and if the persons do not have a distinct personal causality, it follows that when it comes to economic operations the persons can only act indivisibly, given that their nature is shared. Here we have the basis for the generalization of the observed scriptural ascriptions of common actions to all divine persons into a metaphysical rule. The rule stipulates that, in virtue of what the persons are in relation to the substance, they cannot be involved in distinct actions proceeding externally (economic) from this substance. To suppose such diversity in their operations either divides the divine substance into separate acting substances or it introduces creation into the very constitution of the persons.

If this is true, then extreme caution must be demonstrated in any analysis of economic relations between the triune persons. Our understanding of the incarnation, of the obedience of the Son to the Father, of the paschal relations between Father and Son, and so forth will need to be very clearly spelled out. This entails a critical rereading of the dogmatic tradition surrounding these loci precisely in light of the nature of divine operation.[14]

To say that there is a single (efficient) causality of the Trinity in creation, however, does not mean that the divine persons have no *distinct* causality *ad extra*. Indeed, in saying that God acts in virtue of his single essence and through his essential properties, one does not say everything that needs to be said about the divine action. The question, though, is what specific contribution the persons make in economic works. In this connection it will be instructive to return to Aquinas's *Summa Theologiae*, where he asks whether to create is proper to any person. Aquinas first responds in the negative, citing the authority of Pseudo-Dionysius, who holds that "all things caused are the common work of the whole Godhead." He then explains as follows:

> To create is, properly speaking, to cause or produce the being of things. And as every agent produces its like, the principle of action can be considered from the effect of the action; for it must be fire that generates fire. And therefore to create belongs to God according to His being, that is, His essence, which is common to the three Persons. Hence to create is not proper to any one Person, but is common to the whole Trinity.[15]

14. See chapters 4–9 below.
15. Aquinas, *ST* 1, q. 45, a. 6.

Réginald Garrigou-Lagrange explains Aquinas's logic: "To create is to produce the being of things as such. Creation therefore belongs to God according to His being, which is His essence and is common to the three persons. That is, God produces the being of things inasmuch as He is subsisting per se."[16] The idea seems to be something like this: There is a similitude between the very nature of the act of creation, which is to produce being, and the divine being; to produce being belongs to God insofar as he is considered as a being—and not as three persons.

Naturally, there is much more to divine action than the production of being, and this fact allows one to wonder whether there is room for a causality specific to the persons in other terms. We will find this supposition to be warranted and will return to it momentarily. To return to Question 45, Article 6, Aquinas immediately argues that the persons do "have a causality respecting the order of things," since the Father creates through his Word, and through the Spirit. So Aquinas concludes that "the processions of the Persons are the type of the productions of creatures in as much as they include the essential attributes, knowledge, and will."[17]

What Aquinas is telling us is that we have not exhausted the knowledge of the nature of the act of creation if we simply mention its efficient cause in the divine essence. In fact the eternal processions themselves are the cause and reason of the entire production of creatures, as long as one bears in mind that a procession involves, in relation to another, a relation to the essence. In other words, because the processions are internal to the substance, they consist in two kinds of relations: to one another, and to the divine essence. It is in their relations to the divine essence that the processions are the cause and reason of the production of creatures.

The divine act is not explained solely by the divine nature, that is, by the essential knowledge and will of the Trinity, but also by the processions, since the persons proceed within these very essential acts. In other words, it makes a difference that the essential attributes of the Trinity, which account for creation, belong to a dynamic eternal communication of divine being. We are not simply speaking about a monadic and undifferentiated being who creates through his intellect and will. Rather, in the triune being, from the intellectual properties of intellect and will proceed Word and Love, as irreducible persons.

Thus, when we say that the Father acts through the Son, the aspect of unity is not lost, as in an agent operating through an instrument or intermediary. In

---

16. Réginald Garrigou-Lagrange, *The Trinity and God the Creator. A Commentary on St. Thomas' Theological Summa, 1a, Q. 27–119* (St. Louis: B. Herder, 1954), 394.

17. Aquinas, *ST* 1, q. 45, a. 6, *responsio*.

this case, as Aquinas intends it, the persons represent the aspect of the procession, insofar as the procession includes the essential causality of the Trinity. When we say that the Father creates through the Son, we must remember that the Father remains in the Son and the Son remains in the Father and that the will and intellect through which God creates is the same divine essence entailed by the processions.

We are beginning to make some progress in our understanding of the nature of triune external operation. Such operation is not entirely explained by the divine essence regarded as such, but only by bringing into view the processions. However, the processions are nothing but the divine essence under the aspect of a dynamic flow of perfection from one person to another. Quite clearly, we are not dealing with an undifferentiated, monadic causality but with a transcendent causality that is irreducibly differentiated yet simple. We are beginning to draw the contours of a dialectic of unity and distinction that respects the integrity of the Trinitarian grammar of persons and essence. But does it make a difference? Is a monadic divine causality experienced in a different way than a differentiated causality would be experienced? Or, what difference does it make for our descriptions of divine action to say that the divine causality is differentiated?

We have established that, since the divine persons do not have different natures, they cannot act divisibly from one another. At the same time, it can be said that the divine persons have the divine essence and perfection in a differentiated way, the Father as unbegotten, the Son as begotten, and the Spirit as spirated. Therefore, just as each divine person can be said to be a unique and incommunicable mode of being (*tropos hyparxeōs*), in the same way each person has its own unique *mode of action*. It may be said that the persons do not have their distinct actions, but they possess a distinct mode of action within the unity of the same action.

Emery argues that "the properties of the divine persons clarify not only their distinction and their subsistence in the immanence of the Trinity, but equally their act in the world."[18] The names "Word" and "Holy Spirit" entail both a relationship to the essence, as well as a relation of person to person. The Father utters himself (necessarily) and every other creature (contingently) in the very same act. At the same time, the Father loves himself (necessarily) and every other creature (contingently) in the same pure act.[19] Thus, the title Word

18. Gilles Emery, "The Personal Mode of Trinitarian Action in St. Thomas Aquinas," *Thomist* 69, no. 1 (January 2005): 33–34.

19. Cf. Aquinas, *ST* 1. q. 37, a. 2, ad. 3.

utters in the same breath both a procession *from* the Father, when regarded relationally, and the procession *of* creatures, when regarded essentially.

So according to Emery's reading of Aquinas, a relation to creatures is "included" in the notion of person, or it belongs in the second place in the proper name of a divine person.[20] In other words, the person may indeed be identified, though not constituted, through its operation toward creatures, as long as one bears in mind that this operation is by reference to the divine essence. Thus, the personal property of the Son and the personal property of the Spirit also bear a relation to creation. In every divine action this personal property of a divine person is present, which leads us to the concept of appropriation, to be dealt with in the second half of the chapter.

Far from obscuring the distinction of persons, the doctrine of inseparable operations identifies the persons through the essential acts of the Trinity, in which the persons possess their own modes of action. Just as ontologically the persons are distinguished as relations within the unity of the essence, so operationally they are distinguished as modes of activity within the single yet undifferentiated work of God.

This differentiated action, however, does not yield effects that are exclusively assigned to this or that person. This may seem to make it impossible, or entirely arbitrary, to discern a personal property in a particular action. Indeed, the thrust of modern Trinitarianism has often been to call for distinct effects as the only possible epistemic access to the distinct personal causalities of the persons. Yet it is possible to discern the distinct persons even if their effects are always common to them. Remember that it may be possible to discern between different kinds of causalities. Efficient causality is the transmission of extrinsic motion from one cause to one effect. On the other hand, the notion of final causality entails the movement of a particular effect toward a cause.

Take for example the action of a magnet upon a particular metallic object. Insofar as its efficient causality is concerned, the magnet produces a change in the state of the object. However, when this operation is regarded as efficient causality it is impossible to differentiate between the magnet's poles. Only when the operation is regarded in terms of its finality, in the attachment of the object discriminately to this or that pole, is the distinction between the magnetic poles made manifest.

This provides a particularly suggestive analogy for the dynamics of unity and distinction in divine action. God's operations *ad extra* are in terms of the divine essence and the essential properties of intellect and will. As we have

20. Emery, "Personal Mode," 39.

seen, such operations cannot be seen to be in any way constitutive of the divine being or of hypostatic identity. As Marshall insists, the immanent Trinity is *not* the economic Trinity, lest we compromise divine transcendence. The way in which we are to properly relate *ad intra* to *ad extra*, Marshall continues, is in terms of the distinctions between processions and missions.[21]

The missions extend the processions by adding a created effect to a particular procession. The created effect, say the human nature of Jesus Christ, is the common production of the Trinity, insofar as something is brought into being. On the other hand, having been brought into being the human nature is assumed specifically by the Son. Much like the metal object, which is moved by the whole magnet yet attaches distinctly to one of the poles, the human nature of Jesus Christ, the created effect of the mission of the Son, is produced by the whole Trinity yet attached to the Son exclusively.

It is precisely for this reason, namely that it has its finality by hypostatic union in the Son, that the human nature of Jesus Christ reveals the Son in his distinction from the Father and the Spirit. It is not because it is efficiently moved to act or brought into being by just the Son.[22] Thus, the revelation and the manifestation of the distinct persons in the economy is a matter of a distinct causality, a causality other than the efficient one, which belongs to the divine essence.

We shall not at this point take up the knotty issue of the precise nature of this causality, in particular Rahner's proposal that we are dealing with a quasi-formal causality. That discussion will need to be delayed until we investigate the formality of the incarnation. However, we are now in a position to suggest that the following positions are perfectly compatible. On the one hand, it may be affirmed that God, as pure actuality, operates in creation in the same act by which he is constituted as divine and triune. The Father utters himself, as Word, and everything else in the same pure act of the divine being. At the same time, it may be said that certain operations of God, although they are products of the essential efficient causation, nevertheless unite creatures to the divine persons distinctly—in a manner yet to be investigated. While the creatures are not moved distinctly *by* a divine person (such a movement would compromise divine aseity and would make the persons depend in their identity upon creation, as we have shown), they are moved *toward* a particular person in distinct ways.

Without wishing to make too much of the magnetic analogy, one may say

21. Marshall, "Unity of the Triune God."
22. For more on this, see chapters 5-6.

that God *draws* creatures to himself. I have no wish to say that this metaphor exhausts the range of possible language about divine action in the world, yet in this case it is particularly revealing and compelling. God acts, so to speak, without himself moving, much like a magnet draws without changing in any way.[23] In acting, the change is not in God—that would imply real relations with the creature, and thus dependence upon the creature—but in the creature.

We have advanced a particular proposal about the dynamics of unity and differentiation in divine action *ad extra*. It was suggested that the dimension of unity is reflected in the fact that, insofar as any divine action is considered under the aspect of efficient cause, it is ascribed to the divine essence. This does not mean that the essence acts, for to act belongs to supposits, or rather a substance only acts insofar as it is itself in act. In this case, the action is accomplished by all the divine persons in virtue of their essential properties. But this is only half of the story. The dimension of plurality is located in terms of the fact that the divine essence is proceeding from the Father through the Son, and from the Father and the Son to the Holy Spirit. Within every action can be discerned—with the eyes of faith—three irreducible *modes of action*. Thus every action manifests each of the persons insofar as the personal property of each is entailed by the essential properties of God, in virtue of which he acts. The differentiation, however, is only visible under the aspect of the missions, that is, in the form of final causality.

It goes without saying that such an account of triune causality begs a number of questions about a proper Trinitarian scriptural hermeneutics. It is to this that we now have to turn.

Knowledge of the Divine Persons and Actions *Ad Extra*

One of the strongest objections against "hard inseparability" is that it obstructs the manifestation of the persons in their distinctness (the *personal description problem*). If actions are merely "appropriated" to the persons, the notion that the persons of the Son and the Spirit acting in the world are a mediation of God the Father is destroyed. This objection, as we have seen, comes from a variety of quarters and we need not rehearse it here in detail.

Notwithstanding the differences between the various objectors, Gunton per-

---

23. Of course, one can say this about God only because he is not static but plenary life, and only because he freely determines himself from eternity for these operations and not others. The intention here is not to sacrifice the personal dimension of divine agency. Unlike a magnet, which attracts indiscriminately, God freely determines whom he will attract and to whom he will be united.

haps expresses most forcefully this objection. He objects against the preponderance of an account of divine causality, formulated in largely apophatic ways, that dominates our understanding of how God relates to the world. To say that we know God by his effects is acceptable only if by his effects "is not meant a cosmologically abstracted first cause, but the *actions* of God—creation, redemption, etc.—towards and in the created world; God not abstracted from matter, but involved in it."[24] Gunton is concerned that a proper recognition of the distinct agencies of the Son and the Spirit is hampered by a language that favors impersonal notions (effects, energies, etc.) and thus tends toward modalism.

Unless we recognize that the Son and the Spirit have their own distinct "forms of action,"[25] specifically the action of *mediating* the actions of creation, redemption, glorification *initiated* by the Father, as agents in their own right, we will quite simply not know God. "If the persons are functionally indistinguishable—that is, indistinguishable in their modes of action—there seems little point in the doctrine of the Trinity."[26]

We cannot restrict our knowledge of the distinction between the persons to their relations of origin. Gunton insists against Aquinas that the notion "person"[27] is univocal between humanity and divinity.[28] Insistence on an analogical approach acts as a cataract that prevents the clear vision of the distinction between the persons.

Gunton also reproaches Reformed theologians for failing to follow through on their insight that the persons need to be distinguished "in more respects than in their relations of origin."[29] He continues, "Yet they are not aware of the chief pitfall, which is the principle of *opera ad extra trinitatis sunt indivisa* (the actions of the Trinity outside are undivided), their conception of which effectively prevents them from distinguishing the forms of action of the distinct albeit inseparable persons."[30] Noting a tendency to ascribe to the Father creation, to the Son redemption, and to the Spirit sanctification, he counters:

24. Gunton, *Act and Being*, 112.

25. Gunton, *Act and Being*, 145.

26. Gunton, *Act and Being*, 27.

27. He defines persons as "those particular beings—hypostases—whose attributes are manifested in particular kinds of action, such as love, relationality, freedom, creativity" (*Act and Being*, 146–47).

28. "What it is to be a human person is in this case identical with what it is to be a divine person, and therefore the word means the same at the levels of creator and creation" (*Act and Being*, 147).

29. Gunton, *Act and Being*, 138.

30. Gunton, *Act and Being*, 139.

The Father is the one who creates, reconciles, sanctifies, and the rest, but does so in every case by the action of his two hands. The exponents of the approach to which objection is here being taken necessarily cannot distinguish between the different kinds of action of the three persons, and are, indeed, always in danger of modalism, for if to the Father is attributed creation, to the Son redemption and to the Spirit sanctification, there is always a temptation to attribute the unity of the divine action to some deity underlying the reality of Father, Son and Spirit.[31]

Gunton quite clearly does not wish to ascribe *diverse* actions to the persons, but he wants to see them as the *agents* of the Father's own actions. He positions himself between "mere appropriation" and "individual—non-perichoretic—agency."[32] "This," he writes, "is not so much a matter of appropriating particular actions to the Father, Son and Spirit as of bringing to the fore the distinctive forms of action of the persons each in relation to the other two: originating, becoming incarnate, perfecting."[33]

It is quite instructive that Gunton self-consciously goes against the creedal tradition of the will as an attribute of nature and insists on making it a personal attribute. He opines that "the decision which was taken to the effect that will is an attribute of nature and not of the hypostasis or person leads to saying that natures have wills, with an inevitably Nestorian outcome."[34] Instead, we must "think of the will as something characterizing the action of a person rather than being the single attribute of the one God."[35]

Gunton's sentiments find something of an echo in Kevin J. Vanhoozer's *Remythologizing Theology*. The latter argues that we should not "confuse the concept of personhood (what it is to be a person) with personal identity (what it is to be just *this* person). The relations that distinguish, for example, the Father from the Son and the Spirit are constitutive of the Father's distinct personal identity rather than the Father's personhood *simpliciter*."[36] What Vanhoozer means is that the divine persons are constituted as the persons that they are prior to their having the relations they do with each other and the world.

This makes it possible to say that

31. Gunton, *Act and Being*, 139.
32. Gunton, *Act and Being*, 144.
33. Gunton, *Act and Being*, 145.
34. Gunton, *Act and Being*, 29.
35. Gunton, *Act and Being*, 30.
36. Kevin J. Vanhoozer, *Remythologizing Theology: Divine Action, Passion, and Authorship* (Cambridge: Cambridge University Press, 2012), 145.

the particular identities of Father, Son, and Spirit follow from the activities that distinguish them—both the eternal activities (i.e., the processions—begetting, spiration) that characterize the immanent Trinity and the historical acts (i.e., the missions—incarnation, Pentecost) that characterize the economic Trinity. If persons are who they are because of their relations to one another, then it is illegitimate to reduce the richness of these Trinitarian relations to relations of origin alone.[37]

Indeed, the divine persons are understood as diverse communicative agents, each with their own "speaking parts."[38] This provides the warrant for our knowledge of God's immanent life: "It is on the basis of God's communicative presence and activity in history that we come to understand divine communicative perfection in eternity."[39] Turning to the biblical communication between divine persons, the intra-Trinitarian dialogues, Vanhoozer suggests that "the three persons relate in dialogical fashion. . . . God is the Father addressing the Son, the Son responding to the Father, and the Spirit overhearing."[40] This sort of differentiation still does not justify "the social rather than the psychological analogy of the Trinity exclusively. For the Bible also attributes certain actions in the economy (e.g., creation; revelation) to all three persons, with each person contributing to the same action in distinct ways."[41]

Vanhoozer is clearly noncommittal here, refusing to opt for either the social or the Latin model and thus leaving room for both loose and hard inseparability. There are actions that are distinctly and exclusively of this or that triune person; and then there are actions that are commonly and inseparably acted, in which there is a distinct "contribution" made by each of the persons. But will this do? A loose inseparability, where the three persons are distinct agents that engage in distinct actions, assumes a particular metaphysical picture, which is indeed very different if not contrary to the picture assumed by hard inseparability. Vanhoozer does not analyze the precise form of the unity of action that would obtain in both of those cases. For that we will turn, in the last section of this chapter, to a discussion of a social Trinitarian model for inseparable action.

For the present point, it suffices to raise this question: What is a "contribution" to, or an "aspect" of,[42] an inseparable action? Secondly, what sort of

37. Vanhoozer, *Remythologizing*, 147–48
38. Vanhoozer, *Remythologizing*, 245–46.
39. Vanhoozer, *Remythologizing*, 245.
40. Vanhoozer, *Remythologizing*, 246.
41. Vanhoozer, *Remythologizing*, 246–47.
42. Vanhoozer, *Remythologizing*, 261.

insight do the intra-Trinitarian conversations between Jesus and the Father actually provide into the intra-Trinitarian relations between them? Are we warranted in taking them at their face value? Or do they indicate something of the immanent Trinity, yet only obliquely, through a created medium (the human nature of Jesus Christ)?

Both Gunton and Vanhoozer insist that the economic relations between the divine persons reveal their personal identities, even if they do not constitute their personhood as such. Gunton makes the bolder claim, however, that will is a personal property and not a natural one. While Vanhoozer does not say as much, one has to wonder whether this is not a tacit, or at least an implicit, assumption of the suggestion that the divine persons are "conversation partners."

The question for the present model is, what are the implications of the metaphysics of Trinitarian causality for our knowledge of the Trinity from its economic actions? It has already been suggested that another mode of knowledge of God is possible from the missions, as opposed to the operations of the persons. While operations *ad extra* are essential, the missions are personal and are not appropriated.

But the Trinitarian logic also implicitly prohibits the kind of Trinitarian epistemology suggested by Gunton. The late British theologian has had to pay the steep price of rejecting conciliar dyothelite logic, according to which Christ has two wills as a consequence of his having two natures. He has argued that natures do not will; only persons do. But, as we have seen in our discussion of Maximus, this is shortsighted and has the consequence of suspending the person in midair, without any clear connections to nature. Gunton's position makes some sense within the personalist logic of modern Trinitarianism, but it would have been foreign to patristic thinking, for which the persons, both divine and human, are supposits of nature. To eliminate from the explanatory apparatus for actions the prepersonal dimension of willing, or natural willing, renders any account of action deficient.

The unhitching of person from nature and of will from nature is pernicious not only for Trinitarian theology but for Christian anthropology as well. It has been developed within the Enlightenment, which Ian McFarland describes as a "resurgence of a much more fundamental desire to distinguish ourselves from our natures, as though our integrity depended on our being essentially other than God made us."[43] McFarland correctly argues that the heart of personal

43. Ian McFarland, "Willing Is Not Choosing: Some Anthropological Implications of Dyothelite Christology," *International Journal of Systematic Theology* 9, no. 1 (2007): 21.

identity should not be located in the will, for the will is first a natural property, and only secondly is it personal. The will is not the source of personal identity, McFarland argues, but rather the means by which we live out our identities before God.[44]

If will is a personal property, it follows that personal identity is located in freely willed actions. It means that a person is most fully herself when freely exercising the prerogative to initiate actions and make decisions. Personal identity is here equated with freedom, and freedom is understood as detachment from nature. The cost at which this understanding of personal identity comes, however, should not be underestimated. If personal identity is located fundamentally in a free-floating will, removed from one's nature and defined fundamentally as freedom, has any personal identity been established at all? Unless one also probes the relationship between one's free choices and one's ontological and natural substrate, do those free choices reveal *anything*? Is there anything to be manifested in one's actions, or is the self that which emerges as the sum total of one's activities and relations?

Personalism, without appropriate corrections, makes it hard to understand what drives our choices and wherein personal identity resides. By abstracting from our natural endowments, it can only capture snapshots of what might be an identity, yet without any hopes to discover a substantial unity. The best it can hope for is the unity of a story, perhaps revealed at the end only—eschatologically, as it were. But does this story reveal anything beyond itself? Is it a revelation of anything at all? The upshot of dyothelite Christology, as McFarland instructs us, is that what we are personally does not come *from* the will (any more than it comes from our natural endowments), but it comes *by* will. Willing is the mode through which we actualize that which we receive by nature.

To return to Trinitarian matters, if the will is personal, and if each person acts distinctly as an agent, it is difficult to understand how monotheism is safeguarded. Several distinct actions certainly reveal several distinct agents, but does it truly reveal their particular identity as perichoretic persons, as inseparable modes of being of one numerically single divine essence? Is a "loose" inseparability capable of preserving the article of faith that God is one?

Gunton wants to oppose the reification of the essence as a fourth entity over and above the persons, a *Deus absconditus* by definition obscured in its transcendence and antithesis to finite matter. This is an appropriate concern. However, if the divine essence and the divine persons are equiprimordial, and

44. McFarland, "Willing," 18.

if the persons simply are the essence, as per a personal property, then failure to attend to the essential unity of the divine action in history results in an incomplete description of that action.

Finally, turning to Vanhoozer, one must ask about the status of the historical intra-Trinitarian conversations and relations. Is he right to say that these are constitutive of the personal identities but not the personhood of the Father, Son, and Holy Spirit? The difficulty with this proposition is that it assumes that the actions that are constitutive of their personal identities can be undertaken in virtue of personal, not essential, properties, such as intellect and will. But this is somewhat circular. Individual action can be undertaken only if one already has those personal properties, which are not shared with the other persons. If, however, every action that the persons undertake (*ad intra* and *ad extra*) is on the basis of the essential divine intellect and will, it is not clear in what way their personal identities can be constituted through these. If the persons can only act in virtue of an essential will, intellect, and power, how is it that they can delineate diverse identities? Vanhoozer insists that personal identities have to be more than the processions, but what more can there be, given the person's sharing in the essential properties, by way of which alone they can act?

The personal properties of the divine persons are a consequence of their processions by way of essential activities of will and intellect. The personal property of the Son is Word; the personal property of the Spirit is to be Gift. These personal properties are not sufficient for the persons to act independently, while they are sufficient to distinguish the persons from one another. The actions of the Trinity do not reveal the personal identities of the persons because they are individual actions. There can be no individual actions, since there are no individual essences, but only one shared essence.

We should not surmise that the economic activities of the Trinity do not reveal the persons in their distinctness. While in divine missions, the divine persons are distinctly related to certain created effects (in the visible missions) or to human persons (in the invisible missions), the operations of the Trinity serve to manifest the divine persons. The name of the gnoseological ascent from the inseparable operations to the distinct manifestation of a person is *appropriation*.

We will not enter into an exhaustive discussion of this complex concept. We would like, however, to show how appropriation is the epistemic and hermeneutical approach best suited to the reality we are dealing with.

The desire to have the actions reveal the persons is correct. But it must respect the manner in which the persons are ordered to each other and to the es-

sence. Because the persons do not have their own natures they do not act separately. Consequently, they are not revealed by discrete personal actions. The
only personal actions that are distinct are the operations that indicate relations
of origin: The Father *speaks* the Word; Father and Son *spirate* the Spirit.

According to Aquinas, the persons are functions of the processions, which
in turn are predicated upon essential attributes. The Son proceeds as Word in
the essential operation of *understanding*. The Spirit proceeds as Love in the
essential operation of love.[45] These biblical names (e.g., John 1:1; Rom 5:5)
indicate the personal property of the Son and the Spirit. According to Nyssen
as well, the power by which the Father generates the Son is the same as the
power by which the Son creates. Hence, the persons are not distinguished by
the essential attributes since they share these. Such a distinction, as Emery
comments, "must belong to a different schema, that of the *order* within the
Trinity, that is at the level of relations of origin."[46]

If the persons are not distinguished by the essential attributes, and the
persons act economically only through their shared essence, their distinction
cannot be gleaned on the basis of their operations. The knowledge that we
gain from the economy of the distinction between the persons is not, strictly
speaking, predicated on their operations but on their missions. It is because the
Trinitarian persons do not merely act in history but act with the end of uniting aspects of creation to themselves that such a revelation of their personal
distinctions can take place. The reader may be referred back to Augustine's
Sermon 52, where he answers the objection that in the baptism of Jesus we
seem to see the Father, Son, and Holy Spirit acting separately, thus posing an
apparently fatal objection to the principle of inseparable operations. Augustine's response, which we need not rehearse fully here, is to invoke a distinction
between the production of created effects, which is common to the whole
Trinity, and, in a divine mission, the attachment of these effects specifically to
just one person: "The Trinity produced the flesh of Christ, but the only one of
them it belongs to is Christ."[47]

So the knowledge of the distinction of the persons is given in the knowledge of the divine missions, by faith. It is through the missions, and what is
communicated in the missions, that we learn about the distinctions and about
the personal properties of the persons. But the essential operations too provide

45. Aquinas, *ST* 1, q. 37. a. 1.
46. Emery, *Trinitarian Theology*, 187.
47. Augustine, *Sermon 52*, section 21, in *Sermons: III (51–94) on the New Testament*, trans. Edmund Hill, OP, ed. John E. Rotelle, OSA (Hyde Park: New City Press, 1992), 61.

additional insight into the personal character of Father, Son, and Holy Spirit. Trinitarian doctrine teaches us that the contemplation of the divine persons does not proceed by way of isolating them from one another, or indeed from the knower. Since the persons mutually indwell each other, they can only be known together. Moreover, since they can only be known through the missions, their contemplation requires both the visible as well as the invisible missions of the Son and the Spirit. As Sarah Coakley puts it, commenting on Nyssen, "We are presented with the idea of a unified flow of divine will and love, catching us up reflexively towards the light of the Father, and allowing to the 'persons' only the minimally distinctive features of their internal causal relations."[48]

Having established these distinctions on the basis of the visible and invisible missions, we return then to the operations. Again, since the persons do not exist or act separately, they cannot be known separately. Thus, contemplation of the persons by way of appropriation from their essential operations toward their personal properties is not simply an anticlimactic consolation prize. The personal properties of Father, Son, and Holy Spirit are manifested in their essential operations because the very subsistence of the persons themselves is through the essential attributes of intellect and will, and through their essential immanent operations of understanding and love.

While contemplation via appropriation is not second best, at the same time it must be understood that appropriation is not the way to get to the personal properties. Appropriation is not individuation. The personal properties must already be established in order for them to be discerned in the operations. One only finds them, in other words, when one knows what to look for. This is not a vicious circularity since it is not expected of the operations to reveal the personal properties, but only to provide additional semantic depth to them. The personal properties are not "given" in historical revelation in the sense that specific empirical data could provide the justification for inferring the divine plurality. On the contrary, God acts as one in the economy, yet drawing and uniting to himself certain created effects. However, such a union is not in itself empirically perceptible—this would disregard divine transcendence. The fact of the union of these created effects with God is available to faith alone and not to empirical knowledge.

48. Sarah Coakley, "'Persons' In the 'Social' Doctrine of the Trinity: A Critique of Current Analytic Discussion," in *The Trinity: An Interdisciplinary Symposium on the Trinity*, ed. Stephen T. Davis, Daniel Kendall, SJ, Gerald O'Collins (Oxford: Oxford University Press, 2003), 137.

So while the appropriated operations do not anchor the distinction between the persons, they are a sort of a second naïveté, a semantic ascent where we glimpse more of the mystery of the persons by dwelling on their common operations. Aquinas defines appropriation as "nothing other than to draw what is shared towards what is proper."[49] Take as an analogy the Barmen declaration, the common work of a number of theologians. We know from other sources, not from the declaration itself, that Barth was one of the main drafters. With this knowledge already in place, when we read the declaration we can hear echoes of Barth's personality. We do not learn these traits from the declaration itself; rather, already knowing these traits, we see them manifested in the final document. This is, then, not so much a case of learning additional attributes as it is of getting a deeper insight into the very meaning of those attributes themselves. Likewise, from the common operations of the Trinity, we ascend into the understanding of the Son's being Word and image, or of the Spirit's property as love.

We may now more fully respond to Vanhoozer's grievance that the personal identity cannot be simply a matter of relations of origin. The particular relation of origin, take *filiation*, is not just a dull, simple property. Being used to a multiplicity of attributes, it looks to us as if a being that has only one property is a poor being. But this is to misunderstand what filiation means. Filiation is a relational property that condenses in itself, under the aspect of order or being-from-another, the whole inexhaustible being of God. It is not a punctual property but an infinitely expansive property, so to speak. In being restricted to the relation of origin, descriptions of the personal property of the Son are not minimalist, but maximalist. They are not expandable by adding further properties because any other properties imaginable are already possessed in common with the other persons. Rather, deepening our contemplation of one of the persons is an exercise of continuous dwelling on their common work under those aspects that are in some way fitting with that person.[50]

The language of Scripture is not disregarded in favor of a philosophical preconception. Quite the contrary: From Scripture, we learn in faith about the distinctions between the persons, namely that the Father begets the Son and spirates (with the Son) the Holy Spirit. Having established these propositions of faith and their mutual coherence, we then return to the material of Scripture in an exercise of *redoublement*: reading the same texts twice, under

---

49. Aquinas, *De Veritate*, q. 7, a. 3, quoted in Emery, *Trinitarian Theology*, 327.

50. For more on appropriation, see the work of Neil Ormerod, *The Trinity: Retrieving the Western Tradition* (Milwaukee: Marquette University Press, 2006), ch. 5; and Bernard Lonergan, *The Triune God: Systematics* (Toronto: University of Toronto Press, 2007), p. 351, assertion 9.

the aspect of unity and under the aspect of plurality. By staying at the level of a first naïveté, we condemn ourselves to a mythological reading of these texts, at risk of taking too literally statements that pertain to transcendence. Procrastinating in philosophical criticism, conversely, we dehydrate ourselves in the desert of speculation. For that reason, the only alternative is to return again to the scriptural well and to drink again and again, contemplating the persons in their common scriptural manifestation.

A Social Trinitarian Account of Unity and Diversity

We have proposed a particular account of the relationship between diversity and unity in the divine action. It is predicated upon a certain understanding of the relationship between persons and essence. If a person is nothing other than the divine essence considered under a certain relational property, it would seem to follow that the divine persons all have the same action in the economy. And yet that is not all that needs to be said about divine action. Rather, there is a causality belonging to the processions, insofar as the divine essence is tripersonal itself and there is a "circulation" of the divine essence between the divine persons. Such a *taxis* warrants the procedure of appropriation as semantic ascent into the personal character of the persons.

At this stage we must reckon with another possibility for divine action, stemming forth from the modern critique of the classical doctrine of the Trinity, often called social Trinitarianism (hereafter ST). The literature on ST is already vast, and we brushed against it already on several occasions. We found the general suggestion to be unpersuasive, but on exclusively historical grounds. On the one hand, we found ST inconsistent with the nature of Jewish monotheism despite claims to the contrary in recent literature. By implication, the monotheism of the New Testament cannot accommodate the conception that there might be three exemplars of "God." Secondly, also on the level of historical analysis, the attempt to enlist the Cappadocians and the Eastern Trinitarian tradition as a whole to shore up the patristic pedigree of the approach is dubious.

Of these two very serious obstacles, the greatest one is the biblical. The patristic resistance to ST is nowhere near as significant as the apparent clash with Jewish constructions of monotheism. But the possibility remains that one can give an account of ST which fulfills the fundamental conditions of monotheism. Richard Swinburne's doctrine of the Trinity aims to do precisely that.[51]

---

51. We are referring to his *The Christian God* (Oxford: Oxford University Press, 1994). Page numbers will be cited in the text hereafter.

Swinburne argues that there are three "individuals" who are God. These individuals are not distinguished by "thisness" but entirely by relational properties. Apart from these relational properties, they cannot be individuated in terms of some distinct "monadic" properties, since all such properties could, in principle, be possessed by the other divine individuals.

The greatest challenge to the possibility of there being multiple divine individuals, Swinburne admits, concerns their omnipotence: "Would not the omnipotence of one such individual be subject to frustration by the other individual and so not be omnipotence?" (171) In responding to this objection, Swinburne observes that the divine attributes are to be discussed in relation to one another and not taken individually. In this case, if omnipotence is properly understood in connection to goodness, the conflict does not arise. We should then define omnipotence as "the power to do good actions within ranges of the kind available to a perfectly good being" (171–72). As Swinburne explains, "each would recognize a duty not to prevent or frustrate the acts of the other, to use his omnipotence to forward them rather than frustrate them" (172).

It is possible, however, that a conflict may arise between their acts, when two acts are both compatible with divine goodness, but incompatible with each other. The example provided is Abraham's settling in Iraq rather than Iran. If one divine individual willed or decided the former, another divine individual the latter, there is a real possibility for conflict, such that it would make it impossible for two divine individuals to exist.

Swinburne's solution is to introduce a "mechanism to prevent interference" that "could not limit their power in the compatibilist sense, only in the absolute sense (by making it no longer good to do acts of a certain sort)" (172). This limitation would mean making it a bad thing for one "to act in an area where the other was operative" (172). Such a distribution of jurisdiction cannot occur spontaneously among the divine individuals, for "there is nothing to guarantee that at the moment at which he draws up a proposal for distributing power, the other divine individual might not draw up a different proposal" (172).

The only solution is to have one divine individual who has the authority to lay down the rules, over against the other divine individuals. Such a difference in authority, Swinburne argues, can only rest in the fact that one of the divine individuals is the source of being for the other divine individuals. Here Swinburne properly admits that arguments for God's existence are only consistent with the derivation of created order from a single source of being. There is thus only one ultimate divine individual. This individual necessarily causes another such divine individual to exist, and then a third divine individual is "actively co-caused by the first and second individuals" (177).

A "viable way of securing the unity of action in shared power among divine individuals" (174) is to have different functions assigned to them. The distribution of functions would be inscribed in the very act of the causation of the divine persons: "The first individual solemnly vows to the second individual in causing his existence that he will not initiate any act (of will) in a certain sphere of activity that he allocates to him, while at the same time the first individual requests the second individual not to initiate any such act outside that sphere" (174). A similar reciprocal limitation would occur in the case of the cocausation of the third individual (176).

How does Swinburne respond to the tritheism worry? He suggests that, in rejecting tritheism, the tradition was only denying that there are "three independent divine beings, any of which could exist without the other; or which could act independently of each other" (180). We shall not challenge, for the moment, the historical claim made here—although our analysis of ancient Jewish monotheism led us to the opposite conclusion—but will instead focus on Swinburne's understanding of inseparable operation.

The "three divine individuals taken together would form a collective source of the being of all other things; the members would be totally mutually dependent and necessarily jointly behind each other's acts" (180). This collective, he further explains, would be indivisible in its being and also "indivisible in its causal action in the sense that each would back totally the causal action of the others" (181). Thus, Swinburne desires to tighten up the unity of the collective both in terms of codependence of being and in terms of indivisible operation, understood as "backing."

Another important objection arises at precisely this point, since the tradition insists that each of the divine persons, taken singly, is fully God. But our writer appears to argue that only taken together are the individuals God. He retorts that what the creeds intend by the statement that each person is "God" is to be broadly understood in the sense that each person is divine (182), that "they are each of the same essential kind, namely divine" (184).

The cocausation provides sufficient warrant, to Swinburne, for speaking of one God acting externally in the world. "In acting towards the outside world (i.e. in creating or sustaining other substances), although (unless there is a unique best action) one individual initiates any action, the initiating act (whether of active or permissive causation) is backed by the co-causation of the others—hence the slogan *omnia opera Trinitatis ad extra indivisa sunt*" (184).

To rehearse, each divine individual is "God" in the sense of sharing the essential properties of God, minus the relational properties pertaining to their causation, in virtue of which the persons are also individuated. A compact between the individuals is inscribed in the very act of causation, the begetting of the Son and the spiration of the Spirit, such that they undertake to abide by their own jurisdictions (when they do not act together in unique best actions). When a divine individual does act in his jurisdiction, the other two are necessarily backing his action by cocausation. The "backing" is thus not a merely passive standing by the sidelines of the other two persons, but an actual cocausation, which preserves the perichoretic presence of each divine person in every divine act. Tritheism is averted because, arguably, the three divine individuals have relationships of dependence upon each other and ultimately upon the Father, who alone is not dependent on another individual. At the same time, Arianism is forestalled by the fact that the begetting of the Son, although an act of the Father involving his will and reason, is necessary.

Swinburne has elucidated the conditions under which three divine individuals can still count as one God. His "functional monotheism," as Brian Leftow has called it,[52] attempts to secure monotheist unity in coordinating the actions of discrete individuals in such a way that they never become competitive with each other. Yet this comes at the cost of neatly apportioning to the divine individuals their own spheres of operation. It also appears to return to a suborthodox doctrine of the subordination of the Son and the Spirit to the Father. These objections will occupy us in the following paragraphs.

On the first issue, what we may call the distribution of labor of the divine persons, one may legitimately ask what constitutes the boundaries of their spheres of operation. Say the Father reserves for himself the act of creation; to the Son is delegated the act of redemption; to the Spirit the acts pertaining to sanctification. But what does one do about overlapping areas? For example, the Scripture often speaks about redemption in terms precisely of new creation (2 Cor 5:17). The incarnation also clearly entails a creative act—the formation of the human nature of the Son. The resurrection too, appears to involve the giving of life. The Scriptures, moreover, seem to involve the Spirit distinctly in the act of creation (Gen 1:2; 2:7), in the very giving of life to the material body of the first humans. Naturally, Swinburne does not have to say precisely which spheres belong to which persons, but the thought that reality can be neatly divided up into spheres, without the possibility of overlap, seems problematic. It is possible that the distribution is made according to some ineffable divine calculus. It is hard, under any scenario, to avoid the impression of a reality that is divided precisely at its most fundamental level. Many modern theologians,

---

52. Brian Leftow, "Anti Social Trinitarianism," in *The Trinity: An Interdisciplinary Symposium on the Trinity*, ed. Stephen T. Davis, Daniel Kendall, SJ, Gerald O'Collins, SJ (Oxford: Oxford University Press, 2002).

including some with an affinity for ST, would reasonably worry that the underlying unity of creation is thus undermined. Theologians have traditionally moored the unity of creation in the unity of the single divine being. By Swinburne's own admission, it is incumbent upon the theologian to speak about a single ultimate cause for the existence of the world. But this proposal, while perhaps theoretically allowing for such a single ultimate cause, introduces into the picture a buffer between this ultimate cause and that divine person who ultimately accounts for certain regions of the world.

The latter worry is supposed to be quelled by the claim that even in those actions that properly belong to the jurisdiction of just one person, the other two persons covenant to back this first person in the cocausation of this act. The difficulty with this account, however, is that such a cocausation cannot be understood to assign certain effects to certain persons, and hence we face the daunting problem of overdetermination. Which is to say that even though we have three causes for a divine action, each cause fully accounts for the effect, such that if one or two of the causes would be removed, the act would be just the same. But in this case we have not explained the act at all by pointing to the three causes. The worry still remains that two of the cocauses are really just idle.

The more portentous objection to this distribution of labor is that it returns us to the Gnostic separation between the Creator God and the Redeemer. Brian Leftow, arguing for the similarity of this view to the Olympian model of the gods, rightly points out that "if the persons are discrete, and only the Son died for our sins, then however much the Father and Spirit helped out, it seems that the Son did more for us than the other two, who neither bled nor suffered."[53]

If the biblical theology we set out in the first chapter hits anywhere near the mark, and if the fathers of the first four centuries were right in their Trinitarian instincts, the very reason we can confess the divine identity of Jesus Christ is that his actions are interchangeably the actions of the Father and the actions of the Spirit! Dispersing the economic activity of God among the persons removes all the grounds for their distinct divinity. The reason Jesus Christ is understood to be God is not merely because he does divine things, although that too is true. Rather, and most fundamentally, it was, as we have shown, because he accomplishes the singular acts of the unique God of Israel.

There is an additional problem. Swinburne hopes that a distribution of labor can help avert a conflict between the divine persons, such that would

53. Leftow, "Anti Social Trinitarianism," 237.

destroy their omnipotence. But should monotheism be a question of mere agreement in practice? As Leftow puts it:

> Even perfect cooperation is cooperation. This introduces a kind of conflict within each individual divine Person, though not between them. . . . For each obtains the good of the others' society at the cost of having henceforth so to act as to avoid conflict with what the others do: the good of sharing in love has a price in terms of the good of freedom of action.[54]

The point is, an agreement in practice may gloss over a certain self-limitation of each person, and thus gloss over a failure of each to fully actualize his potential as a divine person. The surface agreement, in other words, masks a certain repression of individual potential.

This introduces the second line of objections, pertaining to the immanent subordination of the divine persons. A possible response to our argument is that a certain self-limitation is not necessarily problematic, in particular that the divine attributes already limit each other, as we have seen with the dialectic of power and goodness. It could also be stressed that the very causation of the divine persons of the Son and the Spirit puts a limit on their activity. The language of repression is thus out of place since a divine person is fully at peace with the divine compact and will not feel the tension. The Son always lovingly carries out the will of the Father.

This rejoinder does indeed prove persuasive, but only on pain of a hazardous assumption, which is that of an ontological subordination of the Son and Spirit to the Father. It is true that a subaltern, who knows his place within a given society, need not feel repressed by having an unactualized potential. But certainly the divine persons of the Son and the Spirit are not subalterns to the Father (and the Spirit also to the Son). It is true that the Son is begotten by the Father and that the Spirit is spirated by the Father and the Son. But Swinburne ties to these relational properties additional relational properties that in fact only make sense on the background of yet other exclusive monadic properties. To clarify, from the causal properties it follows that the Father has an authority superior to that of the Son. Having superior authority is a relational property, but it can only be predicated if each of the persons have the monadic property of "having a certain authority."

A very "serious inequality among the three"[55] is introduced by the ground-

---

54. Leftow, "Anti Social Trinitarianism," 229–30.
55. Leftow, "Anti Social Trinitarianism," 236.

ing of the schema of authority and submission in the very processions of the persons. The advantage of this move, and its rationale, is to give warrant for a pattern of authority that is not decided *ad hoc*, voted on, or left to the whim of the persons. But the peril is certainly too great, for in this case the persons differ not only in relational properties but also in their absolute properties as well. It is hard to avoid the conclusion that the power of the Son is less than the power of the Father. Leftow's conclusion is particularly well put: "It is hard to see how ST which includes divine 'begetting' can avoid the claim that the Father creates the Son *ex nihilo*. For in ST, the Son comes to exist as one more instance of a nature which pre-exists Him. (The Father bears it logically or causally if not temporally before the Son does.) We do not hesitate to call anything else of which this is true a creature; Thomists would say that any such item has an essence 'really composed' with its existence, and that this is the mark of createdness. If the Father creates the Son, Arius was right in at least one particular: the Son is a creature (though one nearer the Father in status than any other)."[56]

The fact that we have found Swinburne's functional monotheism wanting does not indicate that the best intuitions of social Trinitarians are mistaken. ST is an increasingly complex school of Trinitarian theology, showing little sign of abating. It takes its cue from important scriptural observations as well as from deeply felt intuitions about personhood. Not all social models advance models of divine action that distribute divine labor à la Swinburne. But it is difficult to see anything in between the Scylla of distribution and the Charybdis of overdetermination.

Our proposal hesitates to say just what the Father, Son, and Holy Spirit are, whether persons, divine individuals, or modes of being. They should rightly remain inscrutable. At best, we can hope to clarify the rules of Trinitarian speech about these three, including speech about their work toward us. And in this we have to remain faithful to the claim of Scripture that "there are diversities of activities, but it is the same God who works all in all" (1 Cor 12:6, KJV).

Conclusion

The development of Trinitarian theology, as we saw in the previous chapter, was premised on the scriptural observation that the action tokens of Christ and the Spirit are precisely the Father's action tokens. The doctrine of inseparable operations is part of the biblical datum, the *explanandum* for which the

56. Leftow, "Anti Social Trinitarianism," 242.

developed doctrine of the Trinity serves as an *explanans*. The doctrine of the Trinity and that of the inseparable operations mutually reinforce each other. Like a double helix, they revolve around each other in a reciprocal fortification. From the observation of inseparability we ascend in our knowledge to the processions; there we grasp that the inseparability of their economic operations is not an accident, but a necessary outcome of what the persons are.

The current chapter set out to lay bare the theo-logic of inseparable operations, precisely the logic that controlled the historical development of the two doctrines. We saw that there are essential reasons that require the development of this rule, reasons that have to do with the relationship between persons and nature in the doctrine of the Trinity. Paying attention to what we have called the ontology of triune causality must come before any discussion of the epistemology of divine action. The following represents a summary of our findings.

First, the ontological distinction between creator and creation has certain implications for our understanding of divine action in the world. Theology must always remain mindful of the finite character of its reflection and its observations, whether scriptural or empirical. Any reflection on divine action in the world must not confuse God with an item in the world. Neither must divine causality be confused with a finite, univocal causality. If God does act in the world, as the Christian faith confesses, theology must resist mythologizing divine action. Thus, we have argued that economic actions must not be taken at their face value. We may illustrate this with the idea of a sphere that goes through two-dimensional space—let's call it Flatland, after Edwin A. Abbott's 1884 novella—and changes positions in relation to it. For an observer in Flatland, it will appear as if a circle moves positions, decreases or increases its circumference, shrinks down to being almost a point. The knowledge that what he is experiencing is ultimately a relation with another three-dimensional object will alert him not to take at face value his experience. Something equivalent applies in the theological case. Since God is transcendent, God's movements, his actions in this world, although truly God's, must be approached with great theological responsibility. This is not to deny that these actions manifest God—they truly do! Rather, it is to be mindful of the manner in which they can manifest a transcendent being, a manner necessarily conditioned by the medium in which the unfolding takes place.

We then asked about the nature of this transcendent being, in this case about the relationship between nature and persons. We observed that the tradition carefully affirms the equiprimordiality of persons and nature. A divine person is not one thing and the divine substance another. Rather each divine person is identical with the substance, but under a particular and irreducible relational aspect. It was also established that on the whole this relationship between persons and nature characterizes both historical approaches, Eastern and Western. It is a caricature to affirm that the Cappadocians "start" with the persons while Augustine and the West "start" with the substance. Such simplifications may have an appropriate didactic value, but they also easily lead to distortions.

The notion that a divine person is nothing but the divine essence under a particular relational aspect leads us to the logic of *ad extra* inseparability. If a person is nothing but a relation within the unity of the divine essence, it is inconceivable for two reasons that one such person might have a separate action in the economy. Either this person has this operation under its aspect of essence, or under its aspect of relation. The first option entails that it would have a different substance, not shared with the other persons. The second option would entail that created realities would enter into its constitution, given that a person is a subsistent relation! For this reason also classical Trinitarianism argues that separable operations *ad extra* compromise the Creator-creature distinction. The conclusion is that whatever action the persons have in the created world is in virtue of their essence.

This is not the whole story, however. It was suggested that even though the efficient causality of the persons *ad extra* is one, the persons nonetheless have a causality. As such, we have insisted that the triune causality is not a monadic, simplex causality, but rather a differentiated one. On this score, the tradition of inseparable operations, especially in its Thomistic elaboration, clarifies that the creative and economic work of the Trinity is grounded in the processions. It was shown that this causality pertains to the different "modes of action" of the persons. Just as the persons are different modes of existence of the divine substance, so they have different modes within the selfsame operation of God.

It is this differentiated operative modality that enables us to find the persons despite the fact that they act inseparably. In the process, a particular way of conceiving personal action needed to be uprooted. Against modern personalism, which anchors will in the person, we have sided with dyothelite orthodoxy by grounding will in nature. The modern quest for personal identity by detaching will from nature was shown to be a dead end. True personal identity is to be found in the enactment of one's nature. The triune persons too act on the basis of a common will and power of nature, and yet they enact this will in three irreducible modalities. It thus appears that we will be getting closer to their proper identities not by drifting away from the natural will and power of the Trinity. The identity of the persons is not revealed by separable acts and wills but precisely in the unity of the divine will and action, since the persons are nothing but this will and power under a particular relational inflection.

The doctrine of appropriation has its justification at this point: To know the persons, we pull the common toward what is proper, yet without leaving sight of the unity. Since the persons do not act separably, we cannot individuate the persons on the basis of exclusive actions. But, importantly, this does not mean there is no knowledge of the persons precisely in their *propria*. Once it is understood that this *propria* is not to be sought away from substance but precisely as a modality within the substance, it will be recognized that the way of appropriation is not a mere consolation prize, something that we need to put up with, hoping for our eyes to be finally opened. In a sense that is true, of course, but there is a real contemplation of the divine persons precisely by learning to discern within the unity of their operation (the only place any person may be found!) the modal trace of each person.

One final pit stop for this chapter was an obligatory discussion of social Trinitarian accounts of the unity of divine action. Taking Swinburne as an exemplar, we found his solution to the issue of divine unity to lead into the troubled waters of ontological subordinationism and into problems of overdetermination.

CHAPTER 4

Creation and Trinitarian Mediation

Scripture presents creation as the work of the Trinitarian God. While some "differentiation" between the work of the Word and Spirit is prefigured in the Old Testament,[1] the New Testament explicitly presents Christ as the "through whom" and "by whom" of creation. Paul speaks of creation being "from him (*ex autou*) and through him (*di' autou*) and to him (*eis auton*)" (Rom 11:36). The author of Hebrews also attributes creation to Christ: "You, Lord, laid the foundation of the earth in the beginning, and the heavens are the work of your hands" (Heb 1:10).[2]

We propose to address the following questions: How is creation an action of the whole Trinity? How should the Christological mediation of creation be interpreted? It will be argued that the centrality of the doctrine of inseparable operations for the patristic and medieval tradition does not need to lead to an obscuring of the triune persons in creation. However, such a diversity does not involve separate agencies, and that is most discernible in how the triune persons are *exemplars* of both creation as well as redemption.

TRINITARIAN ACCOUNTS OF CREATION IN THE TRADITION

Creation consists in the absolute positing of the world as a reality existing externally to God, yet in utter dependence on him. As external to God, the act of creation does not change God's essence. The immanent divine relations remain self-sufficiently what they are, even as another relational partner to

---

1. See the account of creation in Genesis 1:1–2; God is understood to create by the Word (Ps 33:9; 148:5), by Wisdom (Prov 8:22), and by the Spirit (Ps 104:30; Job 26:13), but also see the association between Spirit (*ruach*, breath) and life (Gen 2:7; Ps 33:6; Ezek 37:5).

2. See the possible allusions to Ps 102:25; Zech 12:1.

God is brought into existence. Yet the Creator God does not remain aloof from his new partner, creation, but invests himself in it most intimately in terms of knowledge, presence, and sustenance. In these relations, however, God must remain himself as the Wholly Other from creation. God knows creation perfectly; he is present to it more closely than it is present to itself; he carries it to its ordered end in a most fitting way. In none of these relations does he stop being who he was from eternity past. It is axiomatic for classical Trinitarian theology that God's relations to the world, including the very act of creation itself, do not encroach upon the divine transcendence.

In articulating a Trinitarian theology of creation one must not lose sight of this axiom. Failure to do so can lead to disastrous consequences. A failure to properly understand that God's relations to the world are external to the divine essence can lead to making God ultimately dependent upon the world. A nonobservance of the transcendence of God can lead to mythologically reckoning him as another cause in the world, on the same level with other created causes.

Now the doctrine of the Trinity has been understood as a mystery of salvation. This much is appropriate. But the question is: In what way should the doctrine of the Trinity characterize the whole of the divine economy, including the doctrine of creation? Under the influence of the modern Trinitarian renaissance, much pressure has been exerted to characterize every divine act as a Trinitarian act, to the point that the doctrine of the Trinity, and especially Christology and pneumatology, are now often seen as theologies of *mediation*. This takes place in self-conscious abandonment of the older Trinitarian consensus that stresses the inseparable action of the triune persons in the economy. In place of the older consensus, the work of the Son and the Spirit is now understood to *mediate* the work of the Father, the stress being no longer on the unity of the economic work but on the differentiation between the *kinds* of work of the Son and the Spirit. It is hoped that such a renewed stress on the personal differentiation of the divine action may salvage the relationality of God to the world. The classical account, it is felt, ultimately makes it impossible to affirm a genuine divine relationality to the world. God's relations to the world, as Aquinas has put it, are real in the creature but only logical in God. Appreciating the unique and proper role of each divine person in God's acts toward the world more faithfully accounts for the reality of these relations. If God for us is not fundamentally different than God in Himself—that is to say, if the God who is Father, Son, and Holy Spirit in himself also acts toward us in this distinct three-personal way—then God truly self-communicates himself in his revelation, and the economic Trinity truly reveals and is the immanent Trinity.

In the doctrine of creation, the pressure is to give a rendition of the creative act of God that foregrounds its Trinitarian nature. Creation has to be understood, so the request goes, as *mediated* through the distinct works of the Son and the Spirit. As such, the creative contributions of Son and Spirit are not mere appropriations but genuine exercises of their distinct agencies. If creation is something that the Father does through the mediating agencies of Son and Spirit, the foundation is laid for thinking of all God's relations to the world as being thus differentiated. God no longer will be thought as relating to us as a monad, his Trinitarian personhood remaining a mere matter of speculation and appropriation. Rather, the Trinitarian differentiations are concretely characteristic of God's economic acts. In this way, it is thought, the Trinity truly can be affirmed as a mystery of salvation.

Even so, classical Trinitarianism's disinclination to give a Trinitarian account of creation in the terms desired by modern theologians is not a mere omission. Quite to the contrary, it is a studied choice explained by a desire to observe the distinction between Creator and creation. The aim of this brief section is to further explain the logic of the claim that ascribing exclusive causalities to the divine persons in the act of creation undermines the Creator-creature distinction. Secondly, we will make some comments on how classical Trinitarians understood the act of creation as being mediated through the divine ideas as opposed to the desired mediation through the works of the Son and the Spirit. Having laid down the logic of the classical position on the doctrine of creation, we will then turn to two modern theologians who are representative of the pressure to ascribe distinct causalities to the divine persons in the act of creation.

Exclusive Personal Causality and the Creator-Creature Distinction

Why should a distinct causality of the persons undermine the Creator-creature distinction? The answer lies in the discussion in our preceding chapter. We already noted that a divine person is, in Owen's words, "nothing but the divine essence, upon the account of an especial property, subsisting in an especial manner."[3] That is to say that persons do not partition the divine essence, but are identical with it, under the aspect of a particular relational property. The personal properties of the divine persons are given by their relations of origin. These relations are understood to subsist in the divine essence. The relation-

---

3. Owen, *Communion with God*, 407.

ships themselves are constitutive of the divine essence, just as much as they themselves are constituted by it. The personal "notions" of paternity, filiation, and spiration are the only way to identify the divine persons.

The persons are modes of the divine substance, but not accidental modes. They are not secondary to the divine being. Now the divine operation *ad extra* places God in a relationship to other realities. But because the triune persons are nothing but relations, conceiving an exclusive relation between a divine person and a created thing will necessarily mean that this latter relation enters into the constitution of the divine person, and therefore necessarily it enters into the constitution of the divine essence itself. It cannot be said that the relation to creature remains accidental to the divine person, since there is no substrate to the divine person other than the relation (the divine person is a relation that subsists).

This understanding of the persons and their relationship to the divine essence lies at the foundation of the distinction between the *opera ad intra* and the *opera ad extra*. As John Webster explains,

> (a) God's ad intra works are intrinsic, their term remaining within the subject of the action. . . . (b) God's ad intra works are constitutive, not accidental, activities. They are not 'voluntary' in the sense of enacting a decision behind which there lies an agent who might have willed to act otherwise: there is no Father 'behind' the generation of the Son. . . . (c) God's ad intra activities are unceasing, not temporal or transient. . . . (d) God's ad intra activities require us to speak of distinctions between the persons of the Godhead.[4]

By contrast, God's *opera exeuntia*, or His external works, proceed from his essence. Their term remains outside of God's essence; they are accidental and not constitutive of the divine substance; they are temporal and transient; and they do not require us to speak of distinctions between the persons of the Godhead. The latter point does not mean, as we have seen, that certain divine acts *ad extra* do not *illuminate* the personal properties of a divine person. It only stipulates that the explanation of any particular divine act will not identify any causality other than the one causality of the divine essence.

4. John Webster, "Trinity and Creation," in *God and the Works of God*, vol. 1 of *God Without Measure* (Edinburgh: T&T Clark, 2018), 89–90.

Divine Causality and Divine Ideas

God creates and acts according to his essence, as we have seen. That is to say, he acts in and through his knowledge, wisdom, and love. What he causes remains external to his being. He does not enter into composition with his creatures. As products of his knowledge and will, creatures are not necessary emanations from God, but they are freely desired. Though they are many, they come forth from the One, not as though they had fallen from an original unity but as freely desired and good, very good! Their diversity is willed precisely as diversity; their materiality is also a willed materiality. The dignity of creation consists partly in its being created alongside of God, in its being allotted its proper time and space, which represents the mode in which creation has its own being. As such it never competes with God for his space and his time.

Contrary to emanationist schemes, the diversity of creation is never second-rate. Contrary to Platonist schemes, the ideas according to which God creates are not external to himself, but properly and freely his. To say that God creates according to his own ideas is only to say that God creates in a free and rational way. He creates as the free being that he is; he creates as ultimate Intelligence.

Christianity has adopted the construct of the divine ideas but has modified it in significant ways. This conceptuality serves to anchor creation both in its unity and diversity in God. The divine ideas, then, can be said to mediate between the Creator and his act of creation. But this can only be said in a guarded way. Per divine simplicity, the divine ideas are not discrete mental parts of God. There is a single divine act, which is God himself, according to some in this classical tradition. God is pure act. God is as God does. Yet God's act is single and eternal.

Aquinas would famously explain that God knows himself and everything else in the same act of knowledge. He also wills himself and everything else in the same act of will. Yet his self-knowledge is necessary, unlike the knowledge of his creatures, which is contingent. The imagery of a person seeing himself in the mirror gives us an apt illustration. One sees oneself necessarily in the mirror, but at the same time one sees that which is behind oneself in the mirror only contingently. One necessarily sees oneself if one looks in the mirror, but depending on the orientation of the person different backgrounds can appear. Similarly, God eternally knows himself and everything else in the same act.[5]

---

5. For more on this, see Thomas Aquinas, *Summa contra Gentiles*, trans. Anton C. Pegis (Notre Dame, IN: University of Notre Dame Press, 2016), 1.55.

As Thomas explains, "the conception of the divine intellect as understanding itself, which is its Word, is the likeness not only of God Himself understood, but also of all those things of which the divine essence is the likeness."[6]

Aquinas thus argues that in knowing himself, God also knows the manifold ways in which his goodness can be participated in. In the same act he freely decides which of those ways are going to become actual. Those manifold ways in which God understands his goodness to be participable can be called the divine ideas.[7]

The framework of the divine ideas expresses the manner of the divine immanence in the world. God is intimately present to his creation as one who knows it and sustains it. God knows creation more intimately than it can ever know itself because he understands and wills the manner in which creation can be most truly itself, precisely in relation to himself.

In this manner, God's intimacy to creation is appropriate to the Creator-creature distinction. God is to creatures as an *exemplar* cause. His causality with respect to the creature always remains an extrinsic causality. If one were to choose Aristotle's four causes, only the two extrinsic causes may represent this causal relation: the efficient and the final. Conversely, God may never be the formal cause of a thing, or its material cause.

A formal cause is that which makes a particular thing to be the thing that it is. For example, the formal cause of a statue is the substantial form of statue. Since a formal cause enters into composition with the matter that it informs, the formal cause itself is defined and limited in its being by the potentiality of matter. As such, a formal cause always depends on the passive potency of the matter it informs. As Aquinas explains in *Summa contra Gentiles* I.27.4, "the union of form and matter results in a composite, which is a whole with respect to the matter and the form. But the parts are in potency in relation to the whole." For this reason, God cannot be understood to become the formal cause of any created thing. No created thing can be made to be in act by God as formal cause. Were that the case, created things would have the form of God; they would be God. Absurdly, God would be limited by that which he informs.

It is beyond dispute that God cannot be the material cause of anything. Since God is Spirit, and in God there is no potentiality, matter—as sheer potentiality—has no place in God. It stands to reason, then, that the only way in

---

6. Aquinas, *ScG* 1.53.5.
7. Aquinas, *ScG* 1.54.4.

which God acts in the world is as an efficient or final cause. Let us take each of them in turn.

As efficient cause, God is the being responsible for the bringing into existence of the creature. An efficient cause is that responsible for the very *existence* of something. A sculptor is the efficient cause of his sculpture. He is neither its material cause nor its formal cause, while the latter accrues to the statue through his efficient causality. *Efficient* causes are those causes in virtue of which something exists. *Formal* causes are those in virtue of which something is the thing that it is. *Final* causes, on the other hand, are those things for the purpose of which something exists. The final cause of a sculpture is the reason and motivation in the mind of the author for the existence of the statue.

In restricting divine causality to the efficient/final causation, Aquinas plays a familiar tune on the instrument of Aristotelian philosophy. The familiar tune extols the supremacy and aseity of the Creator in relation to his creature. The Aristotelian framework of causality is simply the instrument with which the tune is played.

The divine ideas are the *ratio* of the creatures. That is to say, the divine ideas are the exemplar causes of the creatures. The idea of exemplar causes lies somewhere in between the formal and final causes. An exemplar cause is similar to a formal cause in the sense that it sketches the idea of what a thing will become. But it is never quite the formal cause, since what makes the thing to be itself must be intrinsic to the thing itself. As Aquinas puts it, "by ideas are understood the forms of things, existing apart from the things themselves."[8]

Thomas continues to distinguish between different kinds of external forms: "Now the form of anything existing apart from the thing itself can be of one of two ends; either to be the type of that of which it is called the form, or to be the principle of knowledge of that thing, inasmuch as the forms of things knowable are said to be in him who knows them."[9] In both of these cases one must suppose ideas, Aquinas insists.

Now there are two types of nonaccidental generation. Since in such cases the agent must act according to a form whose likeness resides in himself, this can happen in two ways. First, by natural generation, as when a person begets another person, or fire generates fire. In this case, "the form of the thing to be made pre-exists according to its natural being."[10] Second, by intelligible

---

8. Thomas Aquinas, *Summa Theologica*, trans. the Fathers of the English Dominican Province (Westminster, MD: Christian Classics, 1981), 1, q. 15, a. 1.

9. Aquinas, *ST* 1, q. 15, a. 1, cf. a. 3.

10. Aquinas, *ST* 1, q. 15, a. 1, cf. a. 3.

generation, in which case the form of the thing to be generated also pre-exists "according to intelligible being." Aquinas gives the example of the likeness of a house that pre-exists in the mind of the builder. He then explains that "this may be called the idea of the house, since the builder intends to build this house like to the form conceived in his mind. And then the world was not made by chance, but by God acting by His intellect . . . there must exist in the divine mind a form to the likeness of which the world was made. And in this the notion of an idea consists."[11] By this distinction Aquinas clarifies that creation is not by way of generation, in which case the form of the thing generated would exist by itself and not according to intellectual being, in God.

Conversely, exemplar causes are types of final causes since they indicate the end of the act itself. Since there may be multiple purposes for which something is made, there may be multiple final causes. A builder wishes to build a house in order to build a town or a residential community. The purpose for his activity of moving bricks and mortar is to build a house. So the idea of a house is the *ratio* that explains his activity.

God, however, cannot be thought to act for an end that is external to himself. External ends perfect the agent, "but it does not belong to the First agent, Who is agent only, to act for the acquisition of some end; He intends only to communicate His perfection, which is His goodness; while every creature intends to acquire its own perfection, which is the likeness of the divine perfection and goodness. Therefore the divine goodness is the end of all things."[12]

Final causes thus indicate the orientation of a substance toward its natural ends. They are not at work only in rational agents but in the natural world as well, as Aristotle explains: "For those things are natural which, by a continuous movement originated from an internal principle, arrive at some completion: the same completion is not reached from every principle; nor any chance completion, but always the tendency in each is toward some end, if there is no impediment."[13]

Michael Dodds insists on the strong connection between the idea of nature and final causes. Without the latter idea, the former disappears as well. Final causes work differently in rational and nonrational creatures, to be sure. Rational creatures move toward their ends through the intellect and will as creatures who have knowledge of their ends. But even in rational agents, delib-

11. Aquinas, *ST* 1, q. 15, a. 1.

12. Aquinas, *ST* 1, q. 44, a. 4.

13. Aristotle, *Physics* 2.8 [199b16–18], quoted in Michael J. Dodds, *Unlocking Divine Action: Contemporary Science and Thomas Aquinas* (Washington, DC: Catholic University of America Press, 2012), 31.

erative means are not always employed to reach certain ends. "We may think of a skilled pianist who does not constantly pause to deliberate what key to strike next. Nature, in an analogous way, may be understood to have a kind of built-in art and so does not need to deliberate when acting for an end."[14]

In desiring an end, creatures ultimately desire God: "All things desire God as their end, when they desire some good thing, whether this desire be intellectual or sensible, or natural, i.e., without knowledge; because nothing is good and desirable except forasmuch as it participates in the likeness of God."[15]

The motion of the creature to its final end in God, however, does not hint at a vying for a primordial unity from which it has fallen. Christian teleology must be purged of its Origenistic connotations. Movement is thus not a promethean wrangling with one's natural condition in an effort to transcend it *en route* to the henad. Quite the contrary, the natural motion of the creature is a gift given by God, who thus summons it back to himself. As Hans Urs von Balthasar puts it in connection to Maximus, "movement . . . consists in allowing oneself to be carried by another in the depths of one's being and to be borne toward the ocean of God's rest."[16]

Like Thomas, Maximus connects teleology to the divine ideas. The ideas are the exemplars in God of created essences, calling the latter to themselves. Such a return is actualized through free will, which, however, doesn't act against nature but in response to it. Given the ontological distance between the finitude of the creature and the transcendence of the ideas, the return cannot be completed apart from the free initiative of God. The process is thus only finalized in the Logos, where, as von Balthasar explains, "all the individual ideas and goals of creatures meet; therefore all of them, if they seek their own reality, must love him and must encounter each other in his love. That is why Christ is the original idea, the underlying figure in God's plan for the world, why all the individual lines arrange themselves concentrically around him."[17]

Divine Ideas: Promise or Peril?

This idea of an exemplar cause is essential for properly understanding divine action. It will form the crux of the modern debates about the Trinitarian mediation of creation. God, as Aquinas holds, "is the efficient, the exemplar, and the

14. Dodds, *Unlocking*, 32.

15. Aquinas, *ST* 1, q. 44, a. 4, ad. 3.

16. Hans Urs von Balthasar, *Cosmic Liturgy: The Universe According to Maximus the Confessor* (San Francisco: Ignatius, 2003), 130.

17. Von Balthasar, *Cosmic Liturgy*, 133.

final cause of all things."[18] As such, the divine causality is mediated through his essence. The divine ideas are located in the divine essence, whereby God knows himself and wills himself in a simple and pure act. By locating the divine ideas in the simple essence of God, classical theology does not envisage a fall from this unity but God's freely making proper room for creation.

Creation is thus God's act of his essence and its attributes: knowledge and will. It is not an act mediated through the triune persons in the sense of any exercise of a distinctive and proper causality of the persons, lest the ontological distinction between creature and Creator be blurred. God's relation to his creatures, including their very production, must preserve his aseity, immutability and simplicity. God stands in efficient, exemplar, and final relations of causality with the creature. He is never the formal cause of a creature, or its material cause. He remains extrinsic to the creature despite his intimacy to it. He relates to it through his essential attributes. While he draws the creature to himself, he does it as Other than itself. As he knows the creature better than it knows itself, he knows it precisely as its exemplar and not its form. As he moves and sustains the creature he remains immutable in himself.

The modern complaint is that this account of mediation—through the divine ideas—is fundamentally an *essentialist* and *impersonal* account. God is understood to relate to creation through his essence—and not through the persons. As such, God's relations to creation are understood primarily in terms of causality. Modern theology fears that the divine presence, immanence, and action in creation is entirely extrinsic and therefore impersonal. God acts in the sense of producing created effects, which are anchored in his ideas. But beyond this anchoring of created things in divine ideas, in the essentiality rather than the personality of God, there doesn't seem to be a personal presence of God in creation. His presence, rather, is understood in terms of power (omnipresence) and knowledge (omniscience).

Equally, such an account is thought to jeopardize the New Testament description of the Christological nature of the creative act. In it, Christ—the human Christ—can only be a created effect, and therefore something extrinsic to God himself and to the divine ideas—which are merely reproduced in him yet without becoming his form (no formal causality in the incarnation either!).

This is the modern temptation, then: to say that the act of creation is itself constituted by something created, that is, the human being, Jesus Christ. In this way, God is not merely extrinsic to creation, as eternally thinking our blueprint, but creation itself in some way is folded into the very being of God. The

---

18. Aquinas, *ST* 1, q. 44, a. 4, ad. 4.

push for a Trinitarian mediation of creation hazards the very Creator-creature distinction. To insist that God creates specifically through Jesus Christ—in his human nature—is to insist that creation is not absolutely posited by a self-sufficient God, but that God's own being, including the Father's fatherhood, as Pannenberg will argue, somehow depends on his economic activity.

Two Recent Critiques

Much modern theology has been issuing calls for an understanding of creation as Christologically mediated. We will focus on Wolfhart Pannenberg and Colin Gunton, both of whom suspect that the received Patristic and scholastic doctrine of creation is largely nontrinitarian and non-Christological. They both raise a series of substantive concerns about how this older tradition perceives the divine creative activity. The aim of this section is to take stock of their objections.

Pannenberg's mature thought on the doctrine of creation is expressed in the second volume of his *Systematic Theology*. He expresses misgivings about the dominant patristic and medieval account of mediation, which he regards as unduly influenced by Platonism. He notes the domination of the principle of inseparable operations as late as David Hollaz, whom he quotes: "As the divine essence is one and indivisible, so the act of creation is one and indivisible."[19] This has disastrous consequences for Pannenberg: "The ancient confession of the mediatorship of Christ in creation, while not denied, is stripped of all function" (26). He concludes that the older doctrine of inseparable operations hinders a proper appreciation of specific role of the incarnate Son in the act of creation. Given that God always acts as a single agent, the mediatorship of the Son can only be relegated to his role as the Logos, who contains in his simplicity the manifold divine ideas for creation.

However, in such an account, even the divine ideas must be anchored in the "essentiality of God" as opposed to his personal distinctions (26). Creation is thus anchored in the simplicity of a single being, with all the stress falling on the unity of the divine essence. God creates on the basis of these ideas, which exist within the unity of the divine essence. Pannenberg does acknowledge that Aquinas, for instance, "did, of course, relate the creative action of God to the person of the Son" (26). But it doesn't make enough of a difference and the participation of the Son in the act is not clearly specified. "The basic idea is that

19. Wolfhart Pannenberg, *Systematic Theology*, trans. George W. Bromiley (Grand Rapids: Eerdmans, 1991), 2.26. Hereafter references to this volume will be in the text.

creation as an outward act is to be ascribed to the Trinitarian God as subject, so that we need not differentiate the specific contributions of the individual divine persons" (26).

Pannenberg objects that this Augustinian and Thomistic account is much too anthropomorphic in distinguishing between understanding and will in God: God first understands and knows his own ideas about creation, much like an artist first considers what he wishes to produce. Then God wills to enact these or some of these ideas. This deliberative view of divine agency undergirds a causative account whereby creation is produced as a complete essence by the divine being in the past.

Such an account, he fears, threatens the scriptural notions of the contingency as well as the historicity of creation. In short, given divine simplicity, the divine ideas are identical to the divine essence, with the implication that the nature of creation flows *necessarily* out of the being of God. Secondly, the full historicity of creation is hard to appreciate in an account where it seems to be but the unfolding in time of an eternal divine decree.

In contrast to this, he notes, the modern approach consists in replacing the concept of the intelligible cosmos, organized by the divine ideas, with a principle that generates the plurality and distinctions of creaturely things. The reason for the reality of creation, and for the distinction among creatures, resides not in abstract ideas in the divine essence but in the personal reality of the Son, who exists in unity and distinction with the Father and the Spirit. The particularity of creatures is thus anchored in the particularity of the Son, precisely in his self-distinction from the Father.

Hegel is embraced here, minus his affirmation of the necessity of creation: "In the Trinity the Son is the principle of otherness, the starting point for the emergence of the finite as that which is absolutely other than deity" (28). There has to be an authentic self-demarcation of the Son from the Father as the ground for the reality of the creature itself:

> In the free self-distinction of the Son from the Father the independent existence of a creation distinct from God has its basis, and in this sense we may view creation as a free act not only of the Father but of the trinitarian God. It does not proceed necessarily from the fatherly love of God that is oriented from all eternity to the Son. The basis of its possibility is the free self-distinction of the Son from the Father; even as the Son moves out of the unity of deity, he is still united with the Father by the Spirit, who is the Spirit of freedom (2 Cor 3:17). . . . Thus creation is a free act of God as an expression of the freedom of the Son in his self-distinction from the Father,

and of the freedom of the fatherly goodness that in the Son accepts the possibility and the existence of a creation distinct from himself, and of the freedom of the Spirit who links the two in free agreement (30).

But the reality of the creatures is grounded not simply in the eternal Son, but in his enfleshing: "in the event of the incarnation . . . the Son moved out of the unity of the Godhead" and, by doing so, he "gave validity to the independent existence of other creatures alongside himself. This was part of the humility of the recognition and acceptance of creatureliness" (29). Such creatureliness can only be grounded in the fact that "the Son lets the Father alone be God and is aware that as the one God the Father is distinct from himself" (29).

Thus, for Pannenberg, the very possibility and existence of creation is grounded in the free self-distinction of the Son from the Father, in the "Son's own subjectivity" (30). Creation is not grounded in the eternal deliberation or decrees of a single being as much as in the free undertakings of the particular triune personalities.

Gunton has much sympathy with Pannenberg's critique of the older theologies of creation. He has written extensively on the doctrine of creation without concealing his deep suspicions of the Augustinian and Thomistic traditions. We find in his work some very pointed criticism of both Augustine and Aquinas, while his heroes appear to be Athanasius and Irenaeus. He finds Augustine's conception of divine creativity to be "rather monistically conceived."[20] Aquinas doesn't fare much better. Lamenting the "merely monotheistic" treatment of the doctrine, he charges that "the problem is that the act of willing is rather monistically conceived. The Trinity plays little or no constitutive part in his treatment of the divine realization of creation."[21] The framing of the doctrine of creation in terms of the causality of the single essence of God permits only an underdeveloped account of the distinctive roles of the divine persons in creation and an almost complete neglect of Christological mediation. Referring to Aquinas's discussion, he claims that "the distinctive forms of agency in creation are minimized rather than taken fully seriously."[22]

Such a blatant neglect of the scriptural notions of mediation through the Son and the Spirit was favored by the ready availability of the Platonic and Aristotelian doctrine of the divine ideas. "Because he had Aristotle, Aquinas

20. Colin Gunton, *The Triune Creator: A Historical and Systematic Study: Edinburgh Studies in Constructive Theology* (Grand Rapids: Eerdmans, 1998), 100.
21. Colin Gunton, "The End of Causality? The Reformers and Their Predecessors," in Colin Gunton, ed., *The Doctrine of Creation* (London: T&T Clark, 2004), 67.
22. Gunton, "The End of Causality?" 67.

did not need a christological mediation of the doctrine of creation."[23] The implication of such accounts of creation is that they tend "to concentrate on creation as an act of will or power . . . but at the expense of conceiving it as an act in which God creates that which he loves and wishes to love for its own sake."[24] These Platonizing tendencies have the effect of displacing the Son from his position of mediator of creation even though he remains mediator of salvation, and thus they separate creation from redemption.

Much like Pannenberg, Gunton wants to recover specific roles for the Son and the Spirit, as the two hands of God in creation and in general any divine activity, a conception he takes over from Irenaeus.[25] "Because God is lord of creation he does not need intermediaries, because mediation is achieved through his two hands."[26]

Important consequences follow from this: "It is because God the Father creates through the Son and Spirit, his two hands (Irenaeus), that we can conceive of a world that is both real in itself, and yet only itself in relation to its creator."[27] More specifically, for our purpose, at least two implications must be noted. First: "That God creates the world through Christ, through the one who became flesh, implies that God is able to come into relation with the world while remaining distinct from it."[28] Second: "Because God as a being also is what he is in terms of free personal relatedness, he is not bound to come into relation with the world. But he can, freely, and therefore such relations as there are must be understood as unnecessitated relations of love. The incarnation is the climax and model of the free relatedness of the triune God to the world he has made and holds in being."[29] Thus for Gunton it is quite important to understand the mediatorship of the *incarnate* Son, not simply that of the *logos asarkos*. To ascribe a role to Jesus Christ himself in creation is to refuse to regard creation as an act contained in the past (Augustine and even Barth) and thus to retain a teleological dynamism of creation, with Christ as its culmination.

23. Gunton, *The Triune Creator*, 121.

24. Gunton, *The Triune Creator*, 55.

25. Gunton, *The Triune Creator*, 62.

26. Gunton, *The Triune Creator*, 62–63.

27. Colin Gunton, *Christ and Creation: The Didsburg Lectures, 1990* (Eugene, OR: Wipf and Stock, 2005), 75.

28. Gunton, *Christ and Creation*, 77.

29. Gunton, *Christ and Creation*, 77. This echoes Pannenberg's insistence on the self-differentiation of the Son from the Father in the incarnation. However, Gunton insists, against Pannenberg, that Christology must presuppose the doctrine of the Trinity (76).

Pannenberg and Gunton have thrown down the gauntlet to patristic and medieval doctrines of creation. The common denominator in both critiques is that the older doctrine pays insufficient attention to the distinctive roles of the triune persons in the act of creation due to their emphasis on the unity of the divine being and operations. Whatever account of mediation is present is filtered through the doctrine of the divine ideas, inherited from Plato and Aristotle but insufficiently modified in light of Trinitarian doctrine.

In what follows, we will defend the Augustinian and Thomistic perspective. First, we will revisit the emergence of the rule of inseparable operations, this time in connection to the theological reflection on creation. Second, we will unpack Aquinas's account of creation as a Trinitarian act, to show that many of the concerns expressed by Pannenberg and Gunton are satisfactorily addressed. Finally, we will suggest ways in which Aquinas may need a Christological supplement after all, yet we will argue that such a supplement is entirely consistent with his fundamental approach.

There are at least two desiderata in any account of the Trinitarian mediation of creation. In our opinion both are satisfactorily addressed by, or within the framework of, Thomas Aquinas's account of creation. First, any account of creation (and in fact any divine action *ad extra*) must be able to account not only for the unity of essence but also the diversity of persons and personal Trinitarian relations. While the doctrine of inseparable operations must not be surrendered, it is not the final word on triune agency. Specifically in relation to our question, a Trinitarian doctrine of creation must give due weight to the biblical notion that God creates *through* the Word.

Secondly, a Trinitarian doctrine of creation must relate creation not simply to the Son, but specifically to Jesus Christ. It is an outstanding question whether the incarnate Son shares in the divine efficient causality of creation, or whether some other account can be given of his participation in the activity of creation. However, it is no longer desirable in the context of modern biblical exegesis to explain mediation simply in terms of the participation of the eternal Son. But the question remains as to the nature of the causality exercised by the incarnate Son in relation to creation.

SOME PATRISTIC ACCOUNTS OF INSEPARABLE OPERATIONS AND CREATION

For patristic writers, the affirmation of the divinity of Christ was predicated upon the biblical observation of the inseparability of his works with the Father. Chief among these works is the act of primordial creation. This section reviews the collusion between the doctrines of creation and that of the inseparable operations.

Athanasius of Alexandria articulates the principle of inseparable operations in the context of his debate with the Arians, who had claimed that the Son is a creature of God, even if a superior one. In response, Athanasius leverages the New Testament designation of Christ as creator. If Christ is a created creator, then, absurdly, God cannot be called creator himself. In *Against the Arians* he is rejecting an Arian ontology according to which the divine essence is not "fruitful" itself, predicated on the claim that the Word is a "work" of God. Athanasius insists on the ontological priority of God's knowing to his willing. Whatever God wills to create must first spring from that which is "above the will," namely God's knowledge. Here is Athanasius:

> But if there be not a Son, how then say you that God is a Creator? Since all things that come to be are through the Word and in Wisdom, and without This nothing can be, whereas you say He has not That in and through which He makes all things. For if the Divine Essence be not fruitful itself, but barren, as they hold, as a light that lightens not, and a dry fountain, are they not ashamed to speak of His possessing framing energy? And whereas they deny what is by nature, do they not blush to place before it what is by will? But if He frames things that are external to Him and before were not, by willing them to be, and becomes their Maker, much more will He first be Father of an Offspring from His proper Essence.[30]

The Father's own creatorship, Athanasius argues, can only be affirmed, given the biblical ascription of creation to the Son, by admitting that the Son is intrinsic to the divine essence and not an extrinsic production from it, as the Arians suggested. It is thus precisely by noting the common operations of the Son and the Father that Athanasius makes this claim. Athanasius uses the doctrine of inseparable operations to show, from the fact that the Son does exactly the same works as the Father, that therefore he is not a creature but on the contrary is the Word and Wisdom through whom the Father himself creates. But the Son is not an external instrument, or else the Father would not be Creator himself. He is internal and indeed the Word and Wisdom of the Father himself.

With Basil the Great we find something very similar. He opposes followers

---

30. Athanasius, *Against the Arians*, in *The Nicene and Post-Nicene Fathers*, series 2, vol. 4, ed. Philip Schaff (Peabody: Hendrickson Publishers, 1994), 2.16.2.

of Aëtius, who employed a particular theology of how attributes may be predicated of God, to argue that since we know God's essence to be unoriginate, therefore the Son himself cannot be divine, as begotten. In *On the Holy Spirit* Basil discusses the biblical use of the language "through whom," "from whom," and "in whom." He observes that Aëtius invoked such language to suggest an inferiority and an instrumentality of the Son and of the Spirit. Aëtius had held that "things that are expressed differently are different in nature.... But, 'through whom' is different from 'from whom'; therefore the Son is different from the Father."[31] This leads to an understanding of the Son as a mere instrument of the Father.

Basil's refutation begins with the observation that the same prepositions are predicated of all Trinitarian persons and they are not the exclusive property of any of them.[32] This enables Basil to refute the subordination claim, even though in the process he seems to be weakening the force of these prepositions in the case of the creative agency itself. The prepositions do not indicate, for Basil at least, any sort of necessity of essence: "Let us not, then, think of this economy through the Son as a compulsory service done out of a slave-like subjection, but rather as a voluntary solicitude that acts according to the will of God the Father out of goodness and tender-heartedness for his own creation."[33]

However, even though this subjection of the Son to the Father as the "through whom" of creation is voluntary, Basil insists that they share a single will that reaches timelessly from the Father through the Son, in an instantaneous moment, without mark of time. In other words, there is a movement from the Father, who alone is unoriginate, to the begotten Son, yet without a diminution of power or a separation of energy. Basil is convinced of the importance of the inseparable operations principle. He articulates one consequence of this: "For the Father is seen not in a difference in his works, not by manifesting his own separate energy, for whatever 'he sees the Father doing,' the Son also does (Jn 5.19)."[34] There is a seamless sharing and transmission of the one will of the Father to the Son and to the Holy Spirit. We do not speak, hence, of two acts of willing, but of a single ordered act of willing, from the Father, to the Son and to the Spirit. Hence, we are not to suppose

31. Basil, *On the Holy Spirit*, trans. Stephen Hildebrand (Yonkers: St. Vladimir's Seminary Press, 2011), 30.
32. Basil, *On the Holy Spirit*, ch. 5.
33. Basil, *On the Holy Spirit*, 47.
34. Basil, *On the Holy Spirit*, 49.

that he needs help to act nor in the sense that he has been entrusted by a detailed stewardship with the function of performing each word, for such a function is not at all consistent with the divine dignity. Rather, since the Logos is full of the Father's goodness and shines forth from him, he does all things in a way similar to the one who begot him. For if he is without difference in substance, he will also be without difference in power, and for those whose power is identical, the energy also is wholly identical.[35]

The persons share the same power, the same will, because they share the same essence. At the same time, the order must be observed. The Son has his nature (and will, and power, and energy) from the Father. Contra the Arian reading of John 5:19, however, this entails no inferiority of nature: "Therefore we should not take the command that was spoken as an imperative that is announced through vocal instruments and that legislates for the Son what he must do under obedience."[36] Rather, it is because "his own will is connected in indissoluble union with the Father" that he acts from the Father.

Much like Athanasius, then, we find in Basil an affirmation of the common and inseparable acting of the triune persons in virtue of their possessing the same substance and thus the same power and energy. Although Basil distinguishes the persons much more clearly than Aquinas will, he resists ascribing to them separate wills, not simply in terms of separate objects of will but in separate acts of willing. The persons share a single act of will, which seamlessly flows "in unity and without interruption"[37] from the Father to the Son. But the key distinction is that the Father may not be identified from a difference in his works or by having any separate energy.

Augustine's own opus also exhibits a gradual unfolding of the implications of inseparable operations for the doctrine of creation. Homoian exegesis of 1 Corinthians 8:6 had posited that "the Son is an instrument in the hands of the Father who is the true creator."[38] Against this, Augustine early on in his work uses Romans 11:36 to highlight inseparable operations in creation itself. We see again how the doctrine of inseparability played an essential role in rejecting Arian-leaning heresies. Augustine deploys the Pauline text in *De fide*

35. Basil, *On the Holy Spirit*, 49–50.
36. Basil, *On the Holy Spirit*, 50.
37. Basil, *On the Holy Spirit*, 50.
38. Lewis Ayres, *Augustine and the Trinity* (Cambridge: Cambridge University Press, 2014), 48.

et symbolo (*On Faith and the Creed*, AD 393) and in *Contra Adimantium* (AD 394), although very briefly at the beginning of the treatise.

Augustine is progressively teasing out the implications of the Trinitarian structure of divine agency in terms of the very nature of creation. In *De vera religione*, he posits that the created order's very intelligibility is closely linked to an account of the Trinity as inseparably sustaining the world in existence. A similar claim about the triadic structure of any reality (that it is, what it is, and its permanence) is made in *Letter 11* (to Nebridius). Ayres contends that this too is connected to Augustine's thinking about inseparable operations. For Augustine the Trinitarian nature of divine agency does not imply effects that are separately attributed to the divine persons. Nonetheless, *the result of the creative activity comes to reflect the Trinitarian nature of this agency.* As he puts it in *De vera religione*,

> Not that the Father should be understood to have made one part of the whole creation and the Son another and the Holy Spirit yet another, but that each and every nature has been made simultaneously by the Father through the Son, in the Gift of the Holy Spirit. Every particular thing, you see, has simultaneously about it these three: that it is one something, and that it is distinguished by its own proper look or species from other things, and that it does not overstep the order of things.[39]

In *Letter 11*, however, he studiously avoids ascribing *cause* exclusively to the Father, *form* exclusively to the Son, and *permanence* to the Holy Spirit. Such an account would in fact destroy the unity of the created nature. It is not as if the Father first causes it, then the Son gives it its shape, and then the Holy Spirit assures its permanence.[40]

Here we find a hint of the supposed Platonism of Augustine's doctrine of creation. In thinking of the Son as the very form of creation, Augustine is arguing that creation itself is grounded in the Son, even as the Son remains in inseparable unity with the Father. The connection between Plato's pre-existing ideas and the Son as the divine Logos, or mind of God, seems to be invited precisely at this point. Augustine affirms as much about the Logos in *Sermon 117*: "You see, it is a kind of form, a form that has not been formed, but

---

39. From *De vera religione* 7.13, quoted in Ayres, *Augustine and the Trinity*, 62.

40. Augustine, *The Works of Saint Augustine II/1, Letters 1–99*, trans. Roland Teske, SJ, ed. John E. Rotelle, OSA (Hyde Park, New York: New City Press, 2001), 35–37. Such an account, indeed, would entail that these dimensions are extrinsic to each other and can be thought without one another.

is the form of all things that have been formed; an unchangeable form that has neither fault nor failing, beyond time, beyond space, standing apart as at once the foundation for all things to stand on, and the ceiling for them to stand under."[41]

We have observed Augustine arguing in *De trinitate*, based on the text from 1 Corinthians 1:24, "Christ the power of God and the wisdom of God," that only the relational attributes of origin, such as unbegotten, begotten, proceeding, can be ascribed specifically to the persons. The essential attributes, such as power and wisdom are ascribed to the persons only by appropriation. By the same logic, however, is it permissible to say that the Father is creator or Lord through the creative agency of the Son? Could one argue that the Father is Creator or Lord through the Son's creatorship or lordship, as through an instrument that has a distinct efficient causality? Augustine's answer would be categorically negative. His account of inseparable operations and appropriation regards creation as the Son's (and the Spirit's, and the Father's) inseparable action. Furthermore, God's creatorship, given divine simplicity, is as Anatolios puts it, "co-terminous with the Father-Son relation."[42]

We have seen in this brief patristic flashback that there is a broad employment of the doctrine of inseparable operations in the service of demonstrating the divinity of Christ, first in relation to the Arian claim that the Son is a creature, then in connection to the claim by Aëtius that the Son is a different substance from the Father. Each of the writers above would insist on the inseparability of the divine operations and not simply on the similarity between them. It follows that the doctrine of inseparable operations is not a remnant of "mere monotheism," but it fundamentally buttresses the doctrine of the Trinity by establishing Christ's divinity and coequality with the Father.

The question still remains of how such an insistence on the unity of the divine action can be consistent with the reality of personal distinctions within God's self, and with the biblical notion of the Christological mediation of creation. As J. I. Doedes puts it: "Did the Father and Son jointly create all things? But then it is not creation *by* the Son."[43]

41. Augustine, *Sermon* 117.3, in *The Works of Augustine. Sermons: III/4 (94A-147A) on the New Testament*, trans. Edmund Hill, OP, ed. John E. Rotelle, OSA (Brooklyn: New City Press, 1992), 210.

42. See above, Anatolios, *Retrieving Nicaea*, 117.

43. Quoted in Herman Bavinck, *God and Creation*, vol. 2 of *Reformed Dogmatics*, trans. John Vriend, ed. John Bolt (Grand Rapids: Baker, 2004), 422 (hereafter *RD*).

Aquinas on Creation as a Trinitarian Act

Earlier in the chapter we noted the severe criticism of Aquinas at the hands of both Pannenberg and Gunton. We hope to make good on the suggestion that Aquinas's theology of creation can both accommodate the diverse causalities of the triune persons, thus explaining in what way the Father creates *through* the Son, *and* parse the instrumentality of the Son in a way that relates specifically to his incarnation.

The proper place to start, with respect to Aquinas, is in his exegesis of the relevant biblical passages. Commenting on Colossians 1:15–17, Aquinas explains that "the Son is the first born of every creature because he is generated or begotten as the principle of every creature."[44] He explicitly critiques Platonist conceptions of "different first principles," insisting that all the perfections found in things are from a first principle, which is Christ.[45] "In him all things were created, as in an *exemplar*," Thomas argues. The exemplarity of the Son is essential, although it has to be admitted that Aquinas thinks not so much of the Son in his divine-human unity, an item we will revisit, but of the eternal Son. Aquinas also suggests that the basis for the difference in things is also to be found in the Son.[46] This also clearly runs against the typical Platonist tendencies to relegate difference to material substrate of creation.

In his *Commentary on John*, Aquinas's main interest is to refute readings of "*through* Christ" that undermine the equality of the Son with the Father. One particular foil here is Origen, whose interpretation of the preposition is "as something is made by a greater through a lesser as if the Son were inferior to, and an instrument of the Father."[47] Aquinas counters: "The preposition 'through' (*per*) does not signify inferiority in the thing which is its grammatical object, i.e. the Son or Word."[48] In this commentary, he further explains that the world has been created through the Son as through a *formal cause*.[49]

---

44. Thomas Aquinas, *Commentary on Colossians*, trans. Fabian Richard Larcher (Ave Maria: Sapientia Press of Ave Maria University, 2004), 37.

45. Aquinas, *Colossians*, 40.

46. Aquinas, *Colossians*, 39–40.

47. Thomas Aquinas, *Commentary on the Gospel of St. John. Part I: Chapters 1–7*, trans. James A. Weisheipl, OP (Albany, NY: Magi Books), 75.

48. Aquinas, *John*, 75.

49. Aquinas, *John*, 76. For an excellent discussion of how exemplary causes relate to formal causes, see David L. Greenstock, "Exemplar Causality and the Supernatural Order," *Thomist* 16, no. 1 (1953). Also helpful is Vivian Boland, *Ideas in God According to Saint Thomas Aquinas: Sources and Synthesis* (Leiden, New York: Brill, 1996), and Gregory T.

In the *Summa Theologiae*, he tackles the theme of Trinitarian mediation in Question 45 of the *prima pars*. There his main interest is to establish the coherence of inseparable action with the apparently diverse actions of the triune persons. He establishes that to create is to cause something to exist.[50] He argues that when the principle of the action is considered from the effect of the action, it is common to all persons. In other words, all the effects of God's action are the common production of the divine persons. So far this is the standard interpretation of the inseparability doctrine. But the persons, he insists, do have a causality. God the Father creates through Word and Love.

It is essential to understand this. Even though the triune agency is unified, its unity is not without differentiation. This applies to creation as well, as he notes: "The power of creation, whilst common to the three persons, belongs to them in a kind of order."[51]

For Aquinas the nature of God and his tripersonality are equiprimordial. They are, in fact, one and the same thing, in reality, though regarded from different perspectives, respectively substantial and relational. To speak of a causality that is proper to the divine persons is not something that can be done over and above, or in distinction from, the essential divine causality. *The diverse causalities of the persons and the single causality of the Trinity must be thought together.* Divine action must be doubly parsed, or redoubled,[52] first in terms of the unity of substance, secondly in terms of the distinction of persons. Aquinas argues that "the processions of the persons are the type of the production of creatures inasmuch as they include the essential attributes, knowledge and will."[53] Put differently, the persons are only types, or exemplars, as modes of the existence of the one divine substance. This does not mean, however, that everything that is interesting about mediation can be expressed in essential terms.

Given this, we should not expect to *individuate* separate actions of the persons in creation. But this raises an important question for Aquinas: May we find no traces of the Trinity in creation? Aquinas argues that the processions are also in some way the cause and type of creation. Substantial attributes, such as power of creation, belong to the persons differently, though inseparably. Just as the persons have the divine nature in a certain order, so the power of

Doolan, *Aquinas on the Divine Ideas as Exemplar Causes* (Washington, DC: Catholic University of America Press, 2014).

50. Aquinas, *ST* 1, q. 45, a. 6.

51. Aquinas, *ST* 1, q. 45, a. 6, ad. 2.

52. Ghislain Lafont's term, picked up by Gilles Emery, in "Essentialism or Personalism in the Treatise on God in Saint Thomas Aquinas," *Thomist* 64, no. 4 (2000): 534.

53. Aquinas, *ST* 1, q. 45, a. 6.

creation belongs to them in an ordered way. It follows that the persons, while sharing the same efficient causality, the same causal relation to the world, nonetheless exhibit it in their own proper manner, or, as Katherine Sondereg-ger elegantly puts it, God's "personal *Relatio* to another echoes and is suffused by the Modes of God's very Life, His Processions."[54]

Aquinas is driving the point that, even though creatures are produced by the inseparable Trinity, they nevertheless come to resemble the persons spe-cifically. Of note here is his nuanced answer to the question of the *vestigia Trinitatis*. One may not distinguish between different traces of the Son and of the Spirit, or of the Father. Every production *ad extra* belongs to their com-mon causality. However, certain effects that are brought about may resemble, or *image*, at different levels and in different ways, distinct Trinitarian persons. He explains that there are two ways in which an effect may resemble a cause. In the first, it is only the causality and not the form that is carried over to the effect, as when a fire produces smoke. We can infer the causality of the fire from the effect of smoke. This Aquinas calls a *trace*. The second, however, is what he calls an *image*. Here both causality and form carry over, as when a fire produces another fire.

These examples give us an insight into how we may discriminate between the various causalities of the divine persons. While they all share efficient cau-sality, the persons act as distinct exemplar causes, insofar as the effects of their inseparable action come to resemble them distinctly. "Therefore in rational creatures, possessing intellect and will, there is found the representation of the Trinity by way of image, inasmuch as there is found in them the word con-ceived and love proceeding."[55] All creatures are the products of the common divine causality. Yet intellectual creatures have been created with the potential to also imitate the divine persons. To put it differently, all creatures are traces of the Trinity, but some traces can become images of the Trinity as well.

Note that Aquinas holds that the inseparability principle permits distinct relations between creatures and the divine persons. Such relations, however, are not in the order of efficient causality, but in the order of formal, or more exactly exemplary, causality. While it is impossible to individuate what we will later call the distinct "mode of action" of each person on the basis of diversity of effects, their efficient causality being unique, it remains possible to so indi-

54. Katherine Sonderegger, *Systematic Theology*, vol. 1, *The Doctrine of God* (Minneap-olis: Fortress, 2015), 268.
55. Aquinas, *ST* 1, q. 45, a. 7.

viduate the person's modes of action on the basis of the creature's being made to resemble these. But we are getting ahead of ourselves here.

Let us summarize our conclusions about Aquinas thus far. We have tried to establish that despite his insistence, with the rest of the patristic tradition, on the inseparable operations principle, Aquinas still allows for an *imaging* of the distinct Trinitarian persons, albeit an imaging that is not predicated on different efficient causalities of the persons. Aquinas's "mere monotheism" is considerably more nuanced and complex than Gunton appears to allow for. Yet Aquinas holds his nerve and resists sacrificing either the distinctness of the persons on the altar of the unity of substance, or the unity of substance in favor of the diversity of persons. The two dimensions are equiprimordial and irreducible to one another.

It follows that any account of the "through whom and by whom" and "in whom" must observe these stringencies. The diverse actions of the Trinitarian persons can only be described as diverse *modes of actions*[56] within the unity of the same divine substance. Thus, insofar as the Son has his divine nature from the Father, his "mode of action" within the inseparable triune action is going to be according to the manner of existence of the divine substance in him. The same goes for the Spirit; mode of action refers to the manner of execution of the *same* action by an inseparable person.

Gilles Emery explains that "this proper mode regards the relations between the divine persons themselves: it is a relational mode of action."[57] One may argue, indeed, that the distinction between inseparable action and diverse modes of action is an extrapolation from the distinction between substance and persons.[58] Just as when speaking substantially about God one speaks of the power of God, the wisdom of God, and indeed the creatorship and lordship of God, so when speaking relationally, one speaks of the mode in which the persons share the same power, wisdom, and creatorship. The Father has these from himself, the Son from the Father, and the Holy Spirit from the Father and the Son. By sharing in the same substance they share in the same eternal action of this substance (God is pure act), yet in distinct modes.

Since each person has a different mode of existing,[59] the persons will have

---

56. For this terminology of "modus operandi" in Aquinas, see *ST* I, q. 89, a. 1.

57. Gilles Emery, *The Trinity: An Introduction to Catholic Doctrine on the Triune God* (Washington, DC: Catholic University of America Press, 2011), 165; cf. Emery, *Trinitarian Theology of Thomas Aquinas* (Oxford: Oxford University Press, 2007), 355.

58. The fact that the Latin tradition understands God to be pure act further corroborates the plausibility of this extrapolation, or rather definition.

59. Emery claims that Aquinas makes a "reappropriation of the Cappadocian Trin-

their own *modus operandi*. It follows, against Gunton and Pannenberg, that persons aren't occulted when creation is attributed to the one God. The persons just are the divine nature in this or that relational mode. But there is also an order to the "circulation" of the divine nature among the persons: from the Father, through the Son, in the Holy Spirit. Naturally, then, all divine actions *ad extra* are accomplished from the Father, through the Son, in the Holy Spirit.

There is indeed a quasi-Platonic element in Aquinas's notion of creation through the Logos. But this does not justify Gunton's fear of a creation that either is necessary or is an arbitrary act of will. The Trinitarian description strongly qualifies whatever elements of Platonism remain:

> The Father utters himself and every creature by the Word which he begets, in as much as the begotten Word represents the Father and all creatures. And in the same way loves himself and loves all creatures by the Holy Spirit, in that the Holy Spirit proceeds as love for the original goodness, the motive for the Father's loving himself and all creatures.[60]

The very emergence of creation and the continuing love and care of God for it are anchored in the processions themselves. It is not simply the Son who has an affinity for the creature or for materiality, as Gunton implies,[61] which would only relocate the problem of mediation. Rather, the Father utters both himself (necessarily) and every creature (contingently) in the same act by which he is the *loving* Father of the Son. And thus the processions of the persons are the origin, the principle, and the exemplar of the processions of the creatures.[62] As Emery explains: "The intercommunication of the entire divine nature amongst the persons of the Trinity is the cause and rationale of the communication to creatures of a participation in the divine nature."[63]

This point is fundamental for Thomas's understanding of creation: "The coming out of the persons in their unity of nature is the cause of the coming out of creatures in their diversity of nature."[64] In the *Summa Theologiae*, Thomas explains that the particular causality involved here is exemplary: "The

---

itarian doctrine: their *tropoi tes hyparxeos* or literally modes of existence" (*Trinitarian Theology*, 353).

60. Aquinas, *ST* 1, q. 37, a. 2, ad. 3.
61. Gunton, *The Triune Creator*, 102.
62. Emery, *Trinitarian Theology*, 343.
63. Emery, *Trinitarian Theology*, 345.
64. Aquinas, *I Sent*, dist. 2, quoted in Emery, *Trinitarian Theology*, 345.

comings forth of the divine persons are patterns [*rationes*] of the coming forth of the creatures."[65]

So there is a causality that is proper to each of the persons, yet it is in the order of exemplary, not efficient, causality. The divine action does not spring from a monolithic divine essence, but from within the eternal movement that is constituted by the divine processions, as Emery also explains: "The divine action is not wholly explained by reference to the divine nature, that is, by the creative knowledge and will of the Trinity. It also has roots in the Trinitarian processions which are the exemplar model and rationale of the works God brings about in the world."[66] Within this movement the freedom of God's willing of creation is distinct from the necessity of the processions, although the distinction does not separate the divine pure act. As Aquinas illustrates: "By the same act, the artist is turned toward his art and his work. But God Himself is the eternal art from which creatures are produced like works of art. Therefore in the same act, the Father is turned toward Himself and to all creatures. Hence, by uttering Himself, He utters all creatures."[67]

The distinction between the unified efficient causality and the distinct exemplar causality is analogous to the operations of a magnet. In a magnet the poles north (N) and south (S) are not parts of the magnet, but functions of, and "subsistent relations" within, the magnetic field. N and S are not *parts* because it is impossible to partition the magnetic field in that way. If one of the poles were to disappear, there would be no magnetic field. Yet it is not the magnetic field that magnetically charges one of the poles. The poles do not exist apart from this magnetic relation. Now consider what happens when a metallic object, say a coin, or a pin, is attracted to the magnet. The object attaches to the magnet, to one of the poles of the magnet, and it receives the opposite magnetic charge. Say the pin is attached to that "part" of the magnet we call S. It would then automatically receive a positive charge, which is the opposite of the negative charge of S.

The analogy must not be stretched to the breaking point.[68] It serves my argument by illustrating the distinction between efficient causality and exem-

---

65. Aquinas, *ST* 1, q. 45, a. 6, quoted in Emery, *Trinitarian Theology*, 346.

66. Emery, *Trinitarian Theology*, 345.

67. Thomas Aquinas, *Quaestiones Disputatae de Veritate*, trans. Robert Mulligan, SJ (Chicago: Henry Regnery Company, 1952), q. 4, a. 4.

68. Henri de Lubac also uses the imagery of the magnet to underscore the tendency of creation toward God: "For man, God is not only a norm that is imposed upon him and, by guiding him, lifts him up again: God is the Absolute upon which he rests, the Magnet that draws him, the Beyond that calls him, the Eternal that provides him with the only atmo-

plary causality. When one considers the action of the magnet from the standpoint of efficient causality, the magnet as a whole attracts the object. The action of drawing or magnetizing belongs to the magnet as a whole. Indeed, N and S are relational distinctions within the same single substance of the magnet, not substance terms.[69] No actions may be predicated of these taken singly, not being substantial terms. Note, however, that one may observe a distinction between the fact that the magnet as a whole is drawing the object, and the fact that the object is attaching itself to S specifically.[70] Not only is the object attached to just one of the poles, but it also receives the charge specific to the other pole. One may say that even though both poles are acting inseparably in the drawing of the object, it comes to resemble one of them in particular, at least under a certain description (of electrical charge).

The magnet acts as a whole in drawing the object to itself. Yet the poles of the magnet can be clearly distinguished from one another in the way the objects are attached to them and how objects variously receive some of their properties. N and S are not changed by the fact that various objects either come to resemble them or be attached to them. So in this case it is possible to individuate the poles despite their lack of a unique efficient causality—moreover, precisely because of the kind of substance that it is, a magnet exercises this particular exemplary causality. Similarly, it is precisely because God is this kind of being—existing in the subsisting relations that constitute the persons of Father, Son, and Holy Spirit—that his actions, though inseparable, exhibit this threefold modality.

It can now be more clearly appreciated why the differentiation between the persons is best visible in the divine missions. In the missions, intellectual creatures are drawn to participate in the Trinitarian life and come to resemble the persons distinctly, the Son through knowledge, the Spirit through love. Thus, the distinction between the persons is most clearly exhibited not by way of efficient causality alone but by union with created substances, whereby the

---

sphere in which he can breathe and, in some sort, that third dimension in which man finds his depth." *The Drama of Atheist Humanism* (San Francisco: Ignatius, 1998), 67.

69. Note that I am following the same logic employed by many patristic theologians to refute Arians and Eunomius; terms such as "being begotten" are not substantial terms, hence it cannot be inferred that the Son is substantially inferior to the Father, who is "unbegotten."

70. The rule I am trying to establish here is that, as far as action goes, the persons act together *ad extra*. As far as passion goes, on the other hand, they are "acted on," or related to, distinctly. Or, considered as a principle of a relation to creatures, God acts inseparably; considered as the end term of the same relation, the persons may be distinguished from one another.

persons are not merely extrinsic to the knower but enter a process of union with her, the finality of which is the beatific vision.

We have argued that Aquinas's understanding of divine agency is not that of a monolithic unity, but rather of a differentiated and dynamic unity determined by the divine processions. One final question remains: How is the mediation of creation through the Son specifically related to his incarnation? It needs to be conceded that, on the surface, Thomas's description of the mediation of creation through the Son seems exclusively oriented to his divine nature. The judgment of Leo Scheffczyk, an otherwise sympathetic scholar, seems to be warranted that Thomas "is more concerned here to buttress his view of the causation of Creation by the divine essence (common, of course, to all three Persons) than to single out a special role of the Logos in Creation or to interpret Creation in terms of the economy of salvation."[71] It can certainly be conceded that this is true on one level. While Aquinas does not explicitly support the notion of a Christological mediation of creation, his description of an "essential" action of creation inherently contains the distinction between the diverse causalities of the triune persons. Such causalities are expressed in the mode not of efficiency but of exemplarity.

It is possible, however, to include within the exemplary causality of the Son a relation to his incarnate nature in such a way that Jesus Christ himself may be said to be the one through whom the Father creates. In order to make such a case, we will need to turn to Aquinas's treatise on truth, *De Veritate*. Two articles in particular help us understand how the exemplarity of the Son is related to his incarnation specifically. They are located under Question 4, pertaining to the divine Word.

In Article 4, Thomas asks: "Does the Father utter all creatures in the Word by which he utters himself?" A difficulty in the way of affirming this is that the divine ideas appear to be an essential notion, not a personal one: "The divine archetype of creatures is an idea. Therefore, the divine word of creatures is simply an idea. An idea, however, is predicated of God, not personally, but essentially. Consequently, the Word which is predicated personally of God, and by which the Father utters himself, is not the word by which creatures are uttered."[72] This formulation of the difficulty triggers Pannenberg's and Gunton's objections that, since the divine ideas pertain to the divine essence, creation is not mediated through the personal self-distinction of the Son from the Father.

---

71. Leo Scheffczyk, *Creation and Providence*, trans. Richard Strachan (New York: Herder and Herder, 1970).

72. Aquinas, *De Veritate*, q. 4, art. 4, see Difficulty 4.

Thomas responds to this difficulty by distinguishing between idea and Word: "A word differs from an idea, for the latter means an exemplary cause and nothing else, but the word in God of a creature means an exemplary form that is drawn from something else. Hence, a divine idea pertains to the essence, but the word to a person."[73] Aquinas is in fact consistently engaged here in an exercise of *reduplication*. The archetype of creation can be described first essentially, as an idea, in which case it is rightly predicated of the essence of God. Additionally, and equally importantly, it can be described relationally, in terms of the very expression, in the Word, of the Father's self-understanding. Thus, to say that creation is through the Word, is to say that it takes place through that self-expression of the Father, which is the Son. In this consists the relationality of "Word" as opposed to "idea." They both have the same reference, since the persons are not something in addition to the divine essence, but Word is predicated under the aspect of relation while idea is predicated under the aspect of essence.[74] Thus, there is a sense in which the work of creation is described as taking place, as it were essentially, through the divine ideas. But this is not the whole story. Triune agency is not simply monolithically conceived but is dynamic in its threefold relationality. The Word expresses that relation whereby the Father is expressed.

This brings us to the second, related, point, which Aquinas develops in Article 5 under the same question. Here he develops the argument hinted at in the previous article, that the Word is a relational way of speaking about the divine being, and its creative activity. Thomas clarifies that the title Word implies not only a relation to the Father, but to creatures as well. The Angelic Doctor writes: "Since the Father principally utters himself by begetting His Word, and, as a consequence of this, utters creatures, the Word is principally, and, as it were, essentially referred to the Father, but consequently, and, as it were, accidentally to creatures; for it is only accidental to the Word that creatures are uttered through it."[75]

In this phrase alone we have in fact a response to at least two desiderata expressed by modern critics. First, creation bears only an accidental relation to the Word, which means it does not belong to him essentially. Hence the contingency of creation is fully affirmed. Secondly, included in the very idea of the Word of God is a relation to creatures, including, I will argue, Jesus

73. Aquinas, *De Veritate*, q. 4, art. 4. See the *responsio*.

74. For a similar argument, based on the *ST*, see Matthew Levering, *Engaging the Doctrine of Creation: Cosmos, Creatures, and the Wise and Good Creator* (Grand Rapids: Baker, 2017), 65–67.

75. Aquinas, *De Veritate*, q. 4, art. 5. See the *responsio*.

Christ; but this relationship is consequent from, and not constitutive of, the eternal Son. This last point, we might be reminded, is the question before us: Is there a relation precisely to the human nature of the Son in the eternal Son's mediatorship of creation?

We would argue that a relation between the Son and his incarnate human nature is indeed contained in the very description of the Son as the Word.[76] Admittedly, Aquinas does not stress this point. He restricts himself to the affirmation of an implicit relation between the Word and the Father, on the one hand, and between the Word and creatures, on the other. It is no stretch, but rather the very logical conclusion of this line of thought, to say that the Word also contains a relation to the human nature that became actuated in the incarnation. Not only is the Son the pattern of creation, but also the one in whose incarnate nature creation is redeemed and glorified.

Importantly, the Son is also the one to whom humanity is united specifically, precisely through the incarnation, and the one whom we come to resemble by faith. Thus, the exemplary causality does not simply explicate the production of creation (as pattern), but also indicates the Son as the *terminus* of humanity. Indeed, it is precisely because humanity is drawn to the person of the Son specifically, and not simply by appropriation, that every other appropriation is made possible. In the mission of the Son, whose incarnation is the raising up of a human nature to union with the Son specifically, the Son is discriminated, for our sake, from the Father. Such a union does not enter into the ontological constitution of the Son, which is solely determined by the intra-Trinitarian relations. Yet only because of this union can we individuate the Son, as distinct from the Father, not because of any difference in efficient causalities.

The persons are known from the missions, in particular the visible missions of the Son and the Spirit. In a mission, a union takes place between a particular triune person and a created reality. Apart from such a union in mission, the activity of God in the world would be epistemically undifferentiated. But because of the missions, an insight is gained precisely into the ontological self-differentiation and dynamism of the divine being and action.

---

76. It is crucial, however, to distinguish between the two relations which are implied in the title of the Word: to the Father, and to creatures. While the relation of Word to Father is a real relation, his relation to creatures is conceptual. Of course, what Aquinas means by this is that the former relation is constitutive of the very ontological identity of Word, as one who proceeds from and manifests the Father, whereas the latter does not constitute the Word, but is constituted by it.

But the missions do not alter the persons; they do not enter into their onto-logical constitution.

CONCLUSION

Much recent theology objects to the allegedly non-Trinitarian theology of creation of the likes of Augustine and Thomas. Pannenberg and Gunton have rightly called attention to the importance of Trinitarian description in the doc-trine of creation as well. Moreover, they have—also rightly in my view—called for an understanding of the participation of Christ himself in the work of cre-ation. We have sought to show that the work of Aquinas adequately addresses both of these concerns. The two desiderata we have identified are satisfied.

First, Aquinas's account of divine causality is richer than is often esti-mated. Divine agency is unitary but not monolithic, containing a threefold self-differentiation. Such a differentiation does not, however, characterize the divine efficient causality. As we have shown, the observation of the common and inseparable causality of the divine persons was a central argument against a whole set of Christological heresies. Aquinas rightly understands that the diverse personal causalities must not undermine the unity of God's efficient causality. Such a distinction is located, with Aquinas, at the level of the persons' exemplary causalities. We have sought to illustrate the distinction between efficient and exemplary causality by an appeal to the analogy of the magnet and its magnetic field. A magnet operates as a single substance, yet objects are drawn to its poles and receive their respective charges distinctively. Similarly, the divine efficient causality is unified, yet dynamically differentiated. Such "differences" are, however, only discernible as creation is drawn to the divine persons and made to resemble them distinctively.

Secondly, it was suggested that while Aquinas does not specifically incor-porate the incarnate Son in his account of mediation, his conceptuality not only permits but encourages such an expansion. The Son as the Word is the self-manifestation of the Father to the creatures. In the notion of the Word is contained a consequent relation to creation. The full extent of the nature and ends of these creatures is expressed in the Word. Thus, it is natural to say that the Word manifests not only the Father, but the Father's knowledge of how the divine being can be participated in, and how it (eventually) will be participated in. In expressing the Father, the Word expresses also the Father's fatherhood of creatures, the adoption of the creatures into the Father-Son relation, and their glorification. Creation is after all related to redemption and to consummation, even though Aquinas does not make this quite as explicit as he might have.

What appeared to be so problematic about the Platonizing tendency of patristic thought, was that it anchors creation in "divine ideas," which are at best ambiguous toward materiality and therefore make the relationship between God and the world less than real, invested, or meaningful. Aquinas's account decisively avoids that implication. Creation is not simply grounded in the divine ideas, but in the procession of the Son and the spiration of the Spirit. It follows that creation is not simply the external production of divine ideas but something intended for union with God and participation in him. The eternal Son is not simply the pattern for creation but its terminus as well. Herman Bavinck expresses this well: "In Him the Father contemplates the idea of the world itself, not as though it were identical with the Son, but so that he envisions it and meets it in the Son in whom his fullness dwells."[77] Humanity is created for union with the Trinity precisely in the person of the Son, whom the Father loves in the Spirit. While that union is brought about through the common operation of the whole Trinity, humanity is united with the Son, specifically in his divine-human unity, through whom it then participates in and comes to reflect the other divine persons (the Holy Spirit through love, in particular).

It is in the missions that the differentiation of the processions is revealed. The mission of the Son channels the fatherhood of God the Father. Through the Son we become adoptive sons. The Son, Jesus pointed out, only does what he sees the Father doing. He channels the Father's work, who is also at work (John 5:17, esp. 14:10). Similarly, the mission of the Son is a conduit to the mission of the Spirit. What we receive is not simply the eternal Spirit of God, but precisely the Spirit of Christ (1 Pet 1:11; Rom 8:9, etc.). Creation returns to God in the missions of the Son and the Spirit. The Son and the Spirit are indeed the two hands of God working in creation, but they are most clearly discerned not in their efficient causality, which is unique and common, but in their exemplary causality, insofar as creatures are drawn to them asymmetrically: We are united to the Son, by the Holy Spirit (1 Cor 12:13). Here too, the agency of the Spirit is not a distinct efficient causality but precisely the formality of love, by which we are united to Christ (Rom 5:5: "God's love has been poured into our hearts through the Holy Spirit who has been given to us"). The Son in his divine-human unity is the "through whom" of creation, both as prototype and end of creation, as new Adam, as firstfruits.

77. Bavinck, *RD* 2, 425.

CHAPTER 5

The Incarnation of the Son Alone

A hard version of the doctrine of inseparable operations stands or falls with its ability to account for the orthodox claim that it was the Son of God alone who became incarnate, suffered, died, and was resurrected on the third day. The burden of this chapter is to show not only that there is no logical contradiction between the two claims but also that, when properly approached from the direction of the Trinity, the doctrine of the hypostatic union yields fundamental insights for the rest of Christian doctrine. In light of the inseparability rule, coupled with a doctrine of the divine processions and missions, the incarnation will not be framed in mythological terms of the descent of the Son from the bosom of the Trinity down the ontological ladder to act in the world, followed by his return upon his ascension. As Augustine and Aquinas have shown, such a view misunderstands the nature of the divine mission. Another picture suggests itself instead, that of the *traction* by the whole Trinity of the human nature into union with the eternal Son, resulting in the human existence of Jesus Christ. Christ thus becomes the gateway, the mediator between God and creation. Through his mission we have the self-donation of the Father, as well as the further mission of the Spirit. In and through Christ the whole creation thus returns to its supernatural source to receive its supernatural end, which is nothing less than communion with the Trinity culminating in the beatific vision. The first act of this return is the incarnation. This comprehensive view will be articulated across the next several chapters, resulting in a Christocentric approach that is nonetheless thoroughly Trinitarian.

The primary task of this chapter is to respond to the objection from the in-

---

This chapter adapts material that previously appeared in my article "Trinitarian Inseparable Operations and the Incarnation," *Journal of Analytic Theology* 4 (May 2016): 106–27. DOI: https://doi.org/10.12978/jat.2016-4.000318210820a. Used by permission.

carnation of the Son alone. The first section does that by distinguishing between acts and states and suggesting that the assumption of the human nature of Christ belongs to the whole Trinity insofar as it is regarded as an action, but it belongs to the Son alone when regarded as a state. The second section explains, using John Owen as a conversation partner, what is entailed by this in terms of which divine person can be understood to be the "immediate" operator upon this human nature. Our account raises two fundamental difficulties, addressed in the final two sections. First, should it not follow that the Son is the immediate operator upon his own human nature, since the assumption is an act that *terminates* precisely in him? Secondly, if the whole Trinity acts the incarnation and the Son makes no unique contribution to it, doesn't this make the Son and his human nature entirely extrinsic to each other, thereby obfuscating the reality of revelation?

ACTS AND STATES

We have seen that hard inseparability stipulates that for every token action in which a Trinitarian person is subject, the other two persons are also necessarily subjects. This rule applies to external operations only, and not to processions. As observed, all such internal Trinitarian traffic is constitutive of the personhood of Father, Son, and Spirit. Therefore, if the Son does a particular action *ad extra*, however that action may be described, the Father must also be understood to undertake the same action, and the Spirit as well.

The difficulty with regard to the incarnation is obvious. If one of the Son's actions can be described as "becoming incarnate," it should follow that the Father also "becomes incarnate" and the Spirit also "becomes incarnate." But these statements are obviously not orthodox and therefore must be rejected.

There are two fundamental ways of solving this dilemma that are open to supporters of hard inseparability. The first would be to deny that "becoming incarnate" or "assuming human nature" is an *opus ad extra*. In this case the assumption of a human nature is an act that defines the Son in his eternal identity and not merely in his economic works. This is obviously unacceptable for the following reasons. On the one hand, it would entail that the identity of the Son is determined by a relation he has to created reality. This would compromise his aseity and transcendence since it would make him dependent upon something other than God. On the other hand, it would entail that the personal property of the Son includes more than simply his procession from the Father.[1] As we have seen in the last chapter, such a position inevitably leads to

---

1. It is to be noted that the reaction to the inseparability tradition does gravitate toward

tritheism, since it would imply an ontological substrate distinct from the other person's substrate, on the basis of which such distinctions would obtain.

There is, however, a second possible approach to the difficulty. It rests on the denial that "assuming human nature" or "becoming incarnate" are actions. A brief excursus in the ontology of action can help clarify this distinction. On a broadly accepted definition of action, there are two necessary conditions for personal actions. First, a change needs to take place in the world. That is, there must be an *event* where there is a change from one state of the world to another. The change need not be material, but it can be a change in consciousness, for example counting, memorizing, remembering. The second condition is more interesting: Responsibility for the particular change must be ascribable to an intentional agent. In this way, actions can be regarded as a subclass of events.[2] John MacMurray captures well the distinction between actions and nonagential events: "What is done in action would not be at all but for the doing of it."[3] In this case, the action so identified is ascribed to the agent who caused or brought about the change or event. It is his action and no one else's, even though other agents may also be involved in the event.

Take for example the action of a butler dressing a lord. The event may be described as "the dressing of Lord John by butler Xavier." Here the butler is the active agent while the lord is the passive object of the action. The action of the dressing is ascribed to the butler while to the lord is ascribed the state of "being dressed."

Every action, therefore, insofar as it entails a change brought about in the state of the world, involves both activity and passivity. Thus, the event that the action brings about can be characterized in both of these terms. The event described above as "the dressing of Lord John by butler Xavier" can

---

blurring the line between works *ad extra* and *ad intra*, and these entailments would not be obviously false for these proponents. See for example, Wolfhart Pannenberg, *Systematic Theology*, trans. George W. Bromiley (Grand Rapids: Eerdmans, 1991), 1.308–19, esp. 317–19, where he argues that the economic relationships between the Father and Son are constitutive of the very identity of both Trinitarian persons. Notable is the vigorous rebuttal of Bruce D. Marshall, "The Dereliction of Christ and the Impassibility of God," in Thomas White, OP, ed., *Divine Impassibility and the Mystery of Human Suffering* (Grand Rapids: Eerdmans, 2009) and Paul Molnar, "Classical Trinity: Catholic Perspective," in Stephen Holmes, Paul Molnar, Thomas McCall, Paul Fiddes, *Two Views on the Doctrine of the Trinity*, ed. Jason S. Sexton (Grand Rapids: Zondervan, 2014).

2. One should register the opposing view of Kent Bach, for example, in "Actions Are Not Events," *Mind* 89 (1980): 114–20.

3. John MacMurray, "What Is Action?" In *Action Perception and Measurement*, vol. 17 of *Proceedings of the Aristotelian Society*, Supplemental volumes (1938), 75.

be described either in terms of intentional agency (whether intentional or unintentional), as in "Xavier dresses," or in terms of patiency, as in "John is being dressed," or without making appeal to action at all, as in "the dressing of Lord John."

We could now add some additional detail to our example. Let's assume that the lord is not entirely passive in the event, but he also takes an active role: He stretches out his feet, he inserts them into the shoes and his arms into the sleeves, he lifts his chin, and so on. In this case, the agency belongs to both the lord and the butler, yet it is still only the lord who is being dressed. The following action descriptions are true, then: "Xavier is dressing John," "John is dressing himself with the help of Xavier," and "John is being dressed by Xavier." Note the different kinds of verbs in these descriptions. We have performance verbs ("dressing"), and we have state verbs ("being"). It is nonproblematic to observe that the former designate performances (which together with activities are a subclass of actions) while the latter designate states.[4]

Now what particular kind of event does the "assumption of human nature" refer to? The tradition understands by this a particular relation that obtains between the human nature of Jesus and the second person of the Trinity. The relationship is understood to be one of dependence, whereby the human nature of Jesus depends on the person of the Word for its existence. We thus say that the human nature is *sustained* by the person of the Word, who "indwells" this human nature, to use the terminology of John Duns Scotus. Now this relationship is initiated by agency. Hence the event of the incarnation can be described both in terms of agency that brings about this relationship and in terms of the state created.

We thus have a prima facie plausible way of resolving the dilemma raised by the incarnation of the Son alone: "Assuming" human nature names an event, which has both active and passive dimensions. On the one hand, we have the active agency of an operator that causes the assumption of the human nature. There is a passive patient too, insofar as the assumption is predicated of, or terminates in, a particular person. Keeping in mind the distinction between action and passion is paramount here.

Aquinas, with his usual sensitivity to our *modus significandi*, applies this dual dimension of actions (action and passion) to the assumption: "In the

---

4. Anthony Kenny distinguishes in *Action, Emotion, and Will* (London: Routledge, 1963) between state-verbs, performance-verbs, and activity-verbs. For our purposes, we need only distinguish between states and actions, paying no further attention to the two subclasses of actions: performances and activities (171–86).

word 'assumption' are implied two things, viz. the principle and the term of the act."[5] Then follows the application of this distinction to our problem:

> Hence what has to do with action in the assumption is common to the three persons; but what pertains to the nature of the term belongs to one person in such a manner as not to belong to another; for the three persons caused the human nature to be united to the one person of the Son.[6]

From an action perspective the agency in the case of the incarnation-assumption belongs to the Trinity as a whole. Father, Son, and Holy Spirit are together *causing* the assumption. They are together bringing it about that a relationship of dependence obtains between the human nature and the person of the Son. However, from a state perspective it is said that the action terminates in the Son, namely that the action results in a state that characterizes the Son alone.[7] Similarly, Augustine writes that "the Trinity together produced both the Father's voice and the Son's flesh and the Holy Spirit's dove, though each of these single things has reference to a single person."[8]

The dressing analogy is helpful here: The state of being dressed (with these particular clothes) is predicated of Lord John alone even though both he and Xavier have caused this particular dressing. There is therefore no contradiction in saying that "the Son alone assumed human nature," as long as "assuming human nature" does not designate the action but the state resulting from the action.

The limitations of the dressing analogy should, however, also be pointed out. On a certain description of the action, it does indeed appear that both the lord and the butler are acting out the same operation. On closer inspection, however, it transpires that they are only acting the same action *types*, not however sharing all *token* actions. While both may be "doing the dressing of Lord John," as a specific, time-indexed action, each is doing a completely distinct token action (stretching out an arm versus pulling the sleeve up the lord's arm).

5. Thomas Aquinas, *Summa Theologica*, trans. the Fathers of the English Dominican Province (Westminster, MD: Christian Classics, 1981), 3, q. 3, a. 1.

6. Aquinas, *ST* 3, q. 3, a. 4.

7. Sometimes the Angelic Doctor captures this distinction with the contrast between union and assumption. He points out that the one who unites is not the same as the one who assumes: "For whatever Person assumes unites, and not conversely. For the person of the Father united the human nature to the Son, but not to Himself; and hence He is said to unite and not to assume" (*ST* 3, q. 2. a. 8).

8. Augustine, *The Trinity*, 2nd ed., trans. Edmund Hill, OP (Hyde Park: New City Press, 1991), 4.5.

These distinct sets of token actions are indeed subsets of a larger cooperative action, which is itself a token action (this particular dressing). Nevertheless, they remain individual sets of actions that the other person has no share in.

Manifestly, then, such an analogy, when pushed to its limits is counterproductive. It does illustrate the possibility of two persons sharing the same action token (the dressing of the Lord by the butler) yet not sharing the state (being dressed). Even if in this situation one must acknowledge the existence of other action tokens that are not shared, the existence of one such action token is sufficient to illustrate the distinction.

It may be useful to correct the dressing analogy with our magnetic simile. A needle is going to be pulled toward the magnet by the whole substance of the magnet, even while it will attach itself specifically to just one of its poles. This analogy too has its limitations. It cannot be said that the action of the magnet is an intentional action. But the presence of intention is not necessary for action. The sun's action of heating the earth is not an intentional action, yet it remains an action. Our example illustrates one dimension, and it illuminates a useful distinction that applies to both intentional and nonintentional actions. As we have seen, the ontology of triune action ultimately remains inscrutable. The best we can hope for is a specification of its grammar. Such illustrations must not be taken as being directly descriptive but rather as performing an analogical service.

Personal Causality of the Son upon the Human Nature?

The human nature of Jesus Christ is drawn by the whole Trinity into union specifically with the Son. But what is this relationship between the Son and the human nature? While there is clearly a causality exercised by the whole Trinity in the *tractio* of the created nature toward the Son, is there not also a specific personal causality of the Son upon this human nature, consequent upon the assumption?

This question will need to be approached from two angles spread across the present and the next chapter. From the first angle, it will need to be asked whether the fact that the assumption terminates in the Son requires that the Son possesses some exclusive causality upon his human nature. In this inquiry we will tease out the implications of the fact that this particular action (assumption) *terminates* in the person of the Son. But the question of a personal and exclusive causality of the Son must be asked from a second angle as well. Not only are we dealing with the act of assumption, but specifically with the *enhypostasia*. Does the subsistence of the human nature exclusively in the person of the Son not require a causality proper to him? The first approach to this broad issue is, so to speak, from above, asking about the significance of the fact that a divine act terminates in a divine person; the second is from below, considering the specifics of the hypostatic union and the enhypostatic existence of Christ's human nature.

Richard Cross observes that "the medievals all argue for the possibility of just one person's becoming incarnate by noting that the state of being incarnate does not in itself place an incarnate being in any sort of causal relationship external to that being. For the Son to become incarnate does not require his exercising any causal power other than that exercised by the three divine persons."[9] Where such a causality exists it belongs to the Trinity as a whole.

Duns Scotus advances two reasons why the dependence relationship between the human nature and the second person of the Trinity is not causal: "because that relation is common to the whole Trinity—nor is it a relation of 'what is caused later to what is caused earlier,' because the Word is not anything caused."[10] On the one hand, all creatures have a relationship of causal dependence upon God and hence the dependence of Christ's human nature would be indistinguishable from the broader relation of human dependence on God. Secondarily, where causality is concerned, it belongs to the whole Trinity.

It is tempting to caricature Duns Scotus's theology, together with most of the medieval tradition, as making the claim that it is the nature of God that acts and thus coming into conflict with the Aristotelian claim *actiones sunt suppositorum*. Duns Scotus writes that "essence qua essence as a principle of acting acts only after the manner of nature [i.e., necessarily]. Now God causes nothing extrinsic to himself in this fashion."[11] God's nature—as nature—does not act externally. Divine persons do, on the basis of that nature. Thus to say that the whole Trinity acts externally is not to say that the divine substance acts, but only that the persons do in virtue of the simple divine substance.

On the Protestant side, the argument that no personal causality (of the

---

9. Richard Cross, *The Metaphysics of the Incarnation: Thomas Aquinas to Duns Scotus* (Oxford: Oxford University Press, 2007), 152–53.

10. John Duns Scotus, *The Ordinatio of Blessed John Duns Scotus*, trans. Peter L. P. Simpson 3.1.1. Duns Scotus also argues his claim on the basis of the incommunicability of the persons: "Since there is a twofold idea of entity, namely quidditative and hypostatic, then, just as it belongs to quidditative entity to give being of itself, because it is of itself communicable, so it belongs to hypostatic entity not to be an act giving being, because as 'that in which,' it is of itself incommunicable" (*Ordinatio* 3.1.2n183). Cf. Cross, *Metaphysics of the Incarnation*, 123.

11. John Duns Scotus, *God and Creatures: The Quodlibetal Questions*, trans. F. Alluntis and A. B. Wolter (Princeton: Princeton University Press, 1975), 8.1.1.

Son) is consequent upon his assumption of the human nature has been made by John Owen. He follows the medieval tradition and argues that apart from assuming human nature, no other action of the eternal Word is *immediately* effected upon his human nature. He claims that "the only singular *immediate* act of the person of the Son on the human nature was the assumption of it into subsistence with himself. Herein the Father and the Spirit had no interest nor concurrence . . . 'but by approbation and consent,' as Damascen speaks."[12] He further notes that "the only necessary consequent of this assumption of the human nature, or the incarnation of the Son of God, is the personal union of Christ, or the inseparable subsistence of the assumed nature in the person of the Son."[13] What this means is that the incarnation does not *require* that the Son be the immediate agent of Christ's actions: "all other actings of God in the person of the Son towards the human nature were voluntary, and did not necessarily ensue on the union mentioned."[14] In fact, Owen insists, the Holy Spirit "is the *immediate* operator of all divine acts of the Son himself, even on his own human nature."[15]

Now while Owen seems to be supporting our claim that even incarnate actions do not belong immediately to the Son, he does seem to treat the Son's assuming of human nature as an action rather than a state. We grant that Owen is not availing himself explicitly of the distinction between action and state. However, he is implicitly suggesting something precisely like this. It is clear that Owen does not create exceptions to the inseparability rule, as we have seen. If that is the case, however, either Owen is inconsistent in suggesting that there is an "action" that is not shared by the Son with the other persons, or he is uncareful in his terminology. In his *Christologia*, Owen clarifies that even the assumption is the "act of the divine nature, and so, consequently, of the Father, Son and Holy Spirit" as regards "original efficiency," but "as unto

---

12. John Owen, *The Holy Spirit*, vol. 3 of *Works of John Owen* (Edinburgh: Banner of Truth Trust, 1966), 160.

13. Owen, *The Holy Spirit*, 160.

14. Owen, *The Holy Spirit*, 161.

15. Owen, *The Holy Spirit*, 162. Owen appeals specifically to the *opera ad extra* principle to clarify that "the immediate actings of the Holy Ghost are not spoken of him absolutely, nor ascribed to him exclusively, as unto the other persons and their concurrence in them." Now if the Spirit were a separate agent, this would have the counterintuitive consequence that the Holy Spirit is the immediate agent of another person's actions. This would indeed make little sense, for then these actions would not be this other person's, but the Spirit's. But the Spirit's actions on the human nature are not the Spirit's alone. What Owen has in mind is something more akin to the Spirit's being the proximal cause, or the perfecting cause of all that God works.

the term of the assumption, or the taking of our nature unto himself, it was the peculiar act of the person of the Son."[16] This closely parallels our distinction between action and passion, and it uses the classical terminology of principle and term of the action. In terms of the principle of the action, all persons are acting. Yet the effect of the action is only drawn into union with the second person. Owen, despite being somewhat imprecise in his use of "action" or "act" to denote the receiving by the Son of the human nature, remains unequivocal that even that assumption is efficiently caused by the whole Trinity.

The question before us is whether there is a personal causality of the Son upon his assumed human nature. For Owen there exists such a causality only as shared with the whole Trinity. Whatever divine operation is exercised upon the human nature of Jesus Christ, it is not exclusively the Son's but belongs to the inseparable efficient causality of the Trinity. We have found this to be consistent with our definition of action as the production of effects. It is possible to say that the whole Trinity is producing the effects that come forth from the human nature of Jesus Christ while also refusing to ascribe to the Father and the Spirit some of the resulting action descriptions. While the Son is one of the divine operators upon his own human nature, he is so only in conjunction with the Father and the Spirit.

However, to say that no divine actions operated upon the human nature of the Son belong exclusively to the Son still leaves the question of a whole other sets of operations, namely the natural operations of Christ's human nature in virtue of its enhypostatic existence in the Word specifically. We shall take up that question in the next chapter; now it is time to turn to two substantive objections to the position we have been constructing.

Consequences of Termination

The denial that the Son continues to act upon or through his human nature raises some serious issues. Oliver Crisp is concerned that Owen's proposal "has the consequence that God the Son is one step removed from his human nature."[17] He goes on to say: "If the human nature of Christ is 'owned' by the Son, it seems very strange that he is not the divine person *immediately* acting

---

16. John Owen, *The Glory of Christ*, vol. 1 of *Works of John Owen* (Edinburgh: Banner of Truth Trust, 1965), 225.

17. Oliver Crisp, *Revisioning Christology: Theology in the Reformed Tradition* (Farnham: Ashgate, 2011), 101.

upon, or through, his human nature."[18] Crisp fears that the intermediary role played by the Spirit removes the Son one step away from his nature.

There is a potential counterargument, based on the doctrine of inseparable operations, which Crisp acknowledges: "So even though the sustenance of the human nature of Christ is a Trinitarian act that devolves upon the Spirit in a peculiar manner, it is still a work of all three persons of the Godhead—God the Son included."[19] This inseparability-based reply attempts to remove the problem by suggesting that even though the Spirit is the person who *immediately* sustains the human nature of Christ, the Son is also involved in that same action and thus the perception of remoteness is false.

This response, however, does not assuage Crisp, since "it constitutes an inappropriate application of the *opera trinitatis ad extra* principle."[20] He explains: "This principle safeguards the doctrine of the Trinity whilst allowing for actions that terminate on particular divine persons. But it cannot be used to justify the agency of the Spirit in the incarnation at all moments after the Son assumes human nature *precisely because the Incarnation is the work that terminates upon the Son*."[21]

This is an important but not a fatal objection. It rests upon a certain preunderstanding of the concept of *termination*. But what it means for an action to terminate in a particular divine person is historically ambiguous. In fact, it must be argued that the concept of *terminus* does *not* service the *individuation* of various roles played by divine persons in external actions. I believe it is possible to distinguish between two senses of *terminus*.

A first sense, *terminus1* is characterized by the following usage. One person is the terminus of the action in the sense that such a person, besides sharing in the common Trinitarian causality (and thus agency), is also the passive recipient of this action, as this action necessarily involves an external term. In such a case, the conceptuality of "terminus" seems to fit best with the Aristotelian origins of Aquinas's philosophy of action. As Aristotle puts it in the *Metaphysics*, "the end and that for the sake of which something comes to be is the terminus of some action."[22] Aquinas too: "The end of human acts is their terminus, for that in which a human act terminates is that which the will [of the agent] intends as the end."[23] What is interesting here, though, is

18. Crisp, *Revisioning Christology*, 102.

19. Crisp, *Revisioning Christology*, 102.

20. Crisp, *Revisioning Christology*, 105.

21. Crisp, *Revisioning Christology*, 105 (my emphasis).

22. Aristotle, *Metaphysics* 2:996a18–996b26, in *The Complete Works of Aristotle*, ed. Jonathan Barnes (Princeton, NJ: Princeton University Press, 1984).

23. Aquinas, *ST* 2-I, 1, 3.

that, as Eleonore Stump notes, "the state of affairs sought after as the end of the action must be in some sense intrinsic to the action itself."[24] And Aquinas: "The end [of an act] is not something altogether extrinsic to the act because the end is related to the act as its principle or terminus."[25] In other words the formal quality of the act is determined by its end, or by the terminus. To take a mundane example, compare the action of clapping one's hands in order to trigger a light switch with the action of clapping one's hands in appreciation of a musical performance. The two actions look identical for an observer, but they are obviously distinguished by their ends. Thus their formal quality is determined by the ends they intend to bring about. In the case of the "humanation," or "incarnation," the end that is brought about is the existence of a relationship between a divine person and a created reality (the Word's *esse secundarium*).

There is, however, a second sense, *terminus2*, encountered in the literature. Here the terminus is the divine person at the far end of a divine agential chain. Bruce Marshall writes, "Depending on the action—especially the actions of the divine persons in relation to one another . . . any of the divine persons might be the primary agent (the one with whose propria the action has the greatest likeness) or the immediate agent (the one whose role terminates the action)."[26] In this sense of the notion, it is the Holy Spirit who seems to invariably serve as the terminus of divine actions, since he is the perfecting cause in addition to the originating (or efficient) cause (Father) and "moulding" (or formal) cause (Son).[27] As perfecting cause, the Spirit applies the agency of the three persons and is thus in a certain sense most proximal to its terminus. Care must be taken, however, not to imagine this "agential chain" as a descending ladder of intermediaries, for as we have seen, the essential will and power is equally possessed by the triune persons.

We should observe that termination, like appropriation, is not mutually exclusive and allows for the predication of different "termini" (in their respective senses) for the selfsame divine actions. Thus, the action of the incarnation can be said to terminate in the person of the Son in the first sense of terminus,

24. Eleonore Stump, *Aquinas* (London: Routledge, 2003), 82.

25. Aquinas, *ST* 1a2ae, q. 1, a. 3.

26. Bruce D. Marshall, *Trinity and Truth* (Cambridge: Cambridge University Press, 2000), 260.

27. The language of "agential chain" or what appear to be different kinds of causes should not obscure the fact that these are distinctions, not separations within the single and simple divine causality. The persons are not separate causes, but their contribution to divine agency is distinct, such that an overdetermination of the effect is avoided.

but also in the person of the Spirit in the second sense of terminus. Emery clarifies that according to Thomas a selfsame action can be appropriated to the three persons, respectively, when considered under different aspects: "It is thus that, for instance, our filial adoption is appropriated to the Father who is its author, or to the Son who is its model, or to the Holy Spirit, who engraves it in our hearts."[28]

The fact that we can assign different terms (in different senses) to different persons risks rendering the distinction useless. The whole point of the distinction was to enable us to identify for indivisible actions a sense in which these actions belong *primarily* to a particular person, such that the recognition of the persons is still possible on the basis of their actions in the economy. However, understanding the variety of possible uses of the term alerts us to the complexity of the unfolding of triune identities within each divine action. Also, the various senses also prevent us from univocal explanations of the structure of divine actions (such as cooperation, or chains of intermediaries). The slippage of the "terminus" between the various persons is a natural consequence of the way in which the persons are truly sharing the "principium" of the action.

A perichoresis of action follows from a perichoresis of persons, such that for every action token, including the action of assuming and, as we will show, incarnate actions, there is an entanglement of roles and terms. While this is an ordered entanglement, we should resist assigning neat 'roles' and 'functions', or a superficial mapping out of the structure of economic works. The bottom line here is that the terminology of *principium* and *terminus*, together with the language of appropriation, is not intended as a univocal way of parsing out the ontological structure of divine actions as much as it is a heuristic device to facilitate our communion with distinct persons through reflection on their indivisible actions. It is not a principle of individuating particular "roles" persons play in action tokens. To say that an action terminates in this or that person is relative to the way in which the action is being described.[29]

We may now return to Crisp's objection. He is in essence arguing that, insofar as the incarnation is an action that *terminates* in the Son, at least some of the incarnate actions have to belong *immediately* to the Son. We may begin by noting a terminological equivocation here. Crisp's use of "immediate" seems to

---

28. Gilles Emery, *The Trinitarian Theology of Saint Thomas Aquinas*, trans. Francesca Aran Murphy (Oxford: Oxford University Press, 2007), 335. See Aquinas, *ST* 3, q. 23, a. 2, ad. 3.

29. In other words, *terminus* is an intensional term. Our descriptions individuate this or that person and this or that (appropriated) personal action, but this is done on the basis of the intension rather than the extension of those descriptions.

follow Marshall's distinction between primary and immediate agents and not so much Owen's distinction between eminent and immediate agency. By "immediate" agency Owen means actions accomplished by just one of the persons, with whom the others have no concurrence but by approbation and support. There is only one such "action," our objections to Owen's language having been noted, and this is the assumption of the human nature. Marshall's notion of "immediate agent" closely parallels the subject of our *terminus*2. It refers to the person at the end of the Trinitarian agential chain, the person most proximate to the effect.

If Crisp truly does use Owen's particular sense of "immediate," he would be in effect undermining the doctrine of inseparable operations, or at least creating exceptions to it, and it is not apparent that he wishes to do that.[30] In such a case, what he would mean by "immediate" is actions that would not have the concurrence of the other divine persons.

However, if Crisp has in mind something like Marshall's sense of "immediate," then to claim that at least some of the incarnate actions would need to be immediately Christ's is consistent with the inseparability rule. In this case, it would only insist that there are incarnate actions that, although enacted through the common agency of the three, are nevertheless most *proximate* to the Son. But these actions would still not belong immediately to the Son (in Owen's sense); that is, they would not be exclusively acted by him. Hence Owen's insistence that the incarnation only requires a single immediate action of the Son—the assumption of the human nature—seems to be warranted.

However, one obstacle needs to be overcome in Crisp's objection. He is suggesting that the doctrine of inseparable operations cannot be invoked to parse the action of the incarnation precisely because the incarnation "terminates" on the Son. Crisp appears to hold that the incarnation is an action that has already been "assigned" to the Son, in which case it no longer comes under the jurisdiction of inseparability. But what does this mean? It could mean that the incarnation is that "segment" of an "external operation" that is accomplished by the Son. But this is wrong, for in this case divine actions are after all divided and apportioned neatly to distinct persons. As we have noted, the idea that a given action "terminates" in this or that person should not be turned into a principle of individuation.[31] Thus, to say that an action terminates in one of the persons does not indicate an exclusive operator of that action.

30. Crisp nowhere advocates either abandoning the doctrine of inseparable operations or creating exceptions; on the contrary, he consistently affirms it throughout his work, although he holds that Owen misapplies the rule in this particular case.

31. For more on this, see Bruce D. Marshall, "What Does the Spirit Have to Do?" in *Reading John with St. Thomas Aquinas: Theological Exegesis and Speculative Theology*, ed.

To say that the incarnation is a work that terminates in the Son does not rule out other modes of the same action that may be said to terminate in other Trinitarian persons. The language of *principium-terminus* is not an ontologically univocal way of differentiating between divine actions. Rather, it belongs to our *modus significandi*, such that for selfsame actions we are able to distinguish (under different perspectives) different persons who terminate and to whom these actions are appropriated. In virtue of the state of affairs that it accomplishes, the assumption of a human nature *terminates*1 in the Son; in virtue of the proximity, it may be said, according to the Scriptures themselves, that it *terminates*2 in the Holy Spirit.

This is not to deny that there are actions upon the human nature that are eminently (in Owen's sense) accomplished by the Son. But these are not immediately (or uniquely, exclusively) caused by the Son but are rather brought about through the same indivisible agency that belongs to the three persons together. The actions that are accomplished "through the human nature" of the Son are in fact actions of the whole Godhead, yet these are actions that are executed in virtue of a relationship of dependence between the Son and a human nature.

Does Christ's Humanity Reveal the Son?

The first objection we have taken up concerns the ontological dimension of the incarnation: Shouldn't immediate actions of the Son be required by the fact that the incarnation terminates in the Son? In response to this it was pointed out that the category of *terminus* does not function to individuate the various roles of the divine persons within divine actions. The second objection we have to consider is of an epistemological sort. The worry is expressed that if the human nature of Jesus Christ is merely an effect of the common triune causality it therefore remains extrinsic to the Son himself, considered in his personal distinctiveness, and therefore it cannot possibly be the medium of the revelation of the Son.

It was already noted that this epistemological consideration lies behind much of the sentiment against hard inseparability in modern theology. Robert Jenson writes:

Michael Dauphinais, Matthew Levering (Washington, DC: Catholic University of America Press, 2010), esp. 69. For an alternative perspective, cf. Najeeb Awad, *God Without a Face: On the Personal Individuation of the Holy Spirit* (Tübingen: Mohr Siebeck, 2011).

The Augustinian supposition that there is no necessary connection between what differentiates the triune identities in God and the structure of God's work in time bankrupts the doctrine of the Trinity cognitively, for it detaches language about the triune identities from the only thing that made such language meaningful in the first place: the biblical narrative.[32]

In Jenson's view the pattern of relationships between the divine persons that the biblical narratives exhibit must have a "necessary connection" to that which differentiates the personal identities of Father, Son, and Spirit. He believes the Augustinian principles confine the revelation of the divine persons to a strictly propositional level of what the Scriptures assert. However,

When logically detached from the biblical triune narrative, the Nicene-Cappadocian propositions about the immanent Trinity become formulas without meaning we can know. . . . But meaningless forms of words, or forms of words whose meaningfulness is posited but declared unknowable by us, can be recited but cannot be put to any other use. If propositions about God's immanent triunity are denied cognitive content, they cannot function in the life of the church or elsewhere in the system of theology.[33]

The concern for the divine transcendence is so overbearing for Augustine, in Jenson's view, that he is prevented from taking seriously the unfolding of the personal identities taking place in the Scriptures. The problem is compounded, as we have previously noted, by Aquinas's claim that any of the divine persons might have become incarnate. Aquinas writes that "the Divine power could have united human nature to the Person of the Father or of the Holy Ghost, as It united it to the Person of the Son. And hence we must say that the Father or the Holy Ghost could have assumed flesh even as the Son."[34]

Rahner has serious reservations about the implications of this position. We shall quote him at length:

If we admit that every divine person might assume a hypostatic union with a created reality, then the fact of the incarnation of the Logos "reveals" properly nothing about the Logos himself, that is, about his own relative specific

32. Robert Jenson, *Systematic Theology,* Volume 1: *The Triune God* (Oxford: Oxford University Press, 1997), 112.
33. Jenson, *The Triune God,* 113.
34. Aquinas, *ST* 3, q. 3, a. 5.

features within the divinity. For in this event the incarnation means for us practically only the experience that God in general is a person, something which we already knew. It does not mean that in the Trinity there is a very special differentiation of persons. Although we know (having been told so in statements) that precisely the second divine person exercises a hypostatic function with respect to the human reality visible in Jesus, there would be no difference in our experience if some other divine person constituted the subsistence of this human reality. Since Jesus speaks of the Father and of himself as "Son," the reality which we perceive in salvation history yields us an outlook into the Trinity through words, not through itself. Since that which happens in salvation history might have happened through each other person, since it is but the neutral vehicle of a merely verbal revelation, not the revelation of some intra-trinitarian occurrence, it tells us nothing about intra-trinitarian life.[35]

Rahner stresses that the Western classical approach, through the doctrine of inseparable operations, reduces revelation to propositional revelation. The immanent relationships within the Trinity are not given to us phenomenologically. Since the created reality of the human nature might have been indifferently assumed by all Trinitarian persons, it bears no intrinsic relation to the Logos.

The consequence of the Augustine-Aquinas position, he argues, is that the incarnation gives us nothing unique about the Son if it is merely the effect of the divine efficient causality. Rahner argues that there are relations between the Trinity and creation that do not pertain to the common efficient causality. The doctrine of inseparable operations applies only in those cases where the "supreme efficient cause" is concerned. But, he continues, there are nonappropriated relations of a single person, where we have a "quasi-formal communication" of God.[36] By "quasi-formal communication" he means that there is a sense in

---

35. Karl Rahner, *The Trinity*, trans. J. F. Donceel (London: Burns and Oates, 2001), 28.

36. Rahner, *The Trinity*, 77. Rahner's notion of "quasi-formal" causality is complex, and we shall examine it in the final chapter. Rahner expands on this notion in his "Some Implications of the Scholastic Concept of Uncreated Grace," in *God, Christ, Mary and Grace*, vol. 1 of *Theological Investigations*, trans. Cornelius Ernst (London: Darton, Longman and Todd, 1961), 328. A more accessible discussion is also present in Rahner, "The Holy Spirit as the Fruit of Redemption," in *The Content of Faith: The Best of Karl Rahner's Theological Writings*, ed. Karl Lehmann and Albert Raffelt (New York: Crossroad, 1994). For more on this, see David Coffey, *"Did You Receive the Spirit When You Believed?": Some Basic Questions for Pneumatology* (Milwaukee: Marquette University Press, 2005), 10–41; William J. Hill, *The*

which a distinct person is not merely the extrinsic cause of an effect, yet without claiming that this divine person enters into composition with another nature.

With regard to the incarnation, Rahner writes: "Something occurs 'outside' the intra-divine life in the world itself, something which is not a mere effect of the efficient causality of the triune God acting as one in the world, but something which belongs to the Logos alone."[37] Hence, the particular type of relation between a divine person and a created effect that occurs in the incarnation serves as a model for other relations between created realities and distinct Trinitarian persons. The incarnation is "a dogmatically certain instance . . . for an economic relation proper to each person, of the divine persons in the world."[38]

The assumption made by Rahner is that unless the Son alone communicates himself to the human nature in the order of quasi-formality, we are left with only a verbal understanding of revelation since the option of unique personal actions is excluded by Rahner (in keeping with the inseparability rule). As the quasi-form of the human nature, the Son is no longer merely extrinsically related to it. In this case, our experience of Jesus Christ is precisely an experience of the eternal Logos in his *proprium*.

Rahner's solution is to tighten the relation between nature, in this case the human nature of Jesus, and the supernatural, in this case the eternal Logos. Reuniting nature and the supernatural (grace) has indeed been the trajectory of much modern Trinitarian theology. Rahner's solution is different from a major kindred option—similarly held by LaCugna, Pannenberg, and Bruce McCormack—which is to make nature constitutive of the supernatural (see chapter 7 below). Whereas Rahner argues that nature and the supernatural are compatible, such that the eternal person of the Word can become the (quasi-)form of a created nature, the others would insist that the natural is constitutive of the supernatural, risking to sacrifice divine aseity, as we shall argue below.

There is much that is at stake in this discussion. While Rahner's and Jenson's appeals touch a sensitive and important chord in Christian sensibility, they are fraught with the danger of obscuring the ontological distinction between

---

Three-Personed God: The Trinity as a Mystery of Salvation (Washington, DC: Catholic University of America Press, 1982), 293; and John P. Galvin, "An Invitation of Grace," in Leo J. O'Donovan, ed., *A World of Grace: An Introduction to the Themes and Foundations of Karl Rahner's Theology* (New York: Seabury Press, 1980).

37. Rahner, *Trinity*, 23.
38. Rahner, *Trinity*, 27.

Creator and creature. In what way could it be said about a reality of an entirely different order that it is *experienced* on the created level of existence? Returning to the imagination of *Flatland*, a sphere cannot be experienced as sphere in a two-dimensional space. To say that it could is to disregard the dimensional difference.

But we also have excellent reason to think that Aquinas's position is entirely defensible and that it satisfies Jenson's and Rahner's common desideratum. The context for Aquinas's statement above is the question of whether each of the divine persons could have assumed human nature. He invokes the principle of the shared power of the three: "Whatever the Son can do, so can the Father and the Holy Ghost, otherwise the power of the three Persons would not be one. But the Son was able to become incarnate. Therefore the Father and the Holy Ghost were able to become incarnate."[39] Aquinas is primarily interested in defending the thought that the incarnation does not indicate any additional ability or capacity possessed by the Son as opposed to the other persons. But he says nothing about how an incarnation of the Father or the Holy Spirit might have looked. He does not, however, assume that it would have been identical. So the claim that the created human nature of Jesus Christ does not reveal the *proprium* of the Son is false.

Dominic Legge clearly explains this:

> This argument says nothing about what would have to change on the created side in a world where the Father or the Holy Spirit became man; Aquinas leaves that question entirely out of account because this article is not exploring counter-factual hypotheticals (contrary to what is often supposed), but rather aims to clarify how the divine power, common to all three persons, is related to the one divine person who did in fact become incarnate.[40]

There are two dimensions to a divine mission: the procession and the created effect. While the created effect is distinct from the procession, and while it is drawn into union with the proceeding person by the common efficiency of the Trinity, it nevertheless receives the mode of existence of the person to whom it is united. So it is possible to say that a created reality, when drawn into union with a divine person, begins to resemble this divine person and

39. Aquinas, *ST* 3, q. 3, art. 5, sed contra.
40. Dominic Legge, *The Trinitarian Christology of Saint Thomas Aquinas* (Oxford: Oxford University Press, 2017), 125–26.

begins to enact, in its created finite existence, the particular *esse* of the divine person, or rather, the divine *esse* as it is manifested by the divine person. In being united to the divine person the created reality is lifted above its created capacities to the supernatural order. Thus, the human nature of Jesus Christ, in being united to the Logos begins to manifest the mode of existence of the Logos. Legge puts it as follows:

> Each of the divine persons has and is the divine esse in its complete perfection. But, as Thomas reminds us here, the personal mode according to which each person subsists is different from each divine person. This means that, while each divine person could equally be a terminus according to being, the personal mode that would characterize the resulting union would be different in each case. Consequently, according to the personal mode that characterizes its every aspect, the incarnation of the Son would be vastly different from a hypothetical incarnation of the Father or the Holy Spirit.[41]

The true consequent upon the union with a particular person, therefore, is not the exercise of that person's unique efficient causality upon the created nature. Rather, it is the elevation of that nature beyond its natural and inherent capacities as it is made to exemplify the unique mode of existence of the person. The assumption does not result in unique actions of the person sent because there is no distinct divine nature in virtue of which such actions could be accomplished.

The magnet as a whole attracts the needle and it attaches the needle to one of the poles of the magnet. Now the receiving pole does not begin to exercise a unique causality through the needle, since it only exists relationally. Neither does the receiving pole become intrinsic to the needle. The needle remains what it is, and so do the magnet and its poles. However, the needle becomes magnetized, and it begins to act as a magnet without itself being a magnet. It receives its new mode of action from the magnet to which it is attached. The union of the two demonstrates that there is a compatibility of the two, but in such a way that the two substances remain what they are. And yet the needle is instrumentalized by the magnet.

With appropriate safeguards we can analogize this to the hypostatic union. The eternal Word remains extrinsic to the human nature in the sense that he is ontologically distinct from it, as uncreated. That said, the human nature upon its union with the Logos begins to manifest the unique mode of existence of

41. Legge, *Trinitarian Christology*, 126.

the Logos on its own created level of existence. To anticipate a further discussion, this means that the eternal receptivity of the Logos, that is, the thought that his entire being and existence are received from the Father, is played out on a human level through the human obedience of Jesus Christ. As Legge puts it, Christ's "human nature is always marked by the filial mode of existing proper to the divine Son who subsists in that human nature."[42]

This is very far indeed from the thought that the human nature is merely extrinsic to the eternal Son and therefore mediates a merely verbal revelation. The human nature mediates the revelation of the Son because it supernaturally acquires the personal *esse* (existence) of the Son as its ultimate metaphysical foundation. But this personal *esse* is nothing but his filial mode of existence, whereby the Son receives everything from the Father—and returns everything back to the Father in love. The personal action of Jesus Christ manifests precisely this receptivity in the mode of obedience. It is thus quite wrong to say that the human existence of Jesus reveals nothing of the Son's *proprium*. Nevertheless, the reason for the true manifestation of immanent *taxis* is not that the Son has become intrinsic to the human nature (as in a formal cause), or that the nature has become constitutive of the eternal person, but rather that the human nature has acquired the mode of existence and action of the Son.

How then does the revelation of the unique identity take place through the human nature of Christ? In addition to the propositional mode, which clarifies and enhances what is experienced, there is an experience of sonship that is consequent upon the assumption of the human nature by the Son himself. Had the Father or the Spirit become incarnate, the assumed nature would have been elevated to a different modality of existence and action, about which we can only speculate. The phenomenological encounter with the human Christ, however, is an encounter with the fullness of God, for in him the fullness of the deity is present but at the same time with the personal *esse* of the Son. This personal *esse* of the Son becomes the metaphysical foundation for everything Christ does, for everything he knows and feels. However, because the personal existence of the Son does not divide the divine essence, it is entirely relational. Therefore, in seeing Christ, one has seen the Father—and the Holy Spirit.

We know Christ as the Son of God because—with the eyes of faith—we discern the supernatural operation of God at work in him. But not only that: We see this operation as a received operation. The Son only does what he sees the Father doing. The divine operation of Christ is in the mode of receptivity, or in a filial mode. The human nature of Christ can only reveal the Son in the

42. Legge, *Trinitarian Christology*, 111.

same breath as it reveals the fullness of God because the person is nothing but the divine essence upon a relational property. We have no experience of God as transcendent, for we are but three-dimensional creatures with a cap on our phenomenological abilities. But we do have an experience of the exclusively divine creative, redemptive, and sanctifying action, and all this is in the person of Jesus Christ.

Conclusion

Far from corseting Christology in the straightjacket of an abstract metaphysical rule, the doctrine of inseparable operations brings out the full religious significance of the incarnation. In Christ we experience not simply one of the Trinity come down with the mere approbation of the others; in Christ we are experiencing the whole Trinity in the mode of sonship. Keen attention to the inseparability rule should convey our experience of the Son and our experience of the full Trinity all in one breath. The Son is never without the fullness of the Godhead, and the Godhead is never an impersonal or suprapersonal abstraction.

Theology confesses that in the person of Jesus Christ we have a visible mission of the Son. As mission, it involves two dimensions. In its dimension of created effect the mission is understood to be appropriated to the Son since the created nature is brought about by the inseparable operation. However, on the side of the procession the mission truly makes available the person of the Son in his *proprium*. In this sense the mission is not appropriated. But the *proprium* of the Son is purely relational and not a set of substantial qualities. For this reason, it cannot be experienced except in inseparable connection with the *propria* of the Father and the Spirit. Nonetheless, the created nature acquires this mode of existence, which includes both the relational properties as well as its substantial properties.

But the rabbit hole goes deeper. If we take seriously the framework of the missions, with all the classical Trinitarian assumptions that it makes, we will have effected a change of perspective. Instead of thinking of Christ in mythological terms of a divine person's ontological descent, we shall have to think of Christ as a sort of cipher of the Trinity. In the mission of the Son it is rather the human nature that is drawn into union with the Word. No change in God is envisioned by this account but only a change in the human nature. The Trinity keeps on doing what it does eternally yet this time with the humanity along for the ride.

In the assumption the two natures remain extrinsic to one another. And yet this is not the last word. Although the human nature does not acquire the quasi-form of the Son, it nevertheless acquires the Son's mode of existence and action. The humanity enters a process of transformation, consequent upon the hypostatic union, whereby its capacities are lifted to share in the power and wisdom of God. The next chapter pays closer attention to the synergy of human and divine operations. But we can anticipate something more than a simple synergy of operation. Because the human nature acquires the mode of existence of the Son, and because this mode entails not simply receptivity (from the Father) but also productivity (the procession of the Spirit), the humanity of Christ in its supernatural existence as the Son not only channels the Father (John 14:9) but also delivers the Spirit. This is the true meaning of Christ as the cipher of the Trinity: The complete fellowship of divine persons is accessible precisely in the humanity of Jesus Christ and yet not as intrinsic to it. This announces a Trinitarian Christocentrism where the humanity of Christ plays a foundational hermeneutical role with respect to our understanding and experience of the Trinity, yet only because by acquiring the modality of the Son it also necessarily mediates the modalities of of the Spirit and the Father.

CHAPTER 6

Christology and Trinitarian Agency

The Christian faith holds that the man Jesus Christ was the incarnate Son of God—that one of the Trinity assumed a human nature, suffered, died, and was resurrected. It is part of the universal confessions of the church that the incarnation is to be predicated of the Son alone. The church similarly condemned *patripassianism*, which is the idea that the Father suffered on the cross. In the background of these crystal clear theological pronouncements stands the thought that the distinction between the triune persons must be preserved. Modalism is thus seen to threaten any account that ascribes the same actions and the same passions to all triune persons.

It would appear, however, that the present account of hard inseparability necessarily implies precisely such a confusion of the persons and their actions. If the Trinitarian operations *ad extra* are indivisible, that is, if they enact the same efficient causality, and moreover if the actions of Christ are the actions of God himself, it seems to follow that the actions of Christ are equally the actions of the Father and of the Spirit. In this case the whole ground is removed from underneath the confession of the distinction between the persons since such distinctions are (at least) epistemologically grounded in the economic distinctions. It is precisely in God's external work that we witness the Father sending the Son, speaking to the Son; and the Son praying to the Father and sending the Holy Spirit. Jewish monotheism is revised precisely under the pressure of these revealed mighty acts of the Trinitarian persons. It is therefore incumbent upon the present account to demonstrate that it does not clash with the church's confession of these distinctions, and especially with the notion of the incarnation of the Son alone.

The previous chapter found no contradiction in affirming both a hard inseparability and the doctrine of the incarnation of the Son alone. We did so by invoking the distinction between the activities involved in the incarnation, which come under the single efficiency of the whole Trinity, and the state of being incarnate, which properly belongs to the Son alone.

One might suppose however that a necessary consequence of the human nature's belonging exclusively to the Son is that the actions that derive from that nature are also properly the Son's and not simply appropriated to him, especially since the human nature is *enhypostatic* in the Son. The matter at hand concerns specifically the human activity of Christ. Whereas the last chapter spotlighted the activity of the eternal Son in the incarnation, we now have to probe particularly into the human actions of Christ. Do even these human actions belong to the whole Trinity, or must they be attributed to the Son alone? It is important to stress that we are here in a domain not regulated by the church's conciliar statements. The latter authoritatively affirm only the truth of the incarnation of the Son alone. Thus, we are in a territory quite open to a diversity of opinions, as we shall see.

The question before us has to be specified more precisely, however. There are two ways of posing the problem. The first is a question about proper *predication* or *attribution*: Who is the subject of Christ's human activity? Are the human actions of Jesus to be attributed to the Son exclusively, or to the whole Trinity? When Christ is praying in Gethsemane, is it appropriate to say that the Son of God alone, through his human nature, is praying to the Father? Or should we say, the Trinity is praying in and through the human nature of the Son?

A second way of framing the issue is along *ontological* or *causal* lines: Is there an exclusive causality exercised by the eternal Son, by one of the Trinity, proceeding through his human nature toward his human works, a causality in which the other divine persons do not have a share?

Such a distinction is all-important and not merely pedantic. In the case of human actions, such a distinction would indeed appear almost redundant. It goes without saying that the subject of an action (predication) is also causally responsible for it (causation). However, given the unique nature of triune causality, as we have seen, this continuity (between subject of attribution and causality) cannot be simply taken for granted in this case either.

In the following, both ways of posing the question must be considered. We must keep an open mind to the possibility of ascribing, much like in the case of the assumption of the human nature, a common causality to the whole Trinity with a proper assumptive relation to the Son alone. The possibility is at least in principle open for us to affirm that the Son is indeed the subject of Christ's human activity, while the causality of these actions belongs properly to the whole Trinity.

Settling this question is not simply a necessary defensive maneuver for hard inseparability. Rather, it will lead to a constructive unpacking of the relations between Father, Son, and Spirit in their common presence in Christ's redemptive acts. Moreover, as the next chapter will probe, it will shed light on the triune interpersonal dimension of Christ's passion.

We will proceed in the following way. The question posed in general terms is this: What implications follow from the proper and nonappropriated nature of the assumption for the agency of Christ's human actions? Do the human actions belong exclusively to the Son, or are they merely appropriated to him? The first section charts some of the historical positions taken on this issue. What we are asking, then, concerns the relationship between natures and actions. If a nature is exclusively assumed by one of the Trinity, does it follow that its actions also exclusively belong to (predication) or are exclusively caused (ontology) by the same? The second section will further probe the manner in which actions relate to the natures and persons. However, in Christ there are two natures, divine and human, and one person. The person is the eternal Son, one of the Trinity. We shall have to ask in the third section how the divine person and the two natures are ordered to each other in activity. This is where we discuss specifically the consequences of the hypostatic union for Christ's activity. We are no longer simply in the general domain of persons and natures but in the specific Christological domain of divine natures and anhypostatic versus enhypostatic human natures. Our solution to the problem will emerge in this section. The fourth section engages in a discussion of so-called theandric action, which refers to the manner in which the human activity of Christ is instrumentalized by his divine activity, yet without destroying the authenticity of Christ's human nature. In the final section, we will deal with one fundamental question—though by no means the only fundamental one— that follows from this account of Christological agency. Given that the human actions of the Son are allowed to transit (as far as causality is concerned) to the other divine persons, what, if anything, should block the inference that the human passions of the Son should also be allowed to transit to the other divine persons? More simply, can the patripassian consequence be avoided?

The Witness of Tradition

The whole tradition is at one that only the Son of God has assumed a human nature. But does it similarly conclude that only the Son of God acts through his human nature? We shall enumerate a number of instances that pertain to this question, including some more recent statements on this theme.

One of the central and most influential texts on this issue comes from Pseudo-Dionysius the Areopagite, whom we will quote at length here:

> An instance of differentiation [between the triune persons] is that benevolent act of God in our favor by which the transcendent Word wholly and completely took on our human substance and acted in such a way as to do and suffer all that was particularly appropriate and exalted within his divinely human activity. This was something in which the Father and the Spirit had no share, unless, of course, one is talking of the benevolent and loving divine will and of the entire supreme and ineffable act of God performed in the human realm by him who as God and as Word of God is immutable.[1]

Another theological authority, John Damascene, after pointing out that "the divinity is simple and has one simple operation," goes on to say,

> On the other hand, everything that pertains to the divine and benevolent incarnation of the Word of God has a distinct application. For, in these, neither the being Father nor the being Spirit is in any way communicated save by good pleasure and the ineffable wondrous operation which God the Word worked, when, while being God unchangeable and the Son of God, he became a man like us.[2]

And later in the same work, *The Orthodox Faith:* "Let us not be constrained to say that all the persons of the sacred Godhead, the Three, that is, were hypostatically united to all the persons of humanity. For in no wise did the Father and the Holy Ghost participate in the incarnation of the Word except by Their good pleasure and will."[3]

It is not at all apparent that Damascene denies a participation of Father and Spirit in the human works of Christ as much as he denies that they too assumed flesh, or that they were "communicated." On the other hand, Damascene affirms quite clearly that, as far as Christ's divine operation is concerned, this is carried out inseparably with the Father and the Spirit: "Even

1. Pseudo-Dionysius, *The Divine Names* 2.6, in *Pseudo-Dionysius: The Complete Works* (New York: Paulist, 1987), 63.

2. John Damascene, *The Orthodox Faith* 1.10, in *Writings: The Fount of Knowledge, The Philosophical Chapters, On Heresies & On the Orthodox Faith*, ed. F. H. Chase (Ex Fontibus, 2015), 191.

3. John Damascene, *The Orthodox Faith*, 3.6.

after the incarnation He is not only consubstantial with the Father but also has the same operation."[4] This is of a part with the confession by Damascene of the two operations, or energies of Christ: human and divine. With many in the tradition, he ascribes the divine activity to the inseparable agency of the Trinity, while the assumption and the incarnation itself are predicated of the Son alone. Yet Damascene is frustratingly quiet on the subject or agent of the human operation of the Word.

Aquinas, on the other hand, tackles this issue more directly. Quoting from the same section, quoted above, in Pseudo-Dionysius's *Divine Names*, he writes that the Father and the Holy Spirit do not share in what "pertains to the human operation."[5] This is not quite what one would have expected, given Thomas's strong affirmation of our hard inseparability thesis. Yet, Thomas's position is strongly qualified by the distinction between the two operations of Christ. This will need to be borne in mind when we return to a fuller discussion of Thomas below. He writes, "Hence it is clear that the human operation in which the Father and the Holy Ghost do not share, except by their merciful consent, is distinct from His operation, as the Word of God, wherein the Father and the Holy Ghost share."[6]

From this brief survey of some major authorities it would seem to follow quite clearly that the human actions of Christ must be ascribed exclusively to the Word and that the Father and the Spirit have no share in them. It is particularly interesting to note that the clearest ascription of exclusive activity to the Son comes from precisely the theologian we would expect to deny it, given his strong stance on hard inseparability.

Many modern theologians seem to agree that Christological agency belongs exclusively to the Son, at least as far as his human activity goes. Pannenberg writes, for instance, that "the incarnation is a specific instance of the intervention of a divine person in worldly reality" and that "only the persons of the Son and Spirit act directly in creation. The Father acts in the world only through the Son and Spirit. He himself remains transcendent."[7]

Vanhoozer echoes the same position: "The particular identities of Father, Son, and Spirit follow from the activities that distinguish them—both the eternal activities (i.e., the processions—begetting, spiration) that characterize

4. John Damascene, *The Orthodox Faith*, 3.15.

5. Thomas Aquinas, *Summa Theologica*, trans. the Fathers of the English Dominican Province (Westminster, MD: Christian Classics, 1981) 3, q. 19 a. 1, ad. 1.

6. Aquinas, *ST* 3, q. 19 a. 1, ad. 1.

7. Wolfhart Pannenberg, *Systematic Theology*, trans. George W. Bromiley (Grand Rapids: Eerdmans, 1991), 2:328.

the immanent Trinity and the historical acts (i.e., the missions—incarnation, Pentecost) that characterize the economic Trinity."[8]

The logic of the modern approach goes as follows: Activities distinguish persons. Unless Christ is seen to have a distinct activity either at the divine or the human level, or at both, his distinct personhood, or personal identity, cannot be established. That being said, as we have seen in our discussion of the patristic development of Trinitarian doctrine, the church fathers did not quite move directly from activity to persons. Rather, they followed the schema activity-power-nature to demonstrate from the common activity of the Son with the Father that they share the same powers and therefore the same nature.

What are we to conclude then? It would seem that the patristic approach carries the benefit of holding to the divine unity and of demonstrating the divinity of the Son. On the other hand, if inseparability is stressed too much, the personal distinctions seem to be lost. It is quite clear, as we have seen in our exegetical discussion, that one finds both distinction as well as inseparability in Christ's actions. Christ clearly relates to the Father, he prays to him, he obeys, he hands the kingdom to the Father. These distinctions are fundamental to the Christian faith. Conversely, Christ discloses that those who have seen him have seen the Father and that the works he is doing can be attributed to the Father: "The Father who dwells within me does his works" (John 14:10).

Whatever account of Trinitarian agency is formulated, it will have to account for both the personal distinction as well as the inseparable unity without reducing one to the other. It appears that the stalemate between the patristic schema of actions-powers-natures and what may be called the modern schema of actions-persons stems from a difference in conceptual frameworks. Modern thought seems to locate actions in persons; patristic and medieval thought (up to the high middle ages, at least) identifies natures as the spring of actions. It is therefore crucial to get some clarity about how persons and natures are related to actions.

PERSONS, NATURES, AND ACTIONS

We have suggested that in order to understand the discrepancy between the modern and the patristic approach, one must reveal the different philosophical assumptions in regard to action. From Duns Scotus onward, as we shall see, a

---

8. Kevin J. Vanhoozer, *Remythologizing Theology: Divine Action, Passion, and Authorship* (Cambridge: Cambridge University Press, 2012), 147–48.

different account of action becomes influential in Western thought, an account that uproots activity from nature and suspends it by the faculty of the free will, itself understood as standing free from nature.

This was not always the case, though. As Michel Barnes has demonstrated, there is a "technical" sense of power (and activity) that is operative among patristic defenders of the doctrine of the Trinity (Hilary, Ambrose, the Cappadocians) that locates powers in natures and sees operations as activations of these powers. Barnes's analysis of power philosophy can be extended to the philosophy of action. Much like powers, actions were seen to originate in natures.

The modern distinction between natural powers and intellectual powers does not mark off a realm of personal human actions that are somehow qualitatively distinct from natural activities of substances like fire, for example. While the distinction between free personal action and natural activity is most certainly not lost on ancient writers such as Aristotle, it does not indicate two incommensurable realms. As Charlotte Witt explains, "Unlike many philosophers, Aristotle does not draw a fundamental—or ontological—distinction between causal powers operating in nature like heat, and the causal powers, or abilities that originate purposive human actions, like the art of building, or practical reason."[9] The difference between these powers has to do, she goes on to explain, with their conditions of activation, and thus with how they are related to actuality. In rational powers, the form according to which the activity is what it is pre-exists in the artist. The form provides the logos, which guides the active power as a telos. In this case, it explains why the form of the product is different from the form of the cause. To take an example, builders build houses; they do not build other builders. In a nonrational power, on the other hand, the form of the activity is the same as the product. Nonrational powers reproduce themselves in other objects; rational powers, conversely, can produce contrary outcomes.

Even when rational substances (persons) act as causes, these act on the basis of capacities that are given in their natures. So for example a person can walk, but she cannot fly. The action of a person was not reduced to that causality that springs from the free will, but rather it was understood as that which the free will itself presupposes. A person can will only insofar as a person is already in act. A being that is not in act is not a real, concrete being. But to be in act is already to have some form of activity and energy. Moreover, this

9. Charlotte Witt, *Ways of Being: Potentiality and Actuality in Aristotle's Metaphysics* (Ithaca: Cornell University Press, 2003), 59.

energy is not passive with respect to the activity that flows from one's free will, but it conditions it and originates it in important ways.

The concept of will itself was understood to be located in nature and not in the person, as the controversy over monothelitism revealed. This is clearly counterintuitive for us moderns, although it was quite commonplace for fathers such as Maximus the Confessor. The exercise of free will, Maximus knows, already presupposes a will inclined by nature toward this or that object, whether the good in general, some particular good, or its own preservation.

The concept of will, as the monothelite controversy indicates, was extremely nuanced. Maximus distinguishes between many facets of the will, including *thelema*—"a capacity which holds together in being (*sunektike*) all the distinctive attributes (*idiomata*) which belong essentially to a being's nature."[10] Secondly, there is *orexis*, which is the will for itself, "a rational and vital desire (*orexis*), whereas *proairesis* is a desire, based on deliberation, for things that are up to us."[11] So there is a facet of the will that is up to us, so to speak, but it is always a continuation of other aspects of the will that are up to nature.

Richard Sorabji finds in Maximus a derivation of the Stoic notion of *oikeiosis*, which he defines as "that attachment that is felt by newborn infants and animals to their own physical constitution (*sustasis*), and which the adult human can later extend to his entire rational constitution."[12] Moreover, "this penchant for self-preservation is due to nature, not to reason."[13]

Other examples might be supplied: a baby's attachment to her mother, the human desire for nourishment or rest. These inclinations of the will cannot simply be attributed to free choice but pre-exist it. Free will presupposes these inclinations; it is guided by them. One may certainly wish against them, but even in wishing against them one is willing according to some other inclination. The human will certainly has a deliberative aspect, but it does not exhaust its range. Moreover, if will is restricted to that aspect, it becomes more difficult to understand how it remains the will of *this* person. The will becomes a faculty that is detached from one's natural conditions; in fact it becomes detached from one's self. Will as a natural capacity, to use a metaphor, is the particular gravitational pull that, as Sorabji explains, holds a particular individual together in being.

---

10. Maximus, *Letter to Marinus*, quoted in Sorabji, "The Concept of the Will from Plato to Maximus the Confessor," in *Will and Human Action: From Antiquity to the Present Day*, ed. Thomas Pink and M. W. F. Stone (New York: Routledge, 2004), 21.

11. Sorabji, "Concept of the Will," 21.

12. Sorabji, "Concept of the Will," 21.

13. Sorabji, "Concept of the Will," 21.

Today we tend to think of will, and indeed of operations that are willed, less as a natural capacity and more as a faculty of spontaneity. Historically this is due to the gradual detachment of will from nature. Many scholars lay the blame for this separation at the feet of John Duns Scotus.

Although Duns Scotus is otherwise influenced by Aristotle's account of action, he disagrees with the Aristotelian consensus that nothing moves itself. One thing that can move itself, he points out, is the will. The intellect cannot move itself but finds itself caused to know what it knows by the objects that it knows. The intellect is thus in the realm of necessity and is not free. The will on the other hand has the capacity for opposites. Nature, as we have seen, does not have that power. As we have seen, the natural operation of fire is to heat; it does not have the power for opposites. Even though the will is indeterminate, it needs no extrinsic cause to be moved. If this were not possible, Duns Scotus argues, then God himself would not be free. God's will is undetermined by anything external to him, and it has the power to move itself freely toward whatever objects he chooses.

Now for Duns Scotus the will needs knowledge in order to move. But presented with opposite ends it remains indeterminate between them. This raises an interesting question for Duns Scotus. If the will is underdetermined by knowledge, it must remain possible to sin despite having the beatific vision. He accepts the implication and suggests that the impeccability of the blessed is guaranteed by God's blocking the actualization of this potency to sin. Although the blessed can in principle still sin, he is actively prevented by God from sinning. This prevention, however, remains an extrinsic exercise of efficient causality and, one might say, an act of violence against the freedom of the individual.

The approach of Aquinas, who keeps the will tethered to nature, is starkly different. The will is moved in accordance with knowledge. Since the will has a natural inclination toward the supreme good, and this good is received in the beatific vision, the impeccability of the blessed naturally follows.

The account of the person that emerges post–Duns Scotus pushes the essence of personhood further away from the constraints of nature. His theory of individuation rejects the Aristotelian-Thomistic angle, by which a substance is individuated by matter. For Aristotle and Thomas, a form is received into a matter (and thereby is also limited by it), and this suffices for individuation. For Duns Scotus, the principle of individuation is not matter but rather something in nature yet distinct from it, something he calls *haecceitas*, which "is not matter or form or the composite insofar as each of these is a 'nature,' but it is the ultimate reality of the being which is matter or form or which is the composite."[14] This adumbrates the Romantic perspective of the absolute uniqueness of each individual. As Aaron Riches explains,

> The haecceitas of each particular suppositum, then, is inseparable from the existence of a given nature (although formally they remain distinct), such that a suppositum is no longer simply an individuated universal forma of "common nature" (natura communis). Natures always exist as haec natura and never as "nature-in-general." Thus the nature of a suppositum is never purely an individuated universal forma; it is forma "plus" haecceitas.[15]

The takeaway is that for Duns Scotus individuation is not simply the reception of a general *forma* into a matter, implying a modification of the form itself by the matter. Rather, it is the presence of an ultimate ground of real individuality, the *haecceitas*, in the very essence of the thing as distinct from its actual existence.

We shall come to Duns Scotus's specific conception of personality in the next section. At this stage it is sufficient to point out that it presupposes a particular notion of individuation. A particular substance is individuated not so much by its act of existence (by the way its form is received in a particular matter) but by an additional principle that it *receives* in its very essence.

It is instructive to point out that the detaching of will from nature is precisely the position of the monothelites. These had argued that what is truly personal in man is precisely the will. For this reason there can be only one will in Christ since if there are two wills, divine and human, one creates the premises for a conflicted Christ. Maximus challenges precisely this assumption, namely that freedom is something that belongs to the person and not to nature. Von Balthasar captures Maximus's thought nicely: "This freedom, Maximus answered, is, at root, a freedom of human nature itself; only its concrete realization, its 'liberation' by appropriation, is the work of the person, and it is there that freedom comes into its own."[16]

Von Balthasar points out the distinction between the basic activity, *actus primus*, which belongs to nature, and "the express realization of the activity

14. John Duns Scotus, *Ordinatio* 2, dis. 3, pars 1, q. 6, n. 188, quoted in Aaron Riches, *Ecce Homo: On the Divine Unity of Christ* (Grand Rapids: Eerdmans, 2016), 213.

15. Riches, *Ecce Homo*, 213.

16. Hans Urs von Balthasar, *Cosmic Liturgy: The Universe According to Maximus the Confessor* (San Francisco: Ignatius, 2003), 227.

(*actus secondus*),"[17] which belongs to the person. Thus, "to act and to achieve reality is the work of nature; it is only in the manner, the 'how' of realization that the hypostatic comes into its own. This *head start of nature* [emphasis mine] is, in the creature, the real clue to its 'givenness', its creaturehood."[18]

This is a pivotal distinction for the present project. On the one hand, there is a dimension of will and operation in its aspect as nature; on the other hand, there is a dimension of will and operation in their aspect as hypostasis, or supposit. The first, as von Balthasar so aptly puts it, gives the hypostasis a head start; it orients it according to a plan of nature toward its ends. The second dimension pertains to the *manner*, or the *mode* in which each hypostasis realizes this plan of nature.

We have here a fundamental and all-important distinction. We have not reduced will and operation to nature. Nor have we reduced it to the hypostatic level. A reduction to the level of nature does away with the rationality of the human nature. On the other hand, a reduction to the hypostatic level leads to a nominalist individualism.

Von Balthasar rightly perceives that

> two ultimate conceptions of the person are on a collision course here. For Pyrrhus, person can represent only an irrational dimension, beyond everything natural. He wants to preserve its absolute spontaneity and self-affirmation through negations. Thus, in many respects, Monothelitism is a precursor of the personalistic nominalism of the late Middle Ages and modern culture. For Maximus, on the other hand, person is the realization, the concrete living out, of a rational nature; and because every realization points back to a real source, it is the original, functional center of the rational nature itself, the radiant inner expression of its being.[19]

Von Balthasar is keenly aware of the temptation, to which Duns Scotus himself seems to have succumbed, of unhitching the person from the underlying nature. For Aquinas and von Balthasar, a person is a particular realization of a given nature. Willing and actions do not arise *de novo* in the person, as if that person is not already moved to actualize a particular rational (or natural) order.

We have been arguing that *persons act from their natures*. The claim is not that natures act *solo*. Something acts only insofar as it is in act, and persons are

---

17. Von Balthasar, *Cosmic Liturgy*, 228.
18. Von Balthasar, *Cosmic Liturgy*, 227.
19. Von Balthasar, *Cosmic Liturgy*, 262–63.

the acts of (rational) natures. But it is essential to understand the second half of the statement, *from their natures*, in order to make sense of the development of Trinitarian doctrine and of dyothelite Christology.

It may now be easier to understand the cognitive dissonance between the patristic and the modern approaches to the problem of action. According to the former, actions indicate powers, and powers, in turn, indicate natures. As Aquinas intimates, "we proceed from acts to faculties, and from faculties to essence."[20] This only makes sense in a framework according to which natures possess an *actus primus* that undergirds the personal mode of action, *actus secundus*.

On the other hand, in a framework in which will and operation are *ex nihilo* there is no way to trace them back to a nature except in a loose sense in which nature is a set of neutral capacities. On this view, operations can only be traced back to the actualization of this set of capacities, which actualization belongs to the personal or hypostatic dimension. Thus, operations can only indicate persons.

If operations merely indicate (count) persons, one must conclude either Nestorianism or monothelitism—Nestorianism if one accepts the two operations, divine and human, and proceeds to number the persons; monothelitism if one accepts the unity of person and concludes the unicity of operation. To prevent this false choice, the two schemas must be allowed to inform each other such that actions get their "head start" in nature but are realized by the hypostasis, who is the ultimate subject of activity. And so actions count natures, not persons. Conversely, natures indicate actions. It follows that the single nature of the Trinity indicates a single action in three different manifestations, or realizations. Conversely, the two natures of Christ count two operations, both realized in the same person of the Word.[21]

20. Thomas Aquinas, *Commentary on Aristotle's* De Anima, 2nd ed., trans. Kenelm Foster (Notre Dame, IN: Dumb Ox Books, 1994), 2.6, 308.

21. In a formidable contribution to the theology of divine action (*Divine Agency and Divine Action*, vol. 2, *Soundings in the Christian Tradition* [Oxford: Oxford University Press, 2017]), William J. Abraham expresses hesitation about the patristic location of will in the natures. He argues that it gives rise to "the three-agent problem in Christology," which he defines as follows: "if there is a will, there must be an agent who exercises that will. So we are driven to conclude that there are at least two if not three agents in Christ: the human nature as an agent, the divine nature as an agent, and the *logos* who acts in concert with or by means of both his divine and human nature as a third agent" (99). In addition to this, "there is another problem lurking in the neighborhood. In the Trinity, one nature means one will; and one will means one action; if so, then it is not possible to predicate unique actions to the various Persons of the Trinity. Yet we must take up the latter option, for neither the Father

Where does this leave our inquiry? We set out to ask about the agency behind Christ's works. A distinction was made between the predicative-epistemological and the causal-ontological dimensions of agency. It was now determined that both natures and persons conspire to account for action at their own levels and that abstracting one from the other leads to misconceptions and serious distortions. However, in the case of Christ we are faced not with one nature but with two. An additional complication is that one of the natures, the human, does not have its own subsistence (*anhypostasia*) but subsists in the person of the eternal Word (*enhypostasia*).

The problem can be described as follows: If all we had to say is that it is persons who act, the actions of Christ, both human and divine, should be unproblematically ascribed to the one person of the Word, without appropriation. That would include both his divine actions as well as his human actions. In fact no clear distinction would obtain between his divine actions and his human actions, except perhaps in an abstract sense by way of a subjective classification or by way of a classification in terms of sets of capacities. That is, if nature is removed from the equation of action, Christ must have a single action. In this case, however, Christology itself would collapse, since we would have no way of probing into the underlying natures. This is why it is so essential to connect person and nature. Once the "head start" of nature is obscured, actions seem to be generated *de novo* from the person, with nature making no contribution at all. Christology would in that case languish in a shallow

---

nor the Spirit dies voluntarily for the sins of the world. Thus, if we are to sustain this crucial claim, we must abandon our prior assumptions that one nature means one will means one action" (99–100). Abraham, however, understands the peril of simply shifting will to the hypostasis, for in that case the distinct human and divine ontological substrate of the actions would not be manifest. His solution is to insist that there is a single willer, the person of the Logos, who moves his human will. The human will is not passive, however, but has its own "self-movement" (115), which is nevertheless enabled by God, though not in a sense that would require a separate subjection. Thus, the human will is moved not by the divine will, but by the Son. Specifically, "all the actions of Christ are enacted in, with, and through the full agency of his human and divine natures, as a fitting restatement of the central insight of Maximus" (117). We can take Abraham's proposal as a friendly amendment, as long as the following points are observed: when the Son moves his human nature, inasmuch as an efficient causality is involved, all three persons must be moving it. In response to his worry about Trinitarian distinctions, the *voluntas* of handing over Christ to death belongs to all of them, but in light of the distinction between actions and passions, only the Son undergoes it. Thus patripassianism is successfully avoided. The final section of this chapter addresses this worry specifically.

narrativism, playing around with action descriptions, with no metaphysical or ontological touchdowns.

If, however, we bear in mind that persons do not simply originate actions but that they actualize a natural movement itself, not just a set of neutral capacities in nature, then we shall have to say—as in fact the fathers have maintained—that persons act from their natures. It then follows that two natures originate two sets of first acts, which come together in the one person of Jesus Christ, the eternal Logos. Actions do not originate at the personal level; they are perfected by the person. Thus, the incarnate Logos perfects in himself a human operation that springs from his human nature. This is indeed what we will argue in the next section.

IMPLICATIONS FOR ACTION OF THE *ENHYPOSTASIA*

Let us return, briefly to the distinction between the predicative and the causal dimension of our inquiry. There is universal consensus that the human activity of Christ is to be ascribed to the Logos. However, it remains something of an open question whether this attribution is proper or appropriated. What's the difference? An appropriated attribution indicates that the action is not executed exclusively by the Logos; it is not caused by him alone. The predication dimension depends, in other words, on the metaphysical dimension. Concepts follow things; in this case concepts follow actions.

So the more fundamental question is whether there is an *exclusive causal influence* of the Word upon the human nature of Jesus Christ leading to the activity of this human nature or to the human acts of Christ. One would think that such an exclusive causal influence must be a necessary consequence of the very assumption of the human nature into hypostatic union with the Son. Others would argue that anything that involves a causal influence must imply the common efficient causality of the three persons. The logic of this discussion will have to be clarified before we can move forward.

The framework for this discussion is given by the conciliar Christological consensus. It was determined that in Christ there is a single person in whom the two natures subsist. The divine person of the Word pre-exists and actualizes the human nature, which does not have its own human hypostasis. The conflict between Nestorianism and Chalcedonian Christology carries certain implications for Christ's actions. To anticipate, it would appear that a Nestorian Christology would be more resistant to an exclusive causality of the Word and that, on the contrary, a Chalcedonian Christology properly invites such an exclusive causality. How so? Nestorius had proposed that there are two persons in Christ, a human and a divine person. In this view the actions of the human nature are self-determined, given that it has its own hypostasis (person). Hence, the divine causality upon those actions is simply the providential divine causality that is generally exercised upon all creatures by God and therefore is an inseparable operation of the whole Trinity. The union that exists between divinity and humanity, being a union of grace, does not remove the personal center of Christ's human nature.

On the other hand, in a conciliar Christology the personal center of Christ's human nature is the divine Word. As such, the human nature is moved and actuated by the very person of the Word and not just by the general divine sustenance. In this case, the divine influence operating upon the human nature is specifically that of the Son, in which this nature is personalized.

This would seem sufficient to settle the issue at hand. However, there are several issues that should make us pause before closing the discussion. First of all, if there is an exclusive causality of the Word in the line of Christ's human operation, or an exclusive efficient causality in which the Father and the Spirit have no share, it will necessarily follow that he has a nature in which the Father and the Spirit do not share. If the patristic logic applies—which is precisely the same logic that secured the doctrine of the Trinity in the first place—we do not seem to have much maneuvering room. Insofar as there is a causality exercised by one of the Trinity upon anything outside of God, as we have seen (see chapter 3), it is axiomatically the common divine efficiency. Thus, if one must have a form of causality exclusive to the Word it must not be in the domain of efficient causes. But material and formal causation is similarly ruled out, and in this case a final cause does not seem to help, being as it were extrinsic to the operation itself.

On the other hand, if only a common efficient causality is maintained, it becomes difficult to see in what way this is the incarnation of the Son specifically. This in fact is a fundamental objection raised against hard inseparability. Why should the incarnation reveal to us anything distinct about the Son when in it we encounter the indifferent common divine causality? Moreover, the same divine causality is encountered in any divine action in the world. Even further, if any one of the divine persons might have become incarnate, as Aquinas holds, how does the incarnation of the Son reveal anything specific about the Son?

These types of questions seem to indicate that the crux of the matter has to do with the personalization of Christ's human nature in the person of the Word. To be more precise: Does anything come to the human nature specifically and exclusively from the Son in virtue of the hypostatic union?

The complexity of the medieval debates over the personality of Christ prohibits us from doing them justice. We may nonetheless distill in broad contours the Thomist and the Scotist approaches to this issue, which are relevant for our discussion. Thomas, who distinguishes between essence and existence, sees in personality something positive that a human essence receives prior to its existence, and in virtue of which it has this existence. As Garrigou-Lagrange defines it, "Personality is therefore that whereby the singular nature becomes immediately capable of existence."[22] Thomists would also stress that individuation is not sufficient for personality.[23] An individual essence must receive something additional in virtue of which it may exist. Thus, Peter is not identical with his existence as this individual substance. Peter is the person who exists, not his own existence. In other words, if one removes everything about Peter's actual existence, it still makes sense to speak about Peter as the subject of this existence. Personality is a positive entity that disposes a singular nature for existence; it comes to the individual substance before and as a condition of its existence. As we shall observe, this bears certain implications for the personal subsistence of Christ's human nature.

Duns Scotus disagrees with this conception of personality. If personality is a positive perfection of an individual human substance, it means that it must have had it prior to the hypostatic union, or else the Word assumed a deficient human nature:

> Therefore, if there were some positive entity which made the nature a person in its own right, then this entity would have been assumed by the Word and thus Christ's human nature would be invested with a dual personality, which is impossible. For if it were personalized by something created, this would render it formally incommunicable to another person. Hence it could not be taken up by the person of the Word, and thus be personalized in him.[24]

But Duns Scotus wishes to avoid this Nestorian implication. Hence, he argues that the formal reason our nature is invested with a created personality is not something positive; for in addition to singularity we find no positive entity that renders the singular nature incommunicable. All that is added to

---

22. Réginald Garrigou-Lagrange, *Christ the Savior: A Commentary on the Third Part of St. Thomas' Theological Summa* (St. Louis: Herder, 1957), 164.

23. Garrigou-Lagrange, *Christ the Savior*, 149.

24. John Duns Scotus, *Quodlibetal Questions* in Scotus, Felix Alluntis, Allan B. Wolter, *God and Creatures: the Quodlibetal Questions* (Princeton: Princeton University Press, 1975), 19.61.

singularity is the negation of dependence, or incommunicability.[25] So the formal constituent of personality is the fact that an individuated human substance does not already exist or that it is not otherwise disposed to exist in another or be communicated to another.

These different takes on the formal constituent of personality naturally result in different conceptions of the influence of the Word upon the humanity of Christ. We shall now proceed in the opposite direction, starting with Duns Scotus. For him, as Kevin O'Shea notes, "there is no positive ontological communication of the Word to Christ's humanity in the line of personality."[26] Hence there is no exclusive causal influence of the Son either. The concept of such a causal influence meets with fundamental objections, according to Duns Scotus.

As Duns Scotus sees it, a causal influence of the Word upon the human nature of Christ has two undesirable consequences. First, it risks instrumentalizing the human nature of Christ. Besides the Apollinarian overtones, instrumentalization denies a true causality to the human nature since it would be a merely passive instrument. The result would be a denial of the intrinsic powers of the human nature itself. A second undesirable outcome is that the Trinity would become the cause of Christ's human activity. Given the instrumentalization of the human nature, and given that all divine actions *ad extra* are inseparable, as Duns Scotus also holds, it would follow that the Trinity as a whole instrumentalizes the human nature and is therefore the subject of Christ's actions. Against this, Duns Scotus insists that the Son alone can be the subject of these actions, per the church's confession.

But how can Duns Scotus deny that there is an active causal influence of the Son while at the same time insisting that the actions must be properly predicated to the Son alone? Here we notice the distinction between the predicative and the causal sense of agency.[27] For Duns Scotus, the reason we can and should predicate these human actions of the Son alone is not that he causes them. These actions are caused by Christ's individual human nature itself. However, in virtue of the union that exists between this human nature and the Word, they are properly predicated of the Word alone. As Cross explains: "There is no sense in which the Word is the causal origin of the human actions, nevertheless this human agency can be predicated of the Word in virtue of the communication of properties."[28]

From a Thomistic standpoint, this sounds suspiciously close to Nestori-

25. Duns Scotus, *Quodlibetal Q*, 19.63.

26. Kevin F. O'Shea, "The Human Activity of the Word," *Thomist* 22, no. 2 (April 1959): 157.

27. Richard Cross, *The Metaphysics of the Incarnation: Thomas Aquinas to Duns Scotus* (Oxford: Oxford University Press, 2007), 219.

28. Cross, *Metaphysics of the Incarnation*, 222.

anism. The human nature appears to be accorded an autonomy inconsistent with conciliar Christology. This is clearly the result of the Scotist identification of personality and individuation. By rightly understanding that the human nature is of an individual kind, an autonomy that only properly pertains to personhood is also given it despite the fact that it is said to subsist in the Word. Since nothing positive comes from the Word by way of personality, it follows that the actions of the human nature are also somehow enacted by the human nature itself, understood as an individual substance. There is no direct causal influence of either the Son or the Trinity as a whole.

Duns Scotus's denial of the real distinction between essence and existence seems to land him in Nestorian waters, even if unwittingly. As Garrigou-Lagrange explains:

> It follows from the thesis of Scotus [about the formal constituent of personality] that there are two existences in Christ . . . and then this means that the humanity of Christ has its own ultimate actuality, namely, its own existence. Thus, before its union with the Word, it is absolutely complete, both substantially and subsistentially. Hence there is danger of Nestorianism in this opinion, since the human nature in Christ appears to be a suppositum distinct from the Word, with whom it can be united only accidentally. Scotus does not wish to affirm this, but his principles ought to lead him to this conclusion. There would be two supposita whose union would not have its foundation in anything positive.[29]

The principles Garrigou-Lagrange mentions are the formal unity of essence and existence, namely that the particular essence of Peter is identical with the distinctly existing Peter. If Christ's human essence is concrete it means it is the foundation for its own existence as a person, without any need for any addition. Christ's human nature does not have to be prepared for existence by a "personality." It already exists as an individual nature. But since its existence does not depend on some "personality," neither does it depend on the Logos. So it would appear that Duns Scotus's conception of Christ's human nature accords it a concrete existence quite independently of the personality that it receives from the Son.

Remember that Duns Scotus's worry is the destruction of the reality of Christ's human powers on the one hand, and on the other the predication or attribution of action to the whole Trinity. We may now turn to Aquinas's elaboration of Christological agency.

---

29. Garrigou-Lagrange, *Christ the Savior*, 150.

It is important to remember that for Thomas personality is a positive thing, one that disposes an individual substance for existence. In order for the human nature of Christ, which is already individuated as a single substance, to subsist, it must receive this personality as a condition. Thus, as O'Shea explains:

> Thomism, for which personality is a positive perfection distinct from the substantial individual nature, sees in the sacred humanity a positive supplying of the positive perfection of connatural human personality by the positive perfection of divine personality. This supplying must be achieved by setting up a positive ontological foundation for the real relation of union between the sacred humanity and the divine person of the Word.[30]

The human nature, for Thomas, receives its act of subsistence from the Word itself, for, as we have seen, the existence of a human nature requires a personality, which disposes the nature for existence. Any actions that it may henceforth perform are enacted by the person of the Word as it becomes the existence of the human nature. Thomas denies that there are two existences in Christ, although it may still be possible to distinguish within the same personal existence between the human and the divine modes or dimensions.

Given that the human nature does not have its own act of existence, but only receives it in light of the positive gift of the Word's personality, which prepares it for existence, all of its energy is perfected by the very existence of the Word itself, as we shall later observe. The human nature is indeed instrumentalized by the Word. There seems to follow from this the thesis that there is indeed an exclusive causality of the Word upon the human nature of Christ such that his human actions are indeed properly the actions of the Son and not merely appropriated to him.

Thomas's elaboration of his views regarding the operations of Christ is condensed in Questions 18–19 of the *Tertia Pars* of the *Summa Theologiae*, where he defends Chalcedonian and dyothelite Christology. As is well known he adopts the notion that the Logos instrumentalizes the human nature of Christ. Thus, "Whatever was in the human nature of Christ was moved at the bidding of the Divine will."[31] However, this does not take away the proper operation of the instrument.

Again we observe the principle that will and operation initially belong to nature (*actus primus*). Without this principle, it is difficult to understand

30. O'Shea, "Human Activity," 157.
31. Aquinas, *ST* 3, q. 18, a. 1, ad. 1.

how Chalcedonian Christology would not necessarily degenerate into Apollinarism, as in fact its opponents charged. There is an activity that is proper to the human nature as nature, which retains its integrity precisely as an operation of the nature and not an activity of the hypostasis. Unless this is understood we are liable to misread Thomas's view on the human activity of Christ.

In Question 19, he takes up the task of defending the two operations of Christ given that his human nature is an instrument of the divine. He meets the objection that "there is but one operation of the principal and instrumental agent. Now the human nature was the instrument of the Divine. . . . Hence the operations of the Divine and human natures in Christ are the same."[32] This is precisely Duns Scotus's objection: Instrumentalization entails that the instrument is purely passive and inert. In his *responsio*, Thomas agrees that the sacred human nature was moved by the divine: "as in a mere man the body is moved by the soul, and the sensitive by the rational appetite, so in the Lord Jesus Christ the human nature is moved and ruled by the Divine."[33]

However, Aquinas recognizes a "twofold action" in what is moved by another. We should listen to Thomas at length:

What is moved by another has a twofold action—one which it has from its own form—the other, which it has inasmuch as it is moved by another; thus the operation of an axe of itself is to cleave; but inasmuch as it is moved by the craftsman, its operation is to make benches. Hence the operation which belongs to a thing by its form is proper to it, nor does it belong to the mover, except insofar as he makes use of this kind of thing for his work: thus to heat is the proper operation of fire, but not of a smith, except in so far as he makes use of fire for heating iron. But the operation which belongs to the thing, as moved by another, is not distinct from the operation of the mover; thus to make a bench is not the work of the axe independently of the workman. Hence, wheresoever the mover and the moved have different forms or operative faculties, there must the operation of the mover and the proper operation of the moved be distinct; although the moved shares in the operation of the mover, and the mover makes use of the operation of the moved, and consequently, each acts in communion with the other.[34]

32. Aquinas, *ST* 3, q. 19, a. 1, obj. 2.
33. Aquinas, *ST* 3, q. 19, a. 1, responsio.
34. Aquinas, *ST* 3, q. 19, a. 1, responsio.

This holds the key to understanding Aquinas's apparent failure to ascribe the agency for Christ's human actions to the inseparable Trinity. The distinction that he makes here is commonsense and elegant. Both the mover and the moved have their own proper operations. But the operation of the moved may be given the form of the operation of the mover. In that case the distinction vanishes for Thomas as the conjunction of operations is formed to produce a single work.[35]

But who is doing the moving of the human nature? Is it the Word exclusively or the Trinity as a whole? It is interesting that Thomas's view of this seems to be always mediated by the authorities he is citing. He quotes from Leo's *Epistle to Flavian*: "Both forms (i.e. both the Divine and the human nature in Christ) do what is proper to each in union with the other, i.e. the Word operates what belongs to the Word, and the flesh carries out what belongs to the flesh."[36] And then he quotes the passage we have already noted from Pseudo-Dionysius, where "Whatever pertains to [the Word's] human operation the Father and the Holy Ghost no wise share in."[37]

However, Aquinas also explicitly talks—very much in line with the language of tradition itself—of the divine nature moving the human nature: "The Divine Nature makes use of the operation of the human nature, as of the operation of its instrument."[38]

How may we resolve this conundrum? The answer is that Aquinas ascribes exclusively to Christ only that *actus primus* of the human nature, that head start in nature, which is actualized by the divine hypostasis in his actions. In every action of Christ, Thomas writes, again in line with much of the tradition he relies on, there is a conjunction of the human and the divine. Christ's divine operation employs the human and his human operation participates in the divine operation. Thus, *there is never an autonomous, exclusively human operation in Christ, but always one moved by and participating in the divine operation.* However, insofar as there exists that authentic human movement, obedient in service of the divine will, such an operation is properly human and belongs properly to the Son alone, in whom alone the human nature subsists.

Thomas does write the following: "Hence it is clear that the human operation, in which the Father and the Holy Ghost do not share, except by Their merciful consent, is distinct from His operation, as the Word of God, wherein

---

35. See below, ad. 2.
36. Aquinas, *ST* 3, q. 19, a. 1, responsio.
37. Aquinas, *ST* 3, q. 19, a. 1, ad. 1.
38. Aquinas, *ST* 3, q. 19, a. 1, responsio.

the Father and the Holy Ghost share."[39] Thus, insofar as there is an activity of the Word, an operation of the Word as God, the Father and the Spirit also share in that. But there is precisely such an operation of the Word in the moving of the human nature! And insofar as one may speak of such a dynamic influence of the divine nature upon the human nature, one must speak in terms of the inseparable causality of the triune persons.

Now of course there remains the proper operation of the human nature, the operation according to which it is the nature that it is and without which it would be a mere abstraction. However, per our discussion of personality, the human nature only has such an activity insofar as it is in act, that is, insofar as it subsists, which it does exclusively in the person of the Word. It follows that its *actus primus* is only possessed insofar as the Word draws it to itself and makes it subsist in itself.

The distinction Thomas makes is clear in his response to the second objection, which we have quoted already:

> The instrument is said to act through being moved by the principal agent; and yet, besides this, it can have its proper operation through its own form, as stated above of fire. And hence the action of the instrument as instrument is not distinct from the action of the principal agent; yet it may have another operation, inasmuch as it is a thing. Hence the operation of Christ's human nature, as the instrument of the Godhead, is not distinct from the operation of the Godhead; for the salvation wherewith the manhood of Christ saves us and that wherewith his Godhead saves us are not distinct; nevertheless, the human nature in Christ, inasmuch as it is a certain nature, has a proper operation distinct from the Divine, as stated above.[40]

One may note the "Godhead" (*divinitatis*) language employed by Aquinas. It is likely not accidental that he does not use personal language. Aquinas understands that as long as an instrument is being moved, such a movement can only happen by efficient causation, and therefore must involve the common causality of the Trinity.

Let us rehearse the distinction as established in the quotation. Insofar as the human nature is regarded as an instrument, its operation is properly the operation of the Godhead. However, inasmuch as it is regarded as a nature, as a thing, it has its distinct operation. Now, again, something acts only insofar

---

39. Aquinas, *ST* 3, q. 19, a. 1, ad. 1.
40. Aquinas, *ST* 3, q. 19, a. 1, ad. 2.

as it is in act. The human nature only has an operation, its own distinctive operation, insofar as it is made to subsist in the Word.

Let's go back to where he initially makes this distinction, in the *responsio*. There Aquinas spells out the principle according to which the operations are to be distinguished, namely forms: "Wheresoever the mover and the moved have different forms or operative faculties," there must the operations be distinct. Note that this is precisely the principle of hard inseparability: The activity of the Father, Son, and Holy Spirit is inseparable and one because their form (nature) and their operative faculties are one. Thus, the rule of inseparable operations has been also in this case consistently applied to yield the orthodox doctrine of dyothelitism and dyoenergism. *The rule does not hinder the ascription to the Son alone of a proper human activity*, understood as *actus primus*, but it properly preserves the common triune operation at the level of Christ's instrumentalized actions.

So far we have fought a rearguard action, defending the doctrine of inseparable operations in the case of the incarnation of the Son alone. We have suggested that, insofar as the human nature is instrumentalized by the Godhead, one must not lose sight of the common triune efficiency. On the other hand, the proper operation of Christ's human nature *as nature* is properly and exclusively the Son's. Since the instrumental use of Christ's human operations properly begins with this *actus primus* of the nature, it may be said that the activity of the Godhead of which Thomas speaks can be especially appropriated to the Son. More must now be said about this instrumentalized action, to which we shall refer simply as Christ's *theandric action*. What will emerge is that Christ's human nature and its natural operation is drawn to share in Christ's existence as the Son of God, thus taking on the mode of being of the Son. The sacred human nature becomes a filial nature; Christ's operation also takes on the mode of filiation. It will thus be seen that the Son is distinguished for us from the Father and the Spirit, not because he has an exclusive causality of his own in the incarnation but because the human nature that he assumes takes on the existence of the Son and acquires the personal property of the Son.

THEANDRIC ACTION AND INSTRUMENTALIZATION

The Trinity's actions originate in the processions. We have already established this fundamental principle of Trinitarian agency. God acts through the Son and in the Holy Spirit. These should not be seen as distinct agents carrying out distinct operations, as Pannenberg sees them. Rather, in every divine action these "poles" need to be distinguished since every divine action carries the three modalities of action: from the Father, through the Son, and in the Holy Spirit. Moreover, every divine person acts insofar as he bears the divine essence. This principle is the equivalent of the rule that persons act from their natures or on the basis of their natures. The Son acts as he has the divine nature. But he has the divine nature from the Father. Similarly, since the Spirit has his divine nature from the Father and the Son, he acts from the Father and the Son. Yet these are only modalities that can be distinguished within the same divine activity, not separate operations. Again, this was elaborated in previous chapters, so we shall presuppose the results of those labors.

The corollary of the above principle is that it is supposits that act, not natures. A thing acts only insofar as it is in act. Thus, the subject of actions is always the hypostasis. The divine substance is only improperly called a subject of action, or an agent. The agency always belongs to the triune persons. However, it belongs to them in a way proportionate to their possession of the divine substance. Thus, although the persons are the subjects of actions, their actions will be inseparable since they do not partition the divine essence but exist as a single being. So again, while we may and should distinguish between the poles of the divine being, or between the modes of the action, this must be done in such a way as not to partition the divine existence.[41]

Back to the incarnation, then. If the incarnation can be properly understood in terms of the mission of the Son, as we believe it should be, a certain ontological constitution of the hypostatic union follows. On the one hand, we have the procession of the Son, which is eternal, immutable, unbroken; on the other hand, we have the addition of a created effect, the human nature, which is made to subsist in this procession. Thus, the human nature receives its act of existence, not as its natural act (which would terminate in a human person), but supernaturally, in the existence of the eternal Son. The Son's personal *esse*, existence, is what makes the human nature actual.

We will turn now to Dominic Legge's exposition of the implications of this for Christ's activity. Legge argues that two consequences follow from the hypostatic union, that is from the fact that Jesus Christ receives everything from the Father. The first is that Christ's human nature receives the very existence of the Son and thus "bears the Son's personal property. . . . Consequently, everything in that humanity takes on the filial mode of the Son."[42] This includes Christ's human will, his knowledge, his operation; all of these are the Son's. We have

---

41. This also follows from simplicity: Since God's essence is identical with his existence, there are not three existences in God but three modes of the same existence.

42. Legge, *Trinitarian Christology*, 112.

had ample opportunity to observe precisely this dependence of the Son on the Father in the Gospel of John especially. The Son has life from the Father; he comes from the Father.

A second consequence, according to Legge, is that Christ also acts from the Father. As one is so one acts, and since he has his being as the Son from the Father, he acts always from the Father. Since the incarnation is nothing but the continuation of the Son's eternal procession, Christ's activity is received from the Father and in fact it reveals the Father, as Word. Legge's formulation is particularly felicitous: Because the Son's humanity is an instrument of the Word, it "is drawn into and participates in the Son's filial mode of action. The converse is also true: the Son acts *in* and *through* the properly human operations of his human nature (speaking, touching, suffering, and even dying), so that even these are from the Father and thus manifest the Father."[43]

The language of "drawing" is particularly significant at this point. The human nature does not have its own center of operation, it does not subsist by itself, and thus it cannot act personally by itself. Only insofar as it receives its existence from the Word does it act. However, the language of drawing can also indicate a kind of divine activity that does not imply a separate motion in God himself. As we saw in our discussion of divine action, it is important that our conception of divine action honors the attributes of immutability and simplicity. As David Burrell has shown, Aquinas's theory of action discourages us from thinking of causality in terms of something passed, as in a medium. All that is required for God to causally impact the world is that the agent be in act—and the existence of a certain relation (order) between the agent and the thing capable of being affected. Thus Aquinas "encourages us to explain causality by a set of relationships rather than to look for something passed on."[44]

The upshot is that we need not think of motion in God when God acts. This need not imply that Aquinas's God moves like Aristotle's God, as final cause. Quite the contrary, there is real causality, real efficiency, in God, yet without necessarily implying change. The language of *drawing* is particularly apt to capture this dynamic. God acts by drawing, by bidding secondary causes to do his will. In this case as well, the human nature is drawn into the vortex of the divine processions and instrumentalized to act as the Son.

However, Legge goes on to conclude "that every human action of Christ is an action of the divine Word in person—it belongs *properly* to him and *not* to

43. Legge, *Trinitarian Christology*, 117.
44. David Burrell, *Aquinas: God and Action* (Eugene, OR: Wipf and Stock, 2016), 150.

the Father or the Holy Spirit."[45] Legge's conclusion is reached from the premise that, since the human nature receives its existence specifically from the Word, its actions must be the Word's actions properly and exclusively.

Emery makes a similar claim: The distinct mode of the Son's act is characterized by the action of his humanity. This is a proper act of the Son, namely his actions that have as their formal principle the humanity of Christ. Since only the Son is hypostatically united to the human nature, the human nature is a proper instrument of the Son.[46] If by this Emery means that in Christ's human actions we have properly the Son's *mode of action*, it is perfectly acceptable. In fact, this is precisely what happens: Christ's human operation takes on the filial mode of action. If on the other hand a discrete action is predicated of the Son exclusively, we then seem to attribute to the Son a nature in virtue of which he acts thus—a nature not shared with the Father and the Spirit.

Now it will naturally be retorted that this is precisely the human nature, in virtue of which the Son acts. However, as we have just seen, no actualized energy exists in this human nature, no actual operation except as moved by the divinity. But as soon as we speak of a *moving*, we find ourselves in the domain of the common efficiency of the Trinity. Emery himself explicitly denies that "an action in the world belongs to one person rather than another."[47] Since the human nature is instrumentalized, it is moved by the common efficiency of the divine nature, not by a single person, insofar as such a movement entails an *ad extra* operation.

Moreover, even if the Son receives a human nature, this does not modify his person. The relation between the Son and his human nature is conceptual in the Son, real in the nature. As Heinrich Heppe puts it, "the result of the assumption is that the humanity of Christ becomes not a part of his person but a serviceable instrument or tool, the medium of its effect upon life."[48]

The human nature of Jesus Christ is drawn into the *taxis* of the divine life, where it receives its existence from the Father. This is as far as its being and existence is concerned; it exists as proceeding from the Father. However, when it is instrumentalized, that is, when a created effect is brought about through its operation, the efficient causality belongs to the Trinity as a whole. We have to say this on the one hand against Scotus—who locates such efficient causality in the human nature itself, as an individual human substance—and on

45. Legge, *Trinitarian Christology*, 117.

46. Gilles Emery, "The Personal Mode of Trinitarian Action in St. Thomas Aquinas," *Thomist* 69, no. 1 (January 2005): 62.

47. Emery, "Personal Mode," 65.

48. Heppe, *Reformed Dogmatics* (Eugene, OR: Wipf and Stock, 2007), 428.

the other against that interpretation of Aquinas by Legge and Emery—which appears to unwittingly ascribe an exclusive efficiency to the Son in virtue of his human nature.

We may again invoke the metaphor of a magnet to illuminate these distinctions. When an object is drawn by a magnet, this object attaches specifically to one particular pole. Yet it is the whole magnet that instrumentalizes it to apply its magnetism to another thing capable of receiving this magnetism. The action of this instrumentalized object, such as a needle, is not the action of the needle itself when regarded as an instrument, but the action of the magnet itself. Nor is it the action of just one of the poles, regardless of its being the exclusive recipient of the needle, but again it is the action of the whole magnet.

The three persons exercise a common causality upon the human nature of Jesus Christ yet in their own proper modes of action. However, and this is the core, the human nature only receives the mode of action of one and not the others, since it subsists in just one of them. For that reason, the incarnation is of the Son alone. But notice the shift of imagery: It is not because the Son exercises a motion that the others do not share in; rather it is because the human nature acquires the Son's mode of filiation. Again, the change is not in the Word but in the human nature itself. In fact, it cannot be said that the human nature is changed, because the human nature is actuated; it receives its very existence from the Son.

Herein lies the difference between the common providential or interventional action of the Trinity, which also exhibits the threefold modalities of operation belonging to the persons. As we have seen in the case of creation there is a common efficiency of the Trinity, yet within this efficiency one finds the irreducible distinction between the poles of action: from the Father, through the Son, in the Holy Spirit. However, despite this threefold modality being a characteristic of all divine action, since all divine actions start in the processions, creation as an act of God does not terminate in a mission. No divine person is given in the sense of sharing its existence with a creature. Only in Christ does this happen. Only in Christ, this human creation is brought into existence precisely in the procession of the Son. Every other creature, including creatures indwelled by the Spirit, as we shall see, have their modification in their operations and habits. Christ's human nature receives its modification in its very being.

This provides an additional response to Rahner's charge that it makes no difference that this is the incarnation of the Son specifically. It is telling that Legge, in answering this challenge, does not fall back on what, on a superficial reading, he seems to allow: a distinct and proper activity of the Son alone. Should the incarnation have terminated in a different person, "the personal mode that would characterize the resulting union would be different in each case. Consequently, according to the personal mode that characterizes its every aspect, *the incarnation of the Son would be vastly different from a hypothetical incarnation of the Father or the Holy Spirit.*"[49]

This is absolutely correct. The difference made by this being the incarnation of the Son specifically is not that the Son gets to act separately from the Father. Rather it is that this human nature acts as the nature of the Son. Therefore, it is right and proper to attribute its actions, all its actions, to the Son. However, if one considers the causality according to which this human nature is instrumentalized, one would have to admit that it belongs equally to the Father and the Spirit.

The same divine energy in which all persons share moves the human nature to be in act. But by the common consent of the divine persons, this human nature receives only the modality of the Son. This entails no less of a presence or activity of the other persons, since the efficiency is inseparable and one. Neither does it entail the absence of the other persons, since the processions mutually entail each other (perichoresis). The Father and the Spirit are equally present—both efficiently and in terms of the processions—in the incarnation, yet only one procession serves as the exemplar for the human nature. This means that the theandric operation is not the operation of the Son in the sense of being the effect of an exclusive causality of the Son. Rather it is the operation of the Son in that all Christ's acts are carried out in the *mode* of the sonship.

As we have seen, the human nature has its own proper *actus primus*. Thus it *belongs* specifically and uniquely to the Son—in a very circumscribed way, precisely because it *exists* in the Son. Such an energy, proper to the human nature, is then instrumentalized to carry out the one salvific work of God.

It is fundamentally mistaken, we would argue, to distinguish between discrete activities of Christ: This carried in virtue of his human nature; that carried in virtue of his divinity. By becoming flesh, by entering into time and space, all divine activities unfold in a finite dimension and therefore are necessarily manifested in this way. All of the Godhead's supernatural activity is thus carried out through natural means, the healing (divine) through the touching (human), or the speaking (also human). Christ does everything in a *theandric* way, which is not to deny the distinction between the operations but only to refuse to distinguish different works by this.

The tradition beautifully testifies to this. Sometimes it speaks rather uncarefully in ways that seem to sacrifice the integrity of the human nature,

---

49. Legge, *Trinitarian Christology*, 126.

as Nyssen does: "But death has been swallowed up by life (cf. 1 Cor. 15:54; 2 Cor. 5:4), the Crucified has been restored to life by power from weakness, and the curse has been turned into blessing. And everything that was weak and perishable in our nature, mingled with the divinity, has become that which the divinity is."[50] Despite the language of mingling and the apparent confusion of the natures that is suggested by the immediately following statements, Riches rightly declares, "In this remarkable passage we see how the conquering of death, the purification of dying whereby the curse of sin is transfigured into blessing, does not occur by extrinsic operation but works, rather, from within the finitude of Christ's humanity."[51]

A similar "mingling"[52] is found in Pseudo-Dionysius: "Furthermore, it was not by virtue of being God that he did divine things, not by virtue of being a man that he did what was human, but rather, by the fact of being God-made-man he accomplished something new in our midst—the activity of the God-man."[53]

Leo the Great is somewhat more careful: "For each form does what is proper to it with the co-operation of the other; that is the Word performing what appertains to the Word, and the flesh carrying out what appertains to the flesh. One of them sparkles with miracles, the other succumbs to injuries."[54] Notice the neat demarcation of what pertains to one nature and the other, an item we shall return to shortly. The cooperation of the other nature is paramount, however. No acts were performed by just a single nature: "the Godhead and the manhood being right from the Virgin's conception so completely united that without the manhood the divine acts, and without the Godhead the human acts were not performed."[55]

The Reformed dogmatics reproduce this traditional consensus, as Jerome Zanchius testifies: "In fact Christ the mediator never did or does anything according to his humanity, in which the divinity too did or does not cooperate, and achieved nothing according to his Deity, which his humanity did not subserve and agree to; so that rightly all the operations of Christ the Mediator are called *Theandrikai* [in Greek] by the Fathers."[56]

---

50. Gregory Nyssen, *Ad Theophilum*, as quoted in Riches, *Ecce Homo*, 99.

51. Riches, *Ecce Homo*, 100.

52. Riches, however, prefers to classify this as "inversion"; cf. *Ecce Homo*, 105.

53. Pseudo-Dionysius, *Letter 4*, in *The Complete Works*, 265.

54. Leo the Great, *Letter* 28.4, in *The Nicene and Post-Nicene Fathers*, series 2, vol. 12, ed. Philip Schaff (Peabody: Hendrickson Publishers, 1994), 40.

55. Leo the Great, *Letter* 129.7, in NPNF 12:94; cf. *Sermon* 46.2, in NPNF 12:159.

56. Heppe, *Reformed Dogmatics*, 445.

The *Leiden Synopsis*, furthermore, is explicitly endorsing the point we have been underscoring, that the ultimate cause of the theandric operation is the divine nature: "In the action of Christ the *Theanthropos* the divine nature functions as the principal cause, the human as a less principal and assistant cause."[57] It is essential that the human and the divine operations are properly ordered to one another. The *Leiden Synopsis* affirms the right order. In Christ we have God acting among us. It is not just the Son that is acting but the whole Trinity. However, the divine action is such that it communicates the person of the Son to the human nature. The divine nature actuates (gives existence) and instrumentalizes (gives operation) to the human nature in such a way that this nature acquires the filial mode of being and the filial mode of operation of the Son.

Thus, the human operation is consequent upon the divine operation. This involves two aspects. On the one hand, Christ has the kind of existence and operation that he does because it is the Son, and not the Father or the Holy Spirit, who became incarnate. Secondly, Christ has the kind of existence and operation that he does because the Son became incarnate in a human nature, that is, in a rational nature, not in an irrational nature.

CHRIST'S SUFFERING

It might seem as if patripassianism is an implication of the present view. Since we have argued that Christ's human activity proceeds as from a first principle from his divine nature and only secondarily as through an instrument through his human nature, it follows that in a certain sense, since the divine nature is identical with the divine personal existence, Christ's theandric activity can be predicated of all the divine persons. Since all divine persons share the one efficient divine causality that moves the human nature of Christ, it seems to follow that *in a certain sense* they are the ascriptive subjects of its action. This is true only in a certain sense because we have been careful to distinguish the *actus primus* from the *actus secundus*. The germinal energy of the human nature of Christ is properly ascribed to the Son alone since only in the Son does it exist as a nature. However, the theandric action, which supernaturally perfects this germinal energy, may be ascribed to all the divine persons and only appropriated in a special sense to the Son, given their common causality in it. So it appears that, given this common causality, we allow these ascriptive predicates to transit between the divine persons. Even though the action is in

---

57. Heppe, *Reformed Dogmatics*, 446.

the supposit of the Son, who alone has the human nature, it can be predicated of, ascribed to, all three persons in virtue of the movement that comes to the human nature from them.

This raises a concern about patripassianism. If we allow action predicates to transit between the persons, from the Son to the Father and the Spirit, should we not also allow passion predicates to similarly transit? In other words, should we not infer from "the Son suffers" that "the Father suffers" or "the Spirit suffers"? This section briefly addresses this worry. It will first be shown why there is a qualitative difference between the dynamisms of action and passion. It will then be shown that it is precisely this difference that allows us to see the salvific nature of Christ's suffering.

Although *acta sunt suppositorum*, acts come from supposits, they come so in virtue of their natures. As we have seen, there is an *actus primus* of nature, which belongs to its very essence, which a supposit perfects in a particular mode (*tropos*). It is important to note that the act itself has its head start in nature even though it is properly predicated of the person alone.

This applies in the case of the incarnation itself. But whereas a human existence is not identical with human essence, the divine essence is identical with the divine persons, and this energy of nature is also the energy common to the three divine persons. In fact, it is precisely the processions themselves in their respective fruitfulness or fruition.

Insofar as a divine person acts in virtue of his nature, as divine, the act can be predicated of all the other persons as well, since the persons do not divide the divine nature. So for example Aquinas explains that essential names, that is, names that are given in terms of an activity in virtue of the divine nature, can be predicated in the singular to all the three persons.[58] Thus the Son is one Creator, the Father is one Creator, and the Spirit is one Creator. They are together one creator, not *creators*.

Now in composite substances accidents are modifications of supposits, not of essences, yet in virtue of the powers of the substances themselves. If Peter is a writer it does not follow that humanity is a writer or that all human beings are writers. However, accidents inhere in primary substances (supposits or subjects, in the case of humanity—persons) in virtue of the natures these have. Both actions and passions presuppose active and passive powers. A fire can't be brave, since "being capable of bravery" is not one of the active powers in a fire. Conversely, a concept can't be melted, since "solubility" is not a passive power of a concept.

58. Aquinas, *ST* 1, q. 39, art. 3.

It is thus clear that suffering can only be predicated of a subject in virtue of its passive powers. Now traditionally the fathers have affirmed together with Aquinas that in God there is no passive power.[59] So if suffering is to be predicated of the subject Christ, it must be so in virtue of a nature other than the divine, a nature that has these passive potencies.[60]

As an accident, suffering can only be in a person, in this case the person of the Son, yet in virtue of his human, not divine, nature. As a property of the person and not of the divine essence, suffering can be predicated nevertheless of the divine essence since the divine essence and the divine persons are identical. Thus, it is possible to say that God suffers. However, precisely because it is a personal property of the Son in virtue of the human nature (which the Father and the Spirit do not have), it may not be predicated of the other two divine persons.[61]

Suffering belongs to the Son in virtue of the Son's *esse secundarium*, namely the Son's existence considered from the point of view of his human nature. Unlike the case of his divine *esse*, which is identical with his divine essence, his human existence (*esse*) is not identical with his human essence. Now this human existence of the Son is not only characterized by passion but by activity also. The following principles are true: First, every action entails a corresponding reaction. The billiard ball impacting another billiard ball receives a corresponding reaction; it is both active as well as passive. Yet at the same time, it has to be said that every passion also entails an activity, at least in the case of rational natures. In suffering, a person is not purely receptive but is actively processing the suffering in a certain way. To be entirely passive is no longer to be a person but to be an inert object, which receives all of its operation from external causes. Persons, as we have seen, are distinguished from other kinds of substance in that they are autonomous centers of action.

But the action of Christ in response to his suffering is also double: there is a human reaction to the suffering, an activity of his human nature that the Word permits: a recoil, a fear, a horror in the face of suffering. Yet this is not the only response. There is a divine response to the suffering as well. The Son's *esse* is not overcome with suffering precisely because he remains fully active and in control of it. While permitting his human operation to act naturally and

---

59. Aquinas, *ST* 1, q. 25, a. 1.

60. Note that I am not saying that a nature can suffer. As Marshall rightly explains, natures don't suffer, persons do.

61. See Aquinas's discussion of proper predication between persons and natures, *ST* 1, q. 39.

recoil in the face of suffering, his divine energy makes the suffering salvific; it gives it a nature that elevates it above what it normally is.

John Damascene captures this very well:

> Accordingly, when the flesh is acting, the divine nature is associated with it because the flesh is being permitted by the good pleasure of the divine will to suffer and do what is proper to it and because the operation of the flesh is absolutely salutary—which last does not belong to the human operation, but to the divine. And when the divinity of the Word is acting, the flesh is associated with it, because the divine operations are being performed by the flesh as by an instrument and because He who is acting at once in a divine and human way is one.[62]

We can think of the relationship between the Logos and the human nature as a "mixed relation."[63] The Logos does not receive the human nature into his person. The union, as Aquinas puts it, is not real in God, but it is real in the human nature. Therefore, anything that is normally received as the corresponding reaction to an action is received into the human *esse* of Christ. Moreover, everything that is active is either permitted (as when the Son allows himself to humanly grieve over the death of Lazarus), or actively caused, as when Jesus resurrects Lazarus. However, whatever the Son *undergoes*, whatever affects him, as part of his human lot—the exposure to causal factors outside of himself—only this is to be predicated of the Son alone, because, again, only the Son has the sort of nature that can be affected in such ways. Everything active, on the other hand, every active response that belongs to his *actus secundus* is to be predicated of the whole Godhead.

The human nature, it may be said, acts as a sort of a valve, channeling the existence and operation of the Son yet retaining to itself (in a manner of speaking) the sufferings and experiences that affect it. Again, Damascene has it right: "Therefore the divinity communicates its excellences to the flesh while remaining with no part of the sufferings of the flesh. For his flesh did not suffer through the divinity in the same way that the divinity acted through the flesh, because the flesh served as an instrument of the divinity."[64] The human nature is instrumentalized to bring about supernatural, divine benefits. It retains its human operation and its human passibility but entirely transfig-

---

62. John Damascene, *Orthodox Faith*, 3.19.
63. Riches, *Ecce Homo*, 165.
64. John Damascene, *Orthodox Faith*, 3.15.

ures them. Thus, Christ's suffering becomes obedience, not rebellion; Christ's temptation yields faithfulness, and his death leads to life. All of this because the deifying energy indivisible between the persons flows through the Son's human nature.

To summarize: Father, Son, and Spirit act together, in virtue of their divinity, through the instrument of the Son's human nature. The resulting *passio* can only be predicated, however, of the Son. Action properties may be said to transit between the triune persons, insofar as they are grounded in the divine nature. Passive properties on the other hand do not transit between the persons since they belong exclusively to the Son in virtue of his passible human nature. As we shall see in the next chapter, it is precisely because of this asymmetry of transit that the Son takes on death and vanquishes it, that he experiences the dereliction by the Father yet without being utterly separated from Him.

CONCLUSION

Is there any operation in Christ that exclusively belongs to the Son? This was the question for this chapter. It is a leading question, which hides an objection: Failure to ascribe to the Son alone his incarnate operations results in the concealment of his personality. Where else would one discover his personhood if not through actions that are his alone? The continued viability of hard inseparability, then, depends on its ability to explain the human operations of Christ. Opponents of hard inseparability can point to pivotal texts in the tradition that seem to concede the point that Christ's human operations belong to the Son alone, with the Father and the Spirit merely approving them.

However, on a closer inspection of these texts it was established that the operations of Christ in which the Father and the Spirit have no part are in fact the *acta prima* of nature, the natural operation of Christ's human nature, an operation that exists in the nature by virtue of this nature's being real and not a mere abstraction. On the other hand, the personal action of Christ, what von Balthasar has called his *actus secundus*, belongs to the Trinity as a whole.

To establish this required a twofold discussion: First, on a general level it needed to be determined how actions are related to both persons and natures. The distinction between *actus primus* and *actus secundus* was explained at this point. In addition, there is a second, specifically Christological, level of discussion since in Christ we have two natures and one person. The question then centered on the dynamic of personal action in the framework of the hypostatic union. If persons act from natures, how does the person of the Logos act in relation to his natures?

The metaphysical elaboration of the hypostatic union provides several options. We have discussed only two of these. Orthodox Christology holds that the human nature of Christ does not have its own hypostasis, but it exists hypostatically *in* the person of the Son. But what are the implications for the operations of the human nature if the latter is personalized exclusively in the person of the Son? Two different accounts of what this "personalization" means lead to different conceptions of Christological agency. On the one hand Aquinas, conceiving personality as a positive communication to the human nature prior to its existence (and therefore grounding it), would seem to incline toward a causal influence by the Word upon the human nature, instrumentalizing it. Concerned to avoid this undesirable instrumentalization, Duns Scotus in turn suggests that personality isn't anything positive but is merely the fact that the individuated substance does not already exist in another or is not communicable to another. In this case, there is no exclusive causal influence of the Son. But this means that the human operations of Christ appear to have an autonomy bordering on Nestorianism.

The dilemma could be defined as follows: Either there is (in virtue of the enhypostasis) a positive communication from the Word to the human nature—in this case risking either the instrumentalization of the human nature or clearly breaking the inseparability rule—or there is no positive communication (as a condition of personality) and the human nature of Christ conducts its operations through its own existence, as it were—thus risking Nestorianism.

We have sided with Aquinas and have argued both that his position is consistent with the inseparability rule and that its apparent instrumentalization of the human nature is not pernicious. First, Aquinas is right to attribute the human operations of Christ exclusively to the Son because they are the natural operations of a nature that only exists in the Son. However, these are the operations that belong naturally to the human nature in virtue of its being an individual human nature. No efficient personal causality of the Son is required to actualize these operations. They are only predicated exclusively to him, rather than caused exclusively by him. Moreover, they only exist, they are only real, as being already instrumentalized by the Son. They become real not in themselves (Nestorianism) but only as actions of the Word. But in this case, the causality of the Word is the common causality of the Trinity. And yet the mode in which these natural human operations (which belong exclusively to the Son) are actualized or expressed is that of sonship. Indeed, these natural operations do not exist prior to being drafted into the service of the Word's operations; they only exist, they only happen as the human nature is moved by God.

Using our magnetic analogy, it is as if the needle did not exist prior to its attachment to the magnet, as if it had no natural operation prior to its magnetization. And yet, as the magnetization happens, as it is attached to the magnet, this happens not without its natural operations. The attached nature acquires its operations not before, but precisely through its hypostatic union. As it acquires the mode of action of the Son, it does so by keeping its natural mode of action.

This is the fundamentally religious point of the hypostatic union: The Word did not unite himself to an already existing human substance, with an already existing operation. Rather, the Word's external actions (and thus the Trinity's external actions) exist precisely as the operations of this man Jesus Christ. This is the true mystery of the faith, namely that God can act as man, not as *a* man but as *the* God-man.

As to the harmfulness of the human nature's instrumentalization, we have found that, to the contrary, it contains the most admirable and lovable truths. From the very moment of their existence, Christ's operations have a dual dimension: They are human operations and at the same time are elevated above their natural capacities. All the energies of Christ are already perfected by and in the hypostatic union. Christ communicates eternal life through the human operation of speaking; he gives light to the blind through the human operation of touching; finally, he gives eternal life through the human *passio* of death.

In being magnetized the needle is drawn beyond the limits of its natural operation; nonetheless the needle exists and has its own operation prior to this. The human operation of Christ, which only exists because it is united to the Word, is also drawn beyond its natural capacity as a human operation. Yet crucially it retains its human dimension, it retains the form of its human operations: Christ speaks, sees, sleeps, walks, eats, and so forth. But these are never just human operations; they are always instrumentalized human operations. A flaming sword is still a sword and it still cuts.[65] A magnetized needle is still a needle; it retains its operations as a needle. For instance it stings and it scratches. It also retains its passive properties: It glows when heated, it melts, and so on.

The disturbing sense of "instrumentalization" goes away when one remembers that the human nature of Christ does not exist prior to its being drafted into the service of the divine. It is not a "something" before the union, but it is only a something because of the union. Thus its existence is the Son's exis-

---

65. See Maximus the Confessor's use of this analogy in *The Disputation with Pyrrhus of Our Father Among the Saints, Maximus the Confessor*, trans. Joseph P. Farrell (South Canaan, PA: St. Tikhon's Seminary Press, 1990), §184.

tence and not a separate existence (*esse secundarium*). The natural operations of Christ's human nature properly belong to the Son in virtue of the union with him alone. However, insofar as any efficient causality is exercised upon the human nature, the actions belong to the whole Trinity. Thus, Christological agency could be described as the whole Trinity efficiently causing certain effects precisely through the human operations of the Son, which are raised above their natural capacities yet retain their natural form.

CHAPTER 7

Atonement

The Christian understanding of the atonement must also respect the rule of inseparable operations. Yet not all views on the atonement satisfy the grammar of Trinitarian doctrine. Since the doctrine of the atonement involves a certain distribution of divine agency, failure to observe this grammar leads to possible distortions. A thorough engagement with the doctrine will not be attempted here; nor is this the place for a constructive account of the doctrine. Although in some part suggestive of a broader constructive outlook, the role of this chapter is primarily corrective. These corrections are applicable to a number of atonement theories and do not single out any approach as the right understanding of the doctrine. While our preferences *include* penal substitutionary theories, some of these corrections will also apply to this family of views.

The relevance of the inseparability rule to the doctrine of the atonement is manifold, and it would be impossible to do justice to its full significance in this context. We shall take up two fundamental areas of relevance. First, we will take up the question of the logical and causal role of the human operations of Christ in relation to the divine operation of salvation. On the assumption that salvation is a divine operation and prerogative, the question is whether anything done on the human side *enables* this ultimate divine action. This raises the larger question of the relation between the economic and the immanent Trinity, or between God for us and God in himself. A chief dimension of this question pertains to the role of the death of Christ (as an economic event in the life of the incarnate Son) upon the identity of God and operation of God. Does the death of Christ change God in any way, either in his identity or in his operation, say, from wrath to love? Penal substitutionary theories often credit the sacrificial and penal death of Christ with changing the disposition of God from wrath to love, or with enabling him to "temper his attributes" such that his love would be consistent with his holiness. In this case, something that happens in the economy and specifically to the humanity of the Son seems to play a causal role upon God himself, or at least upon the person of the Father.

A second question is directly related to the first one, and it pertains to the necessity of the death of Christ. In what sense must the Son of man "suffer many things" (Luke 9:22; Mark 8:31)? The answer to this second question depends in part on the findings about the causal role played by any created event upon the ultimate salvific work of God.

A constructive account of the atonement lurks just around the corner, but it will need to be postponed. Its backbone, however, will have been established quite consistently by the end of the chapter. Central to such an account would be the doctrine of the divine missions and in particular the claim that in the mission of the Son we have the gateway for the indwelling of the whole Trinity (John 14:23). A doctrine of the atonement centered on the conviction that in Christ, and specifically in the humanity of Christ, we have communion with the whole Trinity will need to pay attention to the connection between the atoning work of Christ and the sending of the Spirit. In the cross of Christ not only do we find a reconciled Father, but also the indwelling Spirit. If the work of Christ is the work of the inseparable Trinity, we can expect no less.

How Do Human Actions Bear Upon Divine Actions?[1]

One of the most creative and stimulating recent projects in Trinitarian theology has been undertaken by Kathryn Tanner. Her work affirms the fundamental principles of the doctrine of inseparable operations. A common objection against the classical understanding of the inseparability principle is that it leads to a "cloaking" of the immanent Trinity and its relations, stripping us of any genuine way of deriving those relations from the notional (personal) divine acts in the economy. Kathryn Tanner argues in *Christ the Key* that this is not the case.[2] In fact, failure to discern the inseparability of action leads to undesirable Arian consequences since the Son will be isolated from the simple divine essence. There is a "pattern of trinitarian relationships" (158) that is the subject of the gospel stories; "information about these relationships can be

---

1. This section adapts material that previously appeared in my chapter "The Place of the Cross among the Inseparable Operations of the Trinity," in *Locating Atonement: Explorations in Constructive Dogmatics*, ed. Oliver Crisp and Fred Sanders (Grand Rapids: Zondervan, 2015), 21–42. Used by permission.

2. Kathryn Tanner, *Christ the Key* (Cambridge: Cambridge University Press, 2010). Hereafter references will be to this text.

drawn directly from the way they are narrated in the storyline and does [not?][3] have to be inferred from what Jesus says" (158). This pattern of relationships reveals an intra-Trinitarian taxis, the way in which the persons are ordered to one another.

Tanner writes, "Because Jesus' human life exhibits the Word's relationships with the other members of the trinity, one can use it . . . to uncover their general pattern" (147). Atonement, then, is located in a Trinitarian framework by the axiom that the pattern of intra-Trinitarian relationships is mirrored in the economic relations between Father and the Son. For Tanner this is essential, because "This sharing in trinitarian life from the first in Jesus' life by way of the incarnation is what brings about the redemption of the human as his life proceeds" (145). Atonement turns precisely on the unrestricted and genuine presence of God in the midst of the human circumstances of Jesus's life, especially his suffering and death.

We will return to the redemptive significance of this, but for now we must dwell for a moment on this "trinitarian mirroring" of the immanent into the economic. Both the distinction as well as the unity are so mirrored. Tanner writes, "the Word that becomes flesh in Jesus is taken to be clearly distinct from the Father and Spirit because in the gospel stories Jesus talks to the former and sends the latter" (149). While here the distinction between Trinitarian persons is observed, their unity is evident in an "equivalence of power and value among the three" (150). "The whole story of the gospel is taken, moreover, to be their working a single action of salvation together, through equivalently divine capacities; they each act but always jointly by the very same powers for the very same end" (152). The three accomplish the very same thing, through the very same power "but in different, non-interchangeable manners of fashions" (154).

The missions of the Son and Spirit are also described in relation to her account of inseparability. She denies that the missions are "two separable and sequential acts" (162). Again, remember that for Tanner the economic relationships mirror the immanent relationships. Thus, the processions of the persons are mirrored by the economic missions. However, there is a wrinkle in the story at this point, related to the ancient dichotomy between the immanent and economic trinities. Tanner explains: "Even if the very same relations are simply being extended into the mission they undertake for us, when they incorporate the human in a situation of sin and death through the Word's incarnation, the relations that the members of the trinity have with one another come to reflect that fact" (180). In such a case, to continue the visual

---

3. Tanner's text appears to contain a typo here.

analogies, the Trinitarian light is not so much reflected (as in a mirror), but rather refracted, as through a distorting medium. "Not everything, therefore, about the relations among the persons of the trinity in their mission for us also holds for their relations simply among themselves" (180).

Tanner goes on to highlight two aspects of this "deforming." The first bears on temporally indexed acts; the second on the issues of obedience and subordination. While eternally the mission of the Son is simultaneous with the mission of the Spirit, economically they are temporally indexed and sequential events. There is a "spreading out over time in the mission of movements that coincide in eternity" (181). In the economy, "perfect return is delayed, hampered by the sin and death in human life that the Son and Spirit face in the course of the mission" (181). While eternally the Son and the Spirit proceed from the Father "in interwoven, mutually dependent fashion" (181), in the economy this takes time.

Note Tanner's position here: "The Son can send the Spirit—specifically to us—only because he has already received the Spirit and felt the effects of its working within his own human life." Now all of this takes time. Remember, though, that this is crucial for Tanner's argument: "The very life of God itself . . . must be directly *mixed up* with suffering, conflict, death, and disease in the saving action of Christ" (157). The question is, obviously, in what way *can* the life of God be *mixed up* with these? One potential difficulty for Tanner's position can be noted at this point.

In making the Son's sending of the Spirit conditional upon his being first Spirit-filled, Tanner is making the human nature of Jesus a causal (or constitutive) condition not only of the sending of the Spirit *but also of the very ability to send it*. If this is the case it can no longer be asserted, as Tanner would want to do, that the Son and the Father act jointly by the very same power for the very same end. The Son's power to send the Spirit seems to have an additional constitutive condition. As our discussion of the role of the human created effect in the divine missions will bear out, it is problematic to make Christ's human nature into anything more than just a "consequent condition" of his sending the Spirit to us.

Let us address the second aspect of the "economic refraction" identified by Tanner. The subordination of Jesus to the Father is something to be explained on account of his human nature. However, the Son's human obedience to the Father is indicative of something about the personal identity of the eternal Son: "There is something in the relations between Father and Son that corresponds to the suggestion of inferiority in Jesus' relation with the Father. There must be, since Jesus is the Word and behaving as himself in his relations with the

Father. It is just that what corresponds to it is not properly characterized as a relationship of superiority and subordination" (183). Tanner is perfectly right to appeal at this point to two staples of the classic inseparability doctrine: (a) The economic relationships between the persons are constituted by their relationships of origin. Thus, it is fitting that the Son be obedient to the Father because he proceeds from the Father and not vice versa. Secondly, (b) the Son is obedient to the Father in virtue of their common will. The Son does not obey an external will. Rather the Son shares the same will as the Father. In this case the language of "obedience" almost entirely misfires when applied to the eternal relations between the persons.

Tanner places the humanity of Jesus Christ in a "mirroring" role with respect to the immanent Trinity. The incarnate Son exemplifies in his relationships the intra-Trinitarian relationships of procession. However, there remains an open question with respect to the role of the humanity of Christ in the sending of the Spirit. While, on the divine side the processions and the missions are eternal and simultaneous, economically they are separated in time. While this is true, Tanner's explanation raises some questions about the instrumentality of the human nature of Christ, appearing to suggest that the Son acquires certain new capacities as his human nature is filled with the Spirit. This is an important question, and it will need to be taken up again in the next chapter.

All of this is momentous for the doctrine of redemption. If the economic relationships between the Trinitarian persons refract eternal relationships of origin and therefore eternal personal identities, and moreover if even economically distorted relations such as "obedience" reflect something about personal identities, might it be the case that statements such as "it was the Lord's will to crush him" (Isa 53:10) also have their foundation in the personal identities and thus immanent actions of the Father and the Son? In other words, is there any Trinitarian basis for the claim that there is a direct divine punishment of Jesus—of the Son by the Father?

Like Tanner, McCormack applies the classic doctrine of inseparable operations to the paschal events.[4] His primary insistence is on the uniqueness of the subject of Jesus's actions, which the Logos does "in his divine-human unity" (as he often puts it). He feels that the post-Chalcedonian tradition has

---

4. Bruce McCormack, "The Ontological Presuppositions of Barth's Doctrine of the Atonement," in Frank A. James III and Charles Hill, eds., *The Glory of the Atonement: Biblical, Historical, and Practical Perspectives* (Downers Grove, IL: IVP, 2004). Hereafter references will be to this text.

betrayed the spirit of the council by apportioning certain acts—like suffering, submission, ignorance of the last days, dying itself—to the human nature of Jesus and certain other acts—like omniscience or miracles—to the divine nature. "Where this occurred," he comments, "the 'natures' were made 'subjects' in their own right. The singularity of the subject of these natures was lost to view—and with that, the unity of the work" (354).

McCormack too is concerned to rescue the doctrine of penal substitution from a legalistic exchange framework, where God rewards the obedience unto death of Jesus Christ by dispensing his grace. Moreover, he thinks that such a failure of nerve means that "the human nature is reduced to the status of a passive instrument in the hands of the Logos; it is the object upon which the Logos acts" (352). It is not surprising that such a treatment invites critiques of penal substitution along the lines of "divine child abuse." Either the divine Son is being punished, or an innocent human being, in *exchange* for divine favor.

McCormack's remedy to this line of thinking is to take the human nature of Jesus as constitutive of the very being of God such that the Son suffers in his divine-human unity, not in a human nature that remains external to him. While this does indeed seem to preserve the unity of subject in the God-man, it raises issues about divine immutability. How can the human nature of Jesus be truly taken into the divine being without the divine nature being changed? McCormack's response is to reject a substantialist metaphysic in favor of what he takes to be a Barthian understanding of divine actualism.

Conversely, God chooses to be God only in the covenant of grace. Contained in this decision is the determination for incarnation and the outpouring of the Spirit. The human nature of Jesus is part of the very essence of God because it is how God determines to be Godself. Thus, the inclusion of the human nature of Jesus into the essence of God poses no special problem for immutability: "When, in time, he does that which he determined for himself in eternity, no change is brought in him on an ontological level. To God's being-in-act in eternity there corresponds a being-in-act in time; the two are identical in content" (357).

The payout is significant in terms of the doctrine of redemption. The human nature of Jesus, with everything it undergoes, truly belongs to the Logos. Thus, the Logos truly experiences everything, including death, in his divine-human unity. Thus, "death is a human experience that is taken into the divine life and does not remain sealed off from it" (361).

Tipping his hat to Barth again, McCormack appeals to the principle of inseparability: "The force of the axiom is to say that if one member of the Trinity does something, they all do it" (364). The appeal to the *opera ad extra* principle sheds light on the way in which divine persons can be thought to be acting upon one another in the economy. I will allow McCormack to speak here at length:

> First, an economic relation is never merely economic. If the economic Trinity corresponds perfectly to the immanent Trinity, then the relation of the first "person" of the Trinity to the second "person" must be structured in the same way in both. An action by the first person upon the second, then, is not an action of the Father upon the "eternal Son" (conceived along the lines of a Logos simpliciter); nor is it an action of the Father upon a mere human being. It is an action directed toward the Logos as human (the God-human in his divine-human unity). . . . But secondly, the Trinitarian axiom opera trinitatis ad extra sunt indivisa adds to this the thought that if the Father does anything, then all members of the Trinity do it (365).

The significance of the inseparability principle for McCormack is as follows: If the immanent Trinity and the economic Trinity are one and the same it follows that the Son (simpliciter) cannot be the object of the Father's economic actions. However, inasmuch as the Logos in his divine-human unity is the object of divine action, then such an action has to be understood as the action of all Trinitarian persons. McCormack writes, "An action of the eternal Father upon the eternal Son (seen in abstraction from the assumed humanity) would require a degree of individuation between the two such that the 'separation' needed for an action of the one upon the other becomes thinkable" (365). McCormack does not hesitate to draw the conclusion: "The subject who delivers Jesus Christ up to death is not the Father alone. For the Trinitarian axiom *opera trinitatis ad extra sunt indivisa* means that if one does it, they all do it. So it is the triune God (Father, Son, and Holy Spirit) who gives himself over to this experience" (364). The "Father is not doing something to someone other than himself. The triune God pours his wrath out upon himself in and through the human nature that he has made his own in his second mode of his being—that is the ontological significance of penal substitution" (366).

We suggest that McCormack's proposal illustrates a fundamental impasse in conceiving the relation between the immanent and the economic Trinity. The difficulty seems to be that of maintaining a strong immanent-economic identity thesis yet without making immanent Trinitarian relations and identities depend upon economic relationships. McCormack more than Tanner seems to run this particular risk. He implies that what God does "whether in eternity, or in time" (357) is in some sense constitutive of what God is. McCormack is prepared to speak about God choosing his own identity—presumably as Father, Son, and Holy Spirit—only in the covenant of grace. This is his way of solving the immutability puzzle. But at what cost?

There are two related critical issues here. First, if God *truly* gives himself to the experience of death, in virtue of what is death overcome? McCormack somewhat negligently applies the inseparability doctrine to say that if one does it, they all do it. Thus, if one dies, they all do. But that seems to imply that God truly submitted himself to a mortal risk. Unless we say that it was a real possibility for God to be overcome by the experience of death, or for the Father never to recover from his loss of his Son, we haven't truly predicated the experience of death—as we have it—to God himself. So for this type of theology to truly provide the resources it promises, it may have to venture too far: a God who genuinely puts himself at risk. Yet we would still be at a loss to understand *in virtue of what* God still overcomes a genuine death. Either there is nothing "in virtue of which" God overcomes this death, and he just pulls something out of the hat at the last minute. This leaves open the prospect that God might have ultimately failed. But that means that there remains the prospect that divine empathy with our own suffering at some point might become too much even for God. It is difficult in this case to understand the religious significance of "God with us." Or there is something about God that guarantees his victory over death, evil, and suffering. In this case we seem to be faced again with the prospect of a God behind God—precisely the alternative McCormack wishes to avoid.

The second, related issue has to do with how the identities of the Trinitarian persons depend on their economic relations. If the identity of the divine persons depends on their (contingent) economic relations, it follows that these identities are themselves contingent. If, as McCormack (and Barth?) argue, God chooses to be this particular God in relation to salvific actions, it follows that the identity of God is constituted by contingent realities that need not have occurred (creation, the fall, redemption, etc.). According to Marshall,

> When we take this alternative, the Son comes forth from God not by nature, but by will (as the Arians once held, for their own reasons), indeed by the same free act in which God contingently constitutes himself as Father. If we take our lead from the contingency of a free agent's acts, it is just as contingent that God is the Father, the Son, and the Holy Spirit as that God creates, or redeems, a world. Each depends alike, or they all depend together, on a free decision of God, which could have been otherwise.[5]

---

5. Bruce D. Marshall, "The Dereliction of Christ and the Impassibility of God," in James F. Keating and Thomas Joseph White, eds., *Divine Impassibility and the Mystery of Human Suffering* (Grand Rapids: Eerdmans, 2009), 287.

Marshall continues, echoing the critical point above, we are still left to wonder who is this God who just happens to choose this way?

A second example of the modern willingness to make the economic operation of the Son constitutive of the immanent identity and operation of the Trinity comes from Pannenberg. He argues against "seeing the relations about Father, Son, and Spirit exclusively as relations of origin. With this view one cannot do justice to the reciprocity in the relations."[6] Pannenberg resists reducing the persons to "subsistent relations":

> The persons simply are what they are in their relations to one another, which distinguish them from one another and bring them into communion with one another. Yet the persons cannot be reduced to individual relations, as is done especially in the theology of the West. Such reduction is ruled out by the fact that the nexus of relations between them is more complex than would appear from the older doctrine of relations of origin, i.e., the begetting of the Son by the Father and the procession or breathing of the Spirit from him. The persons cannot be identical simply with any one relation. Each is a catalyst of many relations.[7]

It is difficult, though, to envisage intra-Trinitarian relations other than those of origin, especially since those relations are not to be construed as temporally indexed, but eternal. Thus, the Son is begotten from the Father through a process of eternal generation, and the Spirit proceeds from Father and Son from eternity. But Pannenberg envisages extending the identity of the Trinitarian persons to their economic relations. It is at the economic level that a more diverse reciprocity of relations seems to obtain between the persons. Such economic relations, he argues, are constitutive of their very divine identities.

Thus, "The monarchy of the Father is not the presupposition but the result of the common operation of the three persons."[8] More explicitly: "The fact that the monarchy of the Father and knowledge of it are conditional on the Son demands that we bring the economy of God's relations with the world into the question of the unity of the divine essence."[9] Thus, the identity of the divine persons depends partly on what transpires economically: The Father "has made himself dependent upon the course of history. This results from

6. Wolfhart Pannenberg, *Systematic Theology*, trans. George W. Bromiley (Grand Rapids: Eerdmans, 1991), 1:319.

7. Pannenberg, *Systematic Theology*, 1:320.

8. Pannenberg, *Systematic Theology*, 1:325.

9. Pannenberg, *Systematic Theology*, 1:327.

the dependence of the Trinitarian persons upon one another as the Kingdom is handed over and handed back in connection with the economy of salvation and the intervention of the Son and Spirit in the world and its history."[10] God's very identity as God, it follows, depends on the success of the Son's handing the kingdom back to the Father (1 Cor 15:24): "The immanent Trinity itself, the deity of the trinitarian God, is at issue in the events of history."[11]

Pannenberg's approach inverts the principles at the heart of the classic Trinitarian tradition. Here the very essence of God is made to depend upon the ability of the Son to hand the kingdom back to the Father. Now the very reason Pannenberg insists on such a tight correlation between the economic and the immanent Trinity is to prevent an indefinite deferral of the immanent being of God, hidden behind what is only an appearance of diversity and personal action.

But some hard questions still need to be asked. If there is nothing behind the economic action of God, nothing to anchor and be *that-by-which* the persons act, then out of which nature do the persons we experience work? What is the substrate of their operation? Marshall reveals the subtle irony here: "The Son and the Spirit enter the actual economy of salvation, and before that the decision to have an economy at all, with their distinction from the Father and each other already securely in place. Otherwise the Trinitarian economy of salvation is mere appearance, and the source of the appearances remains unknown."[12] But what Pannenberg is affirming is that the very identity of the Father as divine, and by consequence that of the Son as divine, depends on the success of the mission of the Son. Yet if the divinity of these persons is not the presupposition but the conclusion of their mission, then what is the *that-by-which* they accomplish this mission? In virtue of what is the Son able to secure redemption and hand the kingdom back to the Father if not his divinity and equality with the Father? The irony is indeed inescapable: A theological project aimed specifically at making the immanent Trinity transparent instead renders it completely hidden.

Marshall rightly concludes that "the economic attributes of the divine persons cannot contribute at all to making them the unique persons they are, or to making them actually distinct from one another. At most these economic attributes can exhibit distinctions which already obtain."[13] Whatever it is that

10. Pannenberg, *Systematic Theology,* 1:329.

11. Pannenberg, *Systematic Theology,* 1:330.

12. Bruce D. Marshall, "The Unity of the Triune God: Reviving an Ancient Question," *Thomist* 74, no.1 (2010): 13.

13. Marshall, "Unity," 16.

Trinitarian persons do in the economy, and however it is that they relate to one another in the economy, such relations and actions cannot be constitutive for their identities. Marshall again: "If the persons present in the economy are just the same as the persons who are the 'immanent' Trinity, then they cannot add or acquire any identity-constituting property in this, or any possible, economy."[14] This point is indeed continuous with what was highlighted about the doctrine of inseparable operations: that the action of the Son cannot be construed in such a way as to spring from a different set of capacities (from the Father) or to lead to the Father's acquisition of any additional capacity or property.

The Logical Place of the Humanity in a Mission[15]

We have canvassed three theologians who have been paying close attention to the interrelation of the human and the divine in the work of Christ. Tanner understands the human relationships of the Son to mirror and refract the eternal relationships in the immanent Trinity. McCormack and Pannenberg, on the other hand, make the human activity of the Son *constitutive* of his divine activity and power. The plain difficulties of these views have been noted. It will pay off to turn to an account of the divine missions that is especially attentive to the logical relations between the created effect of a mission and its eternal ground in the processions.

Much was said already about the concept of a divine mission. The dual dimension of a mission was previously indicated: a procession plus a created effect. A mission is also called an external procession, meaning that a divine person comes to exist in a created medium and be united to a particular created effect. Of central importance to our current discussion is the logical place of the created nature in relation to the sent person and triune activity. Canadian Jesuit Bernard Lonergan devoted much of his life unpacking the logical structure of the Thomistic doctrine of the Trinity. He realized the importance of getting right the logical place of the human nature of Jesus Christ.

Since a mission is contingent, true statements about the missions are contingent truths. Lonergan writes that "contingent truths, whether predicated of the divine persons commonly or properly, *have their constitution in God,*

---

14. Marshall, "Unity," 16.

15. This section adapts material that previously appeared in my article "The Cross, and Necessity," *Irish Theological Quarterly* 82, no. 4 (2017): 322–41. Copyright © 2017 (Copyright Adonis Vidu). DOI: https://doi.org/10.1177/0021140017724115. Used by permission.

but their term in creatures."[16] This means that such truths are made true exclusively by something in God, but only in relation to a relevant creaturely state of affairs. The logical and ontological status of this created term in relation to the mission is essential here. Lonergan suggests that "the necessary external term is not a constitutive cause but only a condition, and indeed a condition that is not prior or simultaneous, but consequent."[17] In other words the mission in its ontological totality does not causally depend on any created reality. The temporal effect is not a "constitutive cause," though it is a condition of the divine mission. For example, the Son's mission is not causally constituted by the human nature of Jesus, but nevertheless this human nature remains a condition of the Son's coming to be with us.

At stake for Lonergan is the cluster of principles associated with divine aseity and simplicity. Since God does not depend on anything for his identity or action, the particular logical and causal role of these created effects is carefully circumscribed. Lonergan explains that "[the created effect] is not an antecedent or a simultaneous, but a consequent condition, because the divine persons are absolutely independent with respect to all created things."[18]

The idea of a consequent condition is the key to the present proposal. Lonergan does not define the notion in much detail. He does explain that "a condition is either prior or simultaneous or consequent according as the necessity for it precedes or accompanies or follows the constitution or production of something else."[19] One example of an antecedent condition is that the person officiating the marriage be an ordained minister. The condition is antecedent since its truth makes possible the truth of the consequent. A consequent condition, on the other hand, is such that its truth inevitably follows from an antecedent, while it does not itself constitute it. So, to use an example we will return to later, a consequent condition of our swimming out to save a drowning person is that we will be making waves, that we will be getting our clothes wet, that the beach chair standing by the edge of the water will get wet. These consequent conditions are not what make possible, or what *enable* us to save the drowning person; nevertheless, they cannot fail to obtain (all things being equal) if we are to save this person. As Lonergan puts it, "It is only a condition, because it is not the cause, and yet it is necessarily required."[20]

16. Bernard Lonergan, *The Triune God: Systematics*, vol. 12 of *Collected Works of Bernard Lonergan* (Toronto: University of Toronto Press, 2007), 439.
17. Lonergan, *Triune God*, 441.
18. Lonergan, *Triune God*, 443.
19. Lonergan, *Triune God*, 441.
20. Lonergan, *Triune God*, 443.

Lonergan comes closest to clarifying this notion by suggesting the example of divine knowledge:

> For just as God knows that contingent things exist through his own knowledge, and not through an external term, which is nevertheless required, and just as God wills that contingent things exist through his own volition, and not through an external term, which is nevertheless required, and just as God makes contingent things exist through his own omnipotence and not through an external term, which is nevertheless required, so also the [incarnate] Son is all that he is through his own proper divine act of existence and not through an external term.[21]

Thus God's acts in relation to created realities are made possible by, and they take place *through*, his own perfection and in no way depend on any external terms. But these external terms are nevertheless required as consequents, for if God knows these created realities, it follows that these created realities exist. But their existence derives from and is not the basis or cause of God's knowledge of them.

Lonergan is simply following through the logic of divine aseity and that second strand of this classic Trinitarian tradition that stresses that the identity of the triune God in no way depends on anything that takes place economically. The Son is all that he is simply in virtue of his complete sharing in the divine nature and perfections and not because of any capacities that he might acquire economically.

The Necessity of Christ's Death[22]

Our findings about the consequent place of Christ's humanity corroborate our conclusions about theandric operation of Christ. The whole Trinity instrumentalizes the human nature of the Son, drawing it toward an action that manifests the mode of existence and operation of the Son specifically. The action and passion of the human nature do not add further capacities to God, since in whatever it does it is energized by God himself. And yet the human nature requires time to be transformed and filled with the Spirit.

---

21. Lonergan, *Triune God*, 459.

22. This section adapts material that previously appeared in my article "The Cross, and Necessity," *Irish Theological Quarterly* 82, no. 4 (2017): 322–41. Copyright © 2017 (Copyright Adonis Vidu). DOI: https://doi.org/10.1177/0021140017724115. Used by permission.

We are now in a better position to view the truth that Tanner was trying to articulate. It is not that the Son (as divine) must acquire some new capacity to send the Spirit. The sending of the Spirit has its ontological constitution in the one indivisible power of the Trinity. However, when played out on the created scene, the coming forth of the Spirit takes time since it proceeds—as we shall see in the next chapter—precisely through the humanity of Christ.

Whatever comes forth from the humanity of Christ, whether the Spirit or energy, comes from the one Trinitarian efficiency, which is perfect and in no need of supplement. But there is also a proper causality of the creature, which is allowed its own dignity even as it is instrumentalized by the Logos. There is a human will in Christ, which is free and yet is entirely submissive to and elevated by the unity of Trinitarian will. Since the divine efficiency produces an effect in the created world, instrumentalizing created natures, it requires certain conditions, but these conditions are always consequent.

A significant attempt to deploy a similar conceptuality in relation to the atoning death of Christ is made by Nicholas Lombardo's recent work, *The Father's Will*. While Lombardo is mostly concerned with clarifying the moral dimension of God's implication in the crucifixion, in the process he articulates a helpful account of the logical and ontological relations between various actions and events. Lombardo's concept of the "ontological totality" of an action is particularly helpful. Any action participates in what we may call a causal chain, where some actions serve as antecedent conditions for other actions, and other actions are simply consequent conditions. Consider one of his examples: "A woman runs a marathon, knowing that the running will wear down the soles of her sneakers. She clearly intends to run, and she clearly intends to wear sneakers while she runs, but it seems farfetched to say that she also intends to wear down her sneakers."[23] It seems important to distinguish between necessary effects of actions and the means through which those actions are accomplished. Lombardo distinguishes between means that are ontologically necessary and means that are both ontologically and logically necessary. The runner's wearing sneakers is both ontologically and logically necessary for her running the marathon, while her wearing out her soles is only an ontologically necessary effect of her running. It may be added that the destruction of the soles of the shoes is ontologically implied in the action because of the intrinsic and natural effect of friction upon rubber.

Now this is relevant to the relation between means and ends: "Agents can-

---

23. Nicholas E. Lombardo, *The Father's Will: Christ's Crucifixion and the Goodness of God* (Oxford: Oxford University Press, 2013), 36.

not intend an end without also intending the logically necessary means to that end. Or, to put it another way: for something to be the means to an end, in the sense relevant for moral analysis, it must be implied logically, and not just ontologically, by the agent's intending of the end."[24] The distinction between means and ontologically implied effects is significant. The runner does not complete the marathon *by* wearing out her sneaker soles. Her wearing out the soles is merely an additional effect of elements in a causal chain. To use our previous language, the wearing out of the soles is but a consequent condition of the running, while the wearing of shoes is its antecedent condition.

In terms of a hermeneutics of the cross, Lombardo argues that the cross itself is *ontologically implied* in the divine action, though it is not *logically necessary*. Put differently, the cross is not the means of divine redemption but its consequence. Thus the crucifixion is "necessary in the sense of being inevitable. Given the state of fallen humanity and the ubiquity of sin and malice, the words and actions of Jesus could only lead to his death. So it is necessary for Jesus to suffer not because his suffering advances the divinely apportioned mission, but because it is the necessary consequence of his mission."[25]

This is not mere historical inevitability: "The crucifixion is somehow integral to the mechanics of redemption; something in the way that God's plan of salvation 'works' involves Christ's crucifixion."[26] The cross is necessary in some aspect of its ontological totality, but which one? Lombardo rightly claims that under no circumstances can the cross have any kind of instrumental necessity for divine forgiveness. Commenting on Nyssen's *Catechetical Oration*, Lombardo notes that "Christ comes to rescue humanity from its miserable situation. He is not sent to win God's forgiveness; God's forgiveness is presupposed. Gregory does not puzzle about how Jesus could forgive sins before the crucifixion, but he does not need to puzzle: in his understanding, God's forgiveness does not require Christ's crucifixion."[27] Dealing with our miserable

---

24. Lombardo, *The Father's Will*, 38. The stipulation that intention is a necessary condition of instrumentality is problematic. The fundamental reason has to do with the impenetrability to intention (or knowledge) of the causal chain of bodily movements, for example. The means of my crossing the street is my walking, while the means of my walking is putting one foot in front of the other. This does not mean that I must intend every single movement of each of my legs, or every single movement of each muscle and so on. The causal apparatus which makes possible my crossing the street can be broken down into a quasi-infinite causal chain, the links of which are all constitutive of the means by which I cross the street. Yet it is unrealistic to require that each of these causal motions be specifically intended.

25. Lombardo, *The Father's Will*, 142.

26. Lombardo, *The Father's Will*, 142.

27. Lombardo, *The Father's Will*, 223.

condition requires that the Son unite himself to every aspect of that condition. But this includes dealing with its evil.

Recovering the patristic ransom theory, Lombardo suggests that God deals with evil by using it against itself, by luring it to misuse its authority:

> God allows his creatures to misuse their own freedom, and then uses their evil choices to overcome evil and death. By granting evil a genuine role in the drama of salvation, the devil's ransom interpretation avoids any implication that God secretly orchestrates Christ's crucifixion behind the scenes, or somehow secretly condones it. . . . God sends his Son to draw the malice of human society to himself, but he does not want the actual malice; he wants to protect us from ourselves and give evil a chance to undermine itself. Consequently, the necessity of Judas' betrayal rests not in divine ordination but in our fallen condition.[28]

Here the necessity of the cross is an ontological one in the sense that being part of our human condition entails encountering its evil. However, the experience of evil, including the evil of the cross, is not a means to its overcoming but rather an ontological necessity, much like getting wet is not the means by which I save the drowning person.

Lombardo is right about the claim that the crucifixion is not a means to an end. Our own argument denies "instrumental necessity" on the basis of divine freedom, aseity, and simplicity. God does not have to procure the instruments that would enable him to act redemptively. The inherited Trinitarian metaphysic insists that the identity of the divine persons, and their nature, is already established prior to anything they work in the economy. The Father can acquire no new capacity to forgive *through* anything that the Son accomplishes in the economy of the incarnation.

But while Lombardo wishes to do justice to the biblical language of the necessity of the cross, he does so in a way that is ultimately unsatisfactory. I want to address two dimensions of this "ontological necessity" that Lombardo gets wrong. First, Lombardo argues that the crucifixion of Jesus is not logically but ontologically necessary for God's ultimate aim:

> God's intentions in handing over his Son do not logically imply the intending of his death; they merely imply it ontologically. God intends to provoke evil so it overreaches, and then to overcome death through Christ's resur-

28. Lombardo, *The Father's Will*, 233.

rection. Yet neither the idea of provoking evil to weaken it, not the idea of overcoming death, includes the idea of Christ's death. God does not intend his Son's crucifixion as a means to an end; it is the nonintended side-effect of what he does intend.[29]

God, it appears, has two ends here: God's ultimate aim is to defeat death and evil; but the means through which God intends to do that is through coaxing the powers into their unwitting self-destruction. This provocation of evil is the intermediate end, and thus the means, to the ultimate end of the destruction of death. In this logical structure the crucifixion becomes necessary because it is "ontologically implied" by the whole structure of this divine action. The provocation of evil, however, does not logically or ontologically require Christ's death; neither does death's defeat. Nonetheless, Christ's crucifixion is a "nonintended side-effect."

If Lombardo's argument is to succeed, however, this side effect must be ontologically necessary. Remember that he wants to retain the idea that there is a necessity to the cross, that somehow the cross is entailed in the mechanism of redemption. Yet it is difficult to see why the crucifixion should be inevitable in any of those circumstances. After all, the provoked powers might have overextended themselves (which seems to be a divine aim) without killing Jesus. The mere torture of Jesus, for example, would have constituted an abuse of their power.

Neither is the crucifixion ontologically implied in God's defeat of death. God might have defeated death simply by fiat. There is no obvious reason why this defeat needs to imply the dying of Jesus in the same way as, say, the destruction of a dictator's palace ontologically implies the stirring of a dust cloud.

The desired "ontological necessity" of the crucifixion in relation to either the provoking of the powers or the defeat of death hasn't been convincingly established. But the tightness of the ontological relation must fit the scriptural conviction that "the Messiah had to suffer" (Luke 24:26; Acts 17:3).

The second problem with Lombardo's "ontological necessity" argument is that it does not do justice to the New Testament portrayal of Jesus's death as having a penal (or at least a cultic-legal) quality. A full reconstruction of this biblical teaching cannot be attempted here, but some salient features of it clearly can exhibit the problem with Lombardo's account. According to Lom-

---

29. Lombardo, *The Father's Will*, 232.

bardo, God does not intend the killing of Jesus, and this killing is simply the work of the powers. God wills without intending Jesus's death.

Lombardo admits that the New Testament writers frame the crucifixion in terms of the Father's will. But he says they do not clarify "the precise sense in which it is the Father's will, or why."[30] As we saw, he denies attempts to describe the necessity of the cross in terms of mere historical inevitability. To his credit he takes seriously the claim that we are redeemed "with the precious blood of Christ" (1 Pet 1:18–19).[31] Additionally, the historical-inevitability reading does not sit easily with the New Testament affirmation of the necessity of the resurrection (Mark 8:31; Matt 16:21; Luke 9:22, 24:26; Acts 17:3): "Since the crucifixion is what makes the resurrection possible, the New Testament cannot mean that the crucifixion is necessary merely in the sense of being historically inevitable; it must mean that the crucifixion is also necessary in some ontological sense."[32]

His proposal, as we saw, distinguishes between the Father's intending the death of Jesus and his willing to let Jesus die at the hands of the powers. Redemption works precisely by God's tempting the powers into a self-destructive maneuver. But this means that, lacking an intention of the Father, the crucifixion is not to be ascribed to him but to the powers alone.

Certain features of the narratives, though, do not seem to sit well with ascribing the agency for the crucifixion to the powers alone. The growing anxiety of Jesus in the face of his own death (Matt 26:37–38; Mark 14:33; Luke 22:39–44) is not easily explained by any fear of a purely physical death. His agony is clearly related to his relationship with God, as his cry of dereliction reveals (Matt 27:46; Mark 15:34). Jesus's anguish is closely related to a growing sense of God-forsakenness, to his experiencing the curse of death. He is fully aware of the Father's involvement in his upcoming fate. He applies Zechariah 13:7 to himself: "I will strike the shepherd, and the sheep of the flock will be scattered," while also being cognizant of his ultimate resurrection (Matt 26:31–32). Dread before death, as death, fails to capture the totality of Jesus's experience.

Whether this God-forsakenness is penal (penal substitutionary atonement) or sacrificial (satisfaction atonement) is a matter that cannot be decided at this point. That there is a "legal" quality to Jesus's death is clearly supported by the biblical evidence (Gal 3:13). However, reading the crucifixion as exclusively the act of the powers, and Jesus's agony as being simply in the face of physical

---

30. Lombardo, *The Father's Will*, 133.
31. Lombardo, *The Father's Will*, 141.
32. Lombardo, *The Father's Will*, 141.

death, cannot explain this "legal" quality of Jesus's death. This dimension only makes sense if the Father is much more intimately involved in the killing of Jesus than Lombardo allows. Jesus's death has the legal quality that it does precisely because of the Father's action in "[making] him who had no sin to be sin for us" (2 Cor 5:21).

It was precisely the quality of Jesus's death as a death under divine condemnation, in God-abandonment, that is essential for the mechanics of redemption. Paul understands that what is at issue in relation to divine forgiveness is whether God can be simultaneously just and forgiving. He explains that the death of Jesus is somehow related to God's failure to punish "sins committed beforehand" (Rom 3:25), and that God's presentation of Christ as a sacrifice (notice again the clear divine agency here) was "to demonstrate his justice at the present time."[33] For many writers the implication is clear that the death of Jesus has the quality of divine punishment, precisely a punishment that we ought to have received.

We have registered two objections to Lombardo's account of the "ontological necessity" of the cross. First, it was proposed that he fails to demonstrate a clear ontological necessity given his understanding of the divine plan. God might have defeated evil and Satan using other means. If this objection is correct, it follows that his description of the place of the cross in God's plan of salvation fails to map onto the biblical language of the necessity of the cross. The model simply does not provide the sort of necessity that the Bible seems to call for. A second objection raises the worry that Lombardo's proposal does not capture the Father's judicial involvement in the cross, which is implied by the way in which the crucifixion is biblically interpreted as divine curse and punishment.

Despite these hesitations, Lombardo succeeds in distinguishing between logical and ontological necessity. The cross is not the means through which God procures forgiveness but an ontologically necessary consequent of his redeeming action. We are now in a position to sketch the direction of our constructive proposal more explicitly.

Taking our cue from the doctrine of the divine missions, we may regard what happens to the incarnate Christ to be created, temporal effects produced by the common action of the Trinity. As temporal effects, these do not go into the constitution of the divine action, but are only consequent, yet necessary, conditions of it. Christ's action and passion are simply the consequent condi-

---

33. Note that Paul's argument does not cast the crucifixion as a prerequisite to forgiveness, but as integral to its manifestation.

tions of the divine action. In other words, it can only be truly said that God Xs if it is also true that Christ Ys, while Christ's Ying does not make possible or cause God's Xing. However we end up describing God's ultimate action X in relation to fallen humanity—whether it be reconciliation, defeating death, deification, union, or something else—such an action cannot be caused or otherwise enabled in some way by the action of the Son, however we describe it, whether as satisfaction, penal substitution, propitiation, or ransom.

It is an entailment of ancient Trinitarian metaphysics that the simple action of God is not made up of constituent economic parts, including parts or roles played by the Trinitarian persons. The fanning out of this simple action into what appear to be discrete action tokens is simply a consequent of the fact that the divine action is played out on our ontological level. Consider the analogy of colors. The various colorful refractions of the light as it reflects off various surfaces are not constituent parts of the simple light. Rather they are the necessary manifestation of the light as its wavelengths variously interact with various surfaces and are then interpreted by the brain into color. Being consequent upon the light, these various manifestations are what they are precisely because of the nature of the light, while they do not themselves make the light to be the light it is.

Similarly, God's actions in the economy are simply consequent manifestations of the divine decrees in a temporal and fallen world. As such, the necessity that attaches to them is a necessity consequent upon God's decision to redeem. Tanner puts this well: The economic relations are the same as the eternal ones. Yet when these actions are executed on the plane of human history, marked by sin and death, they will come to reflect that fact.[34] One such example is temporality: on the plane of history the actions of God are spread out in what appears as a division of labor, when in fact this is "a single trinitarian movement considered from vantage points that are only analytically distinct."[35]

Similarly, the doctrine of inseparable operations makes it impossible to think about God the Son persuading the Father to X. Insofar as the triune persons share a will and perichoretically indwell each other, the Son's Ying is not a distinct component of the Father's Xing but the selfsame action regarded from distinct vantage points, to echo Tanner. The crucifixion was not a work of the Son alone, leading up to the Father's own role, but God was in Christ reconciling the world to himself (2 Cor 5:19).

34. Tanner, *Christ the Key*, 180.
35. Tanner, *Christ the Key*, 181.

The crucifixion, then, is necessary in the sense of its being ontologically implied by God's *X*ing. Much as the runner's wearing out her shoes is ontologically implied by her running the marathon, or as the surgeon's causing pain to the patient is ontologically implied by his removing the tumor, or as the lifeguard's making of waves is ontologically implied by his saving the drowning person, so is the cross an ontologically necessary consequent of God's ultimate saving action.

This obviously raises the issue of what God's *X*ing is such that it would ontologically imply the cross. That is, how might the transcendent divine action be described such that it ontologically requires the cross? The answer to this question need not be definitive. A number of descriptions of the ultimate divine action might be supplied, each implying the ontological necessity of the crucifixion. One plausible example will suffice. While it does not rule out other descriptions of the same action *X*, it highlights those dimensions of the totality of the action that render the cross ontologically inevitable.

One such possible description is "being *redemptively united* with fallen humanity." God, in Christ, came to assume our human condition for the purposes of redeeming it and healing it. It is possible to give a soteriological account such that it is not just the sheer fact of the incarnation that is redemptive. The precise manner of the incarnation expresses the redemptive nature of the union it brings about. God might have decided to become incarnate for purposes other than redemption. But once God has decreed that he was going to be present to humanity as its savior, rather than as judge, his action will be manifested on our finite plane in a certain way. Being salvifically present to humanity ontologically entails, early patristic writers insisted, that God assumes every dimension of our condition: "What is not assumed cannot be healed."[36] But the totality of our condition also includes our being mortal and under divine condemnation.

Stressing the connection between death, God-forsakenness, and divine condemnation would be one biblically respectable way to get at the "ontological necessity" of the crucifixion. As long as God's ultimate action and aim is to be salvifically united to humanity, it necessarily implies God's taking on every aspect of our human condition. But this human condition has as one of its central

---

36. Gregory Nazianzen, *Epistle* 101.181c, in J. Stevenson, *Creeds, Councils and Controversies* (London: SPCK, 1989), 90. Note that my view is compatible with non-PSA accounts of atonement, including, for example, Schleiermacher's view of atonement as inspiring us with a new divine consciousness even in the face of death. Christ necessarily experiences evil and suffering, though not as punishment. These points are outlined especially in section 104 of H. R. Mackintosh and J. S. Stewart, eds., *The Christian Faith* (Edinburgh: T&T Clark, 1989).

characteristics the fact that it is an existence standing under the reality of divine condemnation and judgment. Thus, Christ takes on our human nature and in doing that he also takes upon himself the experience of divine condemnation, climaxing in his death under divine-forsakenness at the cross.

The crucifixion is ontologically inevitable, yet not merely in Lombardo's sense. The evil agency of the powers does not fully explain the totality of what transpires at the cross. The cross remains an act of divine judgment and condemnation of sin in the flesh of Jesus Christ (Rom 8:3). Yet crucially, this is not the cause or antecedent condition of reconciliation but the necessary manner of manifesting it, given the reality of sin and death. Much as the sun's light necessarily manifests itself as white daylight by being refracted through the atmosphere, analogically, God's saving action, his uniting himself to us redemptively, necessarily takes the form of judgment, of God's "No!" to sin, death, and evil.[37]

ATONEMENT AND THE SPIRIT

Lombardo sees the necessity of the cross to be of an ontological order, in the sense that the intervention of God necessarily triggers a set of reactions on the human side, from the forces of evil it aims to eradicate. The atonement is not about changing something in God but about the defeat of the powers. Eleonore Stump's recent book, *Atonement*, shares this assumption. Additionally, she attempts to understand the intrinsic connection between the death of Christ and the sending forth of the Holy Spirit. Stump's work is a monumental achievement of philosophical theology. She is particularly important for our project because she picks up a thread in the tradition that understands atonement as quite simply "at-one-ment" in the sense of the re-union of God and humanity, or what we have called "redemptive union." If salvation is all about the restoration of communion between God and humanity, then atonement must be fundamentally understood as a unitive action. Moreover, insofar as the indwelling of the Holy Spirit is the manner in which believers are said to be united to God in the life of grace, there must be an intrinsic connection between the mission of the Holy Spirit and the atonement itself. This certainly dovetails nicely with our project, which assumes that whatever *action* Christ

37. For more on this, see Adam J. Johnson's *Atonement: A Guide for the Perplexed* (London: Bloomsbury, 2015), and, for a thorough discussion of Barthian themes, his *God's Being in Reconciliation: The Theological Basis of the Unity and Diversity of the Atonement in the Theology of Karl Barth* (London: Continuum, 2012).

does in the atonement is a work of the whole Trinity and thus the Holy Spirit must be equally involved in Christ's redemptive work. But how?

Given the comprehensiveness of Stump's theology of the atonement, we will only be able to focus on a number of relevant points, particularly those having to do with the relation between the death of Christ and the indwelling of the Spirit. Stump creates a space for her approach between what she calls the Anselmian and the Thomistic interpretations. The Anselmian family, penal substitution being one of its members, explains the atonement in terms of operating a change in God. Stump finds this model inconsistent with what she holds to be the best account of God's love, namely that of Aquinas. However, the Thomistic model of atonement, while it correctly understands that the atonement is meant to operate a change in the human being, is unable to fully account for the necessity of the cross. In addition, it does not explain the relation between the death of Christ and the sending of the Spirit. Stump's position articulates a view of the atonement that builds on a psychological understanding of personal union between God and the human being, which she likes to describe in terms of Paula or Jerome.

Stump defines union as "mutual *within-ness* of individual psyches or persons."[38] In personal union, a mutual closeness develops between, say, Paula and Jerome, such that Paula's feelings and thoughts can be present inside Jerome's psyche and genuinely experienced by Jerome, only precisely as Paula's. Stump draws on the neuroscientific study of the phenomenon of shared attention to corroborate her position. In shared attention, so-called mirror-neurons are activated in the persons that are so connected such that the very same neurological patterns are observed in both persons.

Research into shared attention reveals a most interesting factor, however, which is that a person who is self-alienated will have difficulty sharing attention with others. Perfect mutual closeness, in other words, requires a total integration of the persons around objective goodness. But this means that "even God cannot be close to a person and united with a person who is divided within himself" (127). The barriers standing in the way of one's ability to love and to allow oneself to be loved by God need to be removed in order for this mutual closeness to become a reality. This is exactly the role that is played by the at-one-ing sacrifice of Christ.

The theological category for this mutual closeness is the indwelling of the Spirit, which is only analogically and imperfectly represented by the phenom-

---

38. Eleonore Stump, *Atonement* (Oxford: Oxford University Press, 2019), 117. Subsequent page references will hereafter be found in the text.

enon of shared attention. We shall discuss Stump's specific view of the indwelling in chapter 9, so we can leave aside some of the details of her construction. The significant point for our present discussion is the relation between the death of Christ and the union between the believer and God, or the indwelling of the Spirit.

There are two ways in which the incarnation and specifically the passion of Christ contribute to the indwelling of the Spirit, corresponding to the two sides of mutual closeness. If God and Jerome are to be united in mutual closeness, then Jerome must be in God and God must be in Jerome. In the hypostatic union, on account of which God has a human set of capacities for empathy and bodily communion, Jerome's psyche can be experienced by Christ as interior to and yet distinct from his own psyche. While Christ has a natural human capacity for this kind of sharing, at the cross God supplements this capacity such that Christ acquires an empathy and shared attention with all human beings from all times. "By opening up the mind of Christ to the incursion of all human psyches, God allows all human beings to indwell in himself" (286).

This first dimension of mutual indwelling, the internalization of all human psyches into Christ's own, is what ultimately leads to the cry of dereliction. It is this empathy with sinners, which leaves Christ himself with the "stain of sin." This is how Stump interprets Christ having been "made to be sin" (2 Cor 5:21), though not in the sense of Christ's being an actual sinner since he experiences the sin of all of humanity, yet not as his own sin. Such an experience proves overwhelming for Christ and it leads specifically to the cry of dereliction. Not only does he experience human sin but also the resulting alienation from God, whereby he temporarily fails to sense the closeness of God. "Flooded with such horror, Christ might well lose entirely his ability to find the mind of God the Father" (165). In this trauma Christ is no longer self-integrated, and this makes it impossible for him to sense the closeness of God.

The advantage of this position is that it does not lead to the dubious position that God might have withdrawn his closeness and affection from Christ. Such a position would run directly counter to the rule of inseparability. Trinitarian grammar does not permit any interpretation of the cross that introduces a separation between the Father and the Son. The forsaking of Jesus by the Father (Matt 27:46) cannot be taken to describe an ontological separation or a separation in action.[39] In this case the distinction between the human

---

39. For an excellent discussion of the cry of dereliction, see Thomas H. McCall, *Forsaken: The Trinity and the Cross, and Why It Matters* (Downers Grove, IL: IVP Academic, 2012). McCall helpfully draws on the rule of the indivisibility of divine operations to show that

and divine energies and wills in Christ becomes paramount. In his human existence, Christ experiences precisely the God-forsakenness that is a consequence of sin.

Stump also explains the death of Christ in terms of this experience of human sin. Sin produces such an internal fragmentation and the experience of the sin of the whole human race—past, present, and future—was too much to bear for Christ. Not only is his integration around goodness damaged, but his personal integrity is also affected. "Seen in this light, the death of Christ at this time makes sense. Once the unity in the incarnate Christ begins to loosen through Christ's bearing human sin, then it is not surprising that the unity of the composite Christ should continue to unravel into the separation of Christ's human soul and body in death" (171). Thus the inevitability of Christ's death is also explained in terms similar to Lombardo's. Death has a necessity consequent upon the internalization of the entirety of human sinfulness.

So the first way in which the death of Christ contributes to union and the indwelling of the Spirit is on the divine side: God internalizes through the human nature of Jesus Christ the sin of humanity and is brought as a result to his demise. But there is a second contribution of the death to the indwelling, corresponding to its other dimension, the internalization of God in the sinner.

Mutual closeness takes place when the persons are mutually present within each other. But while the hypostatic union makes it possible for God to internalize human psyches, something that is ultimately achieved at the cross, there are barriers in the way of humans internalizing of God's psyche. The problem is that human persons often do not wish to open themselves up to the love of God. For such persons, as we have seen, even God cannot bring that union about since it is up to them to open their psyches to God.

Here we have the second function of Christ's death: It is a "most promising way for God to help a human person to this surrender" (288). Here Stump seems to be pulling a page out of Peter Abelard's doctrine of the atonement, despite her avowals to the contrary.[40] The cross, she suggests, "gently disarms a human person's resistance to love, so that she is willing to accept the forgiveness that is always there for her in God's love" (288). When a person is so moved to open herself to the divine love and forgiveness, mutual closeness and

---

the Trinity cannot be broken, and that the persons cannot act against each other. He does not specify his understanding of inseparability, but states that there exists a perichoresis of operations (44, 120–21).

40. Stump insists that, unlike Abelard's, her position takes Christ's passion to be moving the human will, not just the intellect. A close reading of Abelard's position, however, does not support this interpretation.

thus the indwelling of the Holy Spirit are possible. The circle is then complete: Paula is present within God through the empathy of Christ's human nature; and God is present in Paula, the Spirit indwells Paula, who is now willing to accept divine forgiveness and love.

It would take us much beyond the scope of the present book to provide a full response to Stump's rich atonement model. We shall have to restrict ourselves to what is immediately relevant to our topic of inseparable operations and to the question of how the whole Trinity is present and active in the atonement. Both Tanner as well as Stump rightly perceive the fact that in and through the humanity of Jesus Christ the whole Trinity is given to us in a redemptive way. Tanner underscores the manner in which the missions of the Son and the Spirit are proceeding in an interwoven fashion, indicative of the eternal processions yet refracted according to the finite and fallen medium in which they take place. Stump's proposal is less articulated in terms of the processions and the missions, but a clear Trinitarian logic is nevertheless assumed throughout, including an affirmation of the inseparability rule. One would nevertheless have to express some hesitation about a couple of significant points in her presentation.

The first concerns Christ's experience of dereliction and death. Stump explains the death of Christ as a consequent of the internal dispossession that results from Christ's internalizing of the mass of human sin. The effect of this experience is that the unity between Christ's human psyche and God is lost, from which follows the separation between Christ's body and soul in death. Stump is articulating here a logic similar to what we have been proposing, whereby the death of Christ is not an instrumental or constitutive cause that turns God from wrath to love. However, the chronology of the dereliction and death does not seem to match Stump's model. While it is true that the experience is overwhelming for Christ, it does not lead to despair. Christ never loses faith and hope in God. Moreover, his demise finds him at utter peace with God in what appears to be a restored shared attention and mutual closeness: "Father, into your hands I commit my spirit" (Luke 23:46).

So if the death of Christ cannot be explained as a consequence of his dereliction, what can account for it other than the obvious contribution of the powers? Here the enduring value of the penal substitutionary position is most evident. At several crucial junctures the Scriptures connect the death of Christ with punishment. Isaiah 53:5 affirms that "the punishment that brought us peace was on him." Additionally, Paul articulates a logic that connects the justice of God's overlooking former sins with the propitiation that was done through the blood of Jesus. This by no means settles the question of the quality of Jesus's death as divine punishment. Even less does it demonstrate that the

Son is punished by the Father. But they provide sufficient cause to hesitate about a view of Jesus's death that bears no marks of God's will.

The position we have been articulating is more consistent with the biblical witness, and it adequately responds to many of the objections against penal substitution. The death that Christ dies has the quality of a divine punishment since all death has a penal dimension after the fall (Gen 2:17; Ezek 18:4; Rom 5:12). Christ's death was a consequent of his assuming a human nature under divine condemnation. This takes us back to Tanner: The particular working out of the eternal divine relationships has to include the condition into which the Son incarnates, namely a humanity under divine judgment. The union of God is not with an ideal humanity but precisely with a humanity in a specific legal standing: condemned. The redemptive value of the mission of the Son is that it draws precisely this humanity into an existence in the mode of Trinitarian sonship. The triune causality flows through the human nature and its operations, elevating them to a new divine-human life. The salvific significance of Christ does not consist in some logic of exchange but rather in a logic of transfiguration. In fact *any logic of exchange is rendered incoherent by the confession of the indivisible Trinitarian operation in the atonement.* A logic of exchange hides either Nestorian presuppositions or some form of adoptionism. God does not reward or react to anything accomplished on the human side, whether it is the obedience of Christ or his sacrifice. Rather, the whole of the Godhead already is in Christ reconciling the world to Godself (2 Cor 5:19). The human nature, its condition and operations, are taken up as they are and transfigured into the divine condition and operation. A new divine-human reality is thus established in the person of Jesus Christ.

It is important to stress the organic nature of this transfiguration. A logic of exchange keeps grace and nature too far apart from each other. A logic of transfiguration keeps them clearly distinct yet organically related: the human nature and its operations, but also its legal condition, are elevated and transformed, passed from death to life, from corruption to incorruptibility. A new humanity is thus made available in Jesus Christ. It was essential for Christ to die for our redemption not because God would reward this sacrifice, but because the way to new and divine life goes precisely through the old nature with its death.

This brings us to the second aspect where Stump's proposal seems wanting. It concerns the role played by the humanity of Christ in the coming forth of the Spirit. Since this is the topic of our next chapter, these remarks will be completed by a more detailed examination below. Christ's humanity accomplishes the following function in relation to the indwelling Spirit. First, the mutual closeness that the indwelling of the Spirit makes possible entails that human psyches are present in God's own mind. This takes place through the human nature hypostatically united to the Son. In virtue of this human nature, the Son (and therefore the whole Trinity) can internalize the subjectivity of the whole of humanity, including its sin and temptation. Secondly, through the passion of Christ, which takes place in the Son's human nature, humans are moved to open themselves to the love of God.

It should be noted that in both of these respects, it is the human nature of Christ in its originally assumed form or mode that is of decisive value. The first function is satisfied in virtue of its natural openness to other psyches; the second function is satisfied in virtue of the humanity's natural passibility. Thus, the coming forth of the Spirit to indwell believers in the life of grace is made possible by the sheer humanity of Christ, including its passibility.

The narratives, however, suggest something else, as we shall see in the next chapter. In addition to the human empathy and passion, the sending of the Spirit appears to be conditional upon precisely the resurrection and ascension. But these events indicate not simply the natural humanity of Christ, but rather its transfiguration, its elevation to supernatural glory. And thus the coming forth of the indwelling Spirit appears to be conditional upon the deification of Christ. But there is more—and here we must refer the reader back to our biblical discussion of the relation between the risen Christ and the Spirit. The Spirit who comes to indwell believers is not simply the Holy Spirit, but precisely the Spirit of Christ and the Spirit of the Lord (Rom 8:9; Gal 4:6). The argument that will be more fully made in the next chapter is that the Spirit who indwells us is not simply the Spirit of God in the abstract or simply the eternal Spirit of God, but rather the Spirit of God that has first permeated the humanity of Christ and now springs from it as a river of living water.

But this indwelling Spirit is precisely the Spirit that results from Christ having first died—in order to be resurrected and ascended. Thus, the death of Christ is not simply a "most promising" modality of moving the will of acerbic sinners but is rather the only means through which the humanity of Christ is fully transfigured such that it fully manifests the existence of the Son in obedience and therefore can spirate the Holy Ghost into human hearts.

To conclude this evaluation of Stump, we have attempted to show that, first, Christ's death is to be explained not simply as consequent upon his identification with the human experience of sin but rather as a consequent of his assumption of the whole of the human condition. Secondly, the coming forth of the Spirit proceeds by way of the transfigured and deified human nature, and therefore as precisely the Spirit of Christ.

CONCLUSION

Attending to the inseparability rule leads to a qualification of Christological agency, as we saw in the previous chapter. The relationship between the human and the divine operations in the hypostatic union must be understood in fidelity to the rule. We have seen that the human actions of Christ, the natural operations of his human nature, belong exclusively to the Son since the human nature only exists in the Son. Nevertheless, the human operation is actuated precisely by the divine causality, which is common to the three. Thus, the human operation exists only as the human presupposition of the theandric action of Christ and never prior to it. While retaining its human form it is always already divine action as well. In the union, the natural activity and passivity of the human nature are transfigured by the divine presence and causality.

The true significance for faith of the death of Jesus, then, is not that this historic and human event was required by the Father to initiate his specific salvific action, under whatever description we might render it—whether forgiveness, reconciliation, or propitiation. Whatever Christ does as man does not *enable* the Father to act as God because whatever Christ does as God is also done by the Father and the Spirit. Whatever Christ undergoes by way of passion describes the Son alone, since only the Son has a passible nature. Yet the transfiguration of his passion is effected by the whole Godhead: It is the Son alone who dies (in his human nature); it is the whole Trinity who passes him from death to life.

One of the central questions in this discussion concerned the relationship between the triune persons in the atonement, whereas the previous chapter attended to the relationship between the divine and human actions. The Trinitarian logic of salvation prevents pitting the Father against the Son, and it also prevents casting the human actions of the Son in a constitutive, antecedent, or causal role with respect to the actions of the Father. Were it not so, divine transcendence would be sacrificed and the identity of the triune persons would depend on temporal and economic outcomes. We have sided with the position that regards the human dimension of the triune action as a consequent of the divine dimension. Historic actions manifest, they express, the divine transcendent action and thus the divine being. For this reason, the cross has no causal power upon God; rather, the cross is the consequent, the necessary manifestation of divine love in the theatre of human rebellion. Its necessity is a consequent necessity. In Christ, God unites himself redemptively with humanity (Eph 1:10), transforming and transfiguring its condition.

The atonement, then, is not about God enabling himself to redeem us through some legal logic, although God is always "in the right." It is fundamentally about God's assuming the human problem. It is not the assumption in itself that is salvific, though. Rather, it is the fact that the assumption is the presupposition of a transfiguration that takes place through what Christ does and undergoes. Everything that Christ does acquires the mode of filial action: he does it from the Father. Everything he undergoes—his passion, temptation, and so on—is sanctified. Even in his passion he is never merely passive but always victor.

The end of the atonement, which in fact determines its character and form, is the mission of the Holy Spirit. The work of Christ has been about the at-one-ment of God and humanity. But this at-one-ment is not *merely* juridical but is ontologically transformative; it is about the full pneumatization of the human nature of the Son himself, resulting in the outpouring of the "Spirit of Christ." This indicates an *intrinsic* connection between the pouring out of the Spirit and the atonement. The Spirit's outpouring is not simply consequent upon the cross but specifically upon the resurrection and especially upon the ascension. It remains to determine more carefully the character of this relation in the next chapter.

CHAPTER 8

Ascension and Pentecost

The previous chapter began to develop the theme that the heart of the Christian doctrine of salvation is union with the Trinity. This presence of the whole Trinity (John 14:23), however, seems to be focused in a particular way on the *indwelling* of the Holy Spirit. The role played by the indwelling of the *specific* person of the Spirit in relation to the presence of the *whole* Trinity is complicated even more by the biblical link between the Spirit's coming and Christ's departure. From the standpoint of the doctrine of inseparable operations we thus have two related issues. First, how does the logic of inseparability handle the apparent handoff between the departing Son and the descending Spirit? If the persons have an indivisible operation, why is the coexistence of Christ and the Spirit apparently impossible? The second question, to be pursued in our final chapter, concerns the relation between the indwelling of a specific person and the presence of the whole Trinity: What is the indwelling, such that by it we can affirm the reality of distinct relations with the whole Trinity?

The present chapter seeks to provide a solution to the first problem by showing the inherent connection between the missions of the Son and the Holy Spirit. The key narrative element of this relation relates to the conditioning of the coming of the Spirit on the departure of Jesus. Jesus makes the puzzling statement, "I tell you the truth: it is to your advantage that I go away, for if I do not go away, the Helper will not come to you. But if I go, I will send him to you" (John 16:7; cf. John 7:39). While John is the only evangelist to recount this instruction, New Testament authors treat it as a known fact that the Spirit descended after

---

This chapter adapts material that previously appeared in my chapter "Ascension and Pentecost: A View from the Divine Missions," in *Being Saved: Explorations in Soteriology and Human Ontology*, ed. Mark Hamilton and Joshua Farris (London: SCM, 2018), 102–23. Used by permission.

Jesus's ascension. Luke, for instance, explains the Pentecostal events in relation to Christ's exaltation: "Being therefore exalted at the right hand of God, and having received from the Father the promise of the Holy Spirit, he has poured out this that you yourselves are seeing and hearing" (Acts 2:33).

The two events, then, are clearly correlated; but what is the logical relation between ascension and Pentecost? Couldn't Christ, the incarnate Son of God, have sent the Spirit without himself departing? Indeed, the same John records the story of Jesus breathing on his disciples and saying "Receive the Holy Spirit" prior to the ascension (John 20:22).

The appropriate dogmatic way of explaining the correlation between the two events is by considering them from the standpoint of the doctrine of the divine missions. More specifically, the meaning of this correlation will only reveal itself once we understand these events in the light of the Trinitarian sendings of the Son and the Spirit. The analysis of these missions, particularly of the relation between the sending of the Son and the sending of the Spirit, will further ground soteriological assertions that inevitably deal with the on-going presence of the Son and the Spirit in Christian life.

The following section explores a problematic, or at least partial, explanation of the relation between ascension and Pentecost. We then move, in the central constructive part of the chapter, to show how the theology of the missions illuminates the logical connection between the two events, or the two sendings. Briefly put, since a mission extends a procession to include a created effect, the mission of the Spirit, extending as it does the procession of the Spirit, repeats in time the procession of the Spirit from the Father and the Son (*Filioque*). This extension in time of the coming forth of the Spirit from the Father and the Son is consistent with the biblical narratives. The proposal is, finally, further refined in conversation with a number of likeminded authors.

Some Historical Explanations

How have the two signal redemptive historical events been correlated historically? We have identified one tradition, sometimes more suggestive than explicit, that builds on Acts 2:33, where Christ receives the "promised Spirit," or the "promise of the Holy Spirit." Some authors have suggested that the reason Christ cannot send the Spirit prior to his ascension is that he has yet to receive the Spirit as a reward. It is not as if Christ did not already have the Spirit, but the ability or prerogative to send the Spirit is conditioned upon the fulfillment of certain duties. The ascended Christ, then, receives this prerogative as a reward for his obedience.

John Chrysostom does not use the language of reward, but he ties the coming of the Spirit to Christ's fulfillment of his duty. The Spirit, he writes, "could not come, since the curse had not yet been lifted, the original sin had not yet been forgiven, but all men were still subject to the penalty for it."[1] Preaching on John 7:39 he ties Pentecost to the restoration of our favorable status and the return to friendship with God, whereupon we would receive the Holy Spirit as a gift.[2]

Protestant writers also use the language of merit in relation to Christ himself. Martin Luther, for instance, writes that "therefore, these are the gifts of God's grace, which Christ received from the Father through his merit and his personal grace, in order that He might give them to us as we read in Acts 2:33."[3]

Herman Witsius, although not asserting explicitly that Christ receives the prerogative of sending the Spirit as a gift, does nevertheless refer to the exaltation of Christ in terms of reward: "The glory of his justice required that his well beloved Son should not be disappointed of that reward, which was due to an obedience so signal, and a service so arduous and so perfect; and which was to be enjoyed only in heaven."[4] According to Witsius, some operations belonging to his office as mediator are only to be accomplished from heaven, including his giving of the gifts of the Holy Spirit to believers. But this exaltation is, according to Witsius, a "right which he had procured for himself."[5]

The nineteenth-century Church of Scotland minister George Smeaton speaks about Christ's "power of bestowing the Spirit upon others" as "the grandest display of Christ's exaltation—the culminating point,—arguing at once reward and divine dignity."[6] He then goes on to state explicitly: "The right to send the Holy Spirit into the hearts of fallen men was acquired by atonement."[7]

Now it is quite clear that none of the examples marshaled here indicate anything like a substantive attempt to answer my question. Overall, it can be

---

1. John Chrysostom, "Homily 78," in *Commentary on Saint John the Apostle and Evangelist*, trans. Sister Thomas Aquinas Goggin (Washington, DC: Catholic University of America Press, 1959), 345.

2. John Chrysostom, "Homily 51," in *Commentary on Saint John the Apostle and Evangelist*, trans. Sister Thomas Aquinas Goggin (Washington, DC: Catholic University of America Press, 1960), 33–43.

3. Martin Luther, *Lectures on Romans*, vol. 25 of *Luther's Works*, ed. Hilton C. Oswald (St. Louis: Concordia, 1972), 306.

4. Herman Witsius, *Sacred Dissertations on the Apostles' Creed*, trans. Donald Fraser (Glasgow: Khull, Blackie & Co, 1823), 2:227.

5. Witsius, *Sacred Dissertations*, 2:227.

6. George Smeaton, *The Doctrine of the Holy Spirit* (Edinburgh: T&T Clark, 1882), 134.

7. Smeaton, *Holy Spirit*, 135.

observed that Protestant theologians retained Calvin's reserve about a substantive answer to this question. He writes that "here we must not put the question 'Could not Christ have drawn down the Holy Spirit while he dwelt on earth?' For Christ takes for granted all that had been decreed by the Father and, indeed, when the Lord has once pointed out what he wishes to be done, to dispute about what is possible would be foolish and pernicious."[8]

But when some of the authors do venture in this direction, the language of reward is not far. But why should one be suspicious about it? Perhaps the most significant concern, one that has been heard increasingly in Catholic theology since Vatican II, has been about the extrinsic nature of grace.[9] If Christ receives the Spirit as a reward, the Spirit must be seen as extrinsic to Christ, something that he receives from the outside, upon the accomplishment of his mission. This raises important Christological and Trinitarian questions. Christologically, one has to ask about the relation between the human nature of Jesus and the person of the eternal Son. Isn't Christ's human nature by virtue of its hypostatic union to the Son already permeated by the Spirit? The question of agency follows immediately: What is the relation between the human operations and the divine operations of the incarnate Lord? Are the divine actions somehow conditioned by the successful completion of human actions? So for example is the human obedience of Jesus somehow a condition of the eternal Son's sending the Spirit?

Of course, one should not presume an answer to whether the sending of the Spirit is a divine action of the Lord, or whether it is a human action. If it is a divine action, in what way may an operation of the omnipotent Lord be seen to be conditioned by something—short of saying that God acquires capacities to act, which is undesirable, as we have just seen? On the other hand, if the Son sends the Spirit through his human nature what significant change does the ascension produce upon Christ's human nature such that only as ascended could he send the Spirit?

This barrage of questions should at the very least alert us that we must tread very carefully over this sensitive dogmatic terrain. The ground rules for such adventures have already been laid down by the Trinitarian theology and Chalcedonian Christology. The doctrine of the divine missions collates and

---

8. John Calvin, *John* (Wheaton: Crossway, 1994), 372.

9. Cf. Karl Rahner's "Some Implications of the Scholastic Concept of Uncreated Grace," in *God, Christ, Mary and Grace*, vol. 1 of *Theological Investigations*, trans. Cornelius Ernst (London: Darton, Longman and Todd, 1961); Henri de Lubac, *The Mystery of the Supernatural* (New York: Crossroad, 1998); Matthias Joseph Scheeben, *The Mysteries of Christianity* (New York: Crossroad, 2008).

applies these rules to our understanding of the temporal missions of the Son and the Spirit.

THE DIVINE MISSIONS, ASCENSION, AND PENTECOST

Two dimensions of a divine mission were so far identified in previous chapters. First, with Augustine and Aquinas, Western theology understands a mission to be the *temporal extension of a Trinitarian procession*. One might put it this way: In a mission we have the repetition in time of an eternal relation of divine origin. In this way a mission is different from an operation, and it augurs a different kind of divine presence than that by intensity. In a mission the Trinity communicates itself to us hypostatically.

The second dimension is that in a divine mission, the creature is drawn to participate in God, as a divine person comes to exist in a new way in it, yet in such a way that the divine person does not change. The dogmatic reasons for this are straightforward: In a mission we are given precisely the person as he proceeds from another—that is, in his relationship of origin—yet in relation to a created term. The created term is precisely that to which or in the form of which the divine person is sent. The sending thus coheres with the person's "coming forth from another." In this way sending is the extension of a procession.

Since a divine person is nothing but a relation of origin within the unity of the divine substance, what is given in a mission is the complete substance of God, but in terms of a relation between a created term and one of the irreducible yet indivisible relations of origin within this substance. There are in God only two such relations of coming forth from another: filiation and spiration. Consequently there are only two such missions, that of the Son and the Spirit. The Father too is present in the mission, only not as sent. As I noted, the whole Trinitarian substance is present in a way fitting with its relationships of origin and mode of existence.

What does "extending the processions" mean? Here we are starting to wade into deeper Trinitarian waters. For both Western fathers the doctrine of the divine missions must be consistent with the doctrine of the divine attributes. One such attribute is omnipresence, or immensity. Since God is already omnipresent, what might it mean for his being to be "extended," or for a divine person to be sent? Both Augustine and Aquinas understand this new presence not in terms of a change in God but rather as a change in the creature's relation to God. For Augustine, for a divine person to be sent just means for that divine person to be known. Aquinas also insists on this. It leads him to two essential insights into the doctrine: "The divine person sent neither begins to exist where he did not previously exist, nor ceases to exist where he was. Hence a mission takes place without a separation, having only distinction of origin."[10] Aquinas further explains that this is a new way of existing in the other: "Thus the mission of a divine person is a fitting thing, as meaning in one way the procession of origin from the sender, and as meaning a new way of existing in another."[11]

The Trinity in other words comes to exist in a new way in another, both visibly and invisibly. Galatians 4 indicates both types of missions, visible and invisible. Both the Son and the Spirit have visible and invisible missions. The visible mission prepares the invisible missions. As Jesus puts it in John 14:23: "If anyone loves me, he will keep my word, and my Father will love him, and we will come to him and make our home with him."

Again, given divine immutability and omnipresence a mission does not indicate a change in God, but a new relation in the creature whereby the creature begins to resemble God.[12] To say that God begins to exist in a new way in the creature, then, is just to say that the creature is lifted to participate in the divine relations. For this reason, Aquinas insists on defining a divine mission as "includ[ing] the eternal procession, with the addition of a temporal effect."[13]

These considerations merely reflect the implications of Trinitarian doctrine in relation to the work of salvation of the distinct divine persons in the economy. They represent the sifting of orthodox reflection on the Trinitarian nature of God in light of revelation. The Christian truth that they express is that God has made his own being available in time, he has gifted his own self through the missions of the Son and the Spirit. Yet we are instructed to resist certain mythological conceptions of the missions along the lines of their coming down and going up an "ontological ladder." The Western tradition has always exhibited great care to preserve the ontological distinction between

10. Thomas Aquinas, *Summa Theologica*, trans. the Fathers of the English Dominican Province (Westminster, MD: Christian Classics, 1981), 1, q. 43, a. 1, ad. 2.

11. Aquinas, *ST* 1, q. 43, a. 1.

12. Aquinas includes the indwelling of the divine persons under the category of exemplary causality, a type of causality situated between the intrinsic "formal" cause and the extrinsic "final" cause. The driving concern here is respecting the divine transcendence. To be distinctly indwelled by the divine persons is thus to receive a participation in their personal properties, to come to resemble them distinctly, as knowledge (the Son) and love (the Holy Spirit). For more on this, see Gilles Emery, *The Trinitarian Theology of Saint Thomas Aquinas*, trans. Francesca Aran Murphy (Oxford: Oxford University Press, 2007), 376-77. Aquinas clarifies some of these distinctions in Aquinas, *De Veritate*, q. 21, a. 4.

13. Aquinas, *ST* 1, q. 43, a. 2, ad. 3.

God and creation, not in the sense that God is unapproachable but that in communing with creatures he remains God.

A mythological approach will tend to regard the missions precisely in the way Augustine and Aquinas reject, as involving the divine persons in a series of departures and arrivals. The fathers rightly sense that such a view would finally dispense with the central mystery of our faith, that in these missions we are given the indivisible God, not some intermediary or an offshoot. Yet at the same time this God is giving himself to us in the only way it is fitting for him, namely by drawing parts of creation into union with him. This is rather essential for this project. In a divine mission, according to this tradition, a created effect is united to a divine person such that this divine person comes to exist in it in a new way.

The limited analogy we have used earlier might help. Take a natural magnet. The magnet is a substance that generates a magnetic field. The magnetic field comprises a relationship between two poles, negatively and positively charged. It must be understood that the two poles are not separable parts of the magnet but inseparable functions of the relations, which define the magnetic field, which is the magnet itself. Now bring a metallic needle to the magnet. It will become attached to only one of the poles of the magnet depending on its own charge. In the process the needle itself will become magnetized, meaning that it will come to exhibit the relations that constitute the magnetic field into which it participates.

This is a feeble analogy for what happens in a divine mission. The needle participates in the whole magnet, not just in one of the poles, since the poles are relational yet real distinctions within the unity of the magnet. The needle becomes attached specifically to one of the poles of the magnet, not to both of them. Finally, the needle acquires the magnetism of the magnet through its being attached to one of the poles.

Now, to cash out the analogy: The human nature of Jesus Christ is the created term that is drawn into union with the eternal Son. The whole of the Godhead resides in the human nature of Jesus Christ, since the Son is not a part of the Godhead but the whole divine nature considered from the standpoint of relation. Even though the whole Godhead creates the human nature and attracts and unites it to the divine Son, nonetheless the human nature is united exclusively to the Son such that it belongs to him alone. The Son alone comes to exist as Jesus Christ, the Son of Man. However, what it means for the Son to exist in this human nature is precisely for this human nature to acquire the "magnetism" of the divine relations, that is, to become in itself a channel for the relations that characterize this divine nature.

Now just as the needle is a substance while the magnetic pole to which it is attached is only a relation, the human nature of Jesus Christ is a substance while the eternal Son to which it is attached is what Aquinas calls a "subsistent relation." What we have here is the picture of a created substance that comes to participate in a relation while remaining the substance that it is. Thus, the human nature of Jesus Christ, without ceasing to be what it is, becomes hypostatically united to the Son and therefore is a channel or instrument for the Son. The Son can be said to exist in it in a new way insofar as the relation of sonship, or filiation, now also characterizes the human substance.

But in Western theology, it is not filiation alone that characterizes the Son. Unlike a magnet, where only two poles constitute the magnetic field, God is Trinity. The filiation of the Son further engenders the spiration of the Spirit as the common love between the Father and the Son. But this means that the relationship into which the human nature of Jesus Christ comes to participate, united to the Logos as it is, is not only filiation, but also active spiration.[14] Not only is the man Jesus Christ the Son, that is, but he also becomes, precisely as human, breather of the Spirit. Herein lies the key to the relation between ascension and Pentecost. To this we can now turn.

Christ's Human Nature and the Sending of the Spirit

The key question is this: How is the mission of the Son related to the *human* actions and passions of Jesus Christ? We have reported a rather timid suggestion—still influential despite its tentativeness—that Christ is glorified as a reward and more or less explicitly receives the prerogative to send the Spirit also as a reward. It may be argued that behind this answer lies a certain reflex of correlating the mission of the Spirit to the human acts and passions of Jesus. The latter are thought to somehow "unlock" or "enable" what is ultimately a divine action. There are solid dogmatic reasons, however, to reject this view. As we have seen in the last chapter, it implies that God enables himself to do this or that through some created action, in this case Christ's human obedience.

Such a view has a respectable pedigree in the West, from Augustine onward. Augustine had held that the sending of the Holy Spirit by the Son is a divine action, not one undertaken through his human nature. Augustine had argued that Christ receives the Spirit as man but sends him as God. His

---

14. The Thomist tradition identifies four relations within the Trinity: paternity, filiation, active spiration, and passive spiration. Active spiration refers to the joint immanent operation of the Father and the Son in spirating the Spirit.

reception of the Holy Spirit is conditioned, moreover, by his obedience but also by his victory over the powers. In his human nature, Christ removes the obstacles to grace by making satisfaction for our sins. In other words, as man he merits grace that is to be then dispensed through his divine offices. The actions through which he merits grace, in other words, unlock the sending of the Spirit as a divine act. This grace, moreover, is an extrinsic substance, acquired by Christ's sacrifice and bestowed upon believers.

Yves Congar has shown that this view has dominated Western theology up to the twelfth century, toward the end of which Robert of Melun and Gilbert de la Porrée make an alternative suggestion. They argue that Christ, precisely in his human nature is the cause of the influx of grace, and implicitly of the Holy Spirit.[15]

Aquinas: Beyond Mere Merit or Reward

When Aquinas argues this same position explicitly in his later thought, he not only modifies his own earlier position, but he stands against an influential way of understanding the connection between the human nature of Christ and the dispensation of grace and the Spirit.

Dominic Legge has pointed out that for Aquinas, Christ's human nature has not only a ministerial causality in sending the Holy Spirit but an instrumental and efficient one as well.[16] Aquinas gently pushes against the Augustinian tradition in asserting that Christ's actions "cause grace in us both through merit and through a certain efficiency."[17]

The merit view, we might be reminded, holds that Christ's human actions "unlock" a capacity to send the Spirit, or to dispense grace. The difficulty with this view, as we have seen, is that grace appears extrinsic to Christ himself. It is something that is merely bestowed on him upon the successful completion of his task. Aquinas, on the contrary, argues that the bestowal of grace results from the overflowing fullness of grace of Christ himself as man. He gives us the Spirit without measure because he has the Spirit without measure. As John 1:16 says, "from his fullness we have all received, grace upon grace." Legge summarizes Aquinas's contribution: "The visible mission of the Son in the incarnation brings with it, *by way of intrinsic relationship grounded in the eternal*

---

15. Yves Congar, "Saint Augustin et le traité scolastique 'De Gratia Capitis,'" *Augustinianum* 20 (1980): 89–91.

16. Dominic Legge, *The Trinitarian Christology of Saint Thomas Aquinas* (Oxford: Oxford University Press, 2017), 216–17.

17. Aquinas, *ST* III, q. 8, a. 1, ad. 1.

processions, the invisible mission of the Holy Spirit to Christ's humanity in the fullest possible measure, and consequently every grace, gift, and charism that a human nature can receive."[18]

This significantly supports our proposal. Aquinas grounds the sending of the Spirit, instrumentally, in the human nature of Christ, which is hypostatically united to the eternal Son. However, being united to one of the persons, it is *ipso facto* united (though differently) to both the others, including the Holy Spirit.[19] The relationship between the human actions and passions of Christ and the Holy Spirit is an "intrinsic" relation, as Aquinas holds, grounded in the processions themselves.

To speak of Christ as "meriting" the Holy Spirit is at least partial. Nevertheless, the biblical narratives seem to suggest that there is something like an "unlocking" (of something) taking place at the ascension. If with Aquinas we hold that we receive the Spirit from Christ's own superabundance, is this superabundance something he always had? If so, why does its pouring out seem to be conditioned by his return to the Father? If he did not possess it from the start, in what way is it acquired? The merit view does have a prima facie biblical plausibility.

A certain development is affirmed of the human nature of Christ. The book of Hebrews makes a particularly strong case for this, precisely in connection to Christ's heavenly session preceded by his human obedience.[20] The author writes in Hebrews 5:7–9: "During the days of Jesus' earthly life, he offered up prayers and petitions with loud cries and tears to the One who could save him from death, and he was heard *because of his reverence*. Although he was a Son he *learned obedience* through what he suffered. And *being made perfect*, he became the source of eternal salvation to all who obey him." Similar themes are encountered in Philippians 2:6–11, where the exaltation of Christ takes place as a reward for his obedience.

The historic adoptionist and Nestorian traditions are predicated precisely on these kinds of texts. But how are these scriptures to be taken if one wishes to avoid Nestorianism, Docetism, or a view that Christ's human nature makes no contribution to the ultimate salvific work of God? Aquinas's ascription of the sending of the Spirit to Christ's human nature raises the issue of whether something transpired in this human nature such that it could only send the

18. Legge, *Trinitarian Christology*, 178 (italics are mine).

19. It needs to be said that the union with the others is different than the union with the Son, in this case. Not all divine persons are incarnate, or come to exist in the human nature of Jesus Christ, which belongs to the Son alone.

20. Cf. also Hebrews 2:10.

Spirit once ascended. The older Augustinian view, as we have seen, holds that Christ's human actions merit the sending of the Spirit as a divine action. But once we make this sending a human action, why must it happen upon the ascension? If some divine capacity is not unlocked, could it be that a human capacity is?

One proposal comes from Catholic theologian Edward Schillebeeckx, an influential Vatican II voice. His contribution to the question of how to relate ascension and Pentecost is forging in the right direction, though his Christology may give us some pause.

Edward Schillebeeckx: Pentecost as Conditioned by the Realization of Christ's Sonship

In a signal piece, "Ascension and Pentecost," Schillebeeckx addresses the question at the heart of this chapter: Why couldn't Christ send the Spirit prior to his going back to heaven?[21] Schillebeeckx argues that this is not because he is on earth while the Father is in heaven, but because of a certain "inappropriateness" or "estrangement" from God.[22] "As man, God the Son enters into a humanity which made the history of the fall, of 'un-salvation,' and was branded with the sign of disobedience and removal from God—death."[23] Consequently, "the Spirit has first to overcome the sarx-condition, the situation of non-redemption of Jesus' humanity and renew and divinize this humanity through and through into its very bodiliness."[24] Only then can the Spirit be bestowed, Schillebeeckx argues, referencing Acts 2:33 and Hebrews 5:9.

Accordingly, Schillebeeckx treats the incarnation as a process, a "growing reality" and not so much a once and for all reality.[25] Along with Rahner and other modern Christological scholars, Schillebeeckx is suspicious of substance Christologies, preferring to analyze the presence of God in Jesus Christ in terms of consciousness. As a result, what Christ does is not simply a consequent of his divine identity, but what seems to be an antecedent condition of it. Such Christologies, when confronted with adoptionist-sounding texts, will tend to take Christ's obedience as what *determines and constitutes* his ultimate divine identity, whether by adoption or in other terms. This is a problem for Schillebeeckx as well, and we shall return to it in due course.

21. Edward Schillebeeckx, "Ascension and Pentecost" in *Worship* 35, no. 6 (1961): 336–63.
22. Schillebeeckx, "Ascension and Pentecost," 350.
23. Schillebeeckx, "Ascension and Pentecost," 350.
24. Schillebeeckx, "Ascension and Pentecost," 350.
25. Schillebeeckx, "Ascension and Pentecost," 348.

However, Schillebeeckx draws excellently on the doctrine of divine missions to explain the necessity of ascension for Pentecost. "In the bosom of the most Holy Trinity, the Son is pure self-giving to the Father. In God, this self-giving does not imply any giving up, any self-dispossession. Still, in the sphere of the incarnation, Christ's self-giving to the Father becomes a sacrifice, a giving up, an offering of his life."[26]

Now Schillebeeckx makes his essential move, which gets to the heart of the explanation: "The actual prerequisite for the sending of the Spirit of salvation is therefore Christ's obedience and attachment to the Father."[27] The move from the order of the processions to the order of the missions is transparent here: Just as the Holy Spirit proceeds immanently from the self-giving of the Son to the Father, as their mutual love, so temporally the Spirit proceeds from the attachment of the incarnate Son to the Father, which, in a condition of fallenness, must be exercised as self-sacrifice. Since in the bosom of the Trinity the Son is the principle of the life of the Holy Spirit, "on the level of the incarnation and thus as man, He will only be able to send us the Holy Spirit when His Sonship is completely realized in human form and therefore utterly given over in love to the Father who answers this gift in the resurrection."[28]

Schillebeeckx demonstrates what a perspective from the missions can yield. If a mission is the repetition in time of a procession, and if the procession of the Spirit follows from the Son's self-giving to the Father, then the procession of the Spirit in time will also be a function of the Son's (temporal) self-giving to the Father.

Before moving on, a number of critiques need to be made of this proposal. First, Schillebeeckx's Christology is at odds precisely with the tradition of the divine missions that is invoked here. If a mission is the extension of a procession to include a relation to a created effect, it has been stressed that the created term does not modify in any way the divine person. Paramount here is Bernard Lonergan's clarification and insistence that the necessary external term in a mission is only a consequent condition.

The nature of consequent conditions is such that their necessity is determined by the conditions of the activity that one is engaging in. They necessarily obtain upon the acting out of the action. Constitutive conditions on the other hand refer strictly to the powers of the agent. They need to be intended as conditions for the action. The fundamental difficulty with Christologies

26. Schillebeeckx, "Ascension and Pentecost," 351–52.
27. Schillebeeckx, "Ascension and Pentecost," 352.
28. Schillebeeckx, "Ascension and Pentecost," 352.

such as those of Rahner, Schillebeeckx, Pannenberg, and others is that they confuse the two types of conditions. More specifically, they interpret the human actions of Christ as antecedent conditions of his divine identity. A Chalcedonian Christology, on the other hand, views the human actions of Christ as consequent terms. In an account from the missions, therefore, Christ's human obedience is consequent upon his being who and what he is—namely the eternal Son of God—so it is not a condition of his sonship!

This is related to other difficulties. Schillebeeckx argues that the giving of the Spirit is predicated upon Christ's sacrifice. But this seems to require that the fullness of the Spirit be given to Christ upon his resurrection, not upon his ascension. Now it may be that Schillebeeckx in fact follows a modern strand that intentionally conflates the two events. Such a conflation is problematic for a number of reasons we do not have space to discuss here. More significantly, however, it reveals another confusion: Schillebeeckx tends to conflate the full realization of Christ's sonship with the full deification or glorification of Christ's human nature.

In his account, once Christ's sonship is realized the Spirit is bestowed. Chalcedonian Christology, on the other hand, holds that his sonship is a once and for all hypostatic union, from conception. The human actions of Christ are instrumentally the actions of the eternal Son of God. As such, they are consequent conditions of his divine actions. While the distinction between the two energies, divine and human, in Christ is an important one, it must not be confused with a separation. The doctrine of the divine missions intends to preserve the absolute aseity of God by insisting on the consequent nature of the created terms: The created effect is not an antecedent or a simultaneous, but a consequent condition, because the divine persons are absolutely independent with respect to all created things. Still, the consequent nature of Christ's human acts is not to be confused with mere human passivity. The eternal Son instrumentalizes a human nature, which nonetheless preserves its own identity (contra monophysitism and Eutychianism), yet is precisely the human nature of the eternal Son.

Whether or not the Chalcedonian balancing act withstands the critiques hurled at it or not, it constrains what might be said regarding Christology. Schillebeeckx has been found wanting in this respect. However, his account of the relation between ascension and Pentecost is appropriate. Before moving on, one question is begged by the foregoing: If Christ is the Son through hypostatic union and not through his acts of obedience, his divine consciousness (Schleiermacher), or his openness to transcendence (Rahner)—all of which are consequent upon his sonship—and if in virtue of this sonship

Christ also had the Holy Spirit from the beginning, shouldn't he be able to send the Spirit prior to his ascension?[29] What, in other words, is the role of the interval between conception and ascension? This problem still remains outstanding.

Schillebeeckx leads us to a dead end with his apparent confusion between resurrection and ascension.[30] He makes the giving of the Spirit a function of Christ's sonship, which is a result of his obedience. But the obedience is completed upon his sacrifice and vindicated in the resurrection. Yet the narratives portray Jesus as unable to send the Spirit even after the resurrection. "Do not cling to me, for I have not yet ascended to the Father," Jesus tells Mary (John 20:17). Certainly, the issue is complicated by the fact that a few verses later Jesus is recounted as breathing on the disciples and giving them the Spirit. This would seem to corroborate the lumping together of Christ's resurrection, ascension, and glorification.

Nevertheless, it can be safely concluded, with the great tradition, that the resurrection and the ascension represent two different events.[31] It is also beyond doubt that Jesus did condition sending the Spirit on his having ascended. How then are we to understand the so-called Johannine Pentecost? Briefly stated, a significant strand of the tradition regards Jesus's giving the Spirit to the disciples within the framework of the Old Testament dispensations of the Spirit. Strictly speaking, then, John 20 does not indicate an indwelling as much as an *empowering* Spirit. The task for this empowering work is also immediately specified in John 20:23: "If you forgive the sins of any, they are forgiven them; if you withhold forgiveness from any, it is withheld."

Back to the question, then: What difference does the ascension make specifically to the humanity of Jesus if it makes no difference to his sonship, contra Schillebeeckx?

---

29. See for example, Karl Rahner, *Foundations of the Christian Faith* (New York: Crossroad, 1994), 206–27; Friedrich Schleiermacher, *The Christian Faith* (Edinburgh: T&T Clark, 1989), §§93–94.

30. He writes that "broadly speaking—provisionally allowing for other positions in the New Testament—we may say that resurrection, exaltation and empowerment denote one and the same undivided reality in the New Testament profession of faith, with resurrection as the *terminus a quo* and exaltation the *terminus ad quem* of one and the same event." Schillebeeckx, *Jesus: An Experiment in Christology*, vol. 6 of *The Collected Works of Edward Schillebeeckx* (New York: Bloomsbury, 2014), 494.

31. See discussion in Douglas Farrow, *Ascension and Ecclesia* (Grand Rapids: Eerdmans, 2009).

Kathryn Tanner: Pentecost Conditioned by
the Gradual Deification of Christ's Human Nature

Kathryn Tanner's *Christ the Key* also supplies an account based on the missions of the divine persons. She writes that the relations among the Trinitarian persons come to take "humanity along for the ride," yet without changing the identity of the Son.[32] This happens in Christ, as "Jesus' human life exhibits the Word's relationships with the other members of the Trinity."[33]

Echoing the idea that the created effect is transformed in the process of being drawn to union with God, she writes about the Son and the Spirit: "They both return and re-ascend with us."[34] There is thus a progression taking place in the human nature of Jesus Christ. She expresses this variously. At one point she indicates that there is "some historical progression in the successful display of the Spirit's power" that is "not apparently displayed at once," which would seem to be related to the fact that he was sent in the form of a servant.[35] This seems to be a merely epistemic progress, in the way that Christ reveals the Spirit's power progressively. On the other hand, she writes about the end of his life that "only then . . . his humanity is *genuinely full of the Spirit* in the sense of being fully transparent to it."[36] "At only that point," she continues, "is he able to send the Spirit to us through his flesh."[37] There is a gradual transformation of the humanity of Christ as a precondition of his dispensing the Spirit, and this requires the passage of time.

But how are we to understand this gradual transformation in terms of Christ's relationship with the Spirit? Tanner argues, correctly in our view, that Christ has the Spirit from the beginning in virtue of his sonship. However, she argues that the mission of the Spirit does not commence at Pentecost. Rather, the workings of the Son and the Spirit are "intertwined" in the very mission of redemption, which they undertake together. "They are sent out at once together on that mission."[38]

Tanner thus challenges the received Western account of the missions of the Son and the Spirit as being sequential. She surmises the simultaneity of the missions by correctly observing that the Spirit already has an activity in

32. Kathryn Tanner, *Christ the Key* (Cambridge: Cambridge University Press, 2010), 145.
33. Tanner, *Christ the Key*, 147.
34. Tanner, *Christ the Key*, 161.
35. Tanner, *Christ the Key*, 170.
36. Tanner, *Christ the Key*, 171 (our italics).
37. Tanner, *Christ the Key*, 171.
38. Tanner, *Christ the Key*, 172.

Jesus's life from his very conception. The Spirit, she argues, provides the power of sonship to the Son. The Son "sends the Spirit from the Father, but not as the Father does. *The Spirit has already been sent out from the Father as a condition of the Son's own incarnation and mission.*"[39]

It follows that it is not Christ's return to the Father that procures the sent Spirit: "The Son can send the Spirit—specifically to us—only because he has already received the Spirit and felt the effects of its working within his own human life."[40] The reason, then, for the ascension prerequisite is that the effects of the Spirit's mission in Jesus's own life need time. Unlike Schillebeeckx, for whom the resurrection-ascension establish Jesus's sonship and thereby lead to the spiration of the Spirit in time, for Tanner the ascension is the climax of the progressive deification of Christ's humanity resulting in an overflowing abundance of the Spirit.

For Tanner, the Spirit does not result from the Son's love of the Father, not economically and therefore not immanently either. "Rather than the Spirit being the love that emerges from the relationship between Father and Son (as it usually is for Augustine), the Spirit is the love that comes forth from the Father to beget the Son."[41] The Spirit is the love through which the Word itself proceeds, Tanner argues. It does not itself result from the Word returning to the Father in love, although the Word does return the Spirit in love. "The Son does breathe back out the Spirit or (to change the metaphor) send back the Spirit of love to the Father, as the West stresses. But, contrary to the Western view, this is not the way the Spirit arises to begin with. The Spirit already exists in the Son; the Son has already received the Spirit as both emerge from the Father."[42]

What may we say about Tanner's proposal? There is much about her proposal that resonates with our account. She works from a perspective of missions, which temporally repeat what is eternally the case. Christ's obedience does not establish his sonship but merely confirms it. Additionally, she rightly insists that it takes time for the deification of Christ's humanity to take place and therefore for the plenitude of the Spirit himself to be realized. But, decisively, Christ is already the beneficiary of a mission of the Spirit, which does not issue through Christ's humanity itself. The Son and the Spirit come together, redeeming and transforming humanity in a double helix of descent and ascent.

39. Tanner, *Christ the Key*, 174 (our italics).
40. Tanner, *Christ the Key*, 174.
41. Tanner, *Christ the Key*, 178.
42. Tanner, *Christ the Key*, 193.

What Tanner has done, however, is to decouple the mission of the Spirit from the success of the Son's mission altogether. True, the Spirit does come to us because of Jesus's being completely overfilled with the Spirit in his humanity. Like Aquinas and Schillebeeckx she rightly retains the instrumental role played by Christ's humanity. Yet in Jesus's own case there already is a mission of the Spirit in his own life, a mission not mediated by his humanity, but one that precisely enables his own humanity. What are we to make of this?

Tanner is right to insist on the work of the Spirit in the life of Jesus himself. But is she entitled to surmise that this *work* of the Spirit is also a *mission* of the Spirit? Certainly there is an activity of the Spirit in the Old Covenant; there is also an activity of the Spirit in John the Baptist's own life, about whom Luke recounts that he was "filled with the Spirit" from his mother Elizabeth's womb (Luke 1:15, 41). But there is also universal agreement that these are dispensations of the Spirit that are not to be confused with the Pentecostal outpouring of the Spirit, which signifies a different sort of presence, one by indwelling. Strictly speaking a theology of the divine missions such as that of Aquinas will restrict the mission of the Holy Spirit to his visible manifestations at Jesus's baptism and Pentecost, followed by his invisible mission that commences thereafter.

The work of the Spirit in Jesus's own conception and life prior to his baptism need not be identified as a mission. Dogmatically it must be said that the whole Trinity is operative efficiently in Jesus's life. The Son is therefore also operative in Jesus's own life jointly with the Father and the Spirit as an efficient cause. Yet only Nestorians would say that the Son indwells his human nature. Thus activity does not necessarily indicate indwelling. From the fact that the Spirit is active in Christ's life from conception it is not necessary to surmise that the Spirit is sent, or *indwells* Christ in a divine mission. In a mission, as we have noted, a relation of union takes place between a created term and a divine procession. But in the case of the incarnation, the human nature is drawn into union with the Son, specifically. No created term is united to the Holy Spirit prior to the hypostatic union with the Son, since no human nature existed prior to that union (*enhypostasia*). Thus, the contribution of the Spirit to the incarnation cannot possibly be explained in terms of a mission. What needs to be distinguished here is an effect that is brought about by the common work of the triune persons, including the Holy Spirit, and the special union whereby a divine person comes to exist in a new way in a created term. Tanner has in other words identified a necessary though not a sufficient condition for the Spirit's indwelling or mission: the existence of an operation of the Spirit. But an operation does not automatically denote a mission, as is immediately obvious from the Old Testament expectation that the Spirit, which was already active then, will one day be more than active, residing in the hearts.[43]

Where does this leave us Christologically? We have in fact argued that the work of the Spirit in the life of Jesus does not denote an indwelling, or a mission of the Spirit from the beginning. Does that mean that Christ was not indwelled by the Spirit? That would indeed be absurd, making him in a certain sense our inferior.

The tradition that stems from Augustine and Aquinas understands the indwelling of the Holy Spirit operationally. To be indwelled by the Spirit is to be united to the third person through a "created grace," in this case love. Appealing to Romans 5:5, the tradition identifies love as the operation through which the Holy Spirit indwells believers. It is only insofar as a human being returns God's love to him that she may be said to be indwelled by the Holy Spirit. Note that indwelling cannot be a matter of sheer presence, given divine immensity and omnipresence. God the Spirit is already present everywhere. It is only insofar as creatures respond operationally (that is, through their created capacities and actions) that the Spirit may be said to indwell persons.[44]

This is true for Jesus as much as it is true for us. While there are a presence and activity of the Spirit in Jesus's life from conception, leading through his circumcision and growth and so on, it is precisely at the moment of his baptism that he may be said to *receive the indwelling of the Spirit in his human nature.* Not incidentally, baptism is an act of *obedience* for Jesus himself, as he puts it: "It is fitting for us to fulfill all righteousness" (Matt 3:15). Immediately after his baptism, Jesus came out of the water and "suddenly the heavens were opened, and he saw the Spirit of God descending like a dove and resting on him" (Matt 3:16). The Father's voice from heaven declares that he is "well pleased" with his Son. Note that Jesus himself ties the coming of the divine persons to obedience and love (John 14:23).

This does not endorse anything like a Christology from below, or a Spirit Christology. While Christ is substantially the divine Son of God from conception, the human acts he accomplishes lead to his human nature being indwelled by the Spirit. In virtue of his divinity, however, he has the Spirit fully. Yet as far as his humanity is concerned, it receives the mission of the Spirit as it learns to obey, trust, and love God himself.[45]

43. On the contrary, operations are common and appropriated, missions are unique to the persons.

44. And thus the invisible mission of the Son is through knowledge and faith, and that of the Spirit is through love.

45. Yves Congar articulates a similar position. It is worth quoting him at length: "In

What we observe in Jesus's human life is a gradual return to the Father in love. His obedience and love for God, consolidated at his baptism, result in the mission of the Holy Spirit upon his humanity. Not all is accomplished upon his baptism however. Christ must still learn obedience and be thereby perfected.

The ascension, then, symbolizes the loving and obedient return of Christ to the Father, with everything the Father gave him, to present to him his completed work. The reason Christ cannot send the Spirit until he ascends is that the Spirit proceeds from the love that the Son reciprocates to the Father. The incarnate Son obediently takes up his position at the right hand of the Father, in full submission to him as far as his human nature is concerned.

This explains why, although there is already a preascension mission of the Spirit commencing at his baptism, Christ is still not ready to pour out the Spirit for us until the ascension. The Spirit whom Jesus receives at baptism is indeed proceeding from the common love between the Father and the Son. But that which commences at baptism is only ready to be poured out once it completes the process of glorification and transformation of Jesus's own human nature. Importantly, the Spirit whom Christ receives at baptism for himself is still mediated by his humanity as it responds to the Father in love. Christ's human nature has been drawn as an external term into the Trinitarian processions and shares in their own (external) fecundity.[46]

Tanner is right to understand that the ascension represents the climax of a process that encompassed Christ's whole human life. But we have to insist that it doesn't simply amount to a "physicalist" filling up with some reified "grace"; rather, it consists in the operational attunement of Christ's will in submission

---

the case of Jesus, it is important to avoid Adoptionism. He is ontologically the Son of God because of the hypostatic union from the moment of his conception. Because of that too he is the Temple of the Holy Spirit and is made holy by that Spirit in his humanity. We have, however, as believers, to respect the successive moments or stages in the history of salvation and to accord the New Testament texts their full realism. Because of this, I would suggest that there were two moments when the *virtus* or effectiveness of the Spirit in Jesus was actuated in a new way. The first was at his baptism, when he was constituted (and not simply proclaimed as) Messiah and Servant by God. The second moment was at the time of his resurrection and exaltation, when he was made Lord." Yves Congar, *I Believe in the Holy Spirit* (New York: Crossroad, 1983), 3:171.

46. We could add, tentatively, that this human love of Christ is precisely the created consequent of active spiration. Just as immanently the Spirit proceeds in active spiration as the mutual love between the Father and the Son, so economically he proceeds from the reciprocated love of Christ for his heavenly Father. We will take this up in greater detail in the final chapter.

to the Father's.[47] The ascension itself may be seen as an act of obedience and submission but this time with Christ's humanity fully transparent to the Holy Spirit, as Tanner indeed also affirms.

Christ's session at the right hand of the Father represents not only the culmination of a process but the continuation of his mediatorship as he serves as a "minister [*leitourgos*] in the holy places" (Heb 8:2). As Christ is finally fully with the Father, he sends us the Spirit from the Father's bosom, precisely as his Spirit (Rom 8:9; Phil 1:19; Acts 16:7; Gal 4:6). As man, he remains submitted to the Father as his head (1 Cor 11:3), not usurping his glory (Phil 2:6–11), but freely receiving it from the Father. As man he spirates the Spirit for us out of his continuing loving obedience to the Father.[48]

Gradual Deification of Christ's Human Nature?

We have arrived at this position partly on the basis of Trinitarian grammar, which does not permit either the separation between the work of the Son and that of the Spirit, or the enabling of the work of the Spirit by the Son (or vice versa). Consistently throughout this volume we have applied the following logic: The changes that the narratives apparently predicate of the divine persons should be understood in terms of the assumed nature or of the created effects of a mission. The reason the Son cannot send the Spirit is not that the Son in himself lacks some capacity. Rather it is the inability of Christ's human nature to fully mediate the coming forth of the Spirit until its full transfiguration.

Again, the role of the humanity of Christ takes center stage in this discussion. Here the risk is to make what happens to this human nature into a constitutive condition for the divine mission. This, as we have seen, is the tendency of much modern Christology with its rejection of the allegedly static

---

47. Dumitru Stăniloae refers to this as the "state of ultimate pneumatization" of Christ's humanity. It "consists not only in the ability to dwell in and be felt by those who believe as the body borne by Christ's person, full of helping power to do good, but also in the supreme intimacy with the Father." He goes on to say that "The Godhead has completely overwhelmed His body, or better said, it is transparent and irradiates unhindered through his body without abolishing it." Stăniloae, *The Experience of God* (Brookline, MA: Holy Cross, 2011), 3:150.

48. Note that I am predicating obedience to the Father strictly of Christ's human actions. Texts such as 1 Corinthians 15:24 and 28 are to be understood to refer to a subjection that characterizes the ongoing incarnate nature of the eternal Son.

Chalcedonian categories of substance. We have observed it at work in Schillebeeckx's notion of the dynamic development of Christ's sonship.

The desire to make the created effect constitutive of the divine self-communication stems from the conviction that if the divine person remains extrinsic to the assumed nature, revelation is reduced to mere words. Rahner makes this point most forcefully and concludes by calling for an intrinsic relationship between human self-transcendence and the hypostatic union. If Christ is to be seen as the terminus of humanity then the hypostatic union must be understood to be in continuity with human nature. "The Incarnation cannot be understood as the end and goal of the world's reality without having recourse to the theory that the Incarnation itself is already an intrinsic moment and a condition for the universal bestowal of grace to spiritual creatures."[49]

Rahner insists on the intrinsic connection and we will allow him to speak at length here:

> If it can be shown that the two realities not only have an extrinsic, factual relationship to each other, but that by the very nature of both realities they are intrinsically and necessarily related, then in spite of the uniqueness of the Incarnation and in spite of the value and the significance of Jesus Christ for each one of us, which this uniqueness implies, the Incarnation does not appear simply as a higher realization of God's self-communication which leaves the rest of the world behind. If we see a relationship of mutual conditioning between the two realities, then we cannot perceive the God-man simply as someone who enters into our existence and its history from outside, moves it a step further and also brings it to fulfillment in a certain sense, but then nevertheless leaves it behind.[50]

The incarnation, then, is a realization of the intrinsic possibilities of the human nature, "an intrinsic moment within the whole process by which grace is bestowed upon all spiritual creatures."[51] The identity of the Son, in other words, is not extrinsic to the actions and passions of the human nature of Jesus Christ. Rather, the latter are the precise meaning and content of the traditional idea of the hypostatic union. They are not consequent upon an ontological reality or, as it has been called, the grace of union.

For Rahner, then, there is nothing additional to the hypostatic union ex-

49. Rahner, *Foundations*, 199.
50. Rahner, *Foundations*, 200.
51. Rahner, *Foundations*, 201.

cept, in Christ's activity, the full realization of human self-transcendence, which is in fact openness to God. In this sense, man is the "cipher of God."[52] Man is what happens when God utters himself as Word: "When God wants to be what is not God, man comes to be."[53]

It is not surprising that Rahner's turn from static to evolutionary categories in Christology enables him to place more weight on the human experiences and history of the Christ, including his self-consciousness. Distinguishing between an "unreflexive consciousness" where his radical and unique closeness to God may be discerned, and an "objectifying and verbalizing self-consciousness," Rahner writes that the latter has a history:

> It shares the horizons of understanding and the conceptualizations of his milieu, and in regard to himself, not just in "condescension" to others. It learns and it has new and surprising experiences. It is threatened by ultimate crises of self-identity, although once again they remain encompassed by the consciousness that even they are hidden in the will of the "Father," but they are not for this reason any less acute.[54]

Thus in the life of Jesus may be observed the gradual transfiguration and transformation of humanity. Christ by grace becomes the self-expression of God through his actions and passions. This transformation was not seamless and automatic, but it was marked by failures too, as Jesus's mistaken conception of the inauguration of the eschatological kingdom shows.[55]

To sum up this brief discussion of Rahner, we have here an example of making the humanity of Christ constitutive of the mission of the Spirit because in a very real sense it is up to the humanity of Christ to fully realize its potential of becoming the self-expression of the Father, as Word, through grace. Until that realization is complete the Spirit may not be sent. In this case, the operations of his human nature are not merely instrumentalized and consequent upon the causality of the Trinity. On the contrary, they are constitutive of the very fact of the hypostatic union itself. The union between the Word and Christ's human nature is not something that precedes and determines its operations but something that results from these operations themselves.

---

52. Rahner, *Foundations*, 224.
53. Rahner, *Foundations*, 225.
54. Rahner, *Foundations*, 249.
55. Rahner claims that "we may speak of an 'error' in the imminent expectation of Jesus. In this 'error' Jesus would only have shared our lot, since to 'err' in this way is better for historical man, and hence also for Jesus, than to know everything in advance." *Foundations*, 250.

There are good reasons to be suspicious of thinking of the development of Christ's human nature in this kind of framework. Thomas Joseph White expresses well the primary concern about Rahner. First, his approach to Christology echoes Nestorius. The human nature of Christ seems to have a distinct ontological reality of its own, such that it appears to be the source of its own operations. The unity between this nature and the Logos "seems to be constituted primarily by what Aquinas would term the accidental quality of habitual grace."[56] Putting it differently, if the union between the Word and human nature is *constituted* by the operations of this human nature, these operations are prior to the union and therefore they require their own subject: the Nestorian human hypostasis. In Christ there is a uniquely intense self-awareness of God and habitual grace.

Resulting from this change of perspective, Rahner entirely discards the traditional thought of the instrumentalization of the human nature of Christ. Additionally, as White notes, Rahner

> almost never speaks either of the hypostatic "subsistence" of a divine person in a human nature or of the union of two natures in a divine person. Instead, it is now the human history of Christ that is seen as a "self-communication" of God to man, and this self-communication of God being united with man acquires its intrinsic form through Christ's human knowledge of God and free obedience toward God.[57]

It would appear that the present proposal in affirming a development of Christ's human nature also risks turning it into an independent principle, thus inviting Nestorian suspicions. We have argued, with Tanner, that part of the reason why Pentecost must await the ascension is that the human nature of Christ must be filled with the Spirit and that this filling takes time and is completed upon the ascension. But isn't it contradictory to affirm both that (a) the human operations of Christ subsist precisely in the Son and therefore are operations perfected in the mode of sonship; and (b) there is a development, a growth, a gradual deification of Christ's humanity, the completion of which the Spirit must await? What we must now ask is whether there is a third option between the automatic perfecting of Christ's human nature in the hypostatic

---

56. Thomas Joseph White, *The Incarnate Lord: A Thomistic Study in Christology*, Thomistic Ressourcement Series 5 (Washington, DC: Catholic University of America Press, 2015), 99.

57. White, *The Incarnate Lord*, 99.

union, on the one hand, and its contingent development and growth such as what Rahner imagines, on the other.

If the actions of the human nature of Christ subsist in the filial mode of the Son, does it not follow that they are already perfect? In the Thomistic tradition, Christ's human nature is made substantially perfect by habitual grace. In addition, as man Christ also has the experience of the beatific vision. He takes up the question of Christ's possession of "the knowledge of the blessed or comprehensors" in *Summa Theologiae* III, question 9, article 2, and his argumentation is entirely soteriological. Assuming that the perfection of "the end of beatitude" is brought about by the humanity of Christ, according to Hebrews 2:10, "it was necessary that the beatific knowledge, which consists in the vision of God, should belong to Christ pre-eminently, since the cause ought always to be more efficacious than the effect." White notes that this claim goes uncontested until the middle of the twentieth century,[58] when it becomes increasingly unclear how a real human experience of temptation and growth in knowledge, for example, can co-exist with the beatific vision. As we have seen, Rahner points to the fallible human knowledge of Christ as a necessary corollary of his full humanity.

Thomas also insists on the perfection of Christ's human nature, a perfection that is brought about by the hypostatic union but whose formality is habitual grace. The second reason for the necessity of this habitual grace is relevant in connection to our theme: "On account of the dignity of this soul, whose operations were to attain so closely to God by knowledge and love, to which it is necessary for human nature to be raised by grace."[59] Note the priority of habitual grace to operation: Christ is able to attune his human will and operation to God's will and operation because of this habitual grace.

As we have seen, Christ's human operations are instrumentalized by the divinity and in the process elevated beyond their natural capacities. The soul, Aquinas notes, is not capable of the supernatural acts of knowing and loving God, which in the natural Son must be an uncreated act, "i.e. the same whereby the Father knows and loves himself."[60] Such an elevation takes place by grace, without which the operations would remain entirely human and natural. This grace, then, perfects the theandric operations of Christ.

Aquinas continues by asking whether the grace of Christ is infinite and whether it can increase. He distinguishes between the grace of union, which

---

58. White, *The Incarnate Lord*, 237n1.
59. Aquinas, *ST* 3, q. 7, a. 1, *responsio*.
60. Aquinas, *ST* 3, q. 7, a.1, ad. 1.

"is for Him to be personally united to the Son of God, which union has been bestowed gratis on the human nature,"[61] and which grace is clearly infinite, and, on the other hand, habitual grace, which is finite insofar as it is received into a finite nature. The same habitual grace is infinite in the sense that it contains whatever may be contained by grace. Christ in this sense does not receive only some aspects of grace—such as, say, fear of God and wisdom—but everything that pertains to grace.

In regard to the question of the increase of grace in Christ, Aquinas points out that a form can increase in two ways: first, in regard to the subject that possesses that form; secondly on the part of the form itself. In neither of these respects does the grace of Christ increase. In respect of the person, this is because in union with the Son the human nature has attained its end "since Christ as man was a true and full comprehensor from the first instant of His conception."[62] Finally, "on the part of the form, the possibility of increase is excluded when a subject reaches the utmost perfection which this form can have by nature."[63]

That said, it is instructive to see how Aquinas responds to the objection formulated on the basis of Luke 2:52: "And Jesus increased in wisdom and in stature and in favor [*chariti*] with God and man":

> Anyone may increase in wisdom and grace in two ways. First, inasmuch as the very habits of wisdom and grace are increased; and in this way Christ did not increase. Secondly, as regards the effects, i.e., inasmuch as they do wiser and greater works; and in this way Christ increased in wisdom and grace even as in age, since in the course of time He did more perfect works, to prove Himself true man, both in the things of God, and in the things of man.[64]

It appears, then, that on Aquinas's terms we do not have a third option between the gradual progress of Christ's human nature, such as Rahner entertains, and the absolute perfection from conception of this human nature. This, however, may not be Aquinas's last word on the topic. In order to see another possibility, we must attend to what the Angelic Doctor says about the role of the body in beatific vision.

61. Aquinas, *ST* 3, q. 7, a. 11, *responsio.*
62. Aquinas, *ST* 3, q. 7, a. 12, *responsio.*
63. Aquinas, *ST* 3, q. 7, a. 12, *responsio.*
64. Aquinas, *ST* 3, q. 7, a. 12, ad. 3.

In question 92 of the supplement to *Summa Theologiae* III, Aquinas is asking "whether after the resurrection the saints will see God with the eyes of the body." At stake in this question is the continued usefulness of the body as an essential part of human nature. The problem is created by the fact that, since God is spirit, he may only be seen spiritually, with the eyes of the intellect, rather than bodily. This would seem to render the body superfluous to the eternal life, since if the end for which we have been created is the vision of God then our body would seem to be playing no part in this seeing.

However, this is not the whole story. Aquinas distinguishes between direct and indirect vision:

> An indirect object of sense is that which does not act on the sense . . . but is annexed to those things that act on the sense directly: for instance Socrates; the son of Diares; a friend and the like which are the object of the intellect's knowledge in the universal, and in the particular are the object of the cogitative power in man, and of the estimative power in other animals. The external sense is said to perceive things of this kind, although indirectly, when the apprehensive power (whose province it is to know directly this thing known), from that which is sensed directly, apprehends them at once and without any doubt or discourse.[65]

To continue Aquinas's example, my eye sees "Socrates," or a "friend," even if "Socrates" as such is not visible except to the intellect. The material object of vision, however, is connected to the intellectual object and therefore the eye is said to indirectly see the latter. This illuminates the way in which bodily vision can still see God, even if indirectly. Speaking about bodily sight and sense, Aquinas explains that

> it will be impossible for it to see the Divine essence as an object of direct vision; yet it will see it as an object of indirect vision, because on the one hand the bodily sight will see so great a glory of God in bodies and most of all in the body of Christ, and, on the other hand, the intellect will see God so clearly. That God will be perceived in things seen with the eye of the body, even as life is perceived in speech. For although our intellect will not then see God from seeing His creatures, yet it will see God in His creatures seen corporeally.[66]

65. Aquinas, *ST* 3, Supplement, q. 92, art. 2, *responsio*.
66. Aquinas, *ST* 3, Supplement, q. 92, art. 2, *responsio*.

Why is this relevant? Because it indicates the possibility of surpassing the unsurpassable, so to speak. Even fully experiencing the beatific vision, the soul of the blessed can derive additional joy from beholding the manifold ways in which God may be participated in and from the myriad ways in which his infinite beauty is refracted through his creatures.

This reveals another possibility in which grace may be seen to increase, in addition to the new works that spring from it. That is, grace may be seen to increase in Christ as he faces new situations in which its true nature is revealed. Scripture speaks, as we have seen, about a perfection of Christ through suffering and a learning of obedience by Christ. Neither of these need to entail that the grace of Christ, his personal holiness, was deficient in any way.

But it is possible to speak about an increase of grace in the sense of an increase in one's capacity for grace. In the same way in which, as Aquinas puts it, "our body will have a certain beatitude from seeing God in sensible creatures: and especially in Christ's body,"[67] Christ's own beatitude may increase by seeing how his own life—including his growth in human wisdom and knowledge, but especially his passion and resurrection—reflect God. Thus, on the one hand Christ has the vision of God from conception, while on the other hand throughout his earthly life he discovers (as man) the manifold ways in which God may be participated in and experienced, particularly through the experience of loss and want characteristic of the human condition.

We would be prepared to argue additionally that such an increase in the beatific vision throughout the life of Christ is proportionate and instrumental to an increase in Christ's own human capaciousness for God. In this way Christ recapitulates human destiny, leading to his glorified postresurrection human nature. Just as Adam was destined to arrive at his supernatural end through obedience, so Christ inaugurates that end also through obedience—and yet obedience even unto death (Phil 2:8; Rom 5).

The premise of the foregoing is that Jesus's human nature is progressively deified, culminating in his transfigured resurrection body. This represents the fullness of what is achievable or the fullness of grace in the humanity of Christ, from whence the Holy Spirit comes: "From his fullness we have all received, grace upon grace" (John 1:16). This fullness is realized in time, but not in the sense that at any given moment Christ might have had more grace. Rather, grace is maximized in Christ at each moment of his life—considering the multiple experiences and situations in which he would have known this grace—as

---

67. Aquinas, *ST* 3, Supplement, q. 92, art. 2, ad. 6.

he obeys the Father. Moreover, there is no contradiction between this increase in grace and the perfection of Christ's human nature from its conception.

The growth of the capacity for the Spirit in Christ's human nature is predicated on the priority of the hypostatic union and therefore on the grace of union over Christ's habitual grace. That is to say, the operations of Christ do not flow from a quasi-independent human nature but specifically from the God to whom the human nature is united in the person of the Son. The hypostatic union is not constituted by the ongoing deification of Christ. Rather, the latter is the consequent of the former. That said, the *terminus* of this deification is a fully pneumatized life.[68]

A Life-Giving Spirit

There remains one more piece of the puzzle concerning the interpretation of the ascension-Pentecost sequence. We have asked the question of why the Son cannot send the Spirit before his ascension and have found that the answer cannot be in any set of capacities that the eternal Son must somehow acquire. The puzzle is illuminated when one brings to bear the framework of the divine missions. In Jesus Christ human nature is caught up in the Trinitarian relationships and therefore itself begins to mediate the mission of the Spirit.[69] But the Spirit that comes at Pentecost is not a Spirit extrinsic to Christ but is rather the Spirit that overflows from his deified humanity. It remains for us to make some final clarifications about this relationship and this dynamic identity between the risen and ascended Christ and the Spirit.

On the face of it the sequence ascension-Pentecost seems to convey the story of one of the Trinity departing and another of the Trinity arriving. This is true to the extent that theology must take seriously the absence of Christ in his humanity. But upon more careful consideration, it is not as simple as it appears at first blush.

Jesus concludes his commissioning of the disciples with the encouragement, "Behold, I am with you always, to the end of the age" (Matt 28:20).

---

68. Dumitru Stăniloae writes: "Only when Christ, by ascending as man to the Father is filled bodily with the Holy Spirit—and as such the Father himself as God—can the fullness of the Spirit shine forth from His perfectly pneumatized body." Stăniloae, *The Experience of God* (Brookline, MA: Holy Cross, 2012), 4:4.

69. An Eastern Orthodox account would also stress the link between the sending of the Spirit and his procession. So Gregory Palamas stresses that the Son must ascend as man to the Father in order to send the Spirit from the Father's bosom, from which he proceeds. Palamas, "Homily 24," in *The Homilies*, trans. and ed. Christopher Veniamin (Dalton, PA: Mount Tabor, 2014).

Additionally, we have been assured that the whole Trinity will come to make its home with us (John 14:23), that Christ is in us (Rom 8:10), and so on. As we have seen in our discussion of the Pauline understanding of the relationship between the risen Lord and the Spirit, the church's experience of the Spirit is precisely the experience of the presence of Christ in her midst. Thus the Spirit's function is to make Christ present in the same way as in the Old Covenant the Spirit mediated YHWH's presence to Israel.

We seem to be faced with an apparent contradiction in the teaching of the Scriptures. On the one hand Christ explains to the sorrowful disciples that he must leave to go to the Father and that unless he goes to the Father the Spirit will not come. On the other hand we are promised the continued presence of Christ to the end of the age!

The key lies in thinking through the ascension of Jesus Christ along the lines of the transfiguration and pneumatization of his human nature. Our model has called for an understanding of the economy of salvation in terms of the human nature being drawn into union with the Son, acquiring the mode of existence of the Son and consequently spirating the Spirit, upon its full pneumatization. The second Adam recapitulates the journey of the first Adam, thus becoming a "sheep's gate" (John 10:7) to God. From Christ's humanity and in Christ's humanity all the benefits of salvation flow.

Rahner, for all our hesitation about his position, does point the right direction here:

> Jesus' resurrection is . . . the beginning of the transfiguration of the world. . . . The risen Lord, freed by resurrection from the limiting individuality of the unglorified body, has in truth become present to the world precisely because risen (and so by his "going"), and . . . his return will only be the disclosure of this relation to the world attained by Jesus in his resurrection.[70]

Unfortunately, Rahner seems to conflate the resurrection and the ascension, a slippage quite common in modern theology but one that is not legitimized by Scripture. What Rahner adequately grasps, however, is the fact that the resurrection-ascension sequence does not leave Christ as it found him. The sequence involves a transformation, though not to the point of an abandonment of the humanity of Christ.

---

70. Karl Rahner, *Theological Investigations* 4:353, as quoted in Douglas Farrow, *Ascension and Ecclesia: On the Significance of the Doctrine of the Ascension for Ecclesiology and Christian Cosmology* (Grand Rapids: Eerdmans, 2009), 215.

Greek theologian John Zizioulas articulates a similar point in relation specifically to the work of the Spirit:

> Now if becoming history is the particularity of the Son in the economy, what is the contribution of the Spirit? Well, precisely the opposite: it is to liberate the Son and the economy from the bondage of history. If the Son dies on the cross, thus succumbing to the bondage of historical existence, it is the Spirit that raises him from the dead. The Spirit is the beyond history, and when he acts in history he does so in order to bring into history the last days, the eschaton.[71]

For Zizioulas, the Spirit's transfiguration of the humanity of Christ acquires the shape of ecclesiology as well, creating what he has called the "corporate personality" of Christ.[72] And so in the final act of the history of Christ we have, according to Zizioulas, the presence of all times, the *eschaton*, and indeed the presence of all believers, the church.

There is much risk in talk of transfiguration, however. Take for example the Lutheran notion of the ubiquity of Christ's post-ascension body. Many fear that any such transformation renders the ascended Christ no longer recognizably human. Ubiquity may be taken to entail that Christ in his humanity is no longer located in space and thus is no longer a body. To speak, as Zizioulas and others do, of the corporate personality of Christ may seem to destroy the individuality and thus the particularity of Christ. Much caution must be exercised here indeed.

However, the attendant risks are not sufficient to deter us from this important task: to think through a transformation of the humanity of Christ as its pneumatization, namely its being made entirely transparent to the Spirit. But this means that the Spirit who comes down at Pentecost is precisely the Spirit of Christ, as we have seen especially in Paul, and more specifically the Spirit that has been first assimilated by Christ, processed by Christ. The Pentecostal Spirit, sent by the Son from the Father, is intrinsic to Christ's humanity—but not in Rahner's sense of intrinsic. Rahner's intrinsicism confuses the Spirit of God with the human spirit. A properly intrinsic relation understands the Pentecostal Spirit as an emergent property of Christ precisely in virtue of his being the eternal Son of God. To say that the second Adam became a life-giving spirit

71. John Zizioulas, *Being as Communion* (Crestwood, NY: St. Vladimir's Seminary Press, 1985), 130.

72. Zizioulas, *Being as Communion*, 130.

is not to confuse the Spirit and Christ, or the Spirit and the Son (this indeed seems to be one of the primary functions of the historical separation between ascension and Pentecost). It is to say that the indwelling Spirit is shaped,[73] it is formed for us, precisely by the humanity of Christ.

CONCLUSION

The doctrine of inseparable operations also sheds light on the biblical conditioning of Pentecost upon the ascension of the resurrected Christ. Here, as elsewhere, mythology must be resisted. This is not the story of one divine being ascending back up the ontological ladder and being substituted by another divine being who comes down the ladder. Nonetheless the bodily absence of Christ needs to be taken seriously and not trivialized by cavalier appeals to ubiquity.

We have suggested that the key to understanding the ascension-Pentecost sequence resides in applying the framework of missions, since the coming of the Spirit is, specifically, a divine mission. As a divine mission, it is not simply appropriated to the person of the Spirit but rather is proper to him insofar as it is an extension of the procession of the Spirit. But the procession of the Spirit is consequent upon the return of the Son to the Father in love. This provides us with a prima facie logic for the sequencing: Just as immanently the Spirit proceeds from the love that the Son shares with and returns to the Father, so in the economic missions the Spirit proceeds externally once the Son has returned to the Father in love and (economic) obedience.

This prima facie logic, however, must be carefully qualified. Doesn't Christ immediately reciprocate the Father's love? Doesn't he obey God from the very beginning of the hypostatic union? As Tanner reminds us, when immanent relations are manifested on an economic plane they take time and they are refracted to a certain extent by the finite medium of their manifestation. And so the temporal manifestation of these eternal relations is natural. However, it must not be supposed, as Schillebeeckx tends to do (and as Pannenberg also suggests), that somehow the sonship of the Son is itself *realized* on an economic plane. Rather, the sonship of Christ must remain the presupposition of his activity, not its outcome.

We found it preferable to speak of a transfiguration of the human nature of Christ, which follows the hypostatic union yet takes time. Thus, Christ's

---

73. Tanner admits that the Son is simply responsible for giving the Spirit its shape, while denying that it comes from the Son also. *Christ the Key*, 192.

human nature is lifted above its natural capacities by the divine action as Christ acts in obedience and suffers. Being united to the Son, it receives the mode of existence of the Son (not having its own *esse*). And the mode of existence of the Son consists in having come from the Father but also, secondarily, in being productive of the Spirit (together with the Father). So the humanity of Christ manifests both his human obedience to the Father and its progressive enabling for the external spiration of the Holy Ghost. As God, Christ could draw the Spirit at any moment; however, God had determined to pour the Spirit precisely through the humanity of Christ, as the "Spirit of His Son" (Gal 4:6). This takes place through the progressive pneumatization of Christ's human nature. Christ becomes a life-giving spirit, not by ceasing to be human or by relinquishing his body. Rather in his existence, from birth to ascension, he recapitulates the Adamic destiny by lifting human nature to its intended state, the same destiny that awaits us (1 John 3:2), yet only insofar as we are in Christ through his eternal priesthood.

In ascending, although he is no longer present bodily he does not vacate but begins to permeate created reality even more fully, as Paul puts it, "that he might fill all things" (Eph 4:10). The deification of reality is thus premised precisely upon the ascension of Jesus Christ. But the flip side of Christ's ascension is precisely the descent of the Spirit. Christ and the Spirit must not be confused, however. The arrival of the Spirit does not undo the bodily absence of Christ; yet the Pentecostal Spirit is precisely the Spirit of Christ. The doctrine of the Trinity and of the inseparable operations helps us understand that in having the Spirit we have the whole Trinity. We shall now take up a final question: How can we understand the indwelling of the Spirit in the light of the inseparability rule?

CHAPTER 9

The Indwelling of the Holy Spirit as Love

The final doctrinal *locus* where we explore the feasibility of the inseparability rule concerns the doctrine of the indwelling of the Holy Spirit. Christian faith announces that as a result of the work of Christ, believers receive the gift of the Holy Spirit. The whole Trinity, in fact, comes to make its home in the Christian. The completed work of Christ inaugurates a new relation between the believer and the divine persons, a relation that is intimate and personal, where the divine persons are present as distinct terms. As a relationship in the supernatural order, the believer does not simply receive created gifts but the uncreated divine persons themselves. But how is this new relation to be conceived?

A first difficulty is constituted by the distinction between created reality and the uncreated, transcendent God. The difficulty does not primarily consist in the possibility of the union, something that the Christian tradition readily grants, but in how to conceptualize the union metaphysically such that the distinction between God and creatures is preserved.

An additional difficulty relates to the inhabitation of the Holy Spirit specifically. Christians confess that all Trinitarian persons are inhabiting the believer in their hypostatic character. In other words, the persons of the Son and Holy Spirit are being given to us, and the Father is giving himself to us. The persons are present with us, moreover, in their hypostatic particularity, as distinguished from one another in their particular identities and not simply as

This chapter adapts material that previously appeared in my chapter "The Indwelling of the Holy Spirit as Love," in *Love, Human and Divine: Contemporary Perspectives in Systematic and Philosophical Theology*, ed. Oliver D. Crisp, Jordan Wessling, and James M. Arcadi (New York: Bloomsbury, 2019). Used by permission of T&T Clark, an imprint of Bloomsbury Publishing Plc.

causes of created effects. For the classic Western tradition of Trinitarian theology, however, this presents a problem. In this tradition (and also in others) the external operations of the Trinity are axiomatically inseparable. In virtue of the unity of the divine substance, which is the foundation for its operations, all external works of the Trinity must be common to the three persons. Now an invisible mission of the Spirit (which is how this tradition often refers to the indwelling), entails an *opus ad extra* and thus must be taken as common to all Trinitarian persons. The perplexity becomes clear at this point: How can the Spirit as well as the Father and the Son be given to us in their hypostatic uniqueness given that their operations are supposed to be common?

While the Western tradition holds that all the economic works of the Trinity are inseparable, it also employs the principle of appropriation.[1] According to our discussion above, the principle holds that although such works are common to all Trinitarian persons certain works are appropriated to certain persons. Such appropriation does not indicate any unique causality of that particular person but that this or that particular work—or particular effect, to be more precise—manifests this Trinitarian person rather than that one. So for example, we speak about sanctification as being a work common to the whole Trinity yet appropriated to the Holy Spirit.

In the case of the indwelling, however, we do not have to do simply with an external effect—such as "sanctification"—but with a self-giving of the person. The Western strictures seem to foreclose precisely what is religiously significant about the concept, namely that the persons are being given to us distinctly, not simply in an appropriated manner.

The question naturally arises whether the Western rule of inseparable operations inherently contradicts the faith that we are united distinctly to the Father, Son, and Holy Spirit as the end of our salvation. The thesis of this chapter is that this conflict is resolvable. It is possible to give an account that both preserves the important strictures about inseparability of action and affirms the indwelling of the Trinitarian persons in their hypostatic character. We propose to reach this goal through the following steps. First, we start with the biblical testimony to the notion of indwelling and its traditional Thomistic interpretation in terms of love. We then present a number of important objections and Karl Rahner's alternative interpretation of the indwelling in

---

1. For additional work on appropriation, see Augustine, *The Trinity*, bks. 6–7; Gilles Emery, *The Trinitarian Theology of Thomas Aquinas* (Oxford: Oxford University Press, 2007), 312–38; Adonis Vidu, "Trinitarian Inseparable Operations and the Incarnation," *Journal of Analytic Theology* 4 (2016): 106–27.

terms of a "quasi-formal" presence of the persons. The next section argues that Rahner's interpretation fails to preserve important theological assumptions. We then return to the Thomistic interpretation and argue that it is able to address the objections formulated by Rahner and others through its notion of exemplary causality. Next we respond to a number of objections, some of which are inspired by Protestant dogmatic sensibilities. Finally, we recover the dogmatic significance for the question of the indwelling of the Pauline concept of "Spirit of Christ."

THE WESTERN INTERPRETATION OF THE INDWELLING: THE APPROPRIATION TRADITION

The Scriptural witness to the operation of the Trinity upon the justified seems to imply that there is a presence of the divine persons that transcends the effects of God's actions. In Catholic theology this presence leads, through sanctifying grace, to the supernatural elevation of the soul into communion with the whole Trinity. For Protestants this denotes a union with Christ in sanctification. For the Orthodox this refers to the deification of the believer. The universal affirmation of the Christian faith is that salvation amounts to much more than either the communication of a moral property, forgiveness, or justification. More than simply a restoration to an original state or even the resumption of a process of spiritual development, salvation's ultimate aim is ontological communion with God. All Christians affirm that such communion is not simply eschatological but is already inaugurated in some way. While there are differences in how this communion is related to other elements of salvation, in how realized it might be, or in how it is connected to the ultimate *visio Dei*, there is universal agreement on the fact that the Christian is indwelled by the whole Trinity.

The scriptural language for this indwelling is sometimes cultic: "Do you not know," Paul asks the Corinthians, "that your body is a temple of the Holy Spirit within you, whom you have from God?" (1 Cor 6:19; cf. 1 Cor 3:16).

John states that God lives in us and we know this by his Spirit: "Whoever keeps his commandments abides in God, and God in him. And by this we know that he abides in us, by the Spirit whom he has given us" (1 John 3:24). At the same time, the other persons are not merely represented by the residing Spirit, but are also indwelling, as John 14:23 implies: "Jesus answered him, 'If anyone loves me, he will keep my word, and my Father will love him, and we will come to him and make our home with him.'" As seen here, John in particular likes to relate the divine indwelling to love, and love to the keeping of Christ's commandments. In John 17, Jesus prays for the apostles (and their followers) that they "may be one," that "they may be in us." In verse 23 he says: "I in them and you in me, that they may become perfectly one, so that the world may know that you sent me and loved them even as you loved me." And then, in verse 26: "I made known to them your name, and I will continue to make it known, that the love with which you have loved me may be in them, and I in them." John further argues that "if we love one another, God abides in us, and his love is perfected in us. By this we know that we abide in him and he in us, because he has given us of his Spirit" (1 John 4:12–13). Here love is some form or condition of God's abiding in us, and thus of the indwelling Spirit.

Paul seems to be echoing a similar theme in Romans 5:5: "God's love has been poured into our hearts through the Holy Spirit who has been given to us." Moreover, the presence of the Spirit is what vivifies our bodies (Rom 8:9–11). Importantly, it is the reason for our confidence in our ultimate vindication. Paul uses the language of seal, of down payment, of earnest, to make this point, as for example in Ephesians 1:13–14. It is precisely through the Spirit that we become sons. This theme is replete in Paul (Rom 8:9–10, 15–16; Gal 4:6, etc.).

To summarize this much too brief glimpse at Scripture, the Holy Spirit lives in believers as in temples, he unites them to the Father and the Son, he seals them in Christ. His indwelling seems especially connected to the love that has been poured into our hearts, just as Christ's indwelling seems especially connected to faith (Eph 3:17). Not only is the Spirit given, but the other Trinitarian persons are also given and they come to make their home with us. This presence of the Trinity, of the Holy Spirit in particular, is taken as an earnest, as an anticipation of what is yet to come. The language of Scripture on this matter seems intensely ontological: We do not merely have gifts from the Spirit but the Spirit himself. We do not merely have the benefits of Christ but the Son himself.

The question is, can the Western tradition handle these texts? How can the Spirit inhabit us, how can he be possessed, received, and so on if he does not have his own exclusive operation? We have reached here another crux of the modern rejection of the inseparability tradition, which is thought to obscure the supernatural relations to the distinct divine persons in grace. The answer given by the Western tradition, especially in its Augustinian-Thomistic version, is that the manner in which the Holy Spirit inhabits us is through love. Aquinas builds on his understanding of the divine missions, according to which in a mission one may distinguish between the inseparably produced created effect and the procession that is extended through it and is proper to the divine person. Even though the created effect is commonly caused by the whole Trinity, it nevertheless refers back in particular to a single person. As we have seen, this pulling from the common toward the proper is called appropriation. Thus the created term can be said to reveal or disclose the particular person, yet necessarily through what this person does in common with the others. Aquinas holds that in an invisible mission of the Spirit something is produced in the soul, and this something relates the soul distinctly to the person of the Holy Spirit.

This provides us with the basic framework for understanding the idea of the inhabitation of the Holy Spirit by love. While the divine love in our soul is the common production of the three persons, it disposes us specifically to receive one of them, the Holy Spirit. As I will explain below this is a so-called intentional or exemplary solution to the problem. The Holy Spirit is given to us in his hypostatic uniqueness as the end term of a relation to which we are elevated and disposed by the created effect of love. Love, as the common production of the Trinity, is, in scholastic language, the "formal reason" of the inhabitation of the Holy Spirit. In other words, love is the form in our soul through which we are disposed to enjoy God and the third person specifically. Our participation in the divine nature takes place precisely through the formality of the divine gifts such as love or wisdom, as Peter puts it, "so that through them [these promised gifts] you may become partakers of the divine nature, having escaped from the corruption that is in the world because of sinful desire" (2 Pet 1:4).

In this way, Aquinas hopes to have provided an account by which we are related distinctly to the third person, all the while preserving the traditional principle of inseparable operations. We will return to this account once we have discussed some major objections to it.

CRITIQUE OF THE APPROPRIATION TRADITION

As we have seen in chapter 2, modern theology finds this general approach to the Trinitarian operations and missions deeply problematic. One difficulty identified is that of the individuation of the persons. If every action *ad extra* belongs to their common causality, there is no way of discriminating between the persons. We thus seem to have been robbed of any possible basis for ascribing real distinctions to the persons within the Godhead.

Most Latin Trinitarians would hesitate to call for efficient causalities that are exclusive to particular divine persons. However, many theologians in this tradition would affirm the reality of distinct relations to individual divine persons. But is it possible to conceive of such distinct relations on a basis other than efficient causality? Or to put it more simply, can one relate distinctly to Father, Son, and Holy Spirit even if they always act inseparably? If we cannot assign different actions *ad extra* to them, can we nevertheless assign different relationships between them and creatures like us?

But what other kinds of relations of presence may be conceived other than in terms of efficient causality? A number of modern Catholic theologians have suggested a return to formal causality as a means of showing a presence of the Trinitarian persons in terms of their hypostatic character, that is, in their uniqueness and not just in terms of their common operation. The appeal to formal, or rather quasi-formal, causality is made in a number of variations. What follows is a brief summary.

Dionysius Petavius argues for a quasi-formal presence of the Holy Spirit, who unites himself to the human person (or the person's will) in a manner analogous to the Son's uniting himself to human nature. According to Petavius, it is the Holy Spirit alone who unites himself to the just in this way: "The three persons dwell in the just man, but only the Holy Spirit is, as it were, the form that sanctifies and renders a man an adoptive son by its self-communication."[2] The presence of the other Trinitarian persons in the soul of the just is mediated through the formal presence of the Holy Spirit. Such a view has been called the "exclusive proprium view."[3] For Petavius, there is a kind of equivalency between the way in which the Son possesses his divine nature and how the Spirit possesses our natures.

Matthias Joseph Scheeben has proposed a so-called "non-exclusive proprium view." Scheeben argues largely within an appropriation approach yet crucially expands it to allow for nonappropriated quasi-formal relations between the just and the Trinitarian persons. His account is nonexlusive in that he argues that each trinitarian person may possess the soul in a manner analogous to how he possesses the divine nature. "Although the divine substance and activity is common to all the persons, the possession of the substance is peculiar to each person. As each distinct person possesses the divine nature in a special way, He can possess a created nature in His own personal way, and to this extent exclusively. We know that this is the case with the Son in the Incarnation. If the Son alone takes physical possession of a created nature, why should not the Holy Spirit be able to take possession of a created being in

---

2. Quoted in David Coffey, *Did You Receive the Holy Spirit When You Believed?* (Milwaukee: Marquette University Press, 2005), 16.

3. As by Malachi J. Donnelly, SJ, for example, "The Inhabitation of the Holy Spirit: A Solution according to De La Taille," *Theological Studies* 3 (September 1947): 450.

a way that is proper to His own person, by means of a less perfect and purely moral possession?"[4] Scheeben further argues that this new possession is of a formal kind: "We shall perceive that by dwelling in our soul as a guest the Holy Spirit is in a most exalted and marvelous manner not only the efficient and exemplary cause but in a certain sense also the formal cause of our supernatural sanctity, of our dignity as sons of God, and of our union with the divine persons."[5]

While there are other important voices in this conversation, the focus in this chapter will be on Rahner.[6] Scripture and the Greek fathers, Rahner argues, challenge the received scholastic solution to the problem (which appeals to appropriation and makes the created grace the form of the indwelling). While the scriptural statements about the divine self-communication include a created effect, Rahner feels that the order should be reversed. Created grace, he argues, should be understood as the consequence, not as the form of uncreated grace.[7] In other words, the love we have for God (and for each other) is the consequence, not the basis of the inhabiting Spirit.

Rahner perceives a clear advantage in this solution. The whole Trinity is really given to us, the persons in their hypostatic character even now before the *eschaton*, as it were. Grace is intrinsically supernatural, as it were, because it consists precisely of the indwelling of the persons in their *propria*. As he puts it: "The life of grace, that is to say, and the life of future glory do not stand in a purely moral and juridical relation to each other, such that the latter is the reward of the former as merit; the life of glory is the definitive flowering (the 'manifestation', 'the disclosure') of the life of divine sonship already possessed and merely 'hidden' for the moment."[8]

This requires some clarification. According to the appropriation model, Rahner and others suggest, we only have the Spirit, the Son, and the Father in a way that is mediated by created realities. Their indwelling really consists in this new "entitative" (pertaining to an essential element of the soul) trans-

---

4. Matthias Joseph Scheeben, *The Mysteries of Christianity* (New York: Crossroad, 2008), 166.

5. Scheeben, *Mysteries*, 167.

6. Rahner discusses the inhabitation in terms of God's threefold self-communication in several places, first in "Some Implications of the Scholastic Concept of Uncreated Grace," in *Theological Investigations*, trans. Cornelius Ernst, OP, vol. 1 (Baltimore: Helicon Press, 1961), then in *The Trinity* (New York: Crossroad, 1997), 24–45, and finally in *Foundations of the Christian Faith*, trans. William V. Dych, SJ (New York: Crossroad, 1982), 117–26.

7. Rahner, "Scholastic Concept," 321–22.

8. Rahner, "Scholastic Concept," 326.

formation. The beatific vision and our life of glory, on the other hand, consist in an unmediated participation in the triune being, which consequently is qualitatively different from our fellowship with the Trinity in this life and which can therefore only be understood as reward. At any rate, our relationship to the persons of the Trinity is, as Mackey also has noted, extrinsic rather than intrinsic.

Rahner believes that such a new relationship between God and the creature exceeds the order of efficient causality. First, it is an anticipation of our beatific vision, where we shall contemplate God not through created species but through God's own essence. Moreover, such a relationship is already accepted in the case of the hypostatic union. The incarnation and the vision "have this in common, that in them there is expressed a relationship of God to a creature which is not one of efficient causality (a production *out* of the cause . . .), and which must consequently fall under the head of formal causality (a taking up *into* the ground [*forma*] . . .): the ontological principle of the subsistence of a finite nature in this case, the ontological principle of a finite knowledge in the other."[9]

Rahner is aware that there is a problem with God entering into formal composition with creation. As Aquinas argues, God does not enter into such relations since it would make God a composite being and dependent on matter. Any relationships into which God enters must be construed in such a way as to preserve divine immutability and aseity. Consequently, Rahner prefixes his notion of causality with "quasi." He feels that, despite all the risks, "it cannot be impossible in principle to allow an active formal causality of God upon a creature without thereby implying that this reactively impresses a new determination upon God's being in itself, one which would do away with his absolute transcendence and immutability."[10]

This has consequences for the logical relation between created and uncreated grace: "God communicates himself to the man to whom grace has been shown in the mode of formal causality, so that this communication is not then merely the consequence of an efficient causation of created grace."[11] On the contrary, "the communication of uncreated grace can be conceived of under a certain respect as logically and really prior to created grace: in the mode namely in which a formal cause is prior to the ultimate material disposition."[12]

---

9. Rahner, "Scholastic Concept," 329.
10. Rahner, "Scholastic Concept," 330.
11. Rahner, "Scholastic Concept," 334.
12. Rahner, "Scholastic Concept," 334.

The category of formal causality suggests a presence of the Holy Spirit in a different sense than his presence by his own efficiency. But what kind of presence and what kind of causality is this? If efficient causation concerns the production of an effect *out of* a cause, formal causality concerns the particular actualization of a potentiality that resides in the object. We've seen Rahner calling it a "taking up into the ground." So for example the form of fire causes the wood to burn. The form of *statue* causes this marble to become a statue, and so on. Let us take this second example. In terms of efficient causality, what causes the statue to exist is the sculptor. In terms of material causality, what causes the statue to exist is the particular matter of which it is sculpted (marble is indeed already a formed matter, thus a substance; but a substance may become the matter to be informed by higher form). Formal causality in turn refers to that by which this particular marble is a statue. Aristotle argues that we can speak of causality here because the form of statue accounts for this marble being a statue.

Rahner and others want to be able to individuate a self-communication of one of the persons that is proper to that person alone, in this case a self-donation of the Holy Spirit to the human being. This self-donation must be more than mere appropriation, but it must not be conceived along the lines of an exclusive efficiency.

The Holy Spirit comes to live in the human person, as in a temple; he comes to make us partakers of the divine nature. Rahner and company interpret that participation in the divine nature as the self-communication of each of the divine persons to the just, along the lines of formal causation.

It must be admitted that there is at least a prima facie plausibility and attractiveness to this model, beyond enabling us to preserve the principle of inseparable operations in the case of efficient causality. The language of formal causality seems better suited to explain our supernatural elevation, it is argued. If we become partakers of the divine nature, sanctified, deified, this is best explained through the reception of some supernatural form. A mere created effect—such as supernatural grace—cannot really account for the supernatural in the natural. Malachi J. Donnelly expresses this well: "How can a created physical accident make us truly sharers of the divine nature, and how can uncreated grace, which surely does not inform the soul, truly sanctify?"[13] It thus becomes attractive to think of our supernature in terms of the formal reception of the triune persons inside of us. Moreover, explaining our supernature in terms of the formal self-communication of the persons (either just the Holy Spirit as in Petavius or all three of them as in Rahner and Scheeben,

13. M. J. Donnelly, SJ, "Inhabitation," 452.

Donnelly and others) has the advantage of making uncreated grace the basis of created grace (sanctifying grace).

To be sure, as Catholic theologians all of the above will insist on the consequent necessity of created grace. On occasion the language of seal is used to express the point.[14] Created grace is the concave consequent condition upon our created reality of the uncreated, convex formal self-communication of the persons.[15] In this case, love is the concave created effect of the convex formal self-donation of the Holy Spirit. Moreover, they will insist, with the rest of the tradition and against the Lutheran and Reformed theologians,[16] that this love is a habitual love and not simply an actual love. However, at least in the case of Rahner, his prioritizing of uncreated grace has made some of his Catholic peers suspicious of coming too close to a Lutheran position (see the Finnish School of Luther interpretation).

PROBLEMS WITH THE NONAPPROPRIATION VIEW

Rahner is aware of at least one issue with the language of formal causality, and he devotes much energy to responding to it. We are not aware of whether he addresses some of the other substantial difficulties that we will flag below. The tradition has consistently rejected a formal interpretation of the inhabitation of the Trinity in the just (preferring the appropriation approach) for one fundamental reason. In any formal causation there is a certain act-dependence and act-limitation of the form itself. In other words, the form depends on and is limited by its actualization in its own identity. Thus, the form of fire is dependent on the matter of wood or other combustible materials for its essence.

Thomas rejected the idea that God (as form) might enter into composition with matter[17] since that would yield another substance with God as a component of it, which would thus be superior to God. Even if God were to drive such a process of composition he would still be dependent on the matter itself and his relationship to matter would be real rather than merely conceptual. Thomas is quite clear that at stake here is precisely divine transcendence and aseity.

Now Rahner and company are aware of this issue. But they will not be prevented by this rational consideration from attending to what they take to be a

14. Cf. Scheeben, *Mysteries*, 168–72.
15. M. J. Donnelly uses this pair of concepts ("Inhabitation," 463).
16. See the discussion in the final section of this chapter.
17. Aquinas, *Summa Theologica*, trans. the Fathers of the English Dominican Province (Westminster, MD: Christian Classics, 1981), 1, q. 3, a. 2.

datum of revelation. First, such a formal communication has already taken place in the person of Jesus Christ (the hypostatic union); secondly, the beatific vision also entails it since then we will behold God through his own essence, and thus a certain actuation of our knowledge by the divine essence will take place.

Rahner appeals to something like Maurice de la Taille's notion of "actuation," which the latter develops in his work on the hypostatic union.[18] While in the natural order any actuation is an in-forming,[19] which implies act-dependence and act-limitation, this need not be the case, de la Taille argues, in the case of a supernatural actuation. In such a case, the form does not depend on the matter or its potentialities but simply creates these. In the hypostatic union, for example, the union does not depend on the prior existence of the human nature of Jesus Christ. In fact the union actuates precisely the human nature of Jesus Christ as existing in the Logos. Or, rather, the Logos himself actuates the human nature of Jesus Christ as his own. Again, it should be noted that this actuation is not in the order of efficient, but formal causality. The eternal Logos, in other words, actuates the human nature of Jesus Christ.

At least in the case of the incarnation, then, we have a precedent for a formal actuation that does not entail in-formation, and thus the Thomistic hesitations about formal causality do not apply in this case. We can thus treat the hypostatic union as a paradigm case of the inhabitation of the divine persons. The created realities that are being actuated by the supernatural form of the divine persons (knowledge and faith in the case of the inhabitation of the Son, love in the case of the inhabitation of the Holy Spirit) are the form of the self-communication of the divine persons. The Son comes to exist in our knowledge as its very form; the Holy Spirit comes to exist in our love as its very form. The divine persons do not in-form these capacities; if they did, the persons themselves would depend upon them for their own (new) identity. Rather this is a "created actuation" by "uncreated act."

Yet serious difficulties remain. We may grant for the time being that what takes place in the incarnation is in fact a case of quasi-formal causation, a created actuation by uncreated act. But should the analogy of the incarnation reassure us or should it worry us? A number of theologians are certainly worried about it.[20] The problem has to do precisely with the dissimilitude

18. See Maurice de la Taille, *The Hypostatic Union and Created Actuation by Uncreated Act: Light of Glory, Sanctifying Grace, Hypostatic Union* (West Baden Springs, IN: West Baden College, 1952). For a discussion of the problems of "information," see 29.

19. Rahner also stresses that "such a formal causality of God (a Trinitarian hypostasis, his Being) is not known to us in the realm of nature." "Scholastic Concept," 330.

20. See for example, Yves Congar, who is otherwise sympathetic, ascribing a logical

that is entailed here. While in the case of Christ the prior nonexistence of his created capacities is essential in avoiding Nestorianism, in our case our created capacities (knowledge, love) already exist. And thus to speak about the persons themselves becoming the form of these capacities sounds very much like in-forming since the relationship seems to depend upon a prior reality. The Thomistic tradition for this very reason prefers to speak about an "adaptation," or elevation, or disposing of our already existing realities to enjoy the supernatural persons. But the very reception of the form of the persons into these created capacities either leads back to in-formation or it confuses the ontological orders of created and uncreated. If the form is received into a matter, the matter is in-formed. To avoid this, the matter must not exist prior to the actuation—but this does away with the fact that our existence is already hypostatic. On the other hand, if our already hypostasized beings are to be lifted to the level of the divine communion, such adaptation must be created or connatural, adapted to its own nature.[21] But what is suggested is that the adaptation is itself supernatural, that our (already existing) capacities are actualized by a transcendent form, in fact by a triune person. What appears to transpire here is a confusion between the created and the uncreated orders. How may the Holy Spirit be communicated to an already hypostasized love except by the adaptation of that love?

Thus the first problem associated with the quasi-formal approach seems to be that it blurs important distinctions between the natural and the supernatural, or between created and uncreated.[22] In the case of the hypostatic union, the

---

and causal priority to uncreated grace. *I Believe in the Holy Spirit*, trans. David Smith (New York: Crossroad, 2013), 2:88.

21. Aquinas writes (*In Sent.* 1, dist. 17, Paris version): "Whatever is received into a thing is received according to the recipient's mode. But uncreated love, which is the Holy Spirit, is participated in by the creature; therefore he must be participated in according to the creature's mode. But the creature's mode is finite; thus what is received into the creature must be some finite love. But every finite thing is created. Therefore, in the soul having the Holy Spirit, there is a created charity." Thomas Aquinas, *On Love and Charity*, trans. Peter A. Kwasniewski, Thomas Bolin, OSB, and Joseph Bolin (Washington, DC: The Catholic University of America Press, 2008), 10.

22. The work of Bernard Lonergan on this issue might be mentioned. As Doran explains, he was having hesitations about the perceived priority of created grace at roughly the same time as Karl Rahner but resolved the issue in the opposite direction from him. See the excellent discussion in Robert Doran, *The Trinity in History: A Theology of Divine Missions* (Toronto: University of Toronto Press, 2012), 1:25–26. Lonergan discusses the issue in several places, most centrally in *Early Latin Theology*, vol. 19 of *Collected Works of Bernard Lonergan*, ed. Daniel Monsour, Michael G. Shields, and Robert M. Doran (Toronto: University of Toronto Press, 2011); see especially "Part 7: Supplementary Notes on Sanctifying Grace."

human knowledge and love of Christ were brought into existence exclusively as they were hypostasized in the Logos. Such a logic may not apply in the case of the human persons, who are already hypostasized natures. For us, a formal actuation is out of the question since it would necessarily imply in-formation and thus act-dependence and act-limitation. The only option left for us would be that our own hypostases, remaining what they are, would receive something commensurate with our created existence. Clearly what they receive cannot be the divine essence, since that would entail our becoming divine.

There is an additional problem with the quasi-formal suggestion. Simply put, persons are concrete particulars and thus do not become the form of a matter, although they may certainly be informed by an additional substance. So, for example, when the marble is sculpted, it takes the form of a statue, it becomes a statue. The form that it takes is not this or that statue, but the universal form, statue. The form is concretized in the very act of the in-forming. It is not already formed prior to this act. The resulting composite is certainly *this* statue, rather than statue in general, since the form is actualized in the production of the statue.

William Hill explains it well: "A person cannot be a form in any proper sense. Form belongs rather to the realm of essence and is a determinative principle of composite being which can be 'had' only as constituting an intrinsic aspect of the receiving subject's own being."[23] In other words, a form configures determinate being. To say that a person can come to exist in another matter, or can inform another matter is a categorial confusion since the person is already a configured something. It is already a nature that is "closed-off," actualized.

At this point an objection might be formulated on the basis of a particular metaphysics of the soul. Eleonore Stump has argued for a particular Thomistic metaphysics of the human soul: "For Aquinas, the metaphysical world is ordered in such a way that at the top of the metaphysical hierarchy there are forms—God and the angels—which are configured but which aren't configurational constituents of anything else. These forms are configured but non-configuring. Near the bottom of the hierarchy are forms that configure matter but don't exist as configured things in their own right. The form of an amethyst is like this. Such forms are configuring but non-configured. And in the middle are human souls, the amphibians of this metaphysical world, occupying a niche in both the material and the spiritual realm. Like the angels, the human

---

23. William J. Hill, *The Three-Personed God* (Washington, DC: The Catholic University of America Press, 1983), 293. For a lengthier treatment, see William Hill, OP, "Uncreated Grace—A Critique of Karl Rahner," *Thomist* 27, no. 1 (1963): 333–56.

soul is itself configured; but like the forms of other material things, the human soul has the ability to configure matter."[24]

Why is this significant? Because this ontology might present us with the possibility of a form, the human soul, which exists as configuring matter but which can also be itself configured. The implication is that the soul can exist independently of the body. The soul is thus both a particular (configured) and something that can inform matter (configuring). Putting it differently, the soul is both person and form. It thus seems possible that persons do inform.

Closer attention to this discussion will quickly reveal that it is not an authentic counterexample. Stump defines the soul as something that emerges together with the body.[25] Even as the soul informs the matter of the body, making it *this* body, the soul can survive the expiration of the body, thus creating the appearance that it does not depend on the body. However, it can be argued that the soul that survives the body is this particular soul because of its having informed this particular matter (which became this body, now dead). The very particularity of this soul is its having informed this matter-body. The soul's surviving the body is conceptually distinct from its being independent, as a particular, from the body.

The soul emerges from the matter (which becomes this body through the emergence of the soul). Thus, the soul does not pre-exist the body, as something configured, but becomes something configured (a particular something) precisely through its configuring the matter of the body. Thus it is not at all clear that a person, as a concrete particular actualization of some matter, can be also a form of something. In the case of the human soul, the soul only informs the matter-body as something emerging from it.

It is not true that a person can be both a concrete particular as well as a form for a matter. The soul that is at one point a concrete particular, having emerged from the matter, only informs the matter by having emerged from it. It remains the case that this particular soul is dependent on the matter that it configures since it emerges from it and is not imposed upon it, as in problematic views of the pre-existence of souls.

When this putative counterexample is applied to our problematic the difficulties are insuperable. To say that the person of the Spirit is both a concrete particular mode of existence of the divine substance as well as the (quasi-)form of a concrete human created reality requires identifying the divine substance with the human created reality, or claiming that the eternal Holy Spirit is an

24. Eleonore Stump, *Aquinas* (London: Routledge, 2003), 514.
25. Stump, *Aquinas*, 207.

emergent property of the human soul. To say that one of the triune persons becomes the form of a concrete created substance in an actuation takes us far beyond the accepted use of the categories of person and nature.

I have identified two fundamental problems with using the framework of quasi-formal causality to explain the inhabitation of the divine persons in the souls of the just. The first problem consists in the blurring of the ontological distinctions between created and uncreated. Francis Cunningham puts it well: "All things outside of the Trinity Itself are being by participation, dependent for their very existence on the productive and sustaining power of the subsistent Being."[26] Consequently we can only participate in God in the order of operation, not in the order of nature.[27] But God's operation is common to the three persons. Avoiding the pitfalls of quasi-formal causality has led these theologians to affirm that the Trinitarian persons form our created capacities (faith and love) in a supernatural way. But this begs the question of whether these capacities remain recognizably created and human, or at least proper to us.

The second problem consists in a categorial confusion between person and nature. A divine person cannot become the form of something else simply because a person is already a nature existing in a certain manner. Cunningham explains it well: "The rational creature in the line of essence is a complete being, with his own subsistence, not merely a principle of being. One can, accordingly, find no explanation for his union with the Trinity in the line of nature: God cannot be present to him as a hypostatic term because his nature is closed by his own personality, whereas the human nature of Christ was open to the divine personality. Only in the line of operation, then, can God exist as a term for the rational creature."[28]

Given that a quasi-formal approach to the problem of the inhabitation seems to be plagued with considerable difficulties, it is time to revisit the "appropriation" approach.

26. Francis L. B. Cunningham, OP, *The Indwelling of the Trinity: A Historico-Doctrinal Study of the Theory of St. Thomas Aquinas* (Dubuque, IA: The Priory Press, 1955), 194.

27. Some proponents of the quasi-formal approach are hesitating to describe the invisible missions as *ad extra*, thus confirming the impression that the distinctions between created and uncreated are blurred. Thus, M. J. Donnelly writes, "the uniting of the creature with the divine Person (or Persons) is not strictly an *opus ad extra*, but rather *ad intra*[!]" ("Inhabitation," 459). For a similar critique, see Ralph Del Colle, *Christ and the Spirit* (Oxford: Oxford University Press, 1994), 74.

28. Cunningham, *Indwelling of the Trinity*, 189–90.

Salvaging the Appropriation Approach

For Aquinas and the tradition there are strong Trinitarian reasons why the indwelling may not take place in the order of nature, along the lines of a formal causality for instance. An inhabitation at the level of nature renders the human person passive, which is acceptable in the case of the hypostatic union, where Christ's human nature is instrumentalized. Although it retains its natural operation, such an operation is not actualized by a human hypostasis but by the Logos. Our natures on the other hand are "closed off" (Cunningham) by our personalities and therefore cannot be actuated in the order of nature, where they are already in act. It follows that the inhabitation can only take place in the order of operation, that is, only by the exercise of some causality upon our operations.

The problem, of course, as far as a divine influence upon human operations is concerned, is that no distinct notional (or hypostatic) causality can be detected. All the operations of the Trinity upon created reality are inseparable. It becomes difficult, if not impossible, in this scenario to distinguish between the persons in the life of grace, or to speak about the presence of the persons in their hypostatic uniqueness. It seems that all their relations to creatures are common since all their influence is common.

But is this really the case? Do the persons remain confused in the life of grace? For that we need to look more closely at the answer Thomas gives to the problem of the inhabitation. Aquinas provides two explicit accounts of the inhabitation. The first one appears in his *Commentary on the Sentences*, book 1. The second account appears in his treatment of the divine missions in the *Prima Pars* of the *Summa Theologica*, question 43. The two treatments approach the topic from two different directions. The analysis in the *Sentences* is from the standpoint of the processions, while the analysis in the *Summa* is from the standpoint of the created effect. It would help to reacquaint ourselves with the definition of the divine missions that Thomas retains from Augustine: A mission is a prolongation of a procession in a new relationship to a created effect. Approaching the mission from these opposite directions is thus natural and helpful.

There has been some discussion in the scholarship about whether Thomas's analysis in the *Sentences* may leave some room for a quasi-formal approach. Since this is a matter best left to Aquinas scholars, I will simply appeal to Emery's verdict. The analysis in the *Sentences* commentary is ontological, he argues. It discusses the divine missions in light of the Trinitarian processions as causes. In the *Summa*, an operational or intentional analysis is given from the standpoint of the believer's operations. In this second account, God is taken to be present in grace in the manner in which a thing known and loved is present in the subject.

Even in the *Sentences*, though, the principle is clearly enunciated that the effects that are the formality of the divine indwelling are the product of the whole Trinity. Much of the discussion in *Sentences* 1 distinction 17 (Paris version) is given to a correction Thomas makes to Peter Lombard's understanding of charity. Lombard understands the charity by which the Holy Spirit resides in us to be an act, not a habit.[29] Aquinas's response makes three important points.

The first point is that the reception of uncreated love must itself be created: "Whatever is received into a thing is received according to the recipient's mode. But uncreated love, which is the Holy Spirit, is participated in by the creature; therefore he must be participated in according to the creature's mode. But the creature's mode is finite; thus what is received into the creature must be some finite love. But every finite thing is created. Therefore, in the soul having the Holy Spirit, there is a created charity."[30]

The second point is: "Every assimilation [of one thing to another] comes about through some form. But it is through charity that we are made conformed to God himself, and when charity is lost, the soul is said to be deformed. Therefore, it seems that charity is a certain created form remaining in the soul."[31]

Finally, God is present in the saints differently than how he is present in other creatures. But "that diversity cannot be placed on the side of God himself, who stands uniformly to all things." In other words, the effect that is brought about does not involve a change in God himself but in the operations of the creature. Further, this effect must be a habit in the soul, "which habit is indeed from the whole Trinity as efficient cause, but flows from love, which is the Holy Spirit, as exemplar cause: and therefore it is frequently found that the Holy Spirit is the love by which we love God and neighbor."[32]

This is where the confusion of certain modern theologians lies. For they would argue that we have here an instance where the Common Doctor himself understands the Holy Spirit to be the form of our love, implying something like a quasi-formal communication. By now it should be clear why this won't do. Love is a created capacity that is already in a hypostatic existence. To have

---

29. Peter Lombard discusses this in *The Sentences*, bk. 1, dist. 17, ch. 6.8–9, trans. Giulio Silano (Toronto: Pontifical Institute of Medieval Studies, 2007), 97.

30. Aquinas, *In Sent.* 1, dist. 17.

31. Aquinas, *In Sent.* 1, dist. 17.

32. Aquinas, *In Sent.* 1, dist. 17.

the Holy Spirit to be the (quasi-)form of our love implies in-formation, with all its attendant dangers. If there is a perfection of our love, it cannot come from its being informed by uncreated love, since in that case it would no longer be our love.

Aquinas explains the difference: "For the union of human nature in Christ has its term in the one being of the divine Person, and therefore an act numerically the same belongs at once to a divine person and to the human nature assumed. In contrast, the will of a saint is not assumed into unity of suppositum with the Holy Spirit. . . . Hence one cannot understand that there is a perfect operation of the will through which it is united to the Holy Spirit unless one also understands that there is also a habit perfecting the operative power itself."[33] Thus, in the *Sentences*, a certain causality is ascribed to the Holy Spirit as the notional love (uncreated love). But this is not a formal causality.

As was mentioned, the perspective on the divine missions is different in the *Summa Theologiae*. Aquinas unpacks the notion of a divine mission in the sense of a manifestation of a triune person for the purpose of bringing the creature back to God. In question 43, article 2 of book I he responds to the question "Whether the invisible mission of the Divine Person is only according to the Gift of Sanctifying Grace." Thomas rehearses his conception of mission as a temporal procession. He invokes the authority of Augustine that the Holy Spirit proceeds for the creature's sanctification. But since the creature's sanctification is by sanctifying grace, the mission is by sanctifying grace. The same principle enunciated in the *Sentences* can be observed here: The assimilation of uncreated love takes place through a certain created form.

No other effect can bring about such an attaining to God but sanctifying grace, Thomas argues. While all creatures participate in God in the very act of existing, God already being in all things by his essence, beyond this mode of presence God is present in the rational creature in the same way that the known is present in the knower.

Thomas argues that the rational creature attains to God by knowledge and love. Moreover, in response to the objection that the divine person is not given but only his gifts, Aquinas argues that God not only exists in, but dwells therein as in his temple. "Yet the Holy Ghost is possessed by man, and dwells within Him, in the very gift itself of sanctifying grace."[34] The very gift, then, appears to become the formality of the indwelling of the person. Aquinas articulates this idea in terms of an adaptation of the creature such that it might *enjoy* the divine

33. Aquinas, *In Sent.* I, dist. 17.
34. Aquinas, *ST* 1, q. 43, a. 3.

person that is sent. The just has not merely the gift without the person since to have the person is to be able to enjoy the person, which is what the gift does.

But how can one "enjoy" the Holy Spirit if one is unable to individuate the Spirit in his causality *ad extra*? Francis Cunningham helps us understand this. The gift of sanctifying grace, he argues, produces a certain adaptation of the creature such that it enjoys an "experimental knowledge" of God.[35] God is thus substantially present and attained inasmuch as he is known and loved. However, this knowledge is not a discursive knowledge, it is not a knowledge by inference. Such a knowledge may be present in unbelievers as well; it thus cannot be the form of the inhabitation of the Word, as wisdom and faith.

Cunningham cites Aquinas: "The experiencing of a thing is gained through the senses; but in one way, of a thing present, in another, of an absent thing. Of an absent thing, by reason of sight, smell and hearing; but of a thing present, by touch and taste—of a thing extrinsically present, by touch; by taste, however, of a thing intrinsically present. God, however, is not far from us nor outside of us but in us . . . and therefore the experiencing of the divine goodness is called a tasting."[36] Thus, Cunningham comments, this formality of the divine presence "must be an effect within man, an effect to which God is immediately perceptible, an effect supremely expressive of God."[37]

We can explain this by the magnetic analogy. When a needle is attached to one of the poles of the magnet, one can only know to which pole it is attached by observing the transformation of the needle as it receives the charge of the respective pole. The relation between the needle and the pole, one may say, is not merely conventional but intrinsic. The needle acquires a true resemblance of one of the poles as it begins to bear its magnetic property. The magnetic charging of the needle is brought about by the magnet as a whole, and yet the particular charge it receives "disposes" it to receive one of the poles specifically.

The intrinsic connection desired by modern theologians like Mackey is thus established in the fact that the gift represents an imprint of a divine person. But the imprint is not in the order of formal or efficient causality but in the order of exemplary causality. As Aquinas puts it: The "proper relation belonging to the divine person is represented in the soul through a sort of received likeness, whose exemplar and origin is the property of this same eternal relation."[38]

---

35. Cunningham, *Indwelling of the Trinity*, 197.
36. Cunningham, *Indwelling of the Trinity*, 198.
37. Cunningham, *Indwelling of the Trinity*, 200.
38. Emery, *Trinitarian Theology*, 376.

Aquinas's notion of exemplary cause presents some ambiguity. On the one hand he treats it as a type of formal cause; on the other hand it is not an intrinsic cause, much like final causes. It seems to straddle the usual distinction between extrinsic and intrinsic causes. Arguably, Aquinas is compelled to introduce the exemplary variation into the neat distinction between the four causes because he regards creation as being intentional. The ideas in the divine mind are the exemplary causes and the blueprint of creation. The forms, on the other hand, inhere in the creatures.

An example from his *De Veritate* will help clarify the distinction between formal and exemplary causes. Reflecting on the goodness of creatures, Aquinas argues that "all things are good by a created goodness formally, as by an inherent form, but by uncreated goodness, as by an exemplary form."[39] God, as uncreated goodness, is the *terminus ad quem* of creatures, while the inherent form of goodness, as created, is *that by which* creatures are good. The distinction between formal and exemplary serves to identify God as the end of creation while preserving the ontological distinction between creator and creature.

As to the Holy Spirit, created love is the form through which we come to become more like the Holy Spirit in our union with the Father and Son by love. Through created love we come to enjoy the personal property of the Holy Spirit, which is love.[40] We are distinctly related to Trinitarian persons since "the divine person is sent to transmit a participation in his eternal property."[41] But the eternal property of the Holy Spirit is precisely love. And so love, as a created effect and *opus ad extra*, is the formality in which we come to enjoy uncreated love. We participate in the distinct triune persons not because our created capacities are informed by the respective triune person (our knowledge by the Logos, our love by the Holy Spirit). In other words, we participate distinctly in the persons not because the persons are the form of our souls, or various components of our souls. We participate in them because we participate in their notional relations and echo them.[42] We are sharers in the Holy Spirit not because the Holy Spirit becomes our love, but because our love comes to resemble the Holy Spirit. In this sense and in this sense alone can one speak

39. Aquinas, *De Veritate*, q. 21, art. 4.
40. See, for example, Augustine's appeal to 1 John 4 as the basis for calling the Holy Spirit "charity," in *The Trinity*, bk. 15.31.
41. Emery, *Trinitarian Theology*, 376-77.
42. Admittedly, this approach dovetails more nicely with a definition of an eternal person as a subsistent relation.

about an "imprint" of the divine person. The divine person bears fruit *ad extra* in our enjoyment of the Trinity. The gifts assimilate us to their exemplars.

In a very real sense, while remaining firmly in the appropriation tradition, when the invisible mission of the Spirit is regarded from the standpoint of its *terminus*, it reveals a relationship that is proper to the Spirit and not simply appropriated to him. The relationship, however, is in the order of human operations, augmented by the created habits that make it possible for us to enjoy the distinct persons. This is also consistent with the reorientation of our understanding of divine action in terms of creatures being drawn to their ends, as opposed to ontological change in God. Distinct possession of a Trinitarian person refers not to a separation among Trinitarian actions, but to their common orchestration of a return to God whereby the creature comes to resemble their distinct relations. To be distinctly related to a Trinitarian person is, in this key, understood as participating in his distinct personal property, which in turn is the personal fruition *ad extra* of the immanent processions.

The Scriptures also indicate that our ultimate transformation according to the likeness of the Son takes place in the operational order: "What we will be has not yet appeared; but we know that when he appears we shall be like him, because we shall see him as he is" (1 John 3:2). Our becoming like Christ takes place through our operation of seeing him. In response to Rahner's concern, this transformation is not an exclusively eschatological reality, for we are already being remade in his likeness (2 Cor 3:18). While the form of our ultimate destiny is not yet known or accessible to us ("what we will be has not yet appeared"), the exemplar of our present transformation is the same as that of our ultimate destiny. For the wayfarer, Christ truly is given, yet in a mirror, darkly, since our seeing him is by faith not sight.

Just as the form by which we relate distinctly to the Son and are assimilated to him is our faith, our distinct enjoyment of the Holy Spirit has the form of love. God has poured his love into our hearts through the Holy Spirit (Rom 5:5), so that through this love God and the human person mutually abide in one another (1 John 4), or become mutually assimilated to one another through love.[43] Moreover, not only do we come to enjoy the Holy Spirit, but our love for God is necessarily also a love of others (1 John 4:19-21). Furthermore, we become purveyors of the Spirit, after a manner analogous to Christ's sending the Spirit. As Jesus says, "Whoever believes in me, as the Scripture has said, 'Out

---

43. With all the appropriate precautions in regards to divine aseity and immutability. For more on how a human person is indwelling in God, see Eleonore Stump, *Atonement* (Oxford: Oxford University Press, 2019), 115-76.

of his heart will flow rivers of living water.'" As John explains (John 7:38-39), Jesus is referring to the Spirit who at that time had not yet been poured out.

DOES LOVE "BUFFER" THE SPIRIT?

We have argued that the formality by which the Holy Spirit indwells believers is love. It was further suggested that metaphysical and Trinitarian strictures are compelling us to give such an account. Careful reflection on the metaphysics of the indwelling raises some caution about the danger of blurring the distinctions between created and uncreated realities. The solution proposed by Rahner and others, suggesting that the Spirit is quasi-formally present in the believer, risks ignoring those cautions.

It may be retorted, however, that the proposed alternative courts the opposite danger, namely, buffering the real presence of the Holy Spirit. Sometimes it is charged that the Thomistic account overreaches in its attempt to give a metaphysical description of an incomprehensible mystery. Protestant dogmatic sensibilities sometimes account for the suspicion that an intermediary is interposed between God and the human person, which is supposed to enable the former to be received by the latter. On the contrary, God is in no need of such intermediaries, and no prior disposition needs to be created to enable God to act upon the human soul.

The issues and assumptions involved in this dispute are multiple, ranging from broader metaphysical frameworks (Aristotelianism versus Platonism) to divergent conceptions of the relationship between justification and sanctification. We will have to restrict our remarks to the issues we have addressed in the chapter. Protestant theologians would typically side with Rahner on the issue of the priority of uncreated over created grace. John Owen for instance argues that "all gracious habits are effects of the operation of the Spirit, but not the well itself."[44] Similarly, Hermann Bavinck insists that the infused habits "are distinguished ... from the Holy Spirit, who effects them but does not coincide with them."[45] Owen's and Bavinck's willingness to even speak of infused habits, however, represents a possible correction to Luther's and Calvin's proclivity to avoid the language of habits altogether.[46] Both magisterial reformers were in

---

44. John Owen, Appendix in *Pneumatologia*, abridged by G. Burder from the 3rd London Edition (London: Towar & Hogan, 1827), 327.

45. Hermann Bavinck, *Reformed Dogmatics* (Grand Rapids: Baker Academic, 2008), 4:94; cf also 114 for a discussion of how faith is related to love; and 3:574.

46. See John Calvin's discussion of habits in *Bondage and Liberation of the Will*, bk. 6, ed. A. N. S. Lane, trans. G. I. Davies (Grand Rapids: Baker Books, 1996), 378; cf. also Charles Partee, *The Theology of John Calvin* (Louisville: Westminster John Knox Press, 2010), 91.

fact explicitly siding with Lombard against the broader Western approach.[47] As it has been pointed out, Lombard argues that the Holy Spirit is the very form of the love we have for God, as opposed to the later tradition that insisted that the habit of love is the form of the Holy Spirit's presence.

Part of the reason for the Protestant suspicion of "created grace" is precisely the fear of an intermediary that is "entitative" (or pertaining to an essential quality of the human soul) and thus appearing to lead to semi-Pelagianism. With Augustine and Lombard, Luther and Calvin insist that human love of God is directly caused by God. Consequently, Protestantism tends to regard grace as a divine action rather than a substance, or a reality that is distinct from God's action.

This is a legitimate and significant worry. But it fundamentally misunderstands the Thomist position. To say that created love is the formality in which the Holy Spirit is received is not to say that this love is present in the soul prior to and independently of the presence itself of the Holy Spirit. This would indeed seem as if the Spirit prepares the creature in advance of his coming. But the creature does need to be prepared, in a very carefully circumscribed sense. This is a widespread assumption made by Catholic theologians—rejected by Luther and Calvin but subsequently accepted by, for example, Peter Martyr Vermigli and Jerome Zanchi.[48] While this may be of a piece with their Aristotelianism (or Thomism),[49] it intends to safeguard the ontological difference between creator and creature by the principle that any activity of God upon the creature must take place according to the creature's nature.

However, this adaptation to the creature is not an additional *ens completum* but merely the consequent effect of the divine presence itself. The assimilation of the Holy Spirit to some creature must take place through a form, as we have seen. But this form does not pre-exist the presence of the Spirit. It is precisely the manner of its assimilation.

Grace, therefore, is not something reified, a "something" turned into a substance. Charles Moeller and Gérard Philips explain this well: "The love of God works effectively—a man is changed if the Spirit dwells in him; the *habitus* is the result of this; there is no question, therefore, of a *habitus* being

---

47. For more on this, see J. Todd Billings, *Calvin, Participation, and the Gift* (Oxford: Oxford University Press, 2008), 49; William B. Evans, *Imputation and Impartation: Union with Christ in American Reformed Theology* (Eugene, OR: Wipf and Stock, 2008), 43–52.

48. See the discussion in Evans, *Imputation and Impartation*; Norman Shepherd, "Zanchius on Saving Faith," *Westminster Theological Journal*, 36 (1973–74): 31–47; Marvin W. Anderson, "Peter Martyr on Romans," *Scottish Journal of Theology* 26 (1973): 408; J. P. Donnelly, "Calvinist Thomism," *Viator* 7 (1976): 441–55.

49. See Donnelly, "Calvinist Thomism."

required in advance, or produced by any other causality than that of God himself at the very moment He gives Himself. One must speak in this case of a *reciprocal causality*, an idea that expresses the unbreakable union between God sanctifying and the soul really changed by God's entering it. In other words, the idea of created grace simply expresses the reality of regeneration; it is in no way an intermediate reality, a thing, complete in itself, which man possesses as his own."[50]

Some examples of assimilation may provide some clarity here: In the process of digestion food becomes assimilated into the human body in the *form* of tissues and fluids; in photosynthesis, carbon dioxide and water are assimilated through the *form* of organic molecules; blue paint is assimilated into yellow paint in the form of green paint; in visual perception light is assimilated into the knower through a sequence of forms, both physical (sense impressions) and cognitive (concepts). The presence of an element into another is realized in a way that accords with the nature of the receiver. As these examples show, the resulting form is not what makes possible the assimilation, but is its very form. It may be said that the form is not a constitutive condition but a consequent condition. Strictly speaking, the form does not *enable* or cause the assimilation anymore than the tissues and fluids cause the food to be present in the body. Neither is it, however, a remote consequence or effect of the assimilation. This is what Moeller and Philips's idea of "reciprocal causality" intends to convey.[51]

We can, then, affirm a priority of uncreated grace over the infused habits, including love, but still wish to insist that these habits are precisely the form of the Spirit's presence. As created, they are efficiently caused by the inseparable operation of the Trinity even as they dispose the person to enjoy the Trinitarian persons as distinct from one another.

THE SPIRIT OF CHRIST: AN AUGMENTED THOMISTIC MODEL

The remaining hurdle for the present theology of inseparable operations consisted in the doctrine of the indwelling of the Spirit and the distinction between this indwelling and that of the other two Trinitarian persons. Some

50. Charles Moeller, *The Theology of Grace and the Ecumenical Movement* (Paterson, NJ: Saint Anthony Guild Press, 1961), 19.

51. Cardinal Charles Journet prefers to call created and uncreated grace "correlative." *The Theology of the Church*, trans. Victor Szczurek, OP (San Francisco: Ignatius Press, 1987), 79.

worry that the inseparability rule obfuscates the real and distinct relations between the just and the Trinitarian persons, confusing the presence of the uncreated persons with their common gift of created grace.

Our approach to this issue focused on the response of the classical position to these worries, as expounded by Aquinas. Proper relations with the triune persons are possible for the just not so much in the order of formal or quasi-formal causality—which are best reserved for the Son, who is alone hypostatically united to a human nature—but in terms of exemplary causality. Understood in this way, the just possess distinct relations to the divine persons in the sense that they come to experience and taste the divine persons in their *proprium*. The imprint that is left upon their being, and which must be regarded as a common gift of the Trinity, is the correlative of the divine person's *proprium*. The gift disposes one to receive the divine person. Yet the divine person is never received in isolation from the other divine persons. In the case of the divine persons, knowledge cannot work either by division or abstraction. The divine persons are not tropes of a higher concept.

Aquinas's position, however, triggers a certain Protestant sensibility by its language of "disposing" and the quasi-physical appearance of created grace. We have discovered that most of these Protestant apprehensions are unwarranted. Love need not be understood as "buffering" the Spirit. However, we have also noted, as in the case of Stump, a certain disconnection between the indwelling Spirit and the person of Christ. It appeared in Stump's case that the work of Christ, particularly his passion-resurrection, is not integrally connected to the sending of the Holy Spirit. The sending might have conceivably happened in another way than through the passion. The coming of the Spirit appears in her case to be extrinsic to the whole sequence. A similar concern, we have noted, applies to the understanding of the sending of the Spirit as something merited by Christ.

The language of the New Testament, however, indicates a much more intrinsic connection between the sent Spirit and the sending glorified Christ. We canvassed this briefly in the first chapter. And so it would appear that an account of the indwelling of the Spirit must follow the direction indicated by the New Testament. What might such an account look like? This final section explores this question and it attempts to enhance Aquinas's approach by an account of the indwelling that is specifically and constitutively connected to *Christus praesens*.

The basis for including the glorified Christ in an account of the indwelling Spirit is the fact that Christ sends his Spirit from his human nature. It is therefore not simply the eternal divine Spirit that descends but particularly the Spirit of Christ that proceeds from his divinized and glorified human nature. This is too important a detail to be circumvented by any account of the indwelling.

The suggestion that the Holy Spirit is sent to the just through the humanity of Jesus Christ is not original to the present author. Karl Rahner, for instance, explores the significance of the "Spirit of Jesus Christ" in relation to the so-called anonymous Christians but also in relation to the operation of the Spirit in the lives of the Old Testament saints. The reality of the Spirit's presence at least in the latter case is not under dispute. But this raises the question of the connection between this work and the historical events of the incarnation and the cross, which are supposed to mediate the coming of the Spirit. In terms of the theology of religions, it raises the additional question of how there might be a mission of the Spirit in other religions that is not visibly connected to the mission of Christ. In dealing with these very important difficulties, Rahner does not wish to abandon his fundamental thought that in the incarnation we have an instance of a divine self-communication and that the Holy Spirit is similarly communicated to the just. That is, the Spirit does not simply produce effects in grace but communicates his own being to the saints, and this takes place through the historical circumstance of the incarnation of the Son, that is, through the merits of Christ.

If, Rahner argues, the Spirit is given through the merits of the Son, how can it be that the Spirit is salvifically present in persons who do not possess explicit faith in these merits? In addressing this conundrum, Rahner invokes the logic of consequent conditions that we have also been exploring. Appealing to divine immutability, Rahner insists that the cross cannot be the efficient cause of the Father's salvific will. The logic of Pentecost is similar: "If we cannot say this [that the cross influences God to pour out the grace of the Spirit] in the proper sense because of God's sovereign immutability, because he cannot be influenced or moved, then what does it mean to say that he gives his Spirit because of the merits of Jesus Christ, who is the moral and meritorious cause of this Spirit?"[52]

The solution he suggests is that "the Incarnation and the cross are, in scholastic terminology, the 'final cause' of the universal self-communication of God to the world which we call the Holy Spirit, a self-communication given with God's salvific will which has no cause outside of God."[53] Consequently

---

52. Karl Rahner, *Foundations of the Christian Faith: An Introduction to the Idea of Christianity* (New York: Crossroad, 1994), 317.

53. Rahner, *Foundations*, 317.

the sending of the Spirit is not enabled by the merits of Christ, but rather is the "entelechy of the history of revelation and salvation,"[54] a communication that is oriented toward the incarnation and the cross.

By reversing the polarity of Christ and Spirit, such that the history of the incarnation does not enable the sending of the Spirit but rather presupposes it, Rahner makes a significant pivot toward Spirit Christology as well. It is not so much the hypostatic union that leads to the sending of the Spirit as much as it is the entelechy of the Spirit that intrinsically leads humanity to the high point of its union with the Son in the person of Jesus Christ. This portends an "ascending" Christology whereby the divinity of Christ is *realized* in and through his very humanity, as this humanity is carried along by the Spirit to its ultimate capacities.

The biblical indication that the Spirit is precisely the Spirit of Christ is here given an interpretation that does not tether the Spirit to Christ: "Insofar as the event of Christ is the final cause of the communication of the Spirit to the world, it can truly be said that this Spirit is everywhere and from the outset the Spirit of *Jesus* Christ, the Logos of God who became man."[55] If the Spirit is indeed shaped by Christ in some way, this shaping is not presupposed as a condition by the work of the Spirit in the world but rather as its end point, its culmination. In other words, the Spirit does not have the work that he does in the world because of the way in which he was "shaped" by Christ; rather the perfect self-expression of the Spirit as the Spirit of Christ is the horizon to which all self-communication of the Spirit leads. The connection between the universal work of the Spirit, then, and the historical work of Christ is not causal, lest it compromise divine immutability, but rather intentional and conceptual. In this case, there doesn't seem to be a fundamental difference between the operation of the Spirit in Old Testament saints and in Christians. While this position clearly has the advantage of respecting the real operation of the Spirit prior to the historical work of Christ, it does so at the risk of undermining the significance of this historical event. The placement of the event of the incarnation during the course of history rather than at its end seems to be irrelevant if there is no further historical causality stemming from the Christ event in terms of the manner of the operation and presence of the Spirit. As the final cause for the sending of the Spirit, the incarnation might as well have been the chronological end point of history. Rahner thus fails to find an integral connection between the sending of the Spirit and the histor-

---

54. Rahner, *Foundations*, 317.
55. Rahner, *Foundations*, 318.

ical specificity of Christ's ascension. He thus fails to adequately relate *Spiritus praesens* to *Christus praesens*.

Australian theologian David Coffey pursues a largely Rahnerian project in his work on Spirit Christology. He teases out the significance of the concept of the "Spirit of Christ" in a loaded paper, "The 'Incarnation' of the Holy Spirit in Christ."[56] Taking his cue from James Dunn's exegetical work on this issue, which concludes that the Spirit is "shaped" by Christ, Coffey argues that taking this largely Pauline concept seriously leads to a rethinking of the relationship between Christ and the Spirit.

Noting the typical Western Christological claim that the Son assumes a human nature, which he then adorns with the Holy Spirit, Coffey claims that it does not sufficiently account for the role of the Holy Spirit in bringing about the very existence of Christ. The Spirit doesn't simply come at a later stage in Christ's existence, say as the principle of Christ's habitual grace. Rather, "the Holy Spirit is sent directly by the Father and brings about the existence of the Son in humanity."[57]

The notion that the Spirit is "sent directly" makes a conscious departure from the Thomistic model by way of which the Spirit is present through a created grace even in Christ. Were this the case, there would only be a difference in degree between Christ and the just. It must be possible, then, to speak of a presence of the Spirit in Christ precisely in his *proprium*. Coffey does not hesitate therefore to speak, in explicit quotation marks, about an "incarnation" of the Spirit in Christ. In the same way as Christ is the perfect expression in human nature of the divine Logos, so there is a perfect human expression of the Holy Spirit. This perfect expression is located precisely in Christ and to this extent one may hint at an "incarnation" of the Spirit in Christ.

To understand what this "incarnation" of the Spirit might mean, one must ground it in the doctrine of the immanent Trinity. Here Coffey is aware that his model seems to sit ill with what he calls the "procession" model of the immanent Trinity, whereby the Son proceeds from the Father by intellect and the Spirit proceeds from the Father and the Son by way of love. He appeals to another tradition, inspired by Richard of St. Victor, which he calls the "bestowal model" and which views the Holy Spirit not as a procession but as itself

56. David Coffey, "The 'Incarnation' of the Holy Spirit in Christ," *Theological Studies* 45, no. 3 (1984): 466–80. In the article Coffey expands on the Trinitarian theology he explores in *Grace: The Gift of the Holy Spirit* (Sydney: Faith and Culture, 1979).
57. Coffey, "Incarnation," 470.

the very love between Father and Son. The Spirit, then, is not love proceeding but the mutual love itself.

This second model of the immanent Trinity *can* square with Coffey's proposal regarding the work of the Spirit. In this model, the Father eternally loves the Son and the Son eternally responds to this love, this mutual love being the Spirit itself. On the level of the missions, then, not only does the Father anoint Jesus with the Spirit, but Jesus responds to this bestowal with his human love. We should read Coffey's own explanation:

> Within the Trinity the Father's love, which is the Holy Spirit, rests upon the Son as its proper object. When in execution of the divine plan of salvation this love is directed beyond the Godhead into the world, to bring about the Incarnation, the central component of this plan, it will exhibit, in the most radical possible form, the following two characteristics of personal love. It will be creative and it will be unitive, with the former characteristic subordinated to the latter, as is the case in all love. Its creativeness is seen in the creation of the humanity of Christ, which as a work ad extra is the work of all three divine persons, and its radicalness is evident in the fact that we have here creation in the strict sense. In its unitiveness it draws the humanity of Christ into the unsurpassable union of love with the Father which belongs only to the Son in the immanent Trinity, and here the radicalness is seen in the fact that the result is not a mere union of persons but unity of person with the Son. And as an act of assimilation, i.e., ultimately an inner-Trinitarian act, it is the work of the Holy Spirit alone, or better, of the Father acting by the Spirit.[58]

As the love of the Father, which is the Holy Spirit, springs *ad extra*, it creates the humanity of Christ for the purpose of being united to this humanity. This union, Coffey interestingly suggests, is a union *ad intra* insofar as it is an assimilation of the humanity of Christ into the Trinity, and therefore it is a work proper to the Spirit, or to the Father acting by the Spirit. As the humanity of Christ is assimilated into the intra-Trinitarian relations, it responds to and returns the love of the Father, which is the Spirit.

Here Coffey's proposal aims to make sense of the "Spirit of Christ" conceptuality. If in the Holy Trinity, the love of the Father, requited by the Son, is the Holy Spirit, then in the incarnation this divine love elicits the response of Christ's human love. Coffey distinguishes here between the *basic love* of Christ,

---

58. Coffey, "Incarnation," 472.

which is a "necessary consequence of the hypostatic union,"[59] and the gradual expression and completion of this love, which is personal and individual. The first love is transcendental and "prior to the exercise of all freedom," neither an act nor a habit. It is a kind of love that Jesus does not have in common with other men and that results, as we've said, from the hypostatic union. This love is something that Christ receives in virtue of this union, but it is also something to which he responds in a human way, "for whatever he receives, and then returns to the Father, must be received and returned in a human way."[60] Coffey then raises this question: "Is this the Holy Spirit Himself, or, as with us, a human love enabled by the Holy Spirit?"[61] He opts in favor of the first option. The second option would annul the uniqueness of Jesus's sonship, being separated from us only in degree. On the other hand, according to the first option Coffey argues that the Holy Spirit can be received and returned in a human way without ceasing to be the eternal Spirit, that is, while remaining himself—and this is just what is meant by an "incarnation" of the Spirit.

Now both Christ's divine sonship and the "actualization of the Holy Spirit in Jesus' transcendental love of the Father"[62] are progressively realized. There is a mixture of a priori (Jesus's eternal sonship and his transcendental love of the Father) and a posteriori (the realization of his sonship in obedience and of his transcendental possession of the Spirit in love). This notion leads us again to what the idea of the Spirit of Christ might mean: It is neither simply an a priori possession (which would invite docetism), nor something that can be reduced to an act or a habit (thus courting Nestorianism). If the Spirit is the love of the Father for Jesus returned as the love of Jesus for the Father, "the Holy Spirit, as his transcendental love of the Father, began to assume the characteristics of his very personal and individual love of God."[63] The Spirit of Christ, then, is not simply the presupposition of his incarnation and of the hypostatic union, but the gradual expression of this transcendental love in Christ's "personal and individual love of God."

The personal and individual expression of this transcendental love culminates in the death of Christ, for no greater love can be imagined than a self-sacrificial one unto death. It follows that in this death of Christ, his love of the Father achieves the highest possible expression in this life. Beyond death,

---

59. Coffey, "Incarnation," 475.
60. Coffey, "Incarnation," 476.
61. Coffey, "Incarnation," 476.
62. Coffey, "Incarnation," 477.
63. Coffey, "Incarnation," 477.

Christ's actual love of the Father is perfected by his beatific vision, as his love follows his heavenly knowledge.

In this way Coffey has sought to demonstrate "the Christological character of the Holy Spirit."[64] As the mutual love between Father and Son, the Holy Spirit reaches his perfect human expression in the death and resurrection of Jesus Christ. For Coffey, therefore, the historical events of the passion and resurrection of Christ do play a constitutive role for the identity of the Pentecostal spirit, as we too have argued. The human love of Christ is perfected during his life and in the cauldron of his death, and then beyond it in the beatific vision. This of course requires Coffey to deny the fact that as man Christ possesses the beatific vision prior to his resurrection or ascension. Nevertheless, the precise manner and character of Christ's human love seems to now irretrievably define the Holy Spirit for us. The Spirit takes his shape from the resonance between the Father's love for Christ and Christ's human love of the Father, both transcendental and personal.

The Spirit granted by Christ is not just a created reality or a created love, but the supernatural and eternal person of the Spirit himself. This is the yield of the claim that we have something like an incarnation of the Spirit in Christ. Coffey surmises that on this model no longer must we think of Christ being the mediator of the Spirit since the Spirit is sent by the Father directly. It is the Spirit that binds Christ to the Father and the Spirit who binds us to Christ. Just as the Spirit is the one by whom Christ is one with the Father, he is also the one by whom we also cry "Abba!" (Gal 4:6; Rom 8:15).

As exponents of the *Filioque* tradition, both Rahner and especially Coffey readily appreciate the way in which the Spirit's missionary identity, the form he takes for us, is shaped by Jesus Christ. Having moved East of that tradition, Tanner minimizes the way in which Christ shapes the Spirit. Since the Spirit does not proceed *Filioque* neither does the mission of the Son form the mission of the Spirit as much as the opposite. Christ "does not give *to* the Spirit in the way the Spirit gives to him, by empowering his acts as Son. If the Son gives anything to the Spirit it is, to the contrary, just the Spirit's shape; the power of the Spirit takes on in Christ the form of the Son's missionary action."[65] Just as in the eternal Trinity, the Son proceeds by way of the Father's love, so is the Word spoken into the world by way of the Father's love.

Despite these restrictions, Tanner nevertheless seeks to do justice to the language of the New Testament. She knows that "The Spirit of God will rest

---

64. Coffey, "Incarnation," 478.
65. Kathryn Tanner, *Christ the Key* (Cambridge: Cambridge University Press, 2010), 174.

on us (1 Pet 4:14) because the Spirit first rested on Christ to do the same."[66] Thus, "the Spirit always makes its appearance in the form of the Son: the Son is the shape that such power takes."[67]

The Spirit is "the love that comes forth from the Father to beget the Son."[68] In the intertwined missions of the Son and the Spirit, the love of the Son reflects back this love of the Father as it "is then carried along by the very same Spirit of love."[69]

We shall not say more about Tanner on this issue, having already discussed at some length her contribution on the general topic of the mission of the Spirit and its relation to the mission of the Son. Suffice it to say that while she heeds the biblical language of "Spirit of Christ," she tends to emphasize more the interlacing of the two missions rather than an order according to which the incarnate Christ makes a fundamental contribution to the shape of the Spirit's mission for us. Christ only shapes the Spirit for us inasmuch as the Spirit works and manifests himself to us through and in Christ. While it is true that the Spirit only rests on us because he has rested first on Christ, Tanner does not detect how the Spirit has been affected by his resting on Christ, not in himself, for sure, but in his mission for us. While the Spirit's rest on Christ deifies Christ's humanity, it does not seem to affect the form according to which the Spirit then proceeds from Christ to us.

Tanner approvingly quotes Stăniloae: "The irradiation of the Spirit from the Son is nothing other than the response of the Son's love to the loving initiative of the Father who causes the Spirit to proceed. The love of the Father [that is, the Spirit] coming to rest in the Son shines forth upon the Father from the Son as the Son's love."[70] Like all of the writers previously mentioned, Stăniloae too elucidates the idea of the Spirit of Christ in terms of the love of Christ: "The Son Himself imprints His person more deeply in us as an active and affective model; He also imprints His sonly affection for the Father, thus receiving us in the same intimate relation with the infinity of the Father's love, into which he entered as man."[71]

Like most Eastern Orthodox theologians, Stăniloae appreciates the fact that the Spirit is only given to us as a person in the person of Jesus Christ. But this

66. Tanner, *Christ the Key*, 168.

67. Tanner, *Christ the Key*, 169.

68. Tanner, *Christ the Key*, 178.

69. Tanner, *Christ the Key*, 178–79.

70. Quoted in Tanner, *Christ the Key*, 179, from Dumitru Stăniloae, *Theology and the Church*, 31.

71. Dumitru Stăniloae, *The Experience of God* (Brookline, MA: Holy Cross, 2011), 4:3.

leads to Stăniloae's unique emphasis on the mediation of the Spirit through the body of Christ: "The Spirit works in us from within Christ because Christ's body became radiant through the Word's transparence."[72] At work here is the specifically Eastern account of deification, including the concept of the uncreated energies of God. It is only because the material body of Christ has been deified that he can manifest for us the Holy Spirit. Stăniloae thus explains the delay in the hypostatic manifestation of the Spirit at Pentecost by this condition: "The Spirit cannot fully penetrate within a body unless that body is fully pneumatized and transparent. This means that Christ Himself shows the hypostasis of the Holy Spirit."[73]

Stăniloae's approach also intimately relates the *Christus praesens* with the *Spiritus praesens*. There is no operation of the Spirit that is not also an operation of the Son, through whose body the Spirit is received. More than Tanner, Stăniloae appears to make Christ more constitutive of the indwelling Spirit: "Through the Holy Spirit Christ Himself penetrates into human hearts because His body was made spiritual in an incomparable way through the Spirit, who overwhelmed and utterly penetrated Christ's body."[74] It is impossible, therefore, to give a full account of this dynamic except ecclesially. Christ's ascension—whereby, as Zizioulas would put it, the Spirit liberates Christ from the constraints of history—coincides with his penetration of the whole of reality (Eph 4:10). Thus, the Pentecostal Spirit is the Spirit of Christ in this sense as well, namely that to have the Spirit is precisely to imbibe the glorified, transfigured body of Christ.

That the Pentecostal Spirit is precisely the Spirit of Christ is an exegetical observation of enormous dogmatic significance. From Rahner to Stăniloae it has received a variety of interpretations. It is beyond the scope of this volume to enter into a more detailed analysis of the various proposals. We are in a position, however, to tease out some tentative propositions based on the foregoing. First, the economy of the Spirit is integrally related to the mission of the Son. In Rahner, the Spirit's work is oriented to Christ's work as to a final cause. With Coffey, Christ's human response of love is precisely the Spirit of Christ "incarnate" in him. In Tanner this concept is admittedly more muted as the Son merely reflects to others the Spirit who first filled him. Stăniloae's distinctive contribution, finally, calls attention to the coming of the Spirit from the body of Christ, adding a distinctive ecclesiological note. Second, the precise manner

---

72. Stăniloae, *Experience*, 4:4.
73. Stăniloae, *Experience*, 4:6.
74. Stăniloae *Experience*, 4:3.

in which this relation is to be described must observe the fundamental distinctions between Creator and creature, between the transcendent God and finite realities. To say that the Holy Spirit is precisely the Spirit of Christ does not mean that the Spirit is reduced to its "human" expression. We are only positing that the perfect human expression of the Holy Spirit has been actualized in Jesus Christ. It remains a question whether this human expression is created as Thomists would stress, uncreated as transcendental Christologists would have it, or deified as the Eastern Orthodox would say. But the dogmatic possibility has been established—to wit, that from a finite human being, Christ, proceeds (or, as Coffey would prefer, is bestowed) externally the very Spirit of God.

The decision to take seriously this Christoformation of the Pentecostal Spirit augments Aquinas's thesis that the Spirit is sent externally through the human nature of Christ. It makes explicit the claim that Christ, in his human actions and existence, makes a contribution to the manner in which the Spirit is sent. Fundamentally, we have insisted on the dogmatic significance of the historical sequence of passion-ascension for the coming of the Spirit. The Spirit is intrinsically connected to those events and to the effect of those events upon Christ. We have rejected a reductive explanation that appeals to the notion of merit, where the Spirit is given to the glorified Christ as a reward for his merits to be then bestowed upon the Church. Rather, the Spirit emerges from Christ intrinsically insofar as he is hypostatically united to the Son, from whom the Spirit proceeds eternally.

Christ's undergoing death perfects the human love of Christ for the Father (Heb 2:10), which is in fact the expression of his eternal love for him worked out in the contingent circumstances of human existence. Moreover, in being resurrected Christ passes as a seed from one level of existence to another; he is transfigured and deified, sown a natural body and raised a spiritual body, a life-giving spirit (1 Cor 15:45). The Spirit that we have received is precisely the glorified and transfigured—the pneumatized—body of Christ. There is to be no confusing of the Son and the Spirit here! Christ does not simply become the Spirit, as we shall see. In his ascension, Christ ascends to fill everything (Eph 4:10) and to give gifts to men.

Christ not only *reflects* the Spirit to us (Tanner's emphasis) but he positively *inflects* him. In receiving the Spirit we receive precisely Christ. *Spiritus est praesens* because Christ is present. This refers to the eternal priesthood of Christ, his mediatorship between God and humanity. As the Johannine Jesus puts it, the Spirit "will glorify me, for he will take what is mine and declare it to you" (John 16:14).

The Christomorphization of the Spirit does not unduly subordinate the

Spirit to the Son, for it is by the Spirit himself that Christ is transfigured. That is, Christ has no human capacity by which to become pneumatized. He must first receive the work and mission of the Spirit. As a human being Christ is just as dependent upon the Spirit as any other human being. But the mystery of the faith is that the Trinity found it pleasing to take this human nature in union with the Son and thus turn it into a gateway for a whole new supernatural relation with the rest of the world. In this human nature the fullness of the deity is present and overflowing. The human nature of Christ is like the first needle attached to a magnet, which is magnetized and then serves to draw, unite, and magnetize other needles. He is naturally the Son of God, he belongs in the Trinity by hypostatic union; we all cling to him by grace and therefore receive from him the promised Spirit, as a river of living water (John 7:38–39).

The Protestant worry about love as the form of the Spirit should be decisively dispelled by this nuancing of Thomas's position on the formality of the indwelling. Our initial answer to the Protestant objection has been to insist that love is not an *ens completum*, but simply the shape left by the impress of the Spirit. To use scriptural language, love is the seal left on the wax of our souls by the presence of the Spirit (Eph 1:13; 4:30). The benefit of this explanation of the formality of the Spirit is to uphold the transcendence of the Spirit and properly to distinguish the indwelling from the incarnation.

Now this explanation receives an additional specification: The created form by which the Holy Spirit indwells is not simply the believer's love, but precisely the love of Christ. The Spirit in other words arrives to the believer already formed. The indwelling Spirit is not formed by the believer's habitual love, but rather it comes already shaped, inflected, and translated into human existence, having been "processed" by Christ's humanity. Here the priority clearly pertains to supernatural grace, which initially works in the human nature of Christ, which is pneumatized, and from which the Spirit flows as a river of living water. But the decisive factor is that all the uncreated grace of God first works on God's human son, into whom we are then baptized by the Spirit (1 Cor 12:13). Only because this supernatural grace dwells perfectly and bodily in Christ can it then be passed on to those who belong to him. There is no additional "formation" of the Spirit, no other mediation of the Spirit, except his Christoformation.

From a Protestant perspective it is not an embarrassment but an advantage that the form of the Spirit's indwelling is someone else's (Christ's) love. Not only does this prevent a confusion between indwelling and incarnation but it is a source of Protestant assurance and comfort that the formation of grace does not depend on anything on the recipient's side. Christ has already obeyed

CHAPTER 9

all and loved to the end. It is precisely this obedience and this love (Rom 5:5) which is then given to us.[75] It is true this approach seems to foreground participation in Christ and move the imputation of Christ's merits into the background: It is because we are in Christ that we share his benefits. Imputation is not a condition but an effect of participation. Nevertheless, all hint of synergy in justification is removed by this single-minded emphasis on the priority of Christ. What is infused is not a form with which the believer must cooperate, but precisely a complete and sufficient disposition. As Ray S. Yeo puts it, "the infusion of the human unitive drive of Christ could also, in some sense, be construed as the direct impartation of the Spirit's disposition of love as it is worked out and mediated in and through the humanity of Christ."[76]

A final question must be asked at this point: does this sketch of the indwelling Spirit, which pivots on the concept of the Spirit of Christ, understood as his reciprocating human love of the Father, ultimately cohere with the rule of inseparability? Both Rahner and Coffey show much inclination to create caveats and exceptions to the rule—Rahner by his conception of quasi-formal causality, Coffey by applying the language of "incarnation" to the Spirit. Having resisted Coffey's incarnational language, have we still not effectively broken the rule in identifying the Spirit with the love of Christ for the Father? In light of the argument of this section, can we still say that the love we have for the Father is the product of the whole Trinity, and that this love disposes us to receive the Holy Spirit distinctly? At first blush the answer might appear negative. In identifying our love for the Father precisely with Christ's love for the Father, which in turn seems to refer and properly belong to the Holy Spirit rather than the whole Trinity, we seem to have abandoned that type of argument distinctly. It seems in other words that we have identified a created form that circumvents appropriation to refer to just one divine person.

On this point there are two responses. First, it must be noted that the human love Christ has for the Father is the ultimate consequence of the causal influence of his divine nature upon his human nature. To this extent the same logic that governs the activity of the incarnate Son applies in this case. As we

75. Developed accounts of how the indwelling of the Spirit might be understood as the communication of Christ's disposition to love the Father are to be found in Ray S. Yeo, "Towards a Model of Indwelling: A Conversation with Jonathan Edwards and William Alston," *Journal of Analytic Theology* 2 (May 2014): 210-37, but also, as we have noted, in Stump, *Atonement*. William Alston's interpretation of the indwelling as the sharing of a personal life should also be mentioned: "The Indwelling of the Holy Spirit," in *Divine Nature and Human Language: Essays in Philosophical Theology* (Ithaca, NY: Cornell University Press: 1989).

76. Yeo, "Towards a Model of Indwelling," 232.

have seen (chapter 6), a distinction must be made between the natural human operation and energy of Christ, which properly belongs to the Son alone in virtue of the hypostatic union, and his personal theandric operation, which results from the causal influence of the whole Trinity upon the instrumentalized nature. Coffey's distinction may be seamlessly applied here: The basic, categorial, transcendental love of Christ properly belongs to the Son alone, yet insofar as it becomes the personal and individual love of Christ for the Father it is the common effect of the whole Trinity.

Secondly, insofar as one divine person is identified in relation to an essential attribute it must be remembered that a certain appropriation is always operative. When the Son is called Word an appeal is made to the essential property of knowledge. Thus the Son is said to proceed by way of the essential operation of knowledge. Similarly, the Holy Spirit is said to proceed by way of the essential operation of love. The love from which we name the Spirit, and which designated his personal property, is not exclusively the Spirit's property any more than spirituality is or any more than knowledge is the Son's exclusive property. We have resisted throughout an opposition between common works and personal properties. Thus the love that the Father has for the Son is the same as the love the Son has for the Father; it is the same as the love the Spirit has for the Father and for the Son. Other than the relations of opposition the persons do not have their exclusive properties.

By implication, when we say that the Son receives the love of the Father he does not receive an entity different than the one the Spirit possesses. It is the very same essential love that the incarnate Son receives. The Father does not have one love, the Son another love, and the Spirit yet another love. Nevertheless, in receiving this essential attribute the Son also receives that which proceeds by way of this attribute or operation, namely the Holy Spirit himself. In identifying the Spirit with the love of God, Christian theology has made a judgment that there is a certain affinity between the third person and the attribute or operation of love. Conversely, in identifying the second person as the Logos, an affinity between the Son and knowledge has been recognized. It is thus most fitting that it is the Son who reveals the Father, as Word, and that it is the Spirit who unites us with the Father and Son. Neither of this means that the Son and the Father are any less loving or that the Spirit and the Father are any less knowing.

It is thus important to remember that in singling out one attribute as the personal property, or personal name of one of the persons we have not made an essential distinction between the persons but an appropriation. Now Christ possesses both perfect divine knowledge (beatific vision) and perfect divine love. What makes him, then, incarnate Son and not incarnate Spirit? According to our logic, it is the fact that he is by nature the self-knowledge of the Father and yet by consequence the self-love of the Father, not the other way around. In Christ the fullness of the deity resides, but in an *order* according to the divine mode of existence he has assumed, namely that of the only begotten Word. For this reason, Christ is first intellect, first revelation of the Father, then love. Given the divine unity, it is impossible for the incarnate Son to irradiate only knowledge, without love. But he is ordered first to knowledge and then to love, even though in him the passage from the one to the other bears no mark of time.

The inseparability between the various divine attributes, denoted dogmatically as the doctrine of divine simplicity, must be strictly observed together with the indivisibility of operation. Because of this there can be no discursive knowledge of the divine persons in isolation from one another. The persons can only be known and experienced together. In the very same breath, if it were possible, one must confess that Christ is divine self-knowledge and divine self-love.

The question of having distinct relations with the divine persons must be answered by the clarification that between them no separation and isolation is conceivable. We know Christ to be distinctly the Son of God not because we can isolate him from the Father and the Spirit, but precisely because we cannot! How then do we know that this Christ is the Son and not the Spirit? Because in him we have the *revelation* of the Father. Does the Spirit not equally reside in him? Indeed he does but not by incarnation, not having been hypostatically united to a human nature.

Biblically too, as we have observed, the recognition that Christ is the Son of God is inseparable from the recognition that the Father is at work in him and that he bears the power and authority of the Spirit. We confess Christ's divinity because by faith we "have seen the Father" (John 14:9) in him. Equally, we can only confess Christ's lordship through the Spirit (1 Cor 12:3).

This knowledge (revelation) and this confession of lordship (love and attachment) cannot be merely intellectual gestures, for the human intellect operates precisely by division and abstraction. They are fundamentally experiential, which is to say they do not objectify. Authentic revelation (knowledge by the Son) and transformation (love by the Spirit) are possible to the extent that God is subject and not object. Distinct experience of the persons proceeds not by way of conceptual mastery, but by being under the impress of the divine persons themselves.

It may help to invoke the magnetic analogy again. Knowledge that there are a south pole and a north pole in a magnet is possible only to the extent that something begins to bear their property. Only insofar as a needle is magnetically charged does the needle "experience" the poles distinctly. The knowledge of the persons does not follow the route of conceptual mastery but of experiential transformation. We know the Son insofar as we find ourselves to be imprinted with revelation through Christ. We experience the Spirit insofar as we find ourselves to receive a love that surpasses all understanding. Like the wine taster, who can only detect certain fragrances simultaneously with other notes, and only by having his taste buds "impressed," we can only experience the *distinct* persons *together*, as we come under their "impress" in knowledge and love.

Conclusion

With this discussion about the indwelling of the Holy Spirit we have reached the end of our exploration into the doctrine of inseparable operations and its dogmatic coherence. The precious doctrine of the indwelling Spirit celebrates a relationship between the believer and the third person of the Trinity, a relationship of a most intimate kind. The doctrine of inseparable operations must not be construed in such a way as to cast doubt on this reality. And yet, if all the operations of the Trinity in the world produce effects of their common causality, a distinct relation to the persons seems to be lost in a blur of inseparable triune causality. Out of a desire to prevent such outcomes a host of theologians writing largely in the wake of Rahner have attempted to highlight a new relationship between the believer and each triune person. These theologians eschew efficient causality—where admittedly the inseparability rule applies—and conceive of a quasi-formal relationship between the Spirit and the believer.

While the doctrine of inseparability is not altogether rejected in this move, it is claimed that the domain of its applicability is actually rather limited. By contrast, a whole realm of supernatural relations to the triune persons is disclosed in grace, where the triune persons are not related to humans simply extrinsically, in terms of efficient causality, but intrinsically, in a way that they become quasi-forms of certain created faculties, such as knowledge and love.

Despite commendable intentions, we determined that Rahner and his allies ultimately fail to demonstrate the viability of this alternative, risking the erosion of the Creator-creature distinction, confusing persons and essence, and conflating the hypostatic union and the indwelling of the divine persons in the just. Our only alternative was to return to the Thomistic account of the indwelling in the hope that it would be able to withstand the modern critiques. It emerged, in our opinion, that what we called the *appropriation approach*, which defines the formality of the Spirit's indwelling in terms of the created effect of love, is after all conducive to a relationship with the Spirit that is not merely appropriated. The key here was the ontological distinction between the Spirit and created beings. Because the Spirit is wholly Other, he will not be present as himself, but rather through a created form. This created form is the love poured into our hearts (Rom 5:5).

Far from reifying this love into an intermediary substance, we noted that not only is the love a consequent of the Spirit's personal presence (thus an ontological priority of uncreated over created grace), but this love is specifically Christ's love of the Father. The Spirit who indwells the believer is, then, precisely the Spirit that has first been formed by Christ's humanity. This has provided a Protestant qualification of Aquinas's understanding of the created grace. It is not the believer's own love that enables the Spirit to indwell him. Rather, it is the love by which Christ loves the Father, and the Father loves Christ, that is poured into our hearts. Love is not our contribution to the gift of grace. Rather, love is itself a gift that is prepared for us by Christ.

It may be said that the appropriation model is hospitable to the idea of an intimate relationship with the Spirit because the love (which is the common gift of the Trinity, although coming to us specifically through the instrumentality of the Son's human nature) is *disposing* us to receive the Holy Spirit. Under the regime of inseparable operations, we can still affirm a distinct knowledge and relation to the divine persons. However, there is a major difference: we can no longer think about knowledge and relation in terms of subject and object. We know the triune persons because we are indwelled by them, because they give themselves to us most intimately. This is not a detached form of knowledge, but may be called a "self-involved" knowledge, inextricable from knowledge of self. The persons are no longer known as objects. We have warned against this in chapter 3. They are known as intimate dimensions of ourselves, the Son as knowledge, the Spirit as love, yet without confusion.

Conclusion

Speaking in a theologically responsible way about divine action requires an adjustment in our understanding of the fit between words and reality. Given divine simplicity, aseity, and transcendence, there are no created concepts through which God may be comprehended. Language about him must be taken with a certain reserve—not in a nonrealist manner, to be sure, but in the sense that our concepts cannot bear the load of the description by themselves, that they are only useful insofar as one keeps in mind their defectiveness. Faith is in this respect just the realization that our world has been breached by a reality far exceeding our conceptual ability. But faith comes by hearing and not simply by sight. What our senses communicate to us of this irruption accords with their own capacities and with the form of the incursion. So long as we are inhabitants of Flatland we do not see the sphere as sphere but only as the circle it generates in our ontological domain. Our senses do not have a capacity for three-dimensional objects. We only know that there's more to it than the circle by "listening" to it. This does not reduce revelation to its propositional aspect; it only explains that without propositional guidance the revelation is misguiding.

The revelation of the triune persons requires this propositional guidance too. Without it we would not be able to experience and "see" the divinity of Christ, for the acts of a spiritual (John 4:24), divine being are not observable (John 1:18). What the senses register are merely the visible effects of this divine operation. In faith, though, we learn to interpret what we experience as a manifestation of something that ultimately transcends our finite province as well as our capacities.

But this propositional guidance does not amount to conceptual mastery. Hearing and understanding are not necessarily comprehension. To understand a concept, as Wittgenstein so usefully reminds us, is not necessarily to perceive its essence but to know how to apply it, to know how to go on using it in various "language-games." Similarly, understanding the propositional concepts of revelation does not amount to comprehending what they are about. There can be understanding of the notion of divinity, for example, without grasping the divine essence. The propositions of revelation are understandable in the sense that they are followable and applicable in a practical context of prayer, worship, and proclamation. They make sense, to continue using the Wittgensteinian terminology, within these specific forms of life and language games. Theology in this approach is less the organization of objective insights and propositions, but rather a determination of the appropriate use of these propositions within these forms of life. Being only wayfarers and not comprehensors, we require theology to serve as a map of the terrain. But theology does not map God, since God is simple and therefore not mappable; rather it maps our journey to God and with God, under the guidance of his revelation, not least through propositions.

The doctrine of inseparable operations, then, is not remarkable through any comprehension it might lead to. Its value resides rather in the consistency with which it organizes and regulates our understanding of salvation history. Its ultimate foundation is the propositional content of revelation, the ascription of certain created effects commonly to the Father, Son, and Holy Spirit. Again, since we are not comprehensors, the ultimate divine "movements" behind these effects that we register cannot be seen with the naked eye. It is only in faith that we accept that they are caused by God, and it is only in faith that we understand them to be caused by the indivisible energies of the Trinity. The rule of inseparability is thus premised on the propositional content of revelation.

We do not observe the transcendent triune causality. We only remark upon its effects. Under the guidance of revelation we understand these effects to be the common production of three irreducibly distinct "persons." We have no comprehension as to how this inseparable operation "works." But we know that it makes a difference. The necessity of this doctrine, then, results from maintaining this grammatical consistency. But as we have seen, the role of grammar is not to make assertions about reality; it is to make such assertions possible. In this case as well, the function of the rule is to make other claims possible, and less to provide a privileged insight into the essence of divine causality. When we say that it makes other claims possible, what are these assertions? They are precisely the assertions that we have been discussing from chapter 4 onward: that God creates, that only the Son becomes incarnate, that the Son acts redemptively to unite us with God again, that the Spirit has come.

Inseparability orders these statements in the sense that it circumscribes their use. It explains how they should be used. In this case, it instructs that whenever an action is ascribed to a divine person, it should not be to the exclusion of the other persons. Its value as a doctrine is not limited because it leads to no new "in-sight." At the same time, it is not a purely negative doctrine. Were it so, the modern complaint that it obscures the triune persons would be entirely appropriate. If all the doctrine said was that the economic actions must be ascribed uniformly to all the triune persons, it would not be possible to speak about the persons on the basis of their operations. On the contrary, the doctrine underwrites an understanding of the divine persons that assumes the unity of their operations, and yet it trains a sense for a personal mode of action within this unity. Because the persons subsist as relations within the unity of the divine essence, they can never be experienced without each other and in abstraction from this unity. Yet they are not to be confused with the unity. If there is to be an insight into a unique person it will take place in and through the mediation of this unity.

The doctrine of appropriation indicates the manner in which such a drawing toward the personal distinctiveness is to be realized. In appropriation we proceed toward the personal distinction without leaving the unity behind. For this reason, in appropriation we gain not a new insight but semantic depth. By understanding from propositional revelation the personal property we discern how it is manifested in the persons' common operations. Thus the experience of the persons in their hypostatic distinction takes place through the medium of their common operation, but it is a common operation in which we are drawn toward the persons distinctly. But in this case, the experience is not a mere epistemic experience, where we objectify the person. Rather it is a self-involving experience, where the person gives himself to me precisely through my operations. It is, as we have seen, more of a tasting than a seeing. It is more like recognizing a certain note in the unitary taste of a glass of wine. It is experiential and not discursive knowledge. To experience the Son in his personal property, then, is to know God; to experience the Holy Spirit in his personal property is to love God.

To experience the persons in their distinctness is just to experience the one God and to receive, through adoption, the mode of existence of the Son (not instead of our *esse*, but alongside it) and, through indwelling, the mode of existence of the Spirit, which is just the mutual love between the Father and the Son. This takes place through the invisible missions, which are made possible by the visible missions. Thus, distinct relations with the triune persons obtain on the basis of their inseparable operation; yet through this operation we are drawn to participate in the life of God and therefore we begin to resemble the Son and Spirit as exemplars.

The transcendence and simplicity of God go together with the inseparability doctrine. Separable actions entail a divisible God. But a divisible God does not possess aseity. He would depend on the prior existence of his "parts" or on whatever put him together. Separable operations would entail separate essences as grounds for those operations. Even *ad intra*, if we insist on calling the processions operations, they are operations immanent in the same substance. Thus, all distinctions between the persons can only be relational and not substantial. Any other distinctions introduce composition into God's being, since in that case one person would have a set of properties not shared with the others.

One must be mindful of this transcendence when we come to grips with inseparable operations. This means that we must also be mindful of a certain translation of action from a transcendent domain into finite existence, just as a sphere transitions from a three-dimensional to a two-dimensional space. Lack of caution here easily leads to mythologization. But what is this relation, this translation? We have opted to understand action as the production of effects. So, when we identify his agency—that is, that a particular effect is ascribed to God in a special and not merely providential way—we need not look for an additional *finite* link between the effect and its cause. Unlike finite operation, where actions are (often) produced by the movement of bodies, in the case of God such a mediation is not necessary. We need not ask in virtue of what is God causing the effect; no *transfer* of energy needs to take place in divine action. This doesn't suggest that there are only created effects to divine action, only that their transcendent cause is not another item in the world. We can speak of such a divine economic action only from the standpoint of these effects, yet such action is divine only insofar as these effects are ultimately attributable to God.

Again, we have no comprehension of divine action in itself, of that heavenly energy whereby these effects are fashioned. Such transcendent energy is the divine being itself. Our experience only grasps its marks in our domain, just as the Flatlanders only experience a circle and not the whole sphere. And yet we know that our experience is partial and should not be taken at its face value. In faith we confess that since God is triune—something we have learned not from observing separate effects, but having been taught propositionally to ascribe the same effects to Father, Son, and Holy Spirit—we have to describe every divine action in inseparable-Trinitarian terms. We have thus turned to a number of pivotal doctrines in order to demonstrate both the sustainability and the vitality of the doctrine of inseparability.

For Christian theology, creation is the fundamental positing of a reality distinct from God. Under the rule of inseparability, the Christological mediation of creation is understood not in terms of the Son being God's agent in creation, an instrument. This would play into Gnosticism and destroy divine simplicity, making only the Son to be truly creator. Rather, God creates through Christ in a way analogical to how a craftsman creates through his art. The origin and ground of creation lies in the divine processions, which are the type of creatures.

Far from rendering creation necessary it suggests that it is a free act of God, yet not a capricious act. God's creation is wise and good. It is patterned after the processions and therefore it is the actualization of one possible way of sharing in the divine goodness. In knowing himself (as Word), God also knows the manifold ways in which his goodness may be participated. And yet God intended creation not only to resemble him externally, but to be united to him in Jesus Christ. The goal of creation is union with his Son. That this goal is not merely extrinsic is established by the fact that the incarnate Son deifies and raises humanity above its natural capacities. Creation and humanity have an inherent movement toward God, yet it is a movement that cannot be fulfilled apart from grace, apart from God's free gift of himself to humanity.

It was also determined that given the ontological distinction between Creator and creature, the role of the creature in relation to God is always carefully circumscribed. Divine aseity implies that the creature does not actualize God, that God cannot acquire capacities through the creature. This is of fundamental importance, for when God extends his presence and operation to the creature, the created effects that result cannot be seen as constitutive of the divine being but merely as consequences of his transcendent being and operation. Thus the doctrine of creation institutes an important element of the logic of the divine missions, namely that the created effect is merely a consequent of the mission and not a constitutive part. In Flatland terms, the circle does not *enable* the sphere to pass through the two-dimensional space; it is the consequent—and a necessary consequent at that—of the sphere's passing through that space. Or one might say it is the necessary form of the sphere's presence in Flatland. This parameter of divine action and missions is of an incalculable theological value. It affects everything that is said about Christ and his operations.

In Christ, human nature is actuated not by its own principle but by the Word. It exists in the Word, enhypostatically. In the incarnation creation reaches the beginning of its end; for in Christ it is raised above its capacities to union with the Word. We found the doctrine of the incarnation of the Son alone to pose no real difficulty for the doctrine of inseparable operation since the Son doesn't *do* anything different from the other persons in the incarnation. Rather, the whole Trinity actuates this human substance in the person of the Son. The Son, so to speak, receives this human nature just like the fire "receives" an iron or like a magnet receives a needle. The change takes place in the human nature, not on God's side. We have highlighted the distinction between operation and state. The incarnation is a state of the Son alone, yet not simply conceptually, for the relation is real in the creature. The creature receives, the Creator gives. But what the Creator gives is exactly the mode of being and operation of the Son!

The mystery of the incarnation cannot be explained by any amount of effort. It can only be confessed and revered. Christ's human nature acquires not only the mode of existence of the Son but also the Son's mode of operation. The human nature only acts as the instrument of the divine nature. The human operation is only consequent upon the divine operation. This doesn't make it any less human. Unfathomably, in the person of the Son, God actuates this human nature, with its operations, as an instrument of the divine. The operations are actuated in the mode of the Son: Christ only does what he sees the Father doing (John 5:19). In faith we understand that in God there are these three modes of existence and action. In faith we do not separate them in different action tokens but understand them purely relationally, within the unity of the same action. To call them "modes of action" is not to explain what they are. There aren't more basic categories in which to inscribe them. We can only confess and receive that in God there is a single operation in three of what we tentatively call "modes."

Christ's human operation belongs to the Son alone if by that human operation we understand the natural energy of his human nature. Given the enhypostasis, however, this human energy never exists by itself. It only comes into being once the human nature is energized by the divine nature. This energized action has come to be called the theandric operation of Christ. Christ's theandric operation is the instrumentalizing and transfiguring of the human operation of Christ. Just as a magnet instrumentalizes the needle while allowing the latter to retain its natural operation and properties, so the human operation of Christ is raised above its natural capacities as it is coopted, without being corrupted, into theandric action.

Everything flows from the divinity through the humanity. Yet the humanity retains its natural operations. It therefore retains its natural possibility as well. But because the energy proceeds from the divinity, the last word is inevitably God's. For this reason, death stands no chance. The human nature is allowed to fear and recoil from death, and to die, but only as a transitory phase toward glorified eternal life. But the operation and the passion are absorbed and transfigured by the divine operation. The operation is not simply that of a dying man, but of a conquering Lord. The passion too is that of an obedient and faithful servant, who accepts death in faith and without despair.

Christ's atonement must also be understood in a way consistent with the unity of external operations, but also in line with enhypostatic Christology. The role of Christ's human operations, then, must be seen as consequent, not constitutive. Calvary does not unlock or enable anything on God's side. It is a necessary consequence of God's taking seriously our penal condition and assuming it himself in Christ. We have refused a logic of exchange—often supposed to be obligatory for penal substitution—in favor of a logic of union. A logic of union, however, will have to give an integral role to the Holy Spirit. The effect of the union is that the human nature of Christ now participates in the external processions of the Trinity. Just as a needle does not only receive the property of one of the poles in being magnetized but this magnetism passes through it to other needles, the human nature not only receives the property of the Son but also participates in the further mission of the Holy Spirit. The Holy Spirit does not come merely extrinsically, as reward upon the completion of Christ's work. He flows from the pneumatized humanity of Jesus Christ. This reveals, perhaps, why Pentecost must wait upon the ascension. In the ascension the full realization of Christ's sonship is completed as the Son returns everything to the Father in love and obedience, precisely as man. Just as the Spirit proceeds immanently from the Son's return to the Father in love, so externally he proceeds from the Son's return to the Father in human love and obedience.

The logic of union is clearly on display here: Just as by being united to the Son the human nature of Christ acquires the modes of existence and operation of the Son, so it acquires the productivity of the Son, As sheer receptivity it does not require time for Christ to have the existence of the Son; as productivity, however, his human nature must first be disposed to spirate the Spirit externally, as a transfigured human operation!

The mediation of the indwelling Spirit through the human nature of Christ influences our account of the formality of the indwelling. We have resisted throughout a Lombardian and a Rahnerian account of this formality, judging them insufficiently attentive to divine transcendence. At the same time we found it necessary to supplement Aquinas's account of love as the form of the inhabitation. If the Spirit comes down not as the generic Spirit of God but as the Spirit of Christ, then he already has a human form. He is already formed for our reception, precisely by Christ. From a Protestant perspective, this form is not one of my habits but is precisely Christ's habit of love. This preserves the distinction between indwelling and incarnation yet closely orders the former to the latter. As Tanner has put it, Christ forms the Spirit for us; he gives the Spirit a "digestible" form such that he may be assimilated. No modalistic confusion between Christ and the Spirit is lurking here. Rather, just as the Spirit mediates God's presence in the Old Testament, so he mediates the presence of the ascended Christ in the new dispensation. That Christ acquires in his humanity such a pneumatized existence is the presupposition or objective basis for the descent of the Spirit. The Spirit who binds us to Christ is not a being distinct from Christ, but the same God who works all things.

Bibliography

Abraham, William J. *Divine Agency and Divine Action*. Vol. 2, *Soundings in the Christian Tradition*. Oxford: Oxford University Press, 2017.

Alston, William. *Divine Nature and Human Language: Essays in Philosophical Theology*. Ithaca, NY: Cornell University Press, 1989.

Anatolios, Khaled. *Retrieving Nicaea: The Development and Meaning of Trinitarian Doctrine*. Grand Rapids: Baker Academic, 2011.

Anderson, Marvin W. "Peter Martyr on Romans." *Scottish Journal of Theology* 26, no. 4 (1973): 401–20.

Aquinas, Thomas. *Commentary on Aristotle's* De Anima. 2nd ed. Translated by Kenelm Foster. Notre Dame, IN: Dumb Ox Books, 1994.

Aquinas, Thomas. *On Love and Charity: Readings from the Commentary on the Sentences of Peter Lombard*. Thomas Aquinas in Translation. Translated by Peter A. Kwasniewski, OSB, Thomas Bolin, and Joseph Bolin. Washington, DC: Catholic University of America Press, 2012.

Aquinas, Thomas. *Quaestiones Disputatae de Veritate*. Translated by Robert Mulligan, SJ. Chicago, IL: Henry Regnery Company, 1952.

Aquinas, Thomas. *Summa Contra Gentiles*. Translated by Anton C. Pegis. Notre Dame, IN: University of Notre Dame Press, 2016.

Aquinas, Thomas. *Summa Theologica*. Translated by the Fathers of the English Dominican Province. Westminster, MD: Christian Classics, 1981.

Aristotle. *Metaphysics*. In *The Complete Works of Aristotle*. Edited by Jonathan Barnes. Princeton, NJ: Princeton University Press, 1984.

Athanasius. *Orations Against the Arians*. In vol. 4 of *The Nicene and Post-Nicene Fathers*. Series 2. Edited by Henry Wace and Philip Schaff. Peabody, MA: Hendrickson Publishers, 1999.

Augustine. *Faith and the Creed*. In Augustine, *On Christian Belief*. Augustinian Heritage Institute. Edited by Boniface Ramsey. Hyde Park, NY: New City Press, 2012.

Augustine. *Letters 1–99*. The Works of Augustine. Translated by Roland Teske, SJ. Edited by John E. Rotelle, OSA. Hyde Park, NY: New City Press, 2001.

Augustine. *Sermons 51–94*. The Works of Augustine. Translated by Edmund Hill, OP. Edited by John E. Rotelle, OSA. Hyde Park, NY: New City Press, 1992.

Augustine. *Sermons 94A–147A*. The Works of Augustine. Translated by Edmund Hill, OP. Edited by John E. Rotelle, OSA. Hyde Park, NY: New City Press, 1992.

Augustine. *Tractate 20*. In vol. 7 of *Nicene and Post-Nicene Fathers*. Series 1. Edited by Philip Schaff. New York: Cosimo, 2007.

Augustine. *The Trinity*. The Works of Augustine. Translated by Edmund Hill, OP. Hyde Park, NY: New City Press, 1991.

Awad, Najeeb. *God Without a Face? On the Personal Individuation of the Holy Spirit*. Dogmatik in Der Moderne 2. Tübingen: Mohr Siebeck, 2011.

Ayres, Lewis. *Augustine and the Trinity*. Cambridge: Cambridge University Press, 2014.

Ayres, Lewis. *Nicaea and Its Legacy: An Approach to Fourth-Century Trinitarian Theology*. Oxford: Oxford University Press, 2004.

Ayres, Lewis. "'Remember That You Are Catholic' (serm. 52.2): Augustine on the Unity of the Triune God." *Journal of Early Christian Studies* 8, no. 1 (2000): 39–82.

Bach, Kent. "Actions Are Not Events." *Mind* 89 (1980): 114–20.

Barker, Margaret. *The Great Angel: A Study of Israel's Second God*. Louisville, KY: Westminster John Knox Press, 1992.

Barnes, Michel René. *The Power of God: δύναμις in Gregory of Nyssa's Trinitarian Theology*. Washington, DC: Catholic University of America Press, 2001.

Barrett, Charles K. *The Gospel According to St. John: An Introduction with Commentary and Notes on the Greek Text*. 2nd ed. Philadelphia, PA: Westminster John Knox Press, 1978.

Basil. *On the Holy Spirit*. Popular Patristics 42. Edited by Stephen M. Hildebrand. Yonkers, NY: Saint Vladimir's Seminary Press, 2011.

Bauckham, Richard. *Gospel of Glory: Major Themes in Johannine Theology*. Grand Rapids: Baker Academic, 2015.

Bauckham, Richard. *Jesus and the God of Israel: God Crucified and Other Studies on the New Testament's Christology of Divine Identity*. Grand Rapids: Eerdmans, 2009.

Bavinck, Herman. *Reformed Dogmatics*. Vol. 2, *God and Creation*. Translated by John Vriend. Edited by John Bolt. Grand Rapids: Baker Academic, 2004.

Bavinck, Herman. *Reformed Dogmatics*. Vol. 4, *Holy Spirit, Church, and New Creation*. Translated by John Vriend. Edited by John Bolt. Grand Rapids: Baker Academic, 2008.

Beasley-Murray, George R. *John*. Word Biblical Commentary 36. Nashville, TN: Thomas Nelson, 1999.

Billings, J. Todd. *Calvin, Participation, and the Gift: The Activity of Believers in Union with Christ.* Changing Paradigms in Historical and Systematic Theology. Oxford: Oxford University Press, 2008.

Bird, Michael F. *Jesus the Eternal Son: Answering Adoptionist Christology.* Grand Rapids: Eerdmans, 2017.

Bock, Darrell L. *Blasphemy and Exaltation in Judaism: The Charge Against Jesus in Mark 14:53–56.* Grand Rapids: Baker, 1998.

Boland, Vivian. *Ideas in God According to Saint Thomas Aquinas: Sources and Synthesis.* Studies in the History of Christian Traditions 69. Leiden: Brill, 1996.

Bousset, Wilhelm. *Die Religion des Judentums im Neutestamentlichen Zeitalter.* 2nd ed. Berlin: Reuther and Reichard, 1906.

Bradshaw, David. *Aristotle East and West: Metaphysics and the Division of Christendom.* Cambridge: Cambridge University Press, 2004.

Bultmann, Rudolf. *The Gospel of John: A Commentary.* Philadelphia, PA: Westminster John Knox Press, 1971.

Burrell, David. *Aquinas: God and Action.* 3rd ed. Edited by Mary Budde Ragan. Eugene, OR: Wipf and Stock, 2016.

Calvin, John. *The Bondage and Liberation of the Will: A Defence of the Orthodox Doctrine of Human Choice against Pighuis.* Texts and Studies in Reformation and Post-Reformation Thought. Edited by A. N. S. Lane. Translated by G. I. Davies. Grand Rapids: Baker Books, 1996.

Calvin, John. *John.* Crossway Classic Commentaries. Edited by Alister McGrath and J. I. Packer. Wheaton, IL: Crossway, 1994.

Campbell, Douglas J. Foreword to *Paul's Divine Christology*, by Christopher Tilling, x–xix. Grand Rapids: Eerdmans, 2015.

Childs, Brevard S. *Biblical Theology of the Old and New Testaments: Theological Reflection on the Christian Bible.* Minneapolis: Fortress, 2011.

Chrysostom, John. *Homily 78.* In *Commentary on Saint John the Apostle and Evangelist.* The Fathers of the Church 41. Translated by Sister Thomas Aquinas Goggin. Washington, DC: Catholic University of America Press, 1959.

Coakley, Sarah. "'Persons' in the 'Social' Doctrine of the Trinity: A Critique of Current Analytic Discussion." In *The Trinity: An Interdisciplinary Symposium on the Trinity.* Edited by Stephen T. Davis, Daniel Kendall, SJ, and Gerald O' Collins, SJ. Oxford: Oxford University Press, 2003.

Coffey, David. *Did You Receive the Spirit When You Believed? Some Basic Questions for Pneumatology.* The Pere Marquette Lecture in Theology 2005. Milwaukee, WI: Marquette University Press, 2005.

Coffey, David. *Grace: The Gift of the Holy Spirit.* Sydney: Faith and Culture, 1979.

Coffey, David. "The 'Incarnation' of the Holy Spirit in Christ." *Theological Studies* 45, no. 3 (1984): 466–80.

Congar, Yves. *I Believe in the Holy Spirit: Lord and Giver of Life.* Vol. 2. Translated by David Smith. New York: Crossroad Publishing Company, 1983.

Congar, Yves. *I Believe in the Holy Spirit: The River of Life Flows in the East and in the West.* Vol. 3. Translated by David Smith. New York: Crossroad Publishing Company, 1983.

Congar, Yves. "Saint Augustin et le traité scolastique 'De Gratia Capitis.'" *Augustinianum* 20 (1980): 79–93.

Crisp, Oliver D. *Revisioning Christology: Theology in the Reformed Tradition.* Farnham, UK: Ashgate, 2011.

Cross, Richard. *The Metaphysics of the Incarnation: Thomas Aquinas to Duns Scotus.* Oxford: Oxford University Press, 2007.

Cunningham, Francis L. B. *The Indwelling of the Trinity: A Historico-Doctrinal Study of the Theory of St. Thomas Aquinas.* Dubuque, IA: The Priory Press, 1955.

Damascene, John. *Writings: The Fount of Knowledge, The Philosophical Chapters, On Heresies, and On the Orthodox Faith.* The Fathers of the Church 37. Translated by Frederic H. Chase Jr. n.p. Ex Fontibus, 2015.

Dauphinais, Michael, and Matthew Levering, eds. *Reading John with Saint Thomas Aquinas: Theological Exegesis and Speculative Theology.* Washington, DC: Catholic University of America Press, 2010.

Davies, W. D., and Dale C. Allison Jr. *Matthew 8–18.* International Critical Commentary. Edinburgh: T&T Clark, 2004.

Davis, Philip G. "Divine Agents, Mediators, and New Testament Christology." *Journal of Theological Studies* 45, no. 2 (1994): 479–503.

Davis, Stephen T., Daniel Kendall, SJ, and Gerald O' Collins, SJ, eds. *The Trinity: An Interdisciplinary Symposium on the Trinity.* Oxford: Oxford University Press, 2003.

De La Taille, Maurice. *The Hypostatic Union and Created Actuation by Uncreated Act: Light of Glory, Sanctifying Grace, Hypostatic Union.* West Baden Springs, IN: West Baden College, 1952.

DelCogliano, Mark, Andrew Radde-Gallwitz, and Lewis Ayres, trans. *Works on the Spirit: Athanasius's Letters to Serapion on the Holy Spirit, and Didymus's On the Holy Spirit.* Popular Patristics 43. Yonkers, NY: Saint Vladimir's Seminary Press, 2011.

Del Colle, Ralph. *Christ and the Spirit: Spirit-Christology in Trinitarian Perspective.* Oxford: Oxford University Press, 1994.

De Lubac, Henri. *The Drama of Atheist Humanism.* San Francisco: Ignatius Press, 1998.

De Lubac, Henri. *The Mystery of the Supernatural*. Milestones in Catholic Theology. New York: Crossroad Publishing Company, 1998.

Denzinger, Heinrich. *The Church Teaches: Documents of the Church in English Translation*. Edited and translated by John F. Clarkson. Rockford, IL: Tan Books and Publishers, 1973.

Dodd, Charles H. *The Interpretation of the Fourth Gospel*. Cambridge: Cambridge University Press, 1968.

Dodds, Michael J. *Unlocking Divine Action: Contemporary Science and Thomas Aquinas*. Washington, DC: Catholic University of America Press, 2012.

Donnelly, John P. "Calvinist Thomism." *Viator* 7 (1976): 441–55.

Donnelly, Malachi J. "The Inhabitation of the Holy Spirit: A Solution according to De La Taille." *Theological Studies* 8, no. 3 (1947): 445–70.

Doolan, Gregory T. *Aquinas on the Divine Ideas as Exemplar Causes*. Washington, DC: Catholic University of America Press, 2014.

Doran, Robert. *The Trinity in History: A Theology of the Divine Missions*. Vol. 1. Lonergan Studies. Toronto: University of Toronto Press, 2012.

Dunn, James D. G. *Jesus and the Spirit: A Study of the Religious and Charismatic Experience of Jesus and the First Christians as Reflected in the New Testament*. Grand Rapids: Eerdmans, 1997.

Duns Scotus, John. *God and Creatures: The Quodlibetal Questions*. Translated by Felix Alluntis and Allan B. Wolter. Princeton: Princeton University Press, 1975.

Duns Scotus, John. *Opera omnia*. Vol. 9. Vatican: Quaracchi, 1950.

Duns Scotus, John. *The Ordinatio of Blessed John Duns Scotus*. Translated by Peter L. P. Simpson. Accessed March 17, 2020. http://www.aristotelophile.com/Books/Translations/Scotus%20Ordinatio%20III%20dd.1-17.pdf.

Dupuis, Jacques, and Josef Neuner, eds. *The Christian Faith in the Doctrinal Documents of the Catholic Church*. London: Collins, 1983.

Emery, Gilles. "Essentialism or Personalism in the Treatise on God in Saint Thomas Aquinas?" *Thomist: A Speculative Quarterly Review* 64, no. 4 (2000): 521–63.

Emery, Gilles. "The Personal Mode of Trinitarian Action in Saint Thomas Aquinas." *Thomist: A Speculative Quarterly Review* 69, no. 1 (2005): 31–77.

Emery, Gilles. *The Trinitarian Theology of Saint Thomas Aquinas*. Translated by Francesca Aran Murphy. Oxford: Oxford University Press, 2007.

Emery, Gilles. *The Trinity: An Introduction to Catholic Doctrine on the Triune God*. Thomistic Ressourcement 1. Translated by Matthew Levering. Washington, DC: Catholic University of America Press, 2011.

Evans, William B. *Imputation and Impartation: Union with Christ in American*

Reformed Theology. Studies in Christian History and Thought. Eugene, OR: Wipf and Stock, 2009.

Farrow, Douglas. *Ascension and Ecclesia: On the Significance of the Doctrine of the Ascension for Ecclesiology and Christian Cosmology*. Grand Rapids: Eerdmans, 2009.

Fatehi, Mehrdad. *The Spirit's Relation to the Risen Lord in Paul: An Examination of Its Christological Implications*. Wissenschaftliche Untersuchungen zum Neuen Testament 2. Reihe 128. Tübingen: Mohr Siebeck, 2000.

Fee, Gordon. "Paul and the Trinity: The Experience of Christ and the Spirit for Paul's Understanding of God." In *The Trinity: An Interdisciplinary Symposium on the Trinity*. Edited by Stephen T. Davis, Daniel Kendall, SJ, and Gerald O' Collins, SJ. Oxford: Oxford University Press, 2003.

Fletcher-Louis, Crispin. *Jesus Monotheism*, Volume 1. *Christological Origins: The Emerging Consensus and Beyond*. Eugene, OR: Cascade Books, 2015.

Fossum, J. E., *The Name of God and the Angel of the Lord: Samaritan and Jewish Conceptions of Intermediation and the Origin of Gnosticism*. Waco, TX: Baylor University Press, 2017.

Galvin, John P. "An Invitation of Grace." In *A World of Grace: An Introduction to the Themes and Foundations of Karl Rahner's Theology*. Edited by Leo J. O'Donovan. New York: Seabury Press, 1980.

Garrigou-Lagrange, Reginald. *Christ the Savior: A Commentary on the Third Part of Saint Thomas' Theological Summa*. St. Louis, MO: Herder Book Company, 1957.

Garrigou-Lagrange, Reginald. *The Trinity and God the Creator: A Commentary on Saint Thomas' Theological Summa 1a, q.27–119*. St. Louis, MO: Herder Book Company, 1954.

Greenstock, David L. "Exemplar Causality and the Supernatural Order." *Thomist: A Speculative Quarterly Review* 16, no. 1 (1953): 1–31.

Gruenler, Royce G. *The Trinity in the Gospel of John: A Thematic Commentary on the Fourth Gospel*. Grand Rapids: Baker Books, 1986.

Gunton, Colin E. *Act and Being: Towards a Theology of the Divine Attributes*. Grand Rapids: Eerdmans, 2003.

Gunton, Colin E. *Christ and Creation: The Didsbury Lectures, 1990*. Eugene, OR: Wipf and Stock, 2005.

Gunton, Colin E. "The End of Causality? The Reformers and Their Predecessors." In *The Doctrine of Creation: Essays in Dogmatics, History, and Philosophy*. Edited by Colin E. Gunton. Edinburgh: T&T Clark, 2004.

Gunton, Colin E. *The Triune Creator: A Historical and Systematic Study*. New Studies in Constructive Theology. Grand Rapids: Eerdmans, 1998.

Habets, Myk. *The Anointed Son: A Trinitarian Spirit Christology*. Princeton Theological Monograph Series 129. Eugene, OR: Pickwick Publications, 2010.

Hanson, Anthony T. *Jesus Christ in the Old Testament*. Eugene, OR: Wipf and Stock, 2011. First published by SPCK (London), 1965.

Heppe, Heinrich. *Reformed Dogmatics*. Eugene, OR: Wipf and Stock, 2007.

Hill, Edmund. *The Mystery of the Trinity*. Introducing Catholic Theology 4. London: Geoffrey Chapman, 1985.

Hill, William J. *The Three-Personed God: The Trinity as a Mystery of Salvation*. Washington, DC: Catholic University of America Press, 1982.

Hill, William J. "Uncreated Grace—A Critique of Karl Rahner." *Thomist: A Speculative Quarterly Review* 27.1 (1963): 333–56.

Holmes, Stephen R., Paul D. Molnar, Thomas H. McCall, and Paul S. Fiddes. *Two Views on the Doctrine of the Trinity*. Counterpoints: Bible and Theology. Edited by Jason S. Sexton. Grand Rapids: Zondervan Academic, 2014.

Hooker, Morna D. *Son of Man in Mark: A Study of the Background of the Term "Son of Man" and Its Use in St. Mark's Gospel*. London: SPCK, 1967.

Hurtado, Larry W. *One God, One Lord: Early Christian Devotion and Ancient Jewish Monotheism*. London: SCM Press, 1988.

James, Frank A., III, and Charles E. Hill. *The Glory of the Atonement: Biblical, Historical, and Practical Perspectives*. Downers Grove, IL: IVP Academic, 2004.

Jenson, Robert W. *Systematic Theology, Volume 1: The Triune God*. Oxford: Oxford University Press, 1997.

Johansson, Daniel. "Kyrios in the Gospel of Mark." *Journal for the Study of the New Testament* 33, no. 1 (2010): 101–24.

Johnson, Adam J. *Atonement: A Guide for the Perplexed*. London: Bloomsbury, 2015.

Johnson, Adam J. *God's Being in Reconciliation: The Theological Basis of the Unity and Diversity of the Atonement in the Theology of Karl Barth*. T&T Clark Studies in Systematic Theology 15. London: Continuum, 2012.

Johnson, Aubrey. *The One and the Many in the Israelite Conception of God*. Cardiff, UK: University of Wales Press, 1942.

Journet, Charles Cardinal. *The Theology of the Church*. Translated by Victor Szczurek, OP. San Francisco: Ignatius Press, 2004.

Kenny, Anthony. *Action, Emotion, and Will*. London: Routledge, 1963.

Kirk, J. R. Daniel. *A Man Attested by God: The Human Jesus of the Synoptic Gospels*. Grand Rapids: Eerdmans, 2016.

Köstenberger, Andreas J., and Scott R. Swain. *Father, Son, and Spirit: The Trinity and John's Gospel*. New Studies in Biblical Theology 24. Downers Grove, IL: IVP Academic, 2008.

Koutloumousianos, Chrysostom. *The One and the Three: Nature, Person and Tri-adic Monarchy in the Greek and Irish Patristic Tradition*. Cambridge: James Clarke, 2015.

LaCugna, Catherine Mowry. *God for Us: The Trinity and Christian Life*. New York: Harper Collins, 1993.

Leftow, Brian. "Anti-Social Trinitarianism." In *The Trinity: An Interdisciplinary Symposium on the Trinity*. Edited by Stephen T. Davis, Daniel Kendall, SJ, and Gerald O' Collins, SJ. Oxford: Oxford University Press, 2003.

Legge, Dominic. *The Trinitarian Christology of Saint Thomas Aquinas*. Oxford: Oxford University Press, 2017.

Leithart, Peter J. *Athanasius*. Foundations of Theological Exegesis and Christian Spirituality 1. Grand Rapids: Baker Academic, 2011.

Leo the Great. *Letter 28*. In vol. 12 of *The Nicene and Post-Nicene Fathers*. Series 2. Edited by Henry Wace and Philip Schaff. Peabody, MA: Hendrickson Publishers, 1997.

Leo the Great. *Letter 129*. In vol. 12 of *The Nicene and Post-Nicene Fathers*. Series 2. Edited by Henry Wace and Philip Schaff. Peabody, MA: Hendrickson Publishers, 1997.

Levering, Matthew. *Engaging the Doctrine of Creation: Cosmos, Creatures, and the Wise and Good Creator*. Grand Rapids: Baker Academic, 2017.

Levering, Matthew. *The Theology of Augustine: An Introductory Guide to His Most Important Works*. Grand Rapids: Baker Academic, 2013.

Lincoln, Andrew T. *The Gospel According to Saint John*. Black's New Testament Commentaries. Grand Rapids: Baker Academic, 2013.

Lombard, Peter. *The Sentences, Book 1: The Mystery of the Trinity*. Medieval Sources in Translation. Translated by Giulio Silano. Toronto: Pontifical Institute of Medieval Studies, 2007.

Lombardo, Nicholas E. *The Father's Will: Christ's Crucifixion and the Goodness of God*. Oxford: Oxford University Press, 2013.

Lonergan, Bernard. *Early Latin Theology*. Vol. 19 of *Collected Works of Bernard Lonergan*. Edited by Daniel Monsour, Michael G. Shields, and Robert M. Doran. Toronto: University of Toronto Press, 2011.

Lonergan, Bernard. *The Triune God: Systematics*. Vol. 12 of *Collected Works of Bernard Lonergan*. Translated by Michael E. Shields. Edited by Robert M. Doran and H. Daniel Monsour. Toronto: University of Toronto Press, 2007.

Luther, Martin. *Lectures on Romans*. Vol. 25 of *Luther's Works*. Edited by Hilton C. Oswald. St. Louis, MO: Concordia Publishing, 1972.

MacDonald, Nathan. *Deuteronomy and the Meaning of "Monotheism."* 2nd ed. Forschungen zum Alten Testament 2. Reihe 1. Tübingen: Mohr Siebeck, 2012.

Mackey, James P. *The Christian Experience of God as Trinity*. London: SCM Press, 1983.

MacMurray, John. "Symposium: What Is Action?" Proceedings of the Aristotelian Society, Supplemental Volumes 17 (1938): 69–120.

Malone, A. S. "Distinguishing the Angel of the Lord." *Bulletin for Biblical Research* 21, no. 3 (2011): 297–314.

Marshall, Bruce D. "The Dereliction of Christ and the Impassibility of God." In *Divine Impassibility and the Mystery of Human Suffering*. Edited by James F. Keating and Thomas Joseph White. Grand Rapids: Eerdmans, 2009.

Marshall, Bruce D. *Trinity and Truth*. Cambridge Studies in Christian Doctrine 3. Cambridge: Cambridge University Press, 2000.

Marshall, Bruce D. "The Unity of the Triune God: Reviving an Ancient Question." *Thomist: A Speculative Quarterly Review* 74, no. 1 (2010): 1–32.

Marshall, Bruce D. "What Does the Spirit Have to Do?" In *Reading John with Saint Thomas Aquinas: Theological Exegesis and Speculative Theology*. Edited by Michael Dauphinais and Matthew Levering. Washington, DC: Catholic University of America Press, 2010.

Maximus the Confessor. *The Disputation with Pyrrhus of Our Father Among the Saints, Maximus the Confessor*. Translated by Joseph P. Farrell. South Canaan, PA: St. Tikhon's Seminary Press, 1990.

Maximus the Confessor. *Opuscule 7: Letter to Marinus*. In Andrew Louth. *Maximus the Confessor*. London: Routledge, 1996.

McCall, Thomas H. *Forsaken: The Trinity and the Cross, and Why It Matters*. Downers Grove, IL: IVP Academic, 2012.

McCall, Thomas H. *Which Trinity? Whose Monotheism? Philosophical and Systematic Theologians on the Metaphysics of Trinitarian Theology*. Grand Rapids: Eerdmans, 2010.

McCormack, Bruce L. "The Ontological Presuppositions of Barth's Doctrine of the Atonement." In *The Glory of the Atonement: Biblical, Historical, and Practical Perspectives*. Edited by Frank A. James III, and Charles E. Hill. Downers Grove, IL: IVP Academic, 2004.

McDonough, Sean M. *Christ as Creator: Origins of a New Testament Doctrine*. Oxford: Oxford University Press, 2011.

McFarland, Ian A. "'Willing Is Not Choosing': Some Anthropological Implications of Dyothelite Christology." *International Journal of Systematic Theology* 9, no. 1 (2007): 3–23.

McGrath, James F. *John's Apologetic Christology: Legitimation and Development in Johannine Christology*. Society for New Testament Study Monograph Series 111. Cambridge: Cambridge University Press, 2001.

McGrath, James F. *The Only True God: Early Christian Monotheism in Its Jewish Context*. Urbana, IL: University of Illinois Press, 2012.

Michaels, J. Ramsey. *The Gospel of John*. New International Commentary on the New Testament. Grand Rapids: Eerdmans, 2010.

Moeller, Charles. *The Theology of Grace and the Ecumenical Movement*. Paterson, NJ: Saint Anthony Guild Press, 1961.

Molnar, Paul D. "Classical Trinity: Catholic Perspective." In Stephen R. Holmes, Paul D. Molnar, Thomas H. McCall, and Paul S. Fiddes. *Two Views on the Doctrine of the Trinity*. Counterpoints: Bible and Theology. Edited by Jason S. Sexton. Grand Rapids: Zondervan Academic, 2014.

Nazianzen, Gregory. *Epistle 101*. In *Creeds, Councils and Controversies: Documents Illustrating the Early History of the Church, AD 373–561*. Edited by J. Stevenson. London: SPCK, 1989.

Nazianzen, Gregory. *Oration 31*. Translated by Lionel Wickham. In *On God and Christ: The Five Theological Orations and Two Letters to Cledonius*. Popular Patristics 23. Yonkers, NY: Saint Vladimir's Seminary Press, 2002.

Nyssen, Gregory. *Against Eunomius*. In vol. 5 of *The Nicene and Post-Nicene Fathers*. Series 2. Edited by Henry Wace and Philip Schaff. Peabody, MA: Hendrickson Publishers, 1999.

Odeberg, Hugo. *3 Enoch or the Hebrew Book of Enoch*. Cambridge: Cambridge University Press, 1928.

O'Donovan, Leo J., ed. *A World of Grace: An Introduction to the Themes and Foundations of Karl Rahner's Theology*. New York: Seabury Press, 1980.

Ormerod, Neil. *The Trinity: Retrieving the Western Tradition*. Marquette Studies in Theology 48. Milwaukee, WI: Marquette University Press, 2005.

O'Shea, Kevin F. "The Human Activity of the Word." *Thomist: A Speculative Quarterly Review* 22, no. 2 (1959): 143–232.

Owen, John. Appendix to *Pneumatologia*. Abridged by G. Burder from the Third London Edition. London: Towar and Hogan, 1827.

Owen, John. *Communion with God*. Vol. 2 of *Works of John Owen*. Edinburgh: Banner of Truth Trust, 1965.

Owen, John. *The Glory of Christ*. Vol. 1 of *Works of John Owen*. Edinburgh: Banner of Truth Trust, 1965.

Owen, John. *The Holy Spirit*. Vol. 3 of *Works of John Owen*. Edinburgh: Banner of Truth Trust, 1966.

Palamas, Gregory. *Homily 24*. In Palamas, *The Homilies*. Edited and translated by Christopher Veniamin. Dalton, PA: Mount Tabor, 2014.

Pannenberg, Wolfhart. *Systematic Theology*. 3 vols. Translated by George W. Bromiley. Grand Rapids: Eerdmans, 1991.

Partee, Charles. *The Theology of John Calvin*. Louisville, KY: Westminster John Knox Press, 2010.

Pelikan, Jaroslav. *The Christian Tradition: A History of the Development of Doctrine*. Vol. 2, *The Spirit of Eastern Christendom (600–1700)*. Chicago: University of Chicago Press, 1974.

Pink, Thomas, and M. W. F. Stone, eds. *Will and Human Action: From Antiquity to the Present Day*. London Studies in the History of Philosophy. New York: Routledge, 2004.

Pseudo-Dionysius. *Pseudo-Dionysius: The Complete Works*. Edited by Colm Luibheid and Paul Rorem. New York: Paulist Press, 1987.

Rahner, Karl. *The Content of Faith: The Best of Karl Rahner's Theological Writings*. Edited by Karl Lehmann and Albert Raffelt. New York: Crossroad Publishing Company, 1994.

Rahner, Karl. *Foundations of the Christian Faith: An Introduction to the Idea of Christianity*. New York: Crossroad Publishing Company, 1994.

Rahner, Karl. *More Recent Writings*. Vol. 4 of *Theological Investigations*. Baltimore, MD: Helicon Press, 1963.

Rahner, Karl. "Some Implications of the Scholastic Concept of Uncreated Grace." In *God, Christ, Mary, and Grace*. Vol. 1 of *Theological Investigations*. Translated by Cornelius Ernst. Baltimore, MD: Helicon Press, 1961.

Rahner, Karl. *The Trinity*. Translated by Joseph F. Donceel. London: Burns and Oates, 1970.

Rainbow, Paul A. *Johannine Theology: The Gospel, the Epistles, and the Apocalypse*. Downers Grove, IL: IVP Academic, 2014.

Riches, Aaron. *Ecce Homo: On the Divine Unity of Christ*. Interventions. Grand Rapids: Eerdmans, 2016.

Ridderbos, Herman N. *The Gospel of John: A Theological Commentary*. Translated by John Vriend. Grand Rapids: Eerdmans, 1997.

Rowe, C. Kavin. "Biblical Pressure and Trinitarian Hermeneutics." *Pro Ecclesia* 11, no. 3 (2002): 295–312.

Rowe, C. Kavin. "Luke and the Trinity: An Essay in Ecclesial Biblical Theology." *Scottish Journal of Theology* 56, no. 1 (2003): 1–26.

Rowland, Christopher. *The Open Heaven: A Study of the Apocalyptic in Judaism and Early Christianity*. London: SPCK, 1982.

Sanders, Fred. *The Triune God*. Grand Rapids: Zondervan, 2016.

Scheeben, Matthias Joseph. *The Mysteries of Christianity*. New York: Herder and Herder, 2008.

Scheffczyk, Leo. *Creation and Providence*. Herder History of Dogma. Translated by Richard Stachen. New York: Herder and Herder, 1970.

Schillebeeckx, Edward. "Ascension and Pentecost." *Worship* 36 (1961): 336–63.

Schillebeeckx, Edward. *Jesus: An Experiment in Christology*. Vol. 6 of *The Collected Works of Edward Schillebeeckx*. New York: Bloomsbury, 2014.

Schleiermacher, Friedrich D. E. *The Christian Faith*. Edited by H. R. Mackintosh and J. S. Stewart. Edinburgh: T&T Clark, 1989.

Schwöbel, Christoph. *God: Action and Revelation*. Studies in Philosophical Theology 3. Kampen: Kok, 1992.

Segal, Alan F. *Two Powers in Heaven: Early Rabbinic Reports About Christianity and Gnosticism*. Leiden: Brill, 1977.

Shepherd, Norman. "Zanchius on Saving Faith." *Westminster Theological Journal* 36, no. 1 (1973): 31–47.

Smeaton, George. *The Doctrine of the Holy Spirit*. Edinburgh: T&T Clark, 1889.

Sonderegger, Katherine. *Systematic Theology*. Vol. 1, *The Doctrine of God*. Minneapolis: Fortress, 2015.

Sorabji, Richard. "The Concept of the Will from Plato to Maximus the Confessor." In *Will and Human Action: From Antiquity to the Present Day*. London Studies in the History of Philosophy. Edited by Thomas Pink and M. W. F. Stone. New York: Routledge, 2004.

Stăniloae, Dumitru. *The Church: Communion in the Holy Spirit*. Vol. 4 of *The Experience of God: Orthodox Dogmatic Theology*. Brookline, MA: Holy Cross Orthodox Press, 2012.

Stăniloae, Dumitru. *The Person of Jesus Christ as God and Savior*. Vol. 3 of *The Experience of God: Orthodox Dogmatic Theology*. Brookline, MA: Holy Cross Orthodox Press, 2011.

Stăniloae, Dumitru, ed. *Părinți și Scriitori Bisericești* 81. Bucharest: Editura Institutului Biblic si de Misiune al Bisericii Ortodoxe Romane, 1990.

Stump, Eleonore. *Aquinas*. Arguments of the Philosophers. New York: Routledge, 2003.

Stump, Eleonore. *Atonement*. Oxford Studies in Analytical Theology. Oxford: Oxford University Press, 2019.

Swinburne, Richard. *The Christian God*. Oxford: Oxford University Press, 1994.

Tanner, Kathryn. *Christ the Key*. Current Issues in Theology. Cambridge: Cambridge University Press, 2010.

Thiselton, Anthony C. *The First Epistle to the Corinthians*. New International Greek Testament Commentary. Grand Rapids: Eerdmans, 2000.

Tilling, Christopher. *Paul's Divine Christology*. Grand Rapids: Eerdmans, 2015.

Turcescu, Lucian. *Gregory of Nyssa and the Concept of Divine Persons*. Oxford: Oxford University Press, 2005.

Twombly, Charles C. *Perichoresis and Personhood: God, Christ, and Salvation in John of Damascus.* Eugene, OR: Pickwick, 2015.

Vanhoozer, Kevin J. *Remythologizing Theology: Divine Action, Passion, and Authorship.* Cambridge Studies in Christian Doctrine 18. Cambridge: Cambridge University Press, 2012.

Vidu, Adonis. *Atonement, Law, and Justice: The Cross in Historical and Cultural Contexts.* Grand Rapids: Baker Academic, 2014.

Vidu, Adonis. "Trinitarian Inseparable Operations and the Incarnation." *Journal of Analytic Theology* 4 (2016): 106–27.

Vidu, Adonis. "Triune Agency, East and West: Uncreated Energies or Created Effects." In *Perichoresis* 18, no. 1 (2020): 61–79.

Von Balthasar, Hans Urs. *Cosmic Liturgy: The Universe According to Maximus the Confessor.* Translated by Brian E. Daley, SJ. San Francisco: Ignatius Press, 2003.

Webster, John. "Trinity and Creation." In *God and the Works of God.* Vol. 1 of *God Without Measure.* Edinburgh: T&T Clark, 2016.

White, Thomas Joseph. *The Incarnate Lord: A Thomistic Study in Christology.* Thomistic Ressourcement Series 5. Washington, DC: Catholic University of America Press, 2015.

Wiles, Maurice. "Some Reflections on the Origins of the Doctrine of the Trinity." *Journal of Theological Studies* 8, no. 1 (1957): 92–106.

Witsius, Herman. *Sacred Dissertations on the Apostles' Creed.* Vol. 2. Translated by Donald Fraser. Glasgow: Khull, Blackie, and Company, 1823.

Witt, Charlotte. *Ways of Being: Potentiality and Actuality in Aristotle's Metaphysics.* Ithaca, NY: Cornell University Press, 2003.

Wright, N. T. *Paul and the Faithfulness of God.* London: SPCK, 2013.

Yeo, Ray S. "Towards a Model of Indwelling: A Conversation with Jonathan Edwards and William Alston." *Journal of Analytic Theology* 2, no. 1 (2014): 210–37.

Zizioulas, John D. *Being as Communion: Studies in Personhood and the Church.* Contemporary Greek Theologians 4. Crestwood, NY: Saint Vladimir's Seminary Press, 1985.

Index of Authors

Abelard, Peter, 241
Abraham, 3, 12, 117, 327
Abraham, William J., xi, 191–92
Anatolios, Khaled, xi, 57, 62, 145
Aquinas, Thomas, vii, viii, 52–53, 63,
69–73, 87, 89, 92, 99, 101–4, 107, 113,
115, 127, 130–58, 161–75, 184, 188,
190, 191, 194, 197–206, 210–14, 239,
249–56, 263, 264, 269–73, 280, 282,
283, 286, 288, 290–98, 303, 312, 318,
325
Aristotle, 131, 133, 138, 140, 167, 186,
188, 204, 287
Athanasius, 52–57, 61, 67–68, 96,
138–43
Augustine, 52, 63–70, 73, 86, 89, 97,
113, 124, 138, 139, 143–45, 156, 158,
162, 172–73, 251–54, 262, 264, 280,
294–98, 301
Ayres, Lewis, xi, 54, 65, 143–44

Barker, Margaret, 9
Barnes, Michel, xi, 60, 61, 186
Barth, Karl, 35n110, 82, 115, 139, 222,
224, 238
Basil of Caesarea, 53, 59, 141–43
Bauckham, Richard, 5–26, 29–30, 41,
43, 48
Bavinck, Hermann, 145n43, 157, 300

Bousset, Wilhelm, 2
Bultmann, Rudolf, 37–44

Calvin, John, 250, 300, 301
Campbell, Douglas, 19–21
Chrysostom, John, 249
Coakley, Sarah, 114
Coffey, David, 173, 284, 306–15
Congar, Yves, 255, 264–65, 289
Crisp, Oliver, xi, 166–70
Cunningham, Francis L. B., 293, 294,
297

Damascene, John, 79–82, 98, 165, 183,
184, 212
Davis, P. G., 3
De la Taille, Maurice, 284, 289
Del Colle, Ralph, 293n27
Didymus the Blind, 52–55
Dodd, C. H., 38–39, 46
Dodds, Michael, 133–34
Doran, Robert M., 290n22
Dunn, James D. G., 32–36, 306
Duns Scotus, John, 161, 164, 185,
188–90, 195–99, 205, 214

Emery, Gilles, xi, 69–70, 103–4, 113–15,
147–51, 169, 205–6, 252, 294–98
Eunomius, 58–62, 152

Farrow, Douglas, 260n31
Fatehi, Mehrdad, 33–35

Index of Subjects

action: ascriptions, xiv, xv, xvii, 4, 11–14, 19–23, 26, 29–31, 48–50, 64–66, 83–85, 89, 91, 96, 101, 106–8, 128, 137–45, 160, 165, 166, 180–84, 192–93, 200–202, 209, 213, 296, 320–22; filial mode of, 177, 202–5, 209, 27; forms of, 85; and intentionality, 160–63; modes of, 82, 84, 103–7, 124, 148, 149, 176, 191, 204–6, 215, 321, 324; ontological totality of, 228–31; ontology of, 185–93; and passivity, 160–245, 259; and states, 159–63

action, divine: collective nature of, xiii, xv, 52, 62, 96, 121, 163, 169, 208, 314; concurrence by other persons, 165, 170; participable by humans, 28–29

act token, xv, xvii, xviii, 23, 29, 55, 56, 89, 122, 159–63, 169, 236, 324

act type, xv, 22, 23, 25, 29, 50, 55, 92, 162

actualism, 222

actuation, 155, 194, 206, 209, 265n45, 289–94, 323, 324

actus primus and *secundus*, 212–13, 189–91, 198–202, 209–10

adaptation, 64, 290, 296, 297, 301

agency toggling, 14

analogy, xiv, 12, 33–34, 48, 65–72, 97, 104, 105, 109, 115, 151, 156, 162, 163, 214, 215, 236, 253, 289; psychological, 71, 97, 109

Angel of the Lord, 8–9

angels, 3–11, 22, 25, 50, 82, 291

anointing, 31–32

anonymous Christians, 304

antecedent and consequent conditions, 220, 228–38, 241–59

Apollinarism, 196, 199

appointed agent, 40

appropriation, xvi–xix, 52–53, 63–71, 73, 76, 83–88, 95, 104, 106, 108, 110–25, 128, 145, 155, 167–69, 171–83, 189, 192–93, 198, 202, 209, 264n43, 277, 280–302, 314–15, 318, 320–21

Ark of the Covenant, 3

ascension, xviii, 32, 33, 35, 89, 158, 244, 246, 247–78, 306, 309, 311, 312, 325

ascriptive predicates, 209

ascriptive subject, 209

aseity, 41, 100, 105, 132, 135, 159, 174, 228–32, 259, 286, 288, 299, 319–23

assimilation, 299–302, 326

atonement: dereliction, 160n1, 213, 224n5, 234, 240, 242; divine child abuse, 222; historical inevitability of the cross, 230–38; necessity of Christ's death, 229–38; penal dimension, xviii, 217, 222, 223, 233, 234, 236, 242, 243, 249, 325; ransom theory, 232, 236

attributes, divine: personified, 8, 25; simplicity of, xi, 58–63, 67–68, 130,

Index of Scripture